Vision and Separation:
Between Mother and Baby

Vision and Separation: Between Mother and Baby

KENNETH WRIGHT

Jason Aronson Inc.
Northvale, New Jersey
London

Production Editor: Bernard F. Horan
Editorial Director: Muriel Jorgensen

This book was set in 10/13 Times Roman
by Alpha Graphics
and printed and bound by Haddon Craftsmen of Scranton, Pennsylvania.

Library of Congress Cataloging-in-Publication Data

Wright, Kenneth, 1936–
    Vision and separation : between mother and baby / Kenneth Wright.
      p.   cm.
    Includes bibliographical references.
    ISBN 0-87668-559-9
    1. Child analysis.   2. Face perception in children.   3. Mother and
child.   4. Object relations (Psychoanalysis)   5. Separation
individuation.   6. Psychotherapy.   I. Title.
    [DNLM: 1. Child Development.   2. Ego.   3. Mother-Child Relations.
4. Object Attachment.   5. Psychoanalytic Theory.   WS 105.5.S3
W951v]
RJ504.2.W75   1991
155.2—dc20
DNLM/DLC   90-14553

Manufactured in the United States of America. Jason Aronson Inc. offers books and cassettes. For information and catalog write to Jason Aronson Inc., 230 Livingston Street, Northvale, New Jersey 07647.

*To my mother, who taught me to use words;
my father, who taught me to question; and
Maggie, who gave me a place to be.*

Contents

Acknowledgment

In the development of one's ideas one owes a debt to many people, but perhaps the most difficult thing for any writer is to feel that he has something to say that is worth saying. It is, therefore, to those who have most encouraged me that I feel I owe most. In this respect I would like to thank particularly Dr. J. Miller Mair, who many years ago supervised my M.Phil. dissertation and subsequently, as a friend, believed in the possibility of my writing something valuable, even when I did not. I would also thank Dr. John Padel, who in the early years seemed to be one of the few people who understood what I was talking about.

In relation to the preparation of this book, I would like to thank two good friends, Dr. Craigie Macfie and Neville Symington, who encouraged me when I was in Australia, and my colleague and friend, Dr. Nina Coltart, who carefully read early drafts of the manuscript and made useful critical suggestions as well as appreciative noises.

Once in the publisher's hands, Barry Richards of Free Association Books was immensely helpful in the feedback he gave me, and it was partly through his efforts that the later chapters came to be revised or rewritten. I am grateful to Bernard Horan and the other editors at Jason Aronson Inc., who steered the book through its production stages; to Jill Duncan at the Institute of Psycho-Analysis, who helped me to find some difficult references; and not least to my secretary, Joanne Davis, who helped me tie up so many loose ends.

Thanks are due to my family, who have put up with my prolonged withdrawals into the study, and to my son Tom, who in the early stages of writing helped me overcome my fear of technology sufficiently to become proficient at word processing.

Thanks are also due to those patients who enabled me to see more clearly something that I needed to understand; and last, but not least, to my analyst, John Klauber, who put up with my attacks on his "dogmatism," which were probably misplaced. I think he was rare among analysts in being able to allow his analysands to go their own way without too much guilt.

Thanks are due to the following publishers and individuals for permission to quote from previously published material: Sigmund Freud Copyrights, The Institute of Psycho-Analysis and The Hogarth Press; also Norton & Co., New York—*The Standard Edition of the Complete Psychological Works of Sigmund Freud*, translated and edited by James Strachey; The Hogarth Press (Random Century Group)—*Collected Papers on Schizophrenia and Related Subjects* by H. Searles; Tavistock Publications—*Playing and Reality* by D. W. Winnicott; Metheun and Co. Ltd.—*Being and Nothingness* by Jean-Paul Sartre, translated by Hazel E. Barnes; Faber and Faber Ltd. and Harcourt Brace, San Diego—permission to quote from *Four Quartets* and from the poems "Marina" and "The Love Song of J. Alfred Prufrock" from *The Collected Poems 1909-62* by T. S. Eliot; also to Faber and Faber Ltd. for permission to reprint lines from the poems "Snow" and "Prayer before Birth" from *Collected Poems* by Louis MacNeice; A. P. Watt Ltd. on behalf of The Trustees of the Robert Graves Copyright Trust, and Oxford University Press, New York—the poem "The Three-Faced" and lines from "The Cool Web," both from *Collected Poems 1975* by Robert Graves, published by Cassell; The Hogarth Press and Random House Inc., New York—extract from "Ninth Duino Elegy" from *Duino Elegies* by Rainer Maria Rilke, translated by J. B. Leishmann; and finally to Max Reinhardt of Reinhardt Books for a quotation from "Song of Myself" by Walt Whitman.

Introduction

Every book needs an introduction. The reader deserves an opportunity to learn why the book was written and a chance to judge whether it might say anything to him. It gives the writer a chance to justify himself and to say anything he thinks is relevant to the book that might nevertheless have been out of place in the text.

This book was a surprise. *It* might have intended to be written, but *I* did not know at first that I would write it. The stimulus was a trip to Australia, where there was to be an opportunity to lecture. What was I going to say? No doubt we all feel a mixture of panic and challenge about such occasions. We fear we will have nothing to say, yet at the same time we are pleased to have some reason to put order into our thoughts and to try to answer our own nagging questions. Some people may write because they think they know; for me, it is the other way around—I write in order to discover, to clarify a problem, or to take hold of an idea more clearly.

So I started to write with what for me was a kind of conundrum, my own particular riddle of the Sphinx. I needed to find a way of talking about what was happening when an external image, a *view* of one person, made contact with the feelings, or perhaps the behavior, of another. This everyday experience had always seemed to me to be fraught with significance. It had to do with *looking* and with *being seen*, but the intellectual excitement that I felt about this area never seemed to be accounted for by the sexual connotations of the experience. Of course, sexual looking was exciting, but this was something different. Inevitably, my analyst did not agree, so there may be some sense in which this book is addressed, albeit posthumously, to him. But at least as much it is written for myself. It is an attempt to tease out what this something was, which I have known about but have not been able to explain, and, as it turns out, to pursue the ramifications of that idea through its many gyrations.

This is not really a scholarly book in the accepted sense of the word; it is more a journey of self-discovery. I do not seem to have found in the theory which I have read that which for me needed to be said, and thus the book is my attempt to say it. Whether such a gap existed for others, whether it has all been said before ". . . once, or twice, or several times, by men whom one cannot hope to emulate . . ." (Eliot 1944), whether the gap existed because of my own ignorance of relevant theory, or through my own self-blinding, is in one sense irrelevant. For me, writing the book has illuminated my darkness and answered to a felt need. As such, it has been a therapy, giving ease to my unknowing, and a form to something in myself.

The notion that *seeing gives form* is one that is central to the whole book. This book is the seen form of that which was previously felt but not clearly formed. Seeing *is* forming, and the idea that the self, as a conceivable entity, is formed—or de-formed, or re-formed—at that place where the Other's view meets with the felt substance of the person is an important part of my thesis. Therapy, according to this view, is a process of forming, of finding forms for the self.

What I did not realize when I started the book was that self-forming was an aspect of symbol formation. This realization, however, led me to consider the whole question of symbols, and I have developed the argument that looking plays an important part in their genesis. The book is thus not only about the development of the self; it is a reflection on symbol formation as well.

Symbol formation is related to object loss—that is the prevalent psychoanalytic view, which we owe mainly to Segal and Bion, but before that to Freud and his account of the *Fort-Da* sequence in the baby. Winnicott tackled the question of symbol formation through his work on transitional objects and phenomena, and his emphasis is not so much on object loss, but more on the gradual separation of infant from mother brought about by the mother's diminishing adaptation to her infant's needs. Following Winnicott, I have tried to show how the development of symbols parallels this separation, leading eventually to fully separated representational symbols. In this process, looking, which is the most important distance sense, plays a prominent part.

The central structure around which the book coheres is thus the space or gap that develops between subject and object through their separation.

It is this gap that, according to my thesis, becomes the gap or "space" of consciousness. I think of consciousness as a looking or a searching for the object that is missing. The space of consciousness is thus a "looking space," because within it objects can be looked at but not touched.

If consciousness is indelibly marked by this searching looking, it is also fundamentally concerned with patterns and pattern recognition. It is the pattern of an object that guides the infant's searching, and in this book I attempt to describe how the infant's changing relation to such patterns gradually transforms them into symbols. In this process, the pattern that at first inhered in the object later becomes the possession of the subject— a new symbolic tool through which the world can be explored. But for this transformation to occur, the child first has to disengage from the object and in this way disengage the pattern from the arena of practical events. I argue that all of this takes place in the looking space of consciousness, and that a "looking" divorced from "having" is the means by which it occurs.

The "space" of self-consciousness is a secondary development within the field of consciousness. It arises when the subject (the child) becomes aware of the looking of the object. It is the space within which the person looks at himself through the eyes of the Other. I often speak of consciousness as an interface, or inter-*face*. This is to emphasize that both consciousness and self-consciousness, and the symbols that mediate these experiences, only arise between faces, in other words, in an interpersonal setting, within which relations between persons, and relations with objects governed by those persons, are formative.

It is not the purpose of an introduction to give an account of everything in a book, but to give a foretaste of it. An introduction also gives a chance to indicate areas of intellectual indebtedness that are relevant to a way of thinking but that may not be explicitly referred to in the text.

My training is psychiatric and psychoanalytical, though my interests have always had a philosophical slant. I have had a lasting interest in the phenomenological and existential approach; this is probably apparent in my writing, where I prefer to stay at a phenomenological level of analysis rather than jumping to a reductive one. The advantage of this is that the articulations of a psychological structure can be more closely observed; the disadvantage may be that in some places what I say will not link up with more psychoanalytic formulations. I am thinking particularly of the way in which, from a psychoanalytic point of view, fantasy is understood to distort phenomenology. For example, something that phenomenologically is outer may really be something inner that has been projected. To relate more explicitly to the content of the book, the collapse of subjectivity, which I describe in Chapters 2 and 3, takes no account of the psychoanalytic type of explanation that would see the "look" of the Other as having been invaded by a primitive oral-incorporative aspect of the subject. The fact that I have not made such links does not necessarily mean that I reject them. It is more a question of what could or could not be managed within a particular project.

I have also refrained from using psychoanalytic jargon as much as I can. I know that this is often puzzling and irritating to psychoanalysts, and it therefore requires some explanation. There is no doubt that jargon can sometimes facilitate communication; what is less often noted is that it restricts vision. It provides a set of blinkers, which makes it more difficult to see and describe the things in themselves. There is a sense, of course, in which we can never achieve such a project, in spite of the fact that the watchword of phenomenology is "back to the phenomena." Holding off from jargon, however, may allow us to bring new concepts to bear on things and thus to see things in a different way. Once we commit ourselves to jargon we are lost; having swallowed the first term, we are inevitably drawn into a structure of interrelated ideas and concepts from which it is difficult to escape.

I need to say something about writers who have influenced me, especially those who have not received a great deal of mention in the text. Among nonanalytic writers I would single out Susanne Langer, who has had a powerful influence on my thinking. Over the past twenty years I have returned again and again to her wonderful, door-opening book, *Philosophy in a New Key* (Langer 1942). At times when I could find nothing among analytic writings that seemed to relate to issues with which I was struggling, that book seldom failed to confirm in me the feeling that I was relating to genuine and important issues rather than chimeras. Langer's second book, *Feeling and Form* (1953), has also deeply affected my ideas. I would mention two ideas in particular: that of "psychical distance" as an essential element of aesthetic appreciation, which Langer drew from Bullough (1912); and that of "unhinging from practical action," which she also saw as central to the aesthetic process.

Among analytic writers my indebtedness to Donald Winnicott will be obvious.[1] It could be said I am doing little more than exploring the implications of his ideas. If this is so, I think it is still a worthwhile undertaking. Winnicott writes in such a deceptively simple and lyrical way, it is easy to read him without realizing that he has been exploring fundamental philosophical issues. There is a philosophical slant in my exposition that may help to bridge the gap between a psychoanalytic and a wider readership.

Freud is someone with whom I have to argue. His stature is inescapable, and his shadow is everywhere. His maps are still often the best that we have, yet there is a restrictiveness in his vision and his imagery that can prevent us from seeing things if we follow him too closely. I have tried to take him on over the issue of consciousness, and my exasperation and admiration are bound to be apparent.

Two modern analytic writers live on the fringe of my consciousness, and their admirers will certainly feel I have not done them justice. I have often felt that I may be a fellow traveler with both Wilfred Bion and Jacques Lacan, but their style in each case shuts me out. Bion excludes me with his attempt to make psychoanalysis seem like a branch of symbolic logic, with his symbols and signs for different functions. Lacan excludes with his elliptic and esoteric way of writing, which in my view places too great a demand on the reader. Nevertheless, with both writers I have a sense of overlapping interest, to which I cannot properly relate. If someone told me that either of them had already covered the same territory, I would not be surprised. But I would assert that there is always value in exploring a territory for oneself and attempting to make one's own maps.

Toward the end of the book I resurrect an earlier, though seldom revisited, "friendship" with Jung. As a young man, I read Jung avidly; he spoke to my condition. But eventually I found his mysticism infuriating, and I had to leave him behind. Freud's rigorous mind seemed more relevant to the needs of a young doctor trying to understand the nature of neurotic symptoms. From a distance, I can now relate again to what I found in Jung. Apart from a promise that I read into him, a vague promise of enlightenment, I can now see in Jung the maternal presence

---

[1] I have drawn most on his 1951 paper on transitional objects and transitional phenomena and his 1967 paper on the mirror-role of the mother in infant development, both reprinted in *Playing and Reality* (1971).

that is so lacking in Freud's paternally orientated formulations; and I can see how Jung's structures and gestalts of feeling and theory overlap with my own. I have tried to consider this relation between theory and the structures of the self in Chapter 17.

I cannot finish this introduction without reference to two other analytic writers. The first is John Bowlby, whose attachment theory explicitly underpins Chapter 1 and provides an implicit reference point throughout. The other writer, Ian Suttie, is someone I have scarcely mentioned, though his book, *The Origins of Love and Hate* (1935), made a quiet revolution in my life when I first read it many years ago. He is one of a line of what I have called maternally inspired therapists, and I have little doubt that his work has made it easier to write my own book.

My work is maternally biased, as was Winnicott's, Suttie's, and Jung's. Freud's was paternally biased, tougher, and further from the *prima materia* of feelings. I argue here that such a bias is inevitable, and for each reflects his own history and inner structure. We can try to see what others are talking about and describing, but if it does not resonate with our own structure, with our own forms of feeling, we will never feel the same connection with it or conviction about it.

In spite of my maternal bias, the father is not absent in what I have to say; indeed, the theme of the father, the third who makes the difference, is never far away, and his presence becomes more definite and constitutive as the book progresses. If the book as a whole is tinged with nostalgia for a maternal world that is lost, I hope that the necessity and value of the father nevertheless shine through. He acquires a pivotal role in my theory of symbol formation as the one who underpins the integrity of the representational space of the mind.

By way of general orientation, it can be said that the book falls roughly into five parts. Chapters 1 to 5 concern various aspects of the self and its development; Chapters 6 to 10 focus on the development of symbols and language in our experience; Chapters 11 to 13 are concerned with the structuring of experience and how this relates to the development of symbols and language; Chapters 14 and 15 are an attempt to recapitulate, and to some extent develop, the earlier arguments. Finally, Chapters 16, 17, and 18 relate both therapy and theory formation to some of the ideas that I have developed.

It is easy to overvalue what we have written if it has been important to ourselves. It is also easy to be discouraged, to feel that what we have written is uninformed, redundant, and of no value to anyone. To assess what we ourselves have produced is the most difficult task there is, and that is probably why, in the end, we expose ourselves to the Other's view. If the Other's verdict, the verdict of reality and of the father, is that this piece of subjectivity which we have allowed to become an object is no good, we may be able to defend ourselves with the thought that the Other does not understand us. If, on the other hand, the verdict is favorable, we may then take great satisfaction in the feeling that there is, after all, someone out there who understands and confirms the depths of us and who answers to us across the gap which separates.

True philosophy consists in relearning to look at the world. . . . The philosopher . . . is a perpetual beginner, which means that he takes for granted nothing that men, learned or otherwise, believe they know.
—Merleau-Ponty, *The Phenomenology of Perception*

1　Face-to-Face

Who calls her two-faced? Faces she has three:
The first inscrutable, for the outer world;
The second shrouded in self-contemplation;
The third, her face of love,
Once for an endless moment turned on me.
　　　　　—Robert Graves, "The Three-Faced"

And indeed there will be time
For the yellow smoke that slides along the street . . .
There will be time, there will be time
To prepare a face to meet the faces that you meet . . .
—T. S. Eliot, from "The Love Song of J. Alfred Prufrock"

Have you seen your face before your parents were born?
　　　　　　　　　　　　　　　—Zen koan

FACELESS THEORIES

IN *THE EGO AND THE ID*, Freud (1923) writes: "The ego is first and
foremost a bodily ego. . . . If we wish to find an anatomical anal-
ogy for it we can best identify it with the 'cortical homunculus' of
the anatomists, which stands on its head in the cortex, sticks up its
heels, faces backwards and, as we know, has its speech-area on the left-
hand side" (p. 26).

This cortical homunculus that Freud refers to illustrates the dispropor-
tionate representation of certain areas of the surface of the body in the
sensory cortex of the brain. It creates a rather grotesque impression of a
deformed creature with huge mouth and lips, receding forehead, enormous hands and feet, and a tiny body, graphically suggesting the close
affinity of man with his subhuman ancestors. Such an evolutionary,
biological perspective of man-the-animal had created a furor when first

suggested by Darwin some sixty years before Freud wrote *The Ego and the Id*, but it was a view that was still, to many people, unacceptable; and it was by no means a view that could be taken for granted, as it can be in the second half of the twentieth century.

Freud took his stand firmly within this biological perspective. The view of man it succeeded, which saw him as a rational and spiritual being, had de-emphasized his animal nature. Indeed, that term had become synonymous with all that which had to be and could be largely overcome. Pope's vision of man of more than a hundred years earlier,

> Plac'd on this isthmus of a middle state,
> A being darkly wise and rudely great: . . .
> Created half to rise and half to fall;
> Great lord of all things, yet a prey to all . . .

—a view of man as divided and in conflict—had apparently been lost, superseded by a view of man as the master and ruler of all, including himself. Such a view had led to a de-emphasizing of man's animal affinities, a de-emphasizing of what was primitive and instinctual in him, and an overstating of his rationality. Inevitably, this shift of emphasis had led to a great deal of hypocrisy and self-deception, especially in regard to the body and sexuality, and it became very much a part of Freud's project to reinstate the animal base that had been rejected and disowned.

If Freud's view of man, based on an archeology of the repressed, came to have a certain anthropoid character, we can scarcely be surprised. His homunculus still had the large mouth and hands of the neurologist's cortical projections, but it had in addition a large bottom and phallus, rather like the primitive sculptures Freud himself collected. Clearly Freud's image of man had to emphasize what had been denied and rejected if what he had rediscovered was not to be covered over again.

Looking at Freud from the second half of the twentieth century, we can perhaps begin to see the distortion. We also may wonder if the theory that stood man on his head, with his bottom up, may not, in its turn, have brought about a second repression: Is there not a gap in psychoanalytic theory, even present-day theory, where the face should be? Are those thick lips and large mouth really all there is to the human face?

In this first chapter, I want to put the human face back into psycho-analytic theory. I believe there is a gap, though not a total one, where the face should be, and I believe that taking this gap seriously could bring about a rebalancing of theory that could give the neglected face a greater degree of preeminence. Who knows? It might change therapy, too.

MIRRORING AND IDENTITY

Although it has not been linked explicitly with the face, this rebalancing of theory has already begun. The growth of object relations theory has brought about a shift in our view of what is important, so that the development of the infant has come to be seen increasingly as something happening within, and shaped by a human social context, not, as Freud might at times have liked to think, as a spontaneous unfolding of pre-programmed instincts. Winnicott's often-quoted remark, "There is no such thing as a baby" (1958, p. 99), summarizes this trend, reminding us that the baby does not exist or develop alone, but only within a mother–baby dyad.

At around the same time, psychoanalytic treatment was shifting from dealing with the relatively circumscribed symptoms of the neuroses to the more far-reaching character pathology of borderline and other personality disorders. These more pervasive developmental disorders focused attention much more than hitherto on environmental failures and the ways in which maternal failure, and other vagaries of maternal response, shaped, or misshaped, the developing self. The field of self psychology that has developed as a result has helped to humanize psychoanalytic theory by speaking of the importance of what goes on between mother and child, emphasizing its formative significance. At the same time, such work has led to a questioning of the classical role of the therapist and the traditional stance of interpreting and nothing more.

This altered perspective in theory and practice can be stated in another way. While the traditional neurotic patient can take for granted the ongoing continuity of his self, and the existence, in Winnicott's terms, of a "good enough mother," the person with character problems cannot: the self is always in danger of disintegrating at the slightest hint of failure in the holding or facilitating environment. The person's own self has become the problem, not just some conflict-laden or "bad" part of it.

In spite of this shift in perspective over recent years, very little attention has been given to the face in psychoanalytic writings, and theoretical formulations continue to ignore it. Some years ago I made an informal search of the psychoanalytic indexes, and it was remarkable how few entries could be found under *face*. This was in marked contrast to the plethora of references to *mouth, breast, penis, vagina*—in other words, to the familiar objects of psychoanalytic discourse. There were a few notable exceptions. Most important was the literature on attachment theory (Bowlby 1969), in which the development of the smiling response and facial recognition are deemed to play a central role in mother–infant bonding. (I consider this work in more detail later in this chapter.) Apart from this, references to the face were sporadic and seemed to stem from work with severely disturbed, borderline, or schizophrenic patients, where the therapist's response to the clinical situation had led to patients' being seen in a face-to-face setting. An exception to this was Spitz (1946), whose interest in the infant's early recognition of the facial gestalt stemmed from attempts to link psychoanalytic concepts to the phenomena of direct infant observation.

Erikson (1964), describing the treatment of young patients going through identity crises, noted that several individuals had experienced an almost hallucinatory fragmentation of the therapist's face before their eyes. He linked this with the extreme precariousness of the patients' own identities at that time and concluded that they often could not tolerate the "facelessness" of the normal analytic encounter, in which face-to-face interaction was denied. This connection of the face with a sense of identity is a theme that Erikson returns to at various points throughout his work. For example, he speaks of the forerunners of identity, "beginning with that earliest mutual recognition of and by another face which the ethologists have made us look for in our human beginning." He goes on:

> Their findings, properly transposed into the human condition, may throw new light on the identity-giving power of the eyes and the face which first "recognize" you (give you your first *Ansehen*), and new light also on the infantile origin of the dreaded estrangement, the "loss of face." [p. 95]

Harold Searles (1963) is another writer who realized the importance of face-to-face interaction in his clinical work. For many years he undertook intensive psychoanalytic psychotherapy with severely ill schizophrenic patients at Chestnut Lodge, a private psychiatric clinic in the United States. He writes:

In each of several instances in which deeply and chronically schizophrenic patients have progressed far towards recovery in my work with them, the symbiotic phase has been characterised by, among other manifestations, his or her sitting and staring at my face, in session after session, with all the absorbed wonderment and responsive play of facial expressions of a child immersed in watching a fascinating motion picture. I can now fully believe Spitz's comment that "the child learns to distinguish animate objects from inanimate ones by the spectacle of the mother's face in situations fraught with emotional satisfaction." It is thus, in fact, that the child—or the adult schizophrenic patient—becomes aware of his own limitlessly varied emotional capacities, and even of his very aliveness, seen first as attributes of the mother-therapist. . . .

My work with three schizophrenic women and other psychotic patients has suggested to me that the therapist (and, in particular, his face) comes to serve as a kind of mirror image to the patient [italics added]—as, that is, an *alter ego*—preliminary to the patient's identifying with the increasingly emotionally responsive therapist, who confirms, by his increasingly rich responses, the patient's own redifferentiating emotional capacities. . . .

In these comments about the role, in therapy, of the therapist's face, I have been trying to describe something of the manner in which, in the evolution of the patient's transference to the mother-therapist, the patient becomes able to detect, and make increasingly part of himself, the whole realm of emotion which was too inaccessibly hidden behind the inscrutable face of the actual mother of his infancy and early childhood, and which consequently has heretofore been walled off, within himself, to a comparably impenetrable degree, so that his own emotionality—an emotionality for these very reasons not at all well differentiated, nor yet maturely elaborated—has been . . . as inaccessible to him as was the realm of feeling in his mother. [pp. 645–649]

Searles's sensitive observations could be discussed at length and from many different points of view; but as they so closely prefigure Winnicott's views, which I discuss later, I will only summarize his main points. I have emphasized Searles's central point that the mother's face is the child's first emotional mirror, and that it is through her responsiveness (her reflections) that the child is able to come to know his own emotions. His second point seems equally important: if the mirror is unreflecting, damage is done to the child, who becomes walled off from his own emotional self by a similarly rigid and impervious wall. The third point relates to the role of the therapist, who does not simply interpret, but in some very real way reflects back emotionally with his face and gives the patient an experience that makes good the earlier deficit. One suspects that with such patients, classical technique would merely compound the earlier trauma.

As in the Erikson quotation cited earlier, I think we have here, for the first time, a clear indication of the face as having some special importance in its own right, in emotional development, and perhaps under certain circumstances in therapy.

PERSONA AND EMOTIONAL EXPRESSION

This view, that the face is important in its own right, would certainly fit with ordinary common sense, which treats the face as the center of the person, the main expression of character and individuality. We recognize each other by our faces more readily than by name, and we call someone who has no individuality, who is lost in the crowd, faceless. A person with a damaged face has tremendous difficulty coping with the mutilation to his self-image and also with the normal business of face-to-face interaction; conversely, someone who is troubled by a negative identity or discongruent self-image may, in an almost delusional way, experience his face as disfigured.

In ordinary life, the face plays a central role in interpersonal communication. When someone is speaking, we "read" his face for qualifying messages; if we are prevented from doing this, we have an uneasy feeling that we may not be able to gauge the full import of what is being said. The face is a nonverbal qualifier of verbal messages and may either confirm or disconfirm what is being said. Checking the facial channel against the verbal is one means that we use to establish whether the person is telling the truth or not, and where there is a discrepancy of information we tend to feel very uneasy. When it comes to messages of an emotional import, the face often leads. Emotions are often directly presented, and the verbal channel may in fact be quite silent. Someone who is sad may merely reveal a struggle with his tears and in fact say nothing at all. Only when we have gained the person's confidence and conveyed to him that we have understood the nonverbal message will the individual perhaps trust us enough to put into discursive words the more specific content of his unhappiness. In a similar way, expressions of love, affection, and desire are often communicated first of all on the nonverbal channel, which seems to provide a more subtle means of gauging another person's response than a direct verbal message. Someone who ignores this convention and launches straight into the verbal mode may actually be deemed to be overdirect and lacking in important social skills.

In general, we give more weight to facial expression when the issue is an emotional one. Although less specific in its content than the verbal channel, it is more difficult for the face to lie. It is easier to suppress a verbal message by keeping silent than to suppress an emotional message by controlling the face. The larynx is more under voluntary control than the small muscles of the face, and almost certainly an emotion, together with its characteristic facial gestalt, is organized in an older and more primitive part of the brain than speech.

When one considers the enormous importance of the face in human communication, especially in the communication of emotions, the evaluation of character, and the assessment of the truth or falsity of individual messages, it becomes all the more extraordinary to remember that Freud chose to give up access to the facial channel as he evolved his psychoanalytic technique. After all, he was concerned to dig out the truth from beneath the encrusted layers of hypocrisy and falsity that governed the society in which he lived. Why should he have closed off to himself what is perhaps the major channel of emotional expression?

Freud is reported to have said that he could not stand being looked at for twelve hours a day, and there may well be some truth in this. Communication is a two-way process, and the therapist's face is as open to scrutiny as the patient's. I doubt if there is any therapist who does not feel to some extent on guard when under scrutiny, and it is just as important for the therapist as it is for the patient whether a particular set of circumstances facilitates or impedes his work. Coping with face-to-face interaction requires a different set of skills and a different inner set from the free-floating attention of the analyst or the free association of the patient. Both require a relaxed openness to what is going on within as well as a receptiveness to what is coming from without. Although it may be quite different in other forms of psychotherapy, psychoanalytic psychotherapy is less an interaction and more a kind of shared reverie—at least in its optimal mode of functioning. In this sense, what the patient can communicate to himself and what the therapist can communicate to his own self within the therapy setting are at least as important as what they are able to communicate to each other. Perhaps in this way the reading of the facial emotional channel by the other person is diminished in importance.

We can, of course, overemphasize the value of the face as a revealer of emotion and forget how artful people can be in their social interaction at putting on false faces. The quotation from T. S. Eliot at the beginning of this chapter can serve to remind us of this. "And indeed there will be time . . . to prepare a face to meet the faces that you meet." Social manners and graces, sufficiently practiced over time, can no doubt eventually become effective and habitual concealers of the true face of feeling. In the end we have to acknowledge that the face is an ambiguous, though rich, source of emotional messages.

Whether the exclusion of facial communication from analytic discourse is, in the end, a loss or something that facilitates the discovery of personal truth is a matter that should go on being debated. What is more certain is that the exclusion of the face from clinical practice contributed to the development of that hiatus in theory where the face should be. I think it is significant that it begins to be brought back into the field of discussion, not only by those patients for whom the face has been a problem, in the various ways discussed here, but also by those therapists who, responding to the needs of such patients, have seen fit to modify their therapeutic techniques.

THE GROWTH OF ATTACHMENT

I want to open up this inquiry in two directions: in relation to the first face that we ever come to recognize, the mother's face, and, in relation to our own faces—an infinitely more complicated story. In talking about the first aspect, the child's relationship to the mother's face, I shall lean heavily on the wealth of data summarized by Bowlby (1969).

It seems likely that the infant has an inbuilt bias to respond to features of the environment that have a human significance. Even within the first week after birth there seems to be a differential responsiveness to stimuli, such that pattern is preferred to plain color and a plain drawing of the face is preferred to concentric circles. There is a similar early preferential response to the human voice. All of this would make sense in a situation where the development of attachment is a key issue. Attachment to the mother has a clear biological survival value, and I follow Bowlby in seeing the significance of the mother–infant interaction within the overall framework of attachment behavior.

Attachment to the caring person—I will assume this is normally the mother—occurs gradually during the first few months of life. While earlier theories saw it as secondary to feeding and handling, Bowlby argues that attachment is a primary process, not secondary to anything else, and mediated by social interchange (i.e., communication). Within this social interchange, it is the visual channel that appears to have particular importance—it is through smiling, eye-to-eye contact, and playful face-to-face interaction between mother and baby that attachment proceeds. The baby's smile is the essential catalyst that gets the mother–baby interaction going, but this interaction then grows through positive feedback on both sides until it becomes a conversation of visually perceived gestures.[1] Obviously, from the baby's side, an essential part of this process is the increasing ability to recognize perceptual patterns that are discriminated and unique to the mother. The face would seem to have preeminence in this respect.

The development of this early "conversation" of mother and child is of such importance that I will sketch its development (from Bowlby again) in greater detail. First, I will discuss the development of the baby's smile, then the development of facial recognition.

SMILING

Smiling starts at birth. At first, it is fleeting and incomplete and leaves the spectator wholly unmoved. During the fourth and fifth weeks it is still

---

[1]"Conversation of gestures" is a term of G. H. Mead's (1934), though I am using it differently. I do not mean to imply that the preverbal interchange with the mother is a silent process—it obviously includes the mother talking to the baby, the baby's babbling and whole body gestures, and so on. I am only emphasizing the importance of the visual channel in the growth of this social matrix out of which later symbolic and verbal communication will develop. Bowlby mentions the problems of blind children in this respect. The voice to some extent substitutes for vision, but the development of attachment seems to be an altogether slower process.

fleeting but more nearly complete, and it begins to have social effects. The triggers for the smile become gradually more specific: initially the voice, then the face, but neither of these yet specific for a particular person. The response by the fifth or sixth week is fully formed, and though still difficult to elicit, it is fully effective in evoking a playful and loving response in the mother. Over the next few weeks the baby becomes more discriminating. He smiles more readily in response to a familiar voice, and by ten weeks, the mother's face evokes a more immediate and generous smile than any other. Over the next few months, the response to the mother's face and to other familiar faces becomes more dominant; the response to strange faces becomes weaker. Finally, perhaps by eight months, the specificity of response becomes firmly established. Strangers are responded to quite differently from familiar faces, and the mother's face usually evokes the strongest response of all.

RECOGNITION OF FACIAL GESTALT

Until the fifth week, the voice has been the most effective stimulus for eliciting a smile, but around this time it loses much of its power and the face assumes preeminence. From this point on, says Bowlby, it is in happy visual interchanges that the baby's smile comes into its own. It would seem that from about six to fourteen weeks the baby is learning the characteristics of human faces. Before the baby starts to smile at what he sees, he goes through a phase during which he stares intently at faces. During the first three weeks he seems to track them, though not to focus on them; shortly after that he seems to focus and engage in eye-to-eye contact. This is the point at which the mother starts to feel that her baby can see her, and when this occurs she seems to spend much more time with her baby.

Wolff (1963) describes the baby's scanning of the face and the evident importance of eye-to-eye contact. The child searches the face, looking at the hairline, the mouth, and the rest of the face; then, as soon as eye-to-eye contact is made, he grins. Experiments with masks tend to confirm that the eyes are the most important part of the visual gestalt that elicits smiling. For example, at two months, a pair of black dots on a face-sized card will elicit the response. Gradually, however, the complexity of the gestalt must be increased, until at eight months nothing short of an actual human face will do. Overall, a moving human face, seen frontally, is the optimum stimulus; a profile face (i.e., without eyes) will not be effective.

Starting from the beginning, then, the mother's face and the baby's smile soon become central features of a playful social interaction; this social interaction seems to be basic to the attachment process. The baby's responses become increasingly directed and specific; the mother's pleasure in and responsiveness to her baby increase as she feels that her baby recognizes her. Here is a conversation without words, a smiling between faces, at the heart of human development.

Later, I will allow myself a speculation about what the baby's experience of the mother's face might be, and where in our adult experience we might find traces of this earliest era. First, however, I want to develop the idea of this formative "conversation of gestures" between mother and infant.

FACES AND MIRRORS

In a beautiful paper written in 1967, Winnicott observed:

What does the baby see when he or she looks at the mother's face? I am suggesting that ordinarily, what the baby sees is himself or herself. In other words, the mother is looking at the baby, and *what she looks like is related to what she sees there.* All this is too easily taken for granted. I am asking that all this which is naturally well done by mothers caring for their babies shall not be taken for granted. [1967, in Winnicott 1971, p. 112]

In other words, as Winnicott says in the opening lines of the same paper: "In individual emotional development *the precursor of the mirror is the mother's face.*"

The face as mirror—Winnicott offers a rich new metaphor for exploring the meaning and function of the face.[2,3] The face reflects and what it

---

[2]I have noted earlier in this chapter that Searles expressed a very similar idea in his 1963 paper. I do not know whether Winnicott was aware of this aspect of Searles's work, but I suspect that he was not. It seems more likely that they reached a similar conclusion through a certain convergence of clinical work and thinking.

[3]The concept of mirroring is an important one in present-day psychoanalysis. My purpose in this book is not to trace or summarize its development; this has been done admirably in a review article by Malcolm Pines (1984). My aim is far more limited, namely, to focus

reflects back is the other person. The baby looks in the mother's face and sees a reflection of himself. Of course, the baby does see the mother's smiling face, but this, which is in reality her response to his smiles, reflects back to him his own aliveness: "The mother is looking at the baby and what she looks like is related to what she sees there" (p. 112).

I see this as a positively amplifying circuit mutually affirming both partners. The mother is affirmed in her sense of herself as a "good" mother by her baby's smiles of recognition; the baby, we may suppose, feels affirmed in his state of being by the mother's lively and smiling response to him. What, in purely behavioral terms, on the level of the smile, is mutual *reinforcement*, in experiential terms, on the level of communication, is mutual *affirmation*.

We are, I suppose, on dangerous ground when we start to speculate about an infant's experience; but if we do not allow ourselves to imagine and wonder about such things, we may well be closing the door to understanding elements of adult experience that are preverbal yet deeply important. Obviously, we can never *know* what the baby actually feels when the mother smiles at him; but perhaps it would not be too far wrong to think of the experience as quite undifferentiated, whole, and "good." "Smiling face—good smiling feeling," all in one, direct and unmediated. The mother's smiling face is but the most visible part of a total experiential moment. I like to think it is in some such way that the mother's face gets into the baby's experience, not only as the cherished center of his world, but simultaneously as the guiding light of his mind.

Spitz (1955) suggested that the mother's face, perceived in the feeding situation, might become the visual integrator of the earliest and mainly tactile-coenaesthetic experiences of the infant feeding at the breast. What I take Spitz to be saying is something like this. In the beginning, the mother is holding the baby in her arms and the baby is feeding at the breast. In the first three to four weeks the baby cannot see what is going on as it cannot yet focus. But it does have very intense, though vague and diffuse, bodily experiences of feeding and being held, which Spitz calls

---

attention more closely on the face and the part that actual facial interaction plays in the development of our sense of self. Facial interaction also implies different forms of looking and being looked at; I will be arguing that the image of an object that is yielded by looking plays an important part in the whole process of symbol formation, not merely in the formation of those symbols of the self that underpin our "objective" sense of who we are.

primal cavity experiences, as they will be concentrated in the oral cavity and will not in any way differentiate inside from outside. When the infant begins to focus at about five weeks (the time at which the smiling response to the mother's face begins to appear), a visual percept will be added to this early primal cavity experience. This visual percept is the mother's face, it often having been noted that during feeding the infant will look, not at the breast, but at the mother's face. For a long time, then, the mother's face will be but the visual aspect of this experience of satisfaction. It is only later, when the mother's face appears in situations where there is no feeding, no "breast," that it will begin to be differentiated from the primal experience as an external perception.

We do not have to agree with the detail of Spitz's account to take away the idea that, in some way, the mother's face does come to subsume, within a total structure of experience, a whole range of early experiences with the mother, including experiences of being held and fed at the breast. The mother's face then becomes the image of that "good internal object," as well as the perceived face of the actual mother, the attachment figure, increasingly sought after and kept in sight when individuation and separation get under way.

All this can be thought of as happening quite easily and naturally where the mother is responding to her baby's needs and her face reflects her pleasure in the baby's communications. What happens, however, if the mother's face does not respond in this way—if, for example, she is depressed, with a masklike face, or if her smiles are brittle with the rigidity of her own defenses? "In such a case," says Winnicott (1967), "what does the baby see?" (p. 112). He looks and does *not* see himself, but the mother's face. The mother's face is not then a mirror: " . . . perception takes the place of that which might have been the beginning of a significant exchange with the world, a two-way process in which self-enrichment alternates with the discovery of meaning in the world of seen things" (p. 113). The baby's creative capacity begins to dry up.

Winnicott stresses that the child now sees the mother's face, not her mirroring response, and suggests that such children become preoccupied with their mothers' faces in order to read and predict their moods.

Such babies, tantalised by this type of relative maternal failure, study the variable maternal visage in an attempt to predict the mother's mood, just exactly as we all study the weather. The baby quickly learns to make a forecast: "Just now it is safe to forget the mother's mood and to be spontaneous, but any moment the mother's face will become fixed or her mood will dominate, and my own personal needs must then be withdrawn otherwise my central self will suffer insult." [p. 113]

Winnicott thus suggests a sequence in the baby's development of his sense of self—first the *mother* giving back reflections, then the *mirror*. The way the mirror is used will depend on how the mother reflected or failed to reflect. Winnicott, however, does not really explore the idea, implicit in his own paper, that the fixed face of the unresponsive mother could equally be experienced as a reflection, but a distorting one, giving a false feedback of deadness. This actually seems to me more likely. Once the baby knows that it is the mother's face and moods that he sees, he has already moved a long way on the path of differentiation from her. Indeed, my own experience would make me feel that even in adult life, it is hard to free ourselves completely from the feeling that we are the "cause" of expressions we see in the faces of those near us.

This bring us back to the idea of truth or falsity in relation to the face— this time, true or false reflections. This is an idea that could be explored extensively in relation to both development and therapy. I will let Winnicott speak on it in relation to therapy; I can do no more than open the topic in relation to development after that. Winnicott (1967) writes:

This glimpse of the baby's and child's seeing the self in the mother's face and afterwards in the mirror, gives a way of looking at analysis and the psychotherapeutic task. Psychotherapy is not making clever and apt interpretations; by and large it is a long term giving the patient back what the patient brings. *It is a complex derivative of the face that reflects what is there to be seen* [italics added]. I like to think of my work this way, and to think that if I do this well enough the patient will find his or her own self, and will be able to exist and to feel real. Feeling real is more than existing; it is finding a way to exist as oneself, and to relate to objects as oneself, and to have a self into which to retreat for relaxation. [p. 117]

In this brief passage, Winnicott reveals a whole model of therapy, considerably at variance with traditional psychoanalytic technique. It raises many fascinating issues which I will explore further in Chapter 16.

TRUE AND FALSE REFLECTIONS

Before examining the notion of true and false reflections, I will restate the position we have reached. In the beginning, we see the other person's face, but we do not see our own. What we see in the other's face is our own reflection, but not yet as a differentiated experience. This reflection gives back to us our sentient selves, amplified and *real*-ized through a circuit of otherness. It is hard to get back to this experience of having no face of one's own, of never having seen one's actual face, though when we are fully absorbed in our own activities we may temporarily approach this state. What, then, does it mean to discover our own faces, in other words, to see ourselves for the first time in the actual mirror?

Winnicott does not put much emphasis on this precise moment of development in his own writing, but there is an implicit overlap of function between mirror and mother's face, both giving back "reflections"—information about the self. In this context, he makes reference to the psychoanalyst Jacques Lacan and his paper, *Le stade du miroir*, feeling there to be some connection with his own work but not exploring it.

In that paper, Lacan (1949) writes of the importance of the mirror image in the child's developing sense of "I." He describes the child's "jubilant assumption of his own image" when he first recognizes this in the mirror somewhere between the age of six and eighteen months. For Lacan, this image presents, from the beginning, a certain falsity. It is idealized, as it gives back to the child an image of visual completeness and perfection, in sharp contrast to his bodily sense of himself as clumsy and uncoordinated, motor activity being at this time fraught with imprecision and failure. Lacan seems to see this as the start of a dissociation between our own experience of ourselves and our image for others, which increases with time and extends into all our relations with others. The looking glass lies; it makes us look fairer, more whole and complete than we are. Because we believe its lies, we lose touch with our real selves, with the truth of our being, and eventually try to live out the images that have been bestowed upon us by others, by which we have allowed ourselves to be seduced—just as we first allowed ourselves to be seduced by the looking-glass image.

For Lacan, then, the Other (originally the mother) is the one who leads us away from ourselves into this maze of false reflections; for Winnicott, the Other, the "good enough mother," is the one who first reflects back to us our true selves. For Lacan, development and growth into social being and awareness (into the symbolic and language, as he would say) seem to imply an essential and necessary alienation from our true being. It is indeed in the unconscious that our true being lies hidden. Winnicott has a more optimistic view: with an ordinary "good enough mother," most of us more or less make it, with varying degrees of truth or falsity, creativity or compliance. He does not deny pathological "false self" developments, but these are the exception, not the rule.

These theories are built on different views of human nature and, in particular, on different views of mothering. Lacan's mothers would seem to follow the looking-glass model and are false reflectors from the start. The baby is born into an image the mother may have had of the child before he even existed, and there is no escaping from it. Winnicott's mothers can reflect true, so all is not lost, and true being and creativity may still flourish. For all their differences, though, both Lacan and Winnicott might agree that through analysis the person may be led out of the maze in which he has become lost toward his true being. Their techniques, however, would differ quite radically: Winnicott's maternal, empathic, ". . . a complex derivative of the face that reflects what is there to be seen"; Lacan, more like the father perhaps—distanced, standing in language, rigorously translating the text, reading the unspoken book of the unconscious.

THE FACES OF INFANCY

I want to return to the question of where, in our adult experience, we might find traces of that time when the mother's face was the center of our world. I find it unimaginable that so central and pervasive an experience as that early dialogue with the mother could leave no trace, though I have to remind myself that it was preverbal and predominantly visual.

I am going to suggest that it is in the ground from which religion, art, and poetry spring that we should look for such traces—in other words, in those areas where illusion most readily holds sway, which Winnicott (1971) has explored in his writings on transitional experience and transitional phenomena. Such a contention cannot be argued or proved; it can merely be supported by evocative examples. The "proof" is presentational, in Langer's (1942) sense, not discursive. I will give a few illustrations.

Love poetry, particularly the poetry of longing rather than fulfillment, repeatedly returns to the face of the loved object. I believe that the longing of love reactivates imagery from a preverbal past, creating a penumbra of significance that clings to the immediately sought-after person. This view is in line with psychoanalytic ideas about the transference, and I would suggest that the often sacred, almost numinous quality of the loved object's face is the result of this charging with earlier imagery and feeling.

In Robert Graves's poem "The Three-Faced," which I quoted at the beginning of this chapter, we might well ask whose face it is that is "once for an endless moment turned on me." Is it just the face of the poet's current mistress—and we know that Graves had very many? Clearly, it is not. Something else has been added that seems to take the experience out of the mere prosaic present. Perhaps it is the word *endless* that lifts it to a different level and introduces a sense of something timeless and eternal. Jung might have called such an experience archetypal, evidence of some generic memory deep in all of us; but for me, the heightened significance suggests an aura of long-forgotten, and now half-remembered, imagery, the face of the loved object appearing not only in its own right, but representing elements from preverbal memory, when the mother's face filled the child's world with radiance and adoration.

Here is another example:

> Was this the face that launch'd a thousand ships,
> And burned the topless towers of Ilium?
> Sweet Helen, make me immortal with a kiss!

These lines from Marlowe's *Dr. Faustus* open up in a similar way a larger dimension of experience. It is as though the loved face reaches deeply into the soul and resonates there with early memories of the mother. These memories, organized around the central image of the mother's face, may well include feeling images of blissful satisfaction at the breast, as Réné Spitz has suggested. Marlowe's evocative lines suggest this:

> Her lips suck forth my soul: see, where it flies!
> Come Helen, come give me my soul again.

> Here will I dwell, for heaven be in these lips,
> And all is dross that is not Helena.

Religion, at least within the Judeo-Christian tradition, is a further area of experience that makes abundant use of the imagery of the face. The transfiguration (from the French *figure*, face) of Christ would be but one example.[4]

> And after six days, Jesus . . . bringeth them up into an high mountain apart, and was transfigured before them: *and his face did shine as the sun* [italics added], and his raiment was white as the light. [Matthew 17:1–2]

Another example comes from St. Paul:

> For now we see through a glass, darkly; but then face to face: now I know in part; but then shall I know even as also I am known. [1 Corinthians 13:12]

In each of these examples there is a similar image—the face that is hidden and then revealed to show the truth, or the true face of God. The transfiguration is a numinous experience and the shining face is apparently seen for the first time. But in Paul's epistle, there is an intuition that the true face is one that is already, in some sense, known and remembered, and we are again back in the territory of Freud: "The finding of an object is . . . a refinding of it" (1905, p. 222). The mystical poet Henry Vaughan seems to have recognized this conjuncture of the first wonderful face of experience with that which shall be revealed at the end:

> Happy those early days, when I
> Shin'd in my angel infancy.
> Before I understood this place

---

[4]My linking of *transfiguration* with the French word *figure* may not be etymologically accurate. The English word *figure* comes from the Latin *figura* (from *fingere*, to fashion, or form), not from the French word *figure* (one of two French words for *face*; the other is *visage*). Presumably, the French word *figure* comes to mean *face* through the root idea of *form*; the English word *figure* means *form* or *shape*, hence the idea of the face as the form, shape, or pattern by which we recognize the person. This connection between *form* and *face* is interesting for the argument that I develop—namely, that the face is one of the earliest forms or figures (patterns) that the infant learns to recognize, and it provides a prototype for the subsequent recognition of symbolic patterns.

> Appointed for my second race,
> Or taught my soul to fancy aught
> But a white, celestial thought;
> When yet I had not walked
> A mile or two from my first love,
> And looking back—at that short space—
> Could see a glimpse of His bright face.

Is the "white celestial thought" that Vaughan speaks of not more likely to be the first radiant face of the mother? And what of that "white light in the back of my mind to guide me," which Louis MacNeice has written of in his poem "Prayer before Birth"? Certainly Vaughan's feeling is that "His bright face" is something that could be remembered at a very early stage of life, and I suspect MacNeice's image taps a similar area of experience.

It is not a great distance from here to Wordsworth—"Our birth is but a sleep and a forgetting"—and Wordsworth could lead us on to a consideration of nature as a felt presence, something that many people have experienced at some time in their lives. Before I reach that point, I want to mention the benediction that is often given in the Church of England at the end of a service. It is the blessing of Aaron that God gave to Moses in the wilderness:

> The Lord bless thee, and keep thee:
> The Lord make his face shine upon thee, and be
>   gracious unto thee:
> The Lord lift up his countenance upon thee, and give
>   thee peace. [Numbers 6:24–26]

The face that shines upon you and gives you "the peace of God, which passeth all understanding"—surely this soothes and comforts by reaching into that storehouse of early experience deep within the preverbal core of the self where the mother's face "shines" (smiles) upon the baby in her arms and fills its whole perceptual world with its "light." In trying to reach these early experiences, it is worth recalling just how much the mother's face would literally have filled the infant's gaze and world, and even later when the child is taking its first steps in individuation, how centrally important would have been the mother's face and expression as he looked back for reassurance or approval.

I have mentioned the experience of nature as a presence, and I want now to say what I mean in more detail. Wordsworth's poetry epitomizes the kind of experience I have in mind in which the changing scenes and landscapes of the natural world touch the person almost as a living being:

> And I have felt
> A presence that disturbs me with the joy
> Of elevated thoughts; a sense sublime
> Of something far more deeply interfused,
> Whose dwelling is the light of setting suns,
> And the round ocean and the living air,
> And the blue sky, and in the mind of man.

Wordsworth's sentiment may seem somewhat elevated, but I believe that glimpses of such experience are frequently intermingled with our ordinary lives, and ordinary language knows this. The warm wind *caresses* us; the beautiful day *smiles* on us; the quickly moving stream *laughs* as it tumbles over the rocks. The storm clouds *glower*, thunder *roars*, and lightning *flashes* (a wonderful and to some people terrifying image of anger); the soft lines of the hills in the surrounding landscape *enfold* each other and ourselves in their muted lines. On one level, this metaphorical way of speaking of the natural world is quite clichéd. On another level, it still taps in to living experience in which we almost allow ourselves to believe the illusion of such presences. I think the experience is genuinely transitional, in Winnicott's sense, and actually serves to comfort and soothe, even though in the most rational parts of ourselves we would admit that it was all a fiction. It is as though we allow the world to re-present to us those buried memories of a predominantly maternal presence, so that Mother Earth, or Mother Nature, still seems to be all around us as the supporter of our precarious lives. At those times, the changing expressions of this natural world can be felt and experienced as the changing moods on the face of this maternal being.

I am not a painter, but I suspect that it is often these presences and moods that the landscape painter is trying to portray. All art, according to Susanne Langer (1942), is concerned to give form and articulation to human feelings, and a re-creation of such early feelings and states of relatedness to the mother would certainly be in keeping with this view.

Peter Fuller (1980), a well-known art critic, has written at length about the relation of painting to such early feeling states. In his book,

Psychoanalysis and Art, he discusses the work of the American painter Robert Natkin. Natkin's style is largely abstract, although initially he had started by painting portraits. According to Fuller, Natkin gave up figurative portrait painting, "complaining about the limitations and fixity which the physiognomy of facial features imposed on him" (p. 210). In the abstract work that followed, he continued to explore surfaces and textures and their different "feel" and "expressions." Fuller suggests that these expressive sur-*faces* were more than metaphorically in continuity with the faces that Natkin previously had painted. He quotes Natkin as saying that "everything he has ever painted from the time of those early portraits onwards is a face" (p. 210). Even when he returned for a time to a more figurative landscape painting, he felt the same to be true. "Natkin now says that these (Redding View) paintings have about them a quality he can only define as expressing 'The Face of the Earth'" (p. 211). Following this, Natkin painted a major series of abstract canvases, which he called his Face paintings.

Fuller relates these paintings and Natkin's thoughts about his work to elements in Natkin's own life, in particular to his early experiences in relation to his mother, which were often disconfirming and disintegrating. Fuller suggests that creating expressive surfaces on the canvas had become for Natkin a means by which he strove to re-create a preverbal dialogue with the mother. "I am suggesting that, for Natkin, the canvas surface became a surrogate for that reciprocal encounter he had lacked with the 'good' mother's face" (p. 211). It would follow from this that all the subtle variations in mood and texture that the paintings sought to portray could be seen as struggles of the painter to affirm and strengthen a much loved and needed good internal object. That object was his mother's loving face, dimly remembered though maybe insufficiently experienced in the past, now cherished and nurtured in the core of the self.

It could be argued that every picture reaches back into the artist's and our own early experience of the face. The relationship between the picture surface and what it reveals is remarkably similar to that between the face and the expressions that pass across it. The flat picture surface, made up of paints and pigments applied to the canvas, creates an illusion of life and form and space. Life and meaning germinate at this surface; that which was purely a thing lights up through the artist's work, revealing something organized and meaningful. In a similar way, the face is transformed (or transfigured) by an expression that plays across the features, revealing an emotional message. I think that Fuller is very close to saying this in his book, though he is nowhere quite explicit.

The process by which a mere thing is transformed into a symbol that conveys a meaning is one that I will be considering in detail in later chapters. But I want to note here the possibility that the mother's face of infancy, with its capacity to convey emotional messages that foster and modulate the attachment process, could be regarded as a first proto-symbol, the first object in the child's experience to undergo such a transformation. If this were so, it would make very good biological sense, for the face is, from the beginning, an object of recognition, not an object that can be used. It would then be appropriate if that object, which serves the function of attachment, should lead the way toward symbol formation and communication, themselves essential to the maintenance of attachment.

I want to end this chapter by returning to what for me is a wonderful evocation of that early world in which the mother's face plays such a central role. The lines are from T. S. Eliot's poem "Marina" and form a hypnotic journey into that world of forgotten yet not forgotten images:

> What is this face, less clear and clearer
> The pulse in the arm, less strong and stronger
> Given or lent? more distant than stars and nearer
>   than the eye
> Whispers and small laughter between leaves and
>   hurrying feet
> Under sleep, where all the waters meet.

2   The Other's View

And they heard the voice of the Lord God walking in the garden in the cool of the day: and Adam and his wife hid themselves from the presence of the Lord God amongst the trees of the garden.

And the Lord God called unto Adam, and said unto him,

"Where are thou?"

And he said,

"I heard thy voice in the garden, and I was afraid, because I was naked; and I hid myself."

—Genesis 3:8–10

THE SELF AS SPECTACLE

THIS CHAPTER IS, in many ways, a counterpoint to the last. That chapter was a celebration of the "good enough mother," the mother who through her mirroring of emotional responses confirmed and strengthened the infant's embryonic sense of self. This chapter sounds a minor key, the plaintive note of estrangement and loss of self. The mother's face is still here, but no longer as the sun that shines and warms. Her look is cold, and she stands at a distance; she looks *at* me, and the stark outlines of a visual form, the specter of myself as she sees me, haunts the space between us and holds us apart.

The experience that I will explore has many forms; the central feature of all of them is the experience of being looked at.

I will begin with a personal example. When I was an adolescent, I often felt awkward and self-conscious. I would feel that I was being looked at; this feeling inhibited my spontaneity and created a sense of no longer being in touch with myself. I had become a spectacle. I can remember walking down the long aisle in the school chapel feeling that all eyes were on me, and I can recall nightmares in which this experience was replayed in exaggerated form. I would feel that my legs no longer belonged to me;

they seemed to move in a disconnected way, and I had somehow to propel myself as though I were a robot. The look of other people had in some way disintegrated me, displaced me from myself. I no longer lived from the inside out, but instead had lost touch with myself and temporarily seemed to live from the outside in.

It would be easy to offer an interpretation of such an experience—to go for the content. The legs that moved in a disconnected way, for example, might indicate castration anxiety; their giving way, a loss of erection, and so on. Whether or not such interpretations would be true, it is my belief that they do not say all that can be said about the experience. If we can stay closer to the phenomenology and form of the experience, rather than rushing to interpret its content, it may be that they can teach us much that is important about the nature and genesis of the self.

In the last chapter, I asked how it is that we come to discover our own faces, and the answer was in the mirror, but beyond the mirror in the eyes and faces of those who regard us, as a kind of emotional reflection. In this chapter, I will be asking how we come to "see" our own self. Again the answer will be through the eyes and looks of others, through the image that they bestow upon us. I am aware that there is a certain concreteness in the way I am putting this; the Other's view eventually takes its stand in language and is then expressed in words, spoken or unspoken. I am suggesting, however, that the experiential underpinning of this mediation by the Other remains essentially visual and that this fact is enshrined in language in the notion of the Other's view.

If I am right in thinking that the only way we come to know our self is through the Other's view of us, and that all self-consciousness and self-knowledge are thus mediated by an Other, then the importance of exploring the nature of this mediation can scarcely be overemphasized. The self that is offered by this Other arises at the inter-face between this self and the Other and must depend on some kind of symbolic exchange, on communication in the broadest sense. This mediation or reflection is thus exposed to all the risks of distortion and misrepresentation that interpersonal perception and communication are heir to.

I think it is becoming clear that I am using the term *self* in two distinct ways. On the one hand, I am talking about the *self-as-subject*, the experiencing self who exists prior to this encounter with the Other's view. On the other, I am talking of the *self-as-object*, that starkly visual and externally formed image of the self which is constituted by that view. This distinction is one that I will make repeatedly in the next two chapters.

What I want to explore is the relationship, within the person, between these two phases of the self.[1] Does the objective self in some way integrate with or modify the subjective self? Is the objective self repudiated? Or is there a capitulation of the subjective self, a sliding of the subjective self behind the objective form which has been offered? These questions will lead, I believe, into very basic issues of integrity and defense, and ultimately into issues of therapy. They will bring up the relation between different sense modalities in experience, in particular, between the *distance* modality of *vision* and the more *proprio*ceptive modalities of *touch and visceral sensation*.

THE CLAUSTROPHOBIC EXPERIENCE

For my dissertation (Wright 1969), I studied a group of phobic patients, most of whom suffered from claustrophobic-agoraphobic symptoms. I came to note through all the cases a core experience, the upsurge of which was constantly dreaded as a catastrophe of an ultimate kind. What the patient regarded in a distancing and defensive way as an alien symptom repeatedly emerged, on sustained questioning, as a little psychic drama, involving "self" and "others," which might unfold were it not possible to run away from the situation that apparently provoked the anxiety. The essence of the drama was to be forced by the constricting, trapping situation into some kind of uncontrolled state (variously envisaged as shouting, screaming, becoming violent, defecating, or urinating), thereby making a spectacle of oneself. People would gather around and

---

[1]Like the term "conversation of gestures," which I used in the last chapter, the idea of "phases of the self" also owes much to Mead (1934); but again, my borrowing of the term somewhat alters its meaning. Mead's "phases" referred to the "I" and the "me"; the "I" being the subjective source of our actions and behavior that we can never quite get hold of directly, the "me" being the attitudes of all the Others in the social field that I repeatedly take during the course of a social action in order to determine what I will do next. While Mead's "I" may not be so dissimilar to my "subjective self," my "objective self" refers specifically to the self that is objectified through the Other looking at it. I discuss this further in Chapter 15.

look. It was this making a spectacle of oneself that seemed, above all, to be dreaded—"others," people in the street, for example, gathering around and regarding one as mad. There would be no sympathy; none of the spectators would understand what was happening. Instead, they would look on with horror, as though the subject of the drama were an alien being. This was more than simply losing the love of someone who was needed, though that clearly was a part of the fear. It was more than the feeling of painful embarrassment and confusion of being looked at, though that was there as well. The specific trauma seemed rather to reside in the sense of dislocation from oneself, from a center of subjective experiencing to an *external* position, a locus of otherness, from where one would be obliged to look back on this dreadful spectacle of "me." It was as though a new "object" were to be forced on one's awareness, the image of one's self as one appeared to this Other.

I think it is possible to sketch an outline of this drama which is portrayed in the phobic experience. The patient is in a rage against someone who is very controlling and constricting. He is bursting with this rage, and someone, probably the one he is angry with, is standing there and looking at him in a certain sort of way. There is a sense of being alone and uncared for, without sympathy and without love. Also, the way the story is told suggests that the person shares the view of this Other. The *experience* of rage has disappeared, and the only thing left is this *terrible view of oneself* as a mad, less-than-human creature.

This Other who reflects back such an image of the self is concerned with appearances; has no concern for feelings and subjective experience; stands at a distance from the one he confronts; and makes no approach to touch, hold, or comfort. This unempathic Other stands in sharp contrast to the smiling mother of the last chapter, who interacts with her child in a warm and playful way. Since her look freezes the subjective life of feeling, perhaps she is the one who is personified in the myth of Perseus and the Gorgon. The Gorgons were horrific sisters with locks of serpents, tusks of wild boars, and golden wings fixed to their shoulders. Whoever dared to look them in the face was instantly turned to stone. Perseus eventually killed one of these sisters, Medusa, but only by taking elaborate precautions to avoid being turned into stone himself. One of these precautions was making himself invisible (probably so that he could not be looked at); the other was using a mirror so as not to have to look directly at Medusa.

These faces, the face with the loving smile and the face with terrifying eyes, are surely two aspects of the mother of childhood. Together they form the melody and counterpoint of childhood experience. The first face confirms and strengthens the child's subjective being, amplifies it through reverberating circuits of reflection and response. The second face disconfirms, puts the child at a distance, arrests the continuity of subjective feeling, and offers in its place a spectacle of the bad self that puts the continuity of love in question. It may be worth recalling here Freud's theory of the neurotic symptom. Every symptom is a compromise—between the id and the superego; between the impulse and the defense. In this account, the phobic symptom is also a kind of compromise. What is compromised, however, is the person's unfolding action and subjective experience (his rage). It is as though there is a dislocation, a wrenching, of the person from his subjective self, from which he then becomes separated by this image and this distance that the Other interposes.

I want to stress that this "object" that is interposed is purely visual and falls between the child and his subjective self. The self that comes from the Other is a *seen* self, not a *touched* self—maybe it is untouchable. It comes from a look that witholds touching and closeness and emphasizes separation. In contrast, the subjective self feels and does and looks in order to do. It is *in touch* with the world and the Other. "The ego is first and foremost a bodily ego" (Freud 1923, S.E. 19, p. 26).

SCREEN MEMORIES

There is another psychopathological product that I want to consider in light of this analysis—the so-called screen memory described by Freud. This is a childhood memory, often relatively insignificant in content, which stands in front of memories of far greater import that have been repressed. It forms a screen, behind which the repressed experience is hidden. The term itself is an interesting one with a powerful visual reference, but it is the actual characteristics of the screen memories themselves that I want to consider.

In a paper on the subject, Greenacre (1949) writes:

Among these (screen) memories, some were noted as having *special characteristics of brightness and intensity* which generally contrasted with their relatively indifferent, innocuous or patently distorted content. They were not only *predominantly visual*, but Freud further noted, that in contrast to memories from later periods of life, the rememberer was detached and *seemed to watch himself as a child performer*. [p. 73, italics added]

Greenacre attempts to account for these characteristics in a number of ways. She writes of a "superego factor":

It seems, however, that *the detached onlooker quality* characteristic of the typical screen memory may be due, not only to the *paralysis and temporary depersonalization* caused by fright or panic and carried over to the substitute remembered experience, but further and perhaps chiefly to *the arousal of the superego functions* whose force influences decisively the need to deny and the feeling of general intensity, and which are represented by *an actual watchfulness* in the screen memory. [p. 76, italics added]

This is a difficult and somewhat contorted explanation, but the main cause of the typical visual qualities of the screen memory seems to be an aroused "superego function" of "actual watchfulness." In other words, the person reporting the screen memory has apparently identified with this superego function, and thus derivatively with the actual parent of childhood who watched the child (in a disapproving sort of way). It would seem that the screen memory that is presented, the self as a child performer, must, from a formal point of view, be what this detached and watching Other saw, or was imagined to have seen, or more likely a distorted derivative of this. If this is so, then the screen memory is the result of an insertion of an alien fragment into the continuity of subjective self-experience; a piece of felt experience is replaced by a purely visual and externally derived percept, which is not the subject's own, but phenomenologically something the Other saw. There has been an invasion of self by Other.

In the passage quoted above, part of Greenacre's explanation of the heightened visual quality and child performer characteristic of the screen memory is what she calls "paralysis and temporary depersonalization caused by fright or panic." This seems to be another way of putting what I have already said. I would maintain that the substitution of the Other's view for one's own feelings is itself a form of depersonalization. To feel depersonalized is precisely to lose touch with the vitality of one's subjective self. Perhaps this provides a way of looking at the depersonalization syndrome. Anxiety about some unacceptable impulse or feeling and fear of losing the love of the needed person lead to a flight from the self into the Other, and a temporary experiencing of the self from "out there." Depersonalization is often associated with *derealization*, the experience of the world as in some way flat and lacking in vividness. Could it be that the person in this state is also looking at things through the Other's eyes? I will come to this question again in a later chapter when I discuss the integration of looking and doing in development.

SHAME—BEING SEEN AS AN OBJECT

So far I have discussed three kinds of abnormal experience that seem to have something in common. The claustrophobic experience, screen memories, and depersonalization—all seem to involve a positional shift of the person from groundedness in self to looking through the eyes of the Other, correlatively, a substitution in personal experience of visual image from "out there" for lived experience from "in here." In each case, the person suffers a divorce from his own felt experience and personal point of view.

I next want to consider the experience of shame, which I believe shares this characteristic. Shame is a normal, probably universal, human phenomenon, where one's own experience (inner) and the Other's view (outer) invariably meet. It brings me back to the idea that the self is formed or constituted where inner and outer meet, at the interface between persons.

In *Shame and the Search for Identity*, Helen Merrell Lynd (1958) argues that shame has been a relatively neglected experience in psychological writings and in fact merits much closer attention. Although she emphasizes the importance of feeling suddenly exposed in the experience of shame, Lynd puts less emphasis than I do on the experience of being looked at, and so the visual nature of the experience emerges as less important. By arguing that shame can occur in isolation, she also deemphasizes the role of the Other. She does, however, acknowledge that in these circumstances, it is "exposure of oneself to oneself" that is the critical factor. Although Lynd goes on to say that it is falling short of one's own ideal that is in question, she does not seem to make the obvious inference that this ideal is, in fact, an aspect of the Other in oneself. In spite of these reservations, I agree with Lynd's central thesis: shame forces into awareness some aspect of oneself that one had not realized, and can therefore enlarge self-awareness and give a clearer sense of one's own identity.

I would argue that shame is originally grounded in the experience of being looked at by the Other and in the realization that the Other can see things about oneself that are not available to one's own vision. The fact that shame is frequently associated with blushing, which is a visual signal, seems to fit with this view. There may also be a wish to hide oneself or one's face—presumably to escape from this being seen or from the one who sees. Shame is also a sudden experience. It comes upon one unexpectedly, interrupting one's ongoing relation to whatever one is involved in. As in the experiences already discussed, there is a sudden enforced shift in the direction of one's awareness—I see myself from "out there," rather than seeing the world from "in here." Shame is a kind of crisis, a moment of danger that puts in question both my self and my relation to the Other. This self which I am for the Other, will it still be loved? This Other's view cannot be ignored.

My own thinking about the experiences of shame and being looked at and their importance in the development of the self has been strongly influenced by Jean-Paul Sartre. A whole section of *Being and Nothingness* (1957) is devoted to the "The Look" (pp. 252–302); although his purposes are philosophical and mine are psychological, there is much that is of relevance. I want to summarize those parts of Sartre's phenomenological analysis that bear on my subject.

1. For Sartre, self and Other are in opposition because (to speak in the first person, as Sartre does) my subjectivity, my organization of the world about me in terms of my aims and intentions, and my unreflective engagement in these are constantly threatened by the possibility of the Other looking at me. The Other is already a threat, even before he looks at me, becuase *his* looking at the world, *his* organization of this same world in terms of *his* aims and intentions, already introduces a kind of "leakage" into the middle of *my* world: " . . . the world has a kind of drain hole in the middle of its being and . . . it is perpetually flowing off through this hole"

(p. 256). The Other is like a "little particular crack in my universe" (p. 256). He has the capacity to disintegrate my organization of the world about myself and to reorganize it about himself. All of this is still prior to the actual "look," and takes place by virtue of the fact that this Other has consciousness and subjectivity. At a certain point, the Other may look at me and make me an object in his universe.

... (his) space is made *with my space*; there is a regrouping in which I take part, but which escapes me, a regrouping of all the objects which people my universe. . . . Thus suddenly an object has appeared which has stolen the world from me. Everything is in place; everything still exists for me; but everything is traversed by an invisible flight and fixed in the direction of a new object. [p. 255]

2.   This threat that the Other poses is realized when he looks at me. I then become an object in his universe, a fixed something that is defined by him. The catastrophe of this is not that the Other has a view of me that is at variance with my own; rather, that such a view is the death of my own spontaneous subjectivity and causes me to become an object.

Beyond any knowledge which I can have, I am this self which another knows. And this self which I am—this I am in a world that the Other has made alien to me. . . . [p. 261]

It is shame or pride which reveals to me the Other's look and myself at the end of that look. [p. 261]

I grasp the Other's look at the very centre of my *act* as the solidification and alienation of my own possibilities. [p. 263]

Thus in the shock which seizes me when I apprehend the Other's look, this happens—that suddenly I experience a subtle alienation of all my possibilities, which are now associated with objects of the world, far from me in the midst of the world. [p. 265]

3.   The experience of shame seems for Sartre to be immediate and prereflective. It gives me simultaneously the experience of my self as object and the experience of the Other "as he comes toward me from all his transcendence." Self is constituted, experientially, in that same moment that the Other appears. Shame is not an apprehension of particulars—of being this or that guilty object—but

rather an apprehension of object status in the eyes of this Other. It is a question

of *recognising myself* in this degraded, fixed and dependent being which I am for the Other. Shame is the feeling of an *original fall*, not because of the fact that I may have committed this or that particular fault but simply that I have "fallen" into the world in the midst of things and that I need the mediation of the Other in order to be what I am. [p. 288]

4. This leads to the final point—the subject's total dependence on the Other for any apprehension of self as object. Both this basic experience and all further developments of self-knowledge depend equally on the mediation of the Other.

For me the Other is first the being for whom I am an object; that is, the being *through whom* I gain my objectness. If I am to be able to conceive of even one of my properties in the objective mode, then the Other is already given. [p. 270]

That subject's presence without intermediary is the necessary condition of all thought which I would attempt to form concerning myself. [p. 271]

What does Sartre's analysis really add up to? It documents a passage from prereflective living to self-consciousness and self-knowledge, from subjective experience to awareness of self as object. It also demonstrates the essential role of the Other in this process. Developmentally, this is a path that all must take. In terms of current living, it is an oscillation or phasic movement between two modes of being, a passage through the Other to find oneself—though, as Sartre says, to find oneself in the mode of not being, as an object. (There is a gap of "nothingness" between me and myself as object; I can never be the self that I am conscious of.)

LOOKING AT AND LOOKING AFTER

I want to focus for a moment on the dialectic between self and Other that Sartre describes. For Sartre, the Other on whom I depend for my self seems to be a mortal enemy. He is to be feared because he threatens to annihilate my subjective self and reorganize the world in terms of his subjectivity, with me as his object. My only defense against this is for me to make him into my object in order to prevent the eruption of his subjectivity. The Other as object is like a bomb—he can go off at any time, and the upsurge of his subjectivity will then destroy me as subject.

> Therefore my constant concern is to contain the Other within his objectivity, and my relations with the Other-as-object are essentially made up of ruses designed to make him remain an object. But one look on the part of this Other is sufficient to make all these schemes collapse and to make me experience once more the transfiguration of the Other. [Sartre 1957, p. 297]

In psychological terms, we would describe this as an essentially paranoid relation with the Other. Indeed, in *The Divided Self* (1960) Laing drew on this Sartrian analysis to illuminate some of the anxieties and interpersonal maneuvers that schizoid and borderline individuals may engage in. Do we have to believe, though, that all our self-knowledge is based on such a paranoid relation to the Other? Is it this one with terrifying eyes on whom we depend for all knowledge concerning ourselves? Indeed, is all our organized knowledge of the world, all our theorizing about the Other, merely a ruse to keep him in his place and prevent his subjectivity from "exploding"? Surely the answer must be no. Although, formally, Sartre's analysis highlights an essential movement from subjectivity to objectivity and back again, in feeling terms there is an imbalance. Why does objectivity, the Other's view, have to annihilate the subject? And why does there have to be such an either/or, him or me type of situation? Why only one subjectivity, never two subjectivities together?

I now want to insert a counterpoint of experience, which is really a return to Chapter 1—the experience of the Other as horizon of my subjective world. There is a line, which I think comes from Rilke, that beautifully captures this alternative experience of the Other: "Where *you* are a place arises."[2] I would also remind you of Winnicott's idea of the mother's face as the child's first mirror, reflecting back and confirming the child in its being. And I want to remind you of that early playful and smiling interaction between mother and baby that seems to play such an important part in the development of attachment. We could add to this

---

[2] I am attributing this line to Rilke from memory, but I have not been able to find it in his *Collected Poems*.

Winnicott's ideas about play—the mother allowing the child its own space for play and guarding that space from intrusions—and the picture of a benign, nonthreatening maternal space is complete. There seems to be no room in Sartre for a mother or Other of this kind.

It could be argued that all such experiences existed only in some mythical time past, that is, in some early and now superseded period of development, that once we have "fallen" into the world of objects, as Sartre puts it, there is no going back—at least no going back to that mutually confirming, intersubjective experience of infancy. However, ordinary experience seems to put the lie to this. It does seem to be possible in some relationships some of the time, and in a few relationships more of the time, not to have to fight for one's emotional survival. And there does in fact seem to be room for a different kind of dialectic in experience, of the kind envisioned by Martin Buber in *I and Thou* (1937).

Buber certainly saw the prevalence of the objectifying type of connection in our social lives, which he called the I–It relationship. This is the world of ordered experience and ordered events, of people defined by their objective roles and qualities. But for Buber, we repeatedly transcend this I–It world in moments of intersubjective contact with those around us. Such transcending moments are moments of I and Thou. The I–Thou relationship keeps breaking through the objective structures that we have formed. These moments of I–Thou relationship are *mutually* confirming, and without them we are dead as human beings. As Buber says: "Without It man cannot live. But he who lives with It alone is not a man" (p. 34). When we relate to the Other as Thou he is not our object, but present to us in an immediate way. He is not a sum of qualities or defenses or object relationships—all the things that we can "see" about him—"But with no neighbour, and whole in himself, he is Thou and fills the heavens" (p. 8).

Buber thus delineates an area of experience that does not seem to have a place in Sartre. The saying of the primary word *I–Thou* confirms both the speaker and the one addressed. There is a meeting of two subjectivities and neither of them collapses. There is mutuality and meeting *in the present*. Buber affirms an area of mutual confirmation in present experience, which, although it harks back to the early mutuality of mother and child, nevertheless exists in the here and now.

I can now give at least a partial answer to the question I have posed: Why and when does the look of the Other bring about a collapse of the subjective self into the objective image that the look provides? I suggest

that this occurs when there has been insufficient good early experience
with the mother of a comfirmatory kind; when the self is not founded on
the rock of "good enough mothering" it cannot stand firm. This founding
of the self in satisfactory early experience has been written about extensively by Winnicott and many others, and it would go beyond the
confines of this chapter to summarize. (See Chapter 4.) But if we think
for a moment, with Winnicott, of the mother watching over the child's
play, preserving for it a space free from intrusions, we again have a
counterpoint to the kind of mother represented by Sartre's Other, who
looks at but does not *look after*. We might say that the "good mother"
protects the child from the intrusive looking of the "bad mother," just as
Athene, in the Gorgon myth, protected Perseus from the look of Medusa.

Before giving some clinical illustrations, I want to emphasize some
further points about this catastrophic looking which objectifies and destroys. I have already characterized it as a looking at, not a looking after.
It is a distanced, unempathic looking and not a caring looking. Distance
seems to be of its essence; indeed, the look seems to keep the other person
at a distance, out of contact, far from any possibility of touch or closeness. In some ways, this seems like the ultimate act of separation, and the
self that is seen and experienced at that distance does seem to have a
clarity and definitiveness about it that bounds it in some ultimate way.
We could say that the self that is looked at in this way now has an
"outside"; but, of course, the trauma is to feel that this "outside" is not
just a complement to the "inside" and something that can be integrated
with it, but a usurper of it, so that the self becomes completely defined
from the outside. I have said that the Other that does this is distanced and
unempathic. This Other does not "feel with" the one it is looking at,
though it may well be "feeling about"—reacting to behaviors which at
that moment are unacceptable. In this case, the Other's definition of self
is made from within an alien frame of reference, from an outside point of
view. It is clear that this Other's point of view is an inevitable occurrence
in the course of normal development. Every ordinary mother or father is
offering such perspectives on behavior every day. What is in question is
how any particular child deals with this parental view: does he repudiate
it; take account of it, yet hold it at a distance; or succumb to it and in
some way get taken over by it?

We can imagine a whole range of views coming from the actual Other
who is the parent. Some will be cold and distanced, some warm and

empathic, probably many in between. Such views will have varying degrees of consonance or dissonance with the self; as a result, some will be more easily integrated than others. All of this has a great deal of relevance to therapy as well as parenting, as an interpretation is quite clearly a "view" in the sense discussed here. More detailed discussion of the therapeutic issues that are raised by this must wait for a later chapter (Chapter 16), but I want to mention one point to do with timing. Most therapists feel that the timing of interpretations is important and have notions about when the patient is ready for such an intervention. I think the question of timing is also of importance in relation to development: at what point in development does the child become exposed to particular kinds of views emanating from the Other? The distanced view, looking *at*, seems to promote separation. I think we can therefore ask at what stage in the process of separating out from the mother does the child come into contact with such a separating view. What happens, for example, when such a distancing view impinges on a self that has not yet made a sufficiently clear distinction between self and Other to be able to tolerate it? Could this wrong timing be a cause of the sense of dislocation from oneself of which I am talking?

In this chapter I have explored the idea that self-consciousness, in all its many-faceted meanings, is a derivative of the experience of being looked at. I have suggested that this is true, whether we are talking of embarrassed self-consciousness, as in shyness or shame, or of the more neutral kinds of self-awareness that lead to self-knowledge or self-under-standing. I have tried to delineate the dynamic interaction that exists between immediate and unreflective self-experience and the view that the Other takes on that experience or its accompanying behavior. I have suggested that the self is defined or formed in this interaction, rather as for Freud, the ego was formed at the surface of the id through interaction with reality—the external world. Just as I have not really defined the term *self*, so I have avoided where possible defining the term *Other*. *Other*, like *self*, is a vast word that at different times embraces inner and outer, past and present. In experience, though, Other is nearly always "out there." I have tried to show that this dialectic between self and Other can have normal or pathological outcomes depending on the relative strength of the two interacting parties. I have emphasized those situations where there is dissonance between the experience of self and the view of the Other, and related this to a distancing and unempathic look. Some will say that I am merely describing the relations that exist in the psyche between an ego, an id, and a harsh superego. But I believe that something more, or different, emerges from concentrating on a phenomenological and even concrete level of description that emphasizes the visual underpinning of the meeting with the Other and the clash of sensory modalities that it involves.

3   The Self as Visual Object

> *. . . for the roses*
> *had the look of flowers that are looked at.*
> —T. S. Eliot, "Burnt Norton"

Shame is by nature recognition. *I recognize that I am as the Other sees me.*
> —John-Paul Sartre, *Being and Nothingness*

IN THIS CHAPTER I will present some clinical vignettes to illustrate
and perhaps extend the ideas put forward in Chapter 2. In varying
degrees, each of the patients described in the case histories had lost
touch with their alive and feeling selves under the influence of the
Gorgon's stare.

CASE 1

The patient was a woman, forty years old, who had been in weekly
psychotherapy for about two years. She had a grossly impaired
capacity for living—only in playing the piano did she achieve a kind
of freedom.

She felt crushed by her mother and equally crushed by her husband, who seemed in reality to be ruthlessly dominating, inflexible,
violent, and punitive.

In the early stages of therapy the patient felt that I was constantly
watching her, waiting to pounce on her; she would sit in a state of
frozen panic, unable to speak.

As a child, she would sit in her room for long hours, unable to
play. She could only arrange her toys in tidy rows, because she felt
that someone was standing in the doorway watching her.

At home, she was secretive in the extreme. She always felt she had to hide what she was reading, and she would often get up in the middle of the night to play her favorite records when her husband was asleep and therefore not watching her.

She described her feelings in this way: "When I feel watched, I absolutely shrivel up inside. I stop being a person at all, and I become incapable of continuing with what I am doing, or of doing what I was planning to do."

Despite these feelings about her husband, she was quite unable to leave him; the two were locked together, unable to be close but equally unable to separate. Part of this dependence seemed to be because she needed to be watched. Besides believing that her husband watched her every move and detesting him for it, she also felt that he ignored her. This was just as bad, because it made her feel completely nonexistent. There were times when she felt he would enter the room and sit in the chair she was occupying as though she were invisible.

This patient's experience illustrates the catastrophic effects that being looked at can have. Her life was haunted from childhood on by an Other who had the power to freeze her feelings and spontaneous actions and turn her into an object. The original Other was presumably an aspect of her mother, but she had married a man who suited the original role well; in therapy she quickly attributed to me the same characteristics and felt me to be similarly oppressive yet indispensable. This example illustrates the extreme precariousness of the patient's subjective sense of self, which shriveled under the Other's look. But it also suggests a new dimension to the experience; namely, that it is something she needed as well as feared. If the looking stopped, she ceased to exist. This raises an important question. Perhaps she felt the need to be watched and objectified in this way to make up for a more affirmative kind of being seen and recognized that she had lacked. *It is as though she used the look of the Other to try to make real from the outside what had never felt fully real from the inside.* If this were so, it would be her lack of a firm sense of inner reality that had caused her subjective self to collapse and at the same time forced her to hang on to the dreaded experience of being looked at.

CASE 2

This was a young woman, age thirty, who was also in weekly psychotherapy for about two years. Her central complaint was of feeling
unreal and finding the world unreal. But there was a particular
interest in what she said, because she related how she felt to the
traumatic time she had had giving birth to her two children. Her
therapy seemed to raise the question of the relationship between
these actual birth experiences and the original genesis of her self
through the process of psychological birth in infancy.

The patient told me she was afraid of having another baby, which
she thought she wanted, lest it prove a repetition of her experience of
feeling let down by the hospital staff who had cared for her. She felt
they had abandoned her to cope with intolerable pain on her own.

With her first baby she had desperately wanted a natural childbirth; but the pain had proved too much, and she had been left on
her own with inadequate analgesics. With the second she had decided to have an epidural anesthetic if things became too painful; but
again things went wrong, so that again she had intolerable pain. In
both cases, when the pain got to be too much, she just "cut out,"
feeling completely unreal.

After the birth of her first child, the patient had recovered and felt
herself again. Indeed, she felt the best and most real she had been for
many years, and for several months was very close to the baby. After
the birth of her second child, however, she remained depersonalized
and had continued more or less like this until the time of her referral
for therapy.

It seemed at the beginning that she blamed all her problems on the
letdown she had experienced at the birth of her two children. But it
soon became clear that she had felt more or less unreal since childhood. She could pinpoint the onset of this feeling of unreality quite
specifically. She was nine years old. Her family was relocating, a not
infrequent event, and she had been sent away to her grandmother
over the time of the move. She disliked her grandmother, who
preferred her elder brother, and this was the first time she had not
been present at a move.

On her return, she can remember the moment of walking into the new sitting room. Her mother was knitting, as she often did, but it was as though the patient suddenly saw her for the first time. "I'd seen her before, but never objectively," she recounted. Now she *saw her mother terribly clearly*; she had a most unpleasant sensation that she had lost her mother and was completely *out of touch* with her. She said she had "*re-viewed*" her mother, who "now seemed to be a person in her own right." She went to her bedroom after this experience and felt terrible. Everything was unreal. She felt literally miles away from herself, as though she were somewhere out in space. Her parents, the family, the house—all seemed small and insignificant and utterly pointless. She herself felt very small and insignificant. She *saw herself* sitting in front of the fireplace, crying, and wanted to kill herself because there wasn't any point in anything.

She said that up to this time she'd "had a very powerful sense of her own identity," meaning that she'd felt that everything revolved around her. "It sounds ridiculous, I know."

The family was very close knit and didn't involve themselves in the outside world. Her elder brother was so quiet as to be almost nonexistent, and her father particularly had treated her as though she was of central importance. However, the family was also very religious, and she'd grown up in the view that God was everywhere. This meant that He saw everything you did, even blowing your nose. She found this persecuting, because you couldn't ever get away from Him.

There are a number of points I want to make about this case history.

1. It includes a memory from the age of nine. Although this seems to relate to actual events remembered in detail, it is probably also a screen memory relating to an earlier situation. It has two of the features of screen memories noted by Freud and discussed in Chapter 2: a heightened visual clarity (things were "terribly clear") and a recollection of oneself as a child performer (that is, from the outside, from an observer's point of view, rather than from the inside, experientially). In this case, however, the shift to the outside is not complete, and the patient remains to some extent in touch with how bad she feels.

2. It records a catastrophic loss of the mother. This is associated with a change in predominant sensory experience of her: she feels she is

out of touch with the mother, who now appears as a starkly distanced and visual object. There is a catastrophic shift from extreme closeness to the mother to extreme distance from her; from being within her caring orbit to being outside, the distanced and displaced observer. There is a Copernican revolution. Suddenly, there is a shift from an egocentric to an allocentric perspective.

3. This traumatic displacement of the self also involves a changed relation with herself, similar to that described in the last chapter. From unreflectively *being* herself at the center, the patient becomes the one who *looks at herself* from the outside. This is also associated with a change of the dominant sensory modality through which she experiences herself. Her totally involved bodily experience of the world is replaced by a predominantly visual appreciation of herself as "over there," sitting in front of the fireplace, crying.

4. In fact, there are traces of the patient being in two places at once. She is predominantly outside—the one who is in outer space (in banishment, taking a God's-eye view, perhaps?), looking back at herself and the mother she has lost. She is also present in a muted way in the experience of that Other which she now is to herself, sitting forlornly crying; but one senses that this position is too painful to stay with.

5. If the whole experience sounds like a painful expulsion from Eden—a sudden and violent rupture of a state of oneness or symbiosis, a traumatic and alienating birth of self-consciousness— it is probably because that is exactly what it is. It seems that the memory, whatever its historical validity, is also a vehicle through which the patient expresses an earlier trauma with the mother. I felt inclined to understand it in terms of the original process of separation-individuation, which in her case had been too sudden and wrenching, so that she was precipitated into a premature self-awareness that felt like abandonment. It seemed that her own pregnancies had promised a new beginning (Balint 1952) through which she might somehow put right the earlier trauma. As it turned out, this was not to be, and she merely repeated in her experience of actual childbirth the same trauma of painful loss and abandonment. Only during her first pregnancy did she seem to regain the feeling of the earlier symbiosis with the mother.

If we were to look no further, we could be left with the impression of a child who has been traumatized by the mother in some totally passive way. The child is a passive object, who is distanced and shut out from the mother's caring or actively impinged upon in an unempathic and unfeeling way. The child herself plays no part but merely suffers what happens. There is no doubt that such a view plays into the child's defense, which is, in short, to see herself as nothing but this visual object. All subjectivity and agency are denied, no doubt because it was just this which threatened the continuing love of the mother in the first place.

I think it is useful at this point to return to the core phobic experience outlined in the last chapter. This experience had two main elements: a situation that might trigger the dreaded experience and the dreaded experience itself. The trigger was a constricting and constraining object; the dreaded experience was the person's uncontrollable reaction to this object and in turn the looking reaction of some Other to this uncontrolled behavior. From this it was possible to construct a tentative scenario: The subject is in a rage against someone who is very controlling and constricting. He is bursting with rage, and someone, probably the one he is angry with, is standing there and looking at him in a certain sort of way. He feels alone, at a distance, and unloved. Looking through the eyes of the Other, he sees himself as almost unrecognizable, "mad," beyond the human fold. As one phobic woman said to me: "I feel as though no one would recognize me," though talking, of course, within her present frame of reference and meaning that there would only be strangers about.

I would like to think of this experience as a paradigmatic moment from childhood, engraved indelibly on the memory as an ever to be avoided possibility of the self. I think of it as something that is too painful to contemplate, too threatening to be acknowledged as a part of the self— hence, the symptom formation. It represents a crisis in the self's experience when something happened that seemed to jeopardize the continuing love of the caring person—most likely an eruption of rage, a temper tantrum, in relation to that caring person. It is thus a crisis of love in relation to the mother. As an aside, it is worth recalling how infrequently phobic patients actually lose their tempers, and also how they cling to the current object of their love as though there was a constant threat to this relationship. What they say, of course, is that they need their love object to be present "in case something happens to them" (the passive voice).

Perhaps I can begin to link this with the previous case. This patient's story also enshrined a moment of cataclysm—a sudden turning of the world on its head. It was a moment of losing her mother and finding herself, but finding herself as small and vulnerable and unloved, and at the extreme of distance from the one in whose orbit she had previously moved. I speculated that this was a traumatic birth of self-consciousness, erupting prematurely into a still intact symbiosis with the mother.

What I now want to ask is this: Is this sudden rupture of a symbiosis something that lies often or always at the heart of the experience of this kind of person, and is it what makes the experience so difficult to assimilate? I may not be able to answer this question, but I nevertheless want to sketch a further scenario within which we could see more clearly how such an event could occur.

We can imagine a small child safely "held" within the maternal symbiosis. It is probably a crawling child, or a toddler, not yet "hatched," in Mahler and colleagues' (1975) view, but beginning to experiment with increasing distances from the mother. Its forays will be punctuated by a smiling conversation of gestures with the mother, and frequent returns to the mother for "emotional refueling," to use another term of Mahler's. There is a repeated need for confirmation, for getting back reassuring and smiling reflections of the self (Winnicott 1967). Something now happens. The child explores where it is not allowed, and the mother removes or restrains. The child cries and struggles to achieve the thwarted aim. The mother becomes angry. Her face changes. She is no longer smiling, but looking in a different sort of way. She holds the child tightly to prevent him from doing what he wants. Perhaps at a certain point she becomes afraid of her own anger. She leaves the child, gets up, and walks away. Maybe she leaves the room, afraid that she might hit the child. The child is now screaming in anger and screaming in fear because the mother has gone. And there is the memory of the mother's face, cold and "looking" and then walking away.

We could wonder at what point this lived experience flips over, as it were, into seeing what the mother sees. But there would clearly be a survival value in this occurring, since a behavior that so seriously jeopardizes the relationship with the mother must come to be avoided at all costs. There might even be a renewed feeling of closeness to be gotten from taking the mother's point of view. With an older child we could imagine the mother explaining her point of view afterwards; with a small child we could imagine some primitive conception (image) of the Other's view finally crystallizing in a moment such as this.

What we see in this imagined example is not only a fairly normal piece of child behavior, but a degree of maternal failure in coping with it. The mother has not been able to "stay with" her child and contain its anger. Instead, through her own needs, she has been obliged to distance the child, emotionally and physically, perhaps because of her difficulty in containing her own anger and her fear of the consequences. The child's eruption of anger has thus led to a real emotional loss (a loss of "holding") of the mother, and the only remaining link with her across a distance is her cold and disapproving look.

My hypothesis is that it is this catastrophic consequence which leads the child to abandon his own ship, as it were. He joins forces with this mother who looks, disowns the self which the mother could not contain and which caused the rupture, and thenceforward regards this threatening self as an Other that has the appearance the child imagined it had for the looking mother. This is a self that has been written off. It is one of the *desaparecidos*, one that has disappeared and has no name, has no loving mother keeping it alive in the memory or looking to refind it. It exists only in a kind of limbo, in a state of frozen animation behind its visual form—in a space where the mother is not and where things are not named or recognized.[1]

I could put this slightly differently. I could say that what is looked at first by the mother, and later by the child itself, in this life-denying way is what the mother cannot contain or handle emotionally herself. This failure of containment then leads to the offending part of the feeling self being turned into a visual object that is Other to the self. This feeling self is not truly disposed of, but there is no longer a *place* ("Where you are a place arises") for it to be. It lurks nowhere but can threaten to return at any time.

It is clear that these dispossessed selves have never been integrated into the structure of "the self that mother loves" and thus "the self that I can

---

[1]This reminds me of a severely depressed patient I once had who kept saying: "I don't know where I am. . . . I'm in lu-lu land." She could not say anything about lu-lu land, but it was certainly a land of no hope. To some extent, I think one could consider the unconscious in this way as a place of abandoned objects rejected by the mother. I will explore this idea further in Chapter 12.

safely be." A person in this state can never afford to be spontaneous, in case these banished selves should resurrect themselves. The life of the self, therefore, tends to become one of appearances; and the self's project becomes one of delivering up to the mother acceptable appearances, strung together to form a pseudo-cohesive envelope in her continuing positive regard. This pseudo-cohesiveness of the self in the eyes of the mother then becomes a substitute for a genuine integration of feeling and action selves, which might have occurred if this mother could have "held the situation in time" (Winnicott, 1971). It is a "false self" mode of functioning (a term used by both Winnicott [1958] and Laing [1960]), in which the person attempts to live himself as a visual object, articulated from the outside. The next case will illustrate this further.

CASE 3

The patient was a woman in her thirties whom I had in analysis for several years. For a long time her constant complaint was of not feeling real. She didn't know who she was, she didn't know if the opinions she held were her own or someone else's; there was practically no stability in the way she experienced herself from day to day or from hour to hour. This extended even to her perception of her body, which seemed to change in size as she lay on the couch.

She had a deprived background, with a somewhat mad, chaotic mother who had not really had time for the child because she was so busy pursuing her own professional and artistic activities. Such stability as the patient had came from her outwardly calm and commonsense father, but he, too, was often unavailable because of his work. She had had a succession of *au pairs* and nannies to look after her, but none had stayed for very long. There was much parental strife and quarreling, and there had been a seductive relationship with the father when she was in her teens and the parents' marriage was breaking up.

This woman had a calm, organizing side of herself, a bit like her father. This coped for her, but it did not feel real. There had been times in the past when she had behaved chaotically and madly herself, especially in her relationships; but she was afraid of being like this again, particularly as she now had a child to look after.

There is little doubt that her father wanted to see her as a more stable and sensible alternative to his "mad" wife. There is also little doubt that she tried to be what he wanted, not only to please him and perhaps fulfill some of her own oedipal fantasies at the same time, but to reassure herself that she was not like the mother. This, though, was a false identity, because it denied the existence of her frighteningly disorganized and unintegrated inner self.

For some time the patient suffered from almost constant headaches, which she described as "like someone pressing on her head." She somehow related this to the fact that she was looking at herself all the time, something she had only recently realized. She said that looking at herself in this way was utterly exhausting and wished that she could stop doing it, but she supposed that she had to do it in order to go on existing. She related this to the absences of her own mother as a child and supposed that the looking was an attempt to fill these gaps in mothering by being a kind of mother to herself. She went on to say how difficult it was to get anything done if one must constantly look in this way, and she envied me because I had mentioned one day taking my eyes off someone in order to think. She would never be able to do that.

She admitted that, when she lay on the couch, she felt constantly looked at. If she was silent she could perhaps *feel* something, but she was soon aware of me *looking at her* and getting bored. If she spoke, she felt she was not being herself but was talking about someone else who was with her. She felt like someone who had brought along a child, but the child could not speak and she was talking for it. "I can tell you what I feel, but as soon as I say it I don't feel it anymore." It seemed that as she talked, the child she actually was became "that child" who was not her—perhaps one could say a disowned child, whom she looked at. In making this shift, she became Other to herself and lost touch with her own feeling. She did indeed experience this as the death of her own spontaneity. She despaired that she would ever be herself at all.

To *be* herself was too great a risk; her spontaneity might erupt in dangerous ways, not only in such a way as to threaten her precarious links with those she needed, but also in ways that might actually threaten those whom she loved. She greatly feared such upsurges of aggression, though it seemed to me that her fear was exaggerated mainly because she had never been able to try out her anger and see what its real effects might be. She had not been able to test out her fantasies in reality and discover the limits of the real. In Winnicott's terms, she had never had the experience of a mother who could survive her attacks. This was illustrated by a session shortly after the one I have mentioned.

In this session, the patient was still talking about her headaches, and I had related the feeling that someone was pressing on her head to her wish for me to hold her in the way her mother had apparently failed to do. It so happened that during the previous session I had a terrible cold and had fallen asleep. At the time, she had expressed no anger but had been extremely concerned about me, as though I was the patient or the child who needed looking after by her rather than the one who had let her down. The present session had started in complete silence, and it had been very difficult to get anywhere near her at all. I felt that she had distanced me and distanced her own anger at the same time. She denied my interpretations linking her silence with her anger with me, and we then got into a rather intellectual discussion about her headaches and her need to be held. She became upset and cried, and toward the end of the session she told me a dream that seemed to illustrate the fears she had of her own anger. It was an old dream she had never told me before, from when her son was young. She'd dreamed she wanted to smack him, but when she went to him she couldn't do it and stroked him instead. (Rather like the way she had treated me in the previous session.) She felt reassured by this and looked away, but when she looked back he was lying in a heap on the floor, bruised and bloody.

"Looking" and "being looked at" were, for this patient, ways of achieving a sense of continuity in time. They were a substitute mothering, in which the mother's (or her own) distanced looking provided a flimsy envelope for the self, taking the place of bodily and emotional holding through the vicissitudes of spontaneous emotional experience. What is also clear is that her looking at herself was a kind of vigilance, a watching for the first signs of dangerous eruption and a turning of the mother's frightening face of disapproval (the Gorgon's stare) on such stirring selves to freeze them in their tracks. She is thus permanently identified with this looking mother and can only experience her own threatening emotional selves as frightening Others.

This case seems to illustrate Sartre's statement (quoted in Chapter 2), that the Other is an ever-present threat to the self's subjectivity. He has, at all costs, to be kept as an object, so that his subjectivity does not reemerge. So it is for patients, such as the one described here, who have made their threatening selves into objects (Others) by looking at them through the objectifying eyes of the mother. The flip-over from being to looking can go either way. Just as for Sartre, one look of the Other (his emerging subjectivity) is enough "to make all my schemes collapse" and turn me into an object, so for these patients, one moment's lapse in the looking is enough to allow the subjective self to erupt once more from its objectified form and threaten the precarious continuity of the self that can be loved.

In the last chapter I concentrated on purely formal characteristics of the experience of being looked at and borrowed heavily from the phenomenological analysis of Sartre. I reached the conclusion that this analysis presented as an essential feature of the experience something that was only contingent and based on a particular kind of paranoid relationship with an original Other, the mother. I explored the possibility that deficient mothering underlay this experience of one subjective space collapsing under the look of an Other, and tried to present some philosophical and theoretical underpinning for such a view. In this chapter I have explored the implications of this core experience in a more clinical way, in relation to cases for whom Sartre's description seems a fitting account. This brings out the defensive function that looking can have in the emotional economy of such individuals. I will summarize the main points:

1. Being looked at by the mother or looking at oneself provides a pseudo-integration of the self from the outside—a substitute for true integration of affective selves from within. True integration can only occur if the mother has been able to stay with and emotionally hold her child through its emotional/impulsive expressions.

2. Under these circumstances, being looked at gives the self a precarious sense of continuity that would otherwise be lacking. It is as though such a person can say: "I am seen, therefore I am."

3. This external, visual envelope of the self is like the image in the mirror that creates a false picture of unification of parts which belies the inner situation (cf. Lacan 1949). It can also be thought of as a visual skin, providing a false sense of wholeness or integration.

4. The person who operates in this way has effectively made his feeling self into an object—a frightening Other with the appearance it was imagined to have had for the mother who could not cope with it. In relation to such petrified selves (Laing 1960), continual looking serves a function of vigilance—there must be no resurrection of selves that would threaten the self that mother can love.

5. Such a person leads an emotionally impoverished life lacking in spontaneity. He can be thought of as having a false self, in the sense of living an appearance. His life is articulated from the outside, in terms of appearances aimed at the Other, rather than from the inside, in terms of emotionally invested aims and goals. The individual is other-directed, not self-directed.

6. The maternal failure that underlies the need to be looked at in this way may be complex. It may be emotional or actual unavailability, but the mother's inability to stay with her child emotionally—"to hold the situation in time" (Winnicott 1971)—is likely to be a key factor. Related to this could be a mother's imperviousness to her child's emotional states, a failure in her reflecting or mirror function (see Chapter 1). The child identifies with the mother who has failed to "hold" it or respond to it in this way, and looks and distances instead as a means of disowning its own "unmanageable" selves.

7. Winnicott introduced in a slightly different context the idea of "graduated maternal failure" or "gradual disillusionment" as providing a manageable passage from symbiosis to separation in early development. In the development of self-consciousness the same graduation may be necessary. One of the patients discussed here seemed to describe the trauma of a sudden development of self-consciousness that ruptured a preexisting sense of being still "merged in" with the mother. It raises the question whether such premature self-consciousness may not in itself be traumatic.

4   Looking and Doing

And the Spirit of God moved upon the face of the waters.
And God said: "Let there be light," and there was light.
                                                    —Genesis 1:2–3

I
N THE PRECEDING chapters I have considered, in different ways, events that occur in the space between mother and child, which, in my view, have an essential formative significance in the development of the self. I have emphasized the literal inter-*face* between mother and child so that we look closely at what goes on precisely there, between faces: the eye contact, the nonverbal conversation of smiles and expressions, and the interaction of looks, leading to actual conversation in words. All of this is to stress the role of communication in the genesis of the self. It is not to deny the importance of interactive bodily experience, which has been so much written about, especially by analysts.

This exploration of transactions across a separating space between mother and infant led to a consideration of the *experience* of separation and the part that this played in psychological development. This experience of separation between self and Other introduces a gap, or fissure, into the self that not only keeps us apart forever from our primary wholeness, but creates the conditions within which all our specifically human attributes of consciousness, self-consciousness, and use of symbols can arise.

In the next four chapters, I will explore the consequences of that primary separation more fully. First of all, though, I want to recapitulate some aspects of our very early experience that seem to me to be crucial in understanding later developments. I have already drawn attention to a disjunction between feeling and looking, which characterizes the experience of the self as a separate object. In what follows I shall enlarge on this, paying particular attention to the interweaving and separation of sensory modalities at different stages of the process.

FOUNDING AND FORMING OF THE SELF

I like to think of two processes in relation to the development of the self—founding and forming. Founding is a laying down process—a laying down of basic substance, of *prima materia*, to use Jung's term (1953, p. 304ff.). Forming is a more subtle process, a delimiting and bounding, a sharpening of form out of a primary matrix. Obviously, founding is prior to forming, but it is possible to think of both processes continuing throughout development, and indeed into adult life. I am talking about something that has been written about extensively by analysts in a variety of ways—first an undifferentiated state of symbiosis or "merging in" with the mother, within which a secure foundation of good experience and basic trust is established; then a process of separating out and differentiating from this primary state of oneness. Mahler and colleagues (1975) talk about the psychological birth of the human infant and the process of "hatching" of the self. Kohut (1971) talks about development from the merger with the mother and about "the grandiose self" that includes the mother as part of the self. Winnicott (1958, 1971) has written extensively about this period of development, with particular emphasis on the facilitating role of the mother in both the laying down and separating out phases of the process. Even Freud (1930), who did not write in great detail about the early mother–infant relationship, talked about the "oceanic feeling" as a dim recollection of an earlier state of blissful union with the mother. I want, however, to talk about certain aspects of this period of development in my own way, and not get caught up in comparing all the other attempts that have been made.[1]

---

[1]Freud's concept of the ego as differentiating from the id bears a certain relationship to the general idea of the self differentiating from an original state of oneness with the mother. It bears an even closer relationship to the idea of the self developing at the interface of mother and child. "It is easy to see that the ego is that part of the id which has been modified by the direct influence of the external world through the medium of the Pcpt.–Cs.; in a sense it is an extension of the surface differentiation" (1923, p. 25). However, it is by no means clear how Freud's concept of the ego relates to concepts of the self in recent analytic

Founding of the self, then, is about "good" bodily experience with the mother—about being fed, being held, having one's needs attended to, not being frustrated more than is bearable. It is also about "good" social interaction—having one's liveliness and lovableness confirmed in a playful and loving interaction with the mother (see Chapter 1). Founding of the self is about the establishment of a secure ground, of a good internal object, of basic trust. All of this takes place within the primary mother-infant matrix. This, then, is the background against which forming occurs.

Forming is a kind of creation, though it is not creation *de novo*. Something is formed out of a prior something, not out of nothing; but this prior something is formless, at least in the visual sense:

> In the beginning, God created the heaven and the earth. And the earth was without form, and void; and darkness was upon the face of the deep. And the Spirit of God moved upon the face of the waters. And God said: "Let there be light," and there was light. [Genesis 1:1-3]

Light allows seeing, and seeing has something important to do with creating. Seeing allows limits to be seen, forms to be delineated. That becomes clear which before was vague and inchoate, felt only in some primary tactile way. What would an edge of something feel like if we had never seen it? Seeing and being seen certainly have something to do with the forming of the self.

Consider for a minute the creative process. A form begins to take shape in the imagination. First it is vague, dimly apprehended, intuitively *felt*. Only at a later stage can it be clearly *seen* or *form*ulated. Creating involves feeling something first, and only later seeing what that something is. In *Forms of Feeling* (1985), Hobson has written beautifully about the process of forming in works of creative imagination, in self-discovery, and in psychotherapy. I think my position is close to his, though my stance is somewhat more distanced and analytical—I want to see the formal features of the process more clearly.

In this chapter I will explore some of the relationships that pertain

---

writings. Moreover, Freud's concepts of ego, superego, and id define a certain semantic space that limits the discourse which can be carried on. It is for this reason that I want to write in my own way and develop my own language. The territory we cross is always the same, but different maps highlight different features of the landscape.

between seeing and doing, looking and touching, in the child's development of "self" and "world." I want to create a story about such early events.

Looking and touching are the two major ways in which we explore the world directly. Speech is another way that comes later, but it gives us a world mediated by words and therefore by the Other. Looking and touching are direct and unmediated and are the primary stuff of our first relationship with the world.

In the normal course of events we take it for granted that looking and touching work together. They operate in an integrated fashion, and we do not have to think about them. There are situations where they may not work together or may become, in some degree, uncoupled. It is when this happens that we may start to wonder about them.

For example, if we think about people who are blind, we are forced to wonder how the world may seem to them. We may wonder about their conception of space, or what it feels like never to have seen a smile or never to have had the fleeting fulfillment of meeting someone's eyes. Such situations may help us to realize that the world is not given to us ready-made, but has to be gradually built up out of repeated experiences with it. The inputs through vision and touch, for example, have to be gradually assimilated into an overall notion of the object.[2] I will return to the problems posed by lack of vision in those who are congenitally blind, but first I will continue with my story.

TOUCHING, SEEING, AND THE SENSE OF REALITY

In the beginning is touch, skin contact, being held, the firm pressure of the mother's body (though not yet experienced as Other). *This is the nucleus of the real.* We have to imagine that what is seen through the eyes is, in the beginning, more or less separate from what is felt through the

---

[2]In *The Interpersonal World of the Infant* (1985), Daniel Stern presented evidence suggesting that very young infants have an innate capacity for abstracting patterns across different sensory modalities (amodal perception). This capacity would tend to bring about an integrated perception of objects through an "unlearned yoking" of similar patterns from different sensory modalities, for example, touch and vision. If this is so, then my "story" might have to be rewritten.

skin. The integration of visual images and tactile bodily experiences is something that must be learned—it has to be discovered that the breast that is *seen* is the same as the full, warm softness *felt* in the mouth and the warm, smooth surface that meets the fingers; that the mother's face (seen) is the same as the mother who picks up and kisses and holds (touch and bodily experience). "The same as" probably first means "part of the same moment of experience," or "at the same time." As the baby begins to see more clearly and exploration becomes more important, he will realize that what he sees and what he touches are in the same place—are in fact the same object. And then comes the expanding exploration of objects— exploring with the mouth and hand; seeing with the eye what the hand holds; learning to use the eye to guide the hand, thus achieving finer manipulations of the object and thereby more detailed discriminations of it. The details perhaps do not matter that much. What is important is the idea that visual-tactile schemata have to be built up gradually and are not given from the beginning. As I have said, in the beginning is touch and the kingdom of touch. Touch is the primary modality—what *touches* is real; what is *only seen* might be real or might not be real.

Once these integrated schemata have been built up, seeing means "I want to touch, get hold of that, put it in my mouth" (though not, of course, formulated in words). The reality of the seen object is the knowledge that I can get to grips with it. Looking is preparatory to action. *Looking is anticipatory touching* (MacMurray 1957).

We have, then, both visual and carnal knowledge of objects. Our carnal knowledge is immediate, self-validating, but poorly defined—fuzzy in its outlines. It is intensely pleasurable or painful, immediately rewarding or frustrating. Our visual knowledge of objects is knowledge at a distance. It is sharp and clear knowledge, but it is subject to Cartesian doubts. It puts the object in a definite place and in a definite relation to other objects and ourselves. It is hard to imagine how we could properly order objects at all if we had no experience of visual extension, visual space. Space is, to all intents and purposes, visual. It is within the visual that things are located, held in place.

This is not to say that the experience of visual space is something that is given. Like everything else in our world, it must be laboriously built up through experimentation and exploration, a collating of visual and tactile experience over time. It may well be that space and distance really acquire a clear meaning only when we develop locomotor skills and can map the visually perceived space in terms of sequences of locomotor actions.

Development thus means, first of all, a joining together of carnal and visual knowledge. After that, it means using this integrated knowledge to explore the world. Later still, it means giving gradual preeminence to visual knowledge and subsuming carnal knowledge to the visual. Eventually, it means giving up carnal knowledge and making do with visual knowledge.

THE PREEMINENCE OF THE VISUAL

I want to elaborate on this gradual preeminence of visual knowledge. It begins with the fact that the visual becomes superordinating with respect to the practical—*first* I see, *then* I do. Vision organizes the objects of the world within an "all at once" (synchronic) space, and it orientates me in relation to all the infinite possibilities of the practical. It shows me the range of the possible. It guides me to these possibilities one after the other, steering my locomotion and physical movements. And finally, in the consummation of the motor act, it modulates my physical relations with the object through finely discriminated feedback. All of this is given in vision and accounts for its position of overriding importance in our developing relations with the physical world.

Up to this point, however, our visual knowledge merely facilitates our practical, carnal relation to objects, and guides us in the execution of our intentions and desires. What curbs that practical relation to objects is the intervention of the Other—*"You may not touch this or this, do this or this; you may only look."* The Other places a limit on my activities, communicated and imposed in a thousand ways. I am still free to look, but free to act only within constraints.

This is a momentous step. Looking and seeing, which had so far in development been laboriously integrated with doing, now have to be kept apart from it. Here is the beginning of a separation between the perception and the act. A gap has opened in my relation to the object within which the image of the object may be held, but not the object itself. This is not to say that the practical relation to the object will be totally abandoned, all at once. Indeed, it may well be that the first response to this constraint is to envisage the action that cannot be performed, thus leading to fantasy action instead of real action. Perhaps in time, though, a further development is possible. With the continuance of the limiting parental constraint, the action element may come to be more willingly abandoned. Then we approach a situation within which the image of the object may be contemplated, held in the mind, and explored in its own right.

What we have here is a growing conception of the object as something not necessarily to be engaged with in a practical way. This has several results:

1. A clearer perception of the object as separate from oneself—there is a forbidden distance between oneself and the object.
2. An image of the object that can be held in consciousness and contemplated, which may either be a perceptual image or a memory of such an image.
3. The growing possibility that this perceptual image can be used to re-present the object—in other words, to allow the object to be related to even when the object is absent. This marks the beginning of a path toward symbol formation.

Clearly, it will be a long time from the start of this process to the realization of a pure symbol—of a form that merely indicates the idea of an object, rather than its immediate or approaching presence. Attrition of the action component of the image may never be complete. What I have tried to show is that the possibility of symbol formation does not necessarily depend on an outright loss of the object and the associated mourning, but only on the inevitable limitation of access to the object brought about by the parental figure, the Other, in the normal processes of child rearing.

DISCREPANCY AND THE EXPERIENCE OF OTHERNESS

Symbol formation will form the subject of later chapters, especially Chapter 6. Here, I will look more closely at certain aspects of how the baby comes to separate out from the mother as a separate entity, and the part that different sensory modalities may play in this process. In the previous section, I talked mainly of the baby's relation to inanimate objects. In this section, I am more concerned with the relation to the first object, the mother.

Separating out has two main aspects—the growth of a boundary, and the development of distance between self and other. Psychoanalysis has several stories to describe what happens. The explanations have a good deal in common, though also some differences. I will confine myself to summarizing the essential elements in Winnicott's (1958, 1971) account.

Holding, handling, and object presenting is the way Winnicott (1971) summarizes the necessary "environmental function"—in other words, what the "good enough mother" provides—that enables the baby to get started properly in its emotional development. Holding and handling both have an emotional connotation as well as a physical one; object presenting carries with it the very important idea that the object (the breast) is at first presented in such a way that it meets exactly the baby's need—100 percent fit in terms of timing:

> A baby is held and handled satisfactorily, and with this taken for granted is presented with an object in such a way that the baby's legitimate experience of omnipotence is not violated. The result can be that the baby is able to use the object, and to feel as if this object is a subjective object, and created by the baby. [p. 112]

To these three factors, Winnicott would undoubtedly add a fourth—mirroring, or reflecting (see Chapter 1).

So, bodily contact (holding, touching, rocking, cuddling), communication (smiling, talking to the baby, responding to its smiles), and giving the breast (or the bottle) at just the right moment are the things that lay the foundations for a secure sense of self. At this point, the mother is there, very much there, but she is not the Other, or at least, not in more than a most rudimentary sense. She appears or she disappears like the sun or the moon, with a rhythm that no doubt can begin to be sensed; but it is the rhythm of the baby's needs, and as such, in no way impinges with any sense of otherness.

According to Winnicott, otherness begins to be realized in two main ways. The first of these is through what he calls "gradual disillusionment"—the illusion that the breast is created by the baby out of its own need or wish begins to be eroded by "graduated maternal failure." The baby has to wait a little longer for its needs to be satisfied. There is no longer a perfect fit between the expected and actual satisfaction. The second main path to otherness comes through the mother's survival of the baby's fantasied attacks. When frustration at the maternal failure reaches a certain degree, the baby attacks the picture in its mind of the mother and destroys her. But then the real mother comes and gives the real holding, feeding, and cuddling, invalidating the fantasied state of affairs. The repetition of this experience gradually leads to a distinction between inner and outer, imaginary and real, in whatever primitive way these categories are experienced by the baby.

In each of these paradigmatic situations, the recognition of otherness comes from the realization of discrepancy or difference between the anticipated outcome and the actual one. Yet in each case, it has to be asked what it is that ultimately differentiates one experience as real and coming from the outside, the other as illusory. Perhaps the answer is simply that, in the end, it is the experience that comes from the real mother that feels more real. It is based in real tactile and visceral experiences that are substantial and self-validating. This may sound like a tautology—what *is* real *feels* more real—but perhaps this is the irreducible fact that saves us all from the reef of solipsism. In the beginning is touch, and touch is the foundation of the real.

The reality of the Other resides in the fact that he can be touched and felt. I follow MacMurray (1957) in believing that this is the basis of the real. I am also suggesting that it is true in some rudimentary sense that the child's embryonic yet developing reality sense is based on the presence or absence of actual touch; and that those early imaginary experiences, which later become inner, but at the beginning might be confused with real events, become discriminated because they lack this essential modality. In adult life, the loss of a sense of reality, and of a sense of the reality of the self, can also be traced to a loss of the experience of being in touch with things.

TOUCH AND VISION IN PRIMITIVE BOUNDARY SETTING

I want to look at the question of separation from the mother in a slightly different way. I have said that there are two main aspects—the development of a boundary and the interpolation of distance between infant and mother, self and Other. Distance is something that above all is seen; there is a depth of space that can only be spanned by locomotion. Distance as a mode of separation is probably a relatively late occurrence. The appreciation of distance implies the ability to actually see distance, an ability that is probably not there from the beginning. It also implies the realization of distance, which is something that will have to be built up and probably only is fully grasped when locomotion becomes possible. Touch and pressure are a different matter. Being touched and being held are there from the beginning and from an early stage may give a sense of being surrounded by something firm from the outside, the beginnings of a bounding of the self (Bick 1968). Touching itself, as part of exploring, yields an immediate sense of the resistance of the Other, as that which is over against one.

The resistance of the Other—of things, of the mother's body—through this a first boundary of the self must be formed. Imagine the baby held in the mother's arms, or sitting on her knee. The baby wriggles or arches away from her. The baby's pressure creates an increased sense of resistance, an increasing hardness and firmness. The Other is that which will not give way, which opposes my action. Or imagine the mother with her baby lying on her knee. She presses against the extended feet with her hands. There is the Other again as force and resistance at the limit of my body. So the Other arises in action and reaction at the surface of my body—in handling and holding and exploring. In my story, the visual will link in later. The baby will *see* that which is already there, which it has already *felt* in a dim though immediate way.

Vision, of course, does not just come after; it interweaves with touch in the creation of both boundaries and objects. What I am asserting is the primacy of touch (and pressure) in the establishing of what is real, and the role of vision in clarifying its outline and delineating its form. "That is what it is! Now I see what you mean!" Vision does more than this, however; it manifests space and the position of objects in space. It anchors objects in space in relation to one another; and it places them at a certain distance from me, a distance I understand immediately in terms of motor acts—the stretch of an arm, or a certain distance that I must traverse by walking or crawling.

Vision does not at first imply such a motor understanding of space; this must be built up gradually through experience and learning. We can only wonder what a visual space that lacked such motor coordinates would feel like, just as we can only wonder about a "blind" space that lacked any seen dimensions. Perhaps a premotor visual space is little more than a vague background out of which the mother and other familiar objects will suddenly appear. Perhaps it is something that is scanned for patterns and movements which of themselves have no particular significance.

The point I will take up is that vision gives depth and clarity to separation, and comes to show at the same time the means that I must employ to overcome that separation. If I am a baby, it places my mother "out there" where I can touch her or not touch her, reach her or not reach her, crawl to her, walk to her, call to her, smile at her. It shows me her comings and goings, the door she walks through, the places I can find her or not find her. It shows me the space that not only separates me from her, but joins me to her—for looking, it must not be forgotten, is still anticipatory touching.

I am describing a baby who has moved a long way along the path of separation from the mother, who is confident of its motor skills and its capacity to keep in touch with the mother or to return to her for "refueling" (Mahler et al. 1975). It is the other end of the process from the first vague discrimination of a tactile Other at the limits of my own body.

I know of no better description of the trajectory between these points than that of Mahler and colleagues (1975) in their book, *The Psychological Birth of the Human Infant*. Even if one cannot completely agree with their theoretical reference points in Freudian theory, one can enjoy the richness of their observational material. For my present purposes, I would note only a few points from their account. First, the researchers remark on the apparently innate thrust toward individuation and separation in which mothers play a largely facilitating or inhibitory role. Second, they link this thrust with developing motility and the insatiable exploratory tendency that is probably also a basic given. Third, they emphasize the importance of different sensory modalities at different stages of the developmental process—in particular, the importance of touch in the earlier stages of the process and the increasing importance of vision in the later stages. Vision, they say, is the vital link as the child begins to acquire motility. It is smiling and the visual conversation with the mother that bridges the distance. Mahler and colleagues also make an interesting point that tends to support the view I am adopting here. They describe how children who seem to have been smothered in the symbiotic phase tend to keep their distance from the mother once they have the opportunity to do so; and how children who seem to have had too little close and satisfactory handling in the earlier phase seem reluctant to part from their mothers, and find the insertion of distance something that is threatening and to be avoided. In the second case, it is as though the tactile underpinning of vision is deficient; vision is not then a sufficient means of "keeping in touch."

STRUCTURING OF EXPERIENCE IN THE CONGENITALLY BLIND

As a postscript to this chapter, I want to make a brief foray into the world of the congenitally blind. If vision is so vitally important in the processes of separation and individuation, how do people who are congenitally blind, who have no sense of vision from birth, manage at all?

I certainly cannot answer this question in any detail, but there do, indeed, seem to be specific developmental difficulties for the blind. Nagera and Colonna (1965), for example, have noted that there seems to be a specific defect in superego formation among those who are blind; furthermore, Fraiberg and Freedman (1964) suggest that there is a marked deficit in ego development and self-differentiation which is not present in the congenitally deaf. They stress that hearing and language as such do not seem to be necessary for normal ego development, the establishment of a sense of self, and mutual object relations, but they imply that vision in some way is.

Some interesting observations also come from von Senden (1931). What emerges from his account is the idea that the person who is congenitally blind has no spatial conceptions as such. The world is known only in terms of temporal, sequential action schemata, which serve to link isolated tactile and other sensory experiences with objects into constancies that can be learned and that have a predictive value. But the spatiality of the world as such completely eludes him. He experiences it rather as a kinesthetic/temporal sequence: in terms of duration (how long it takes to get from one place to another) or number (how many steps, how many finger spans make up a certain distance, etc.). Spatiality as such—the experience of a synchronous coherence, grasped all at once, as a whole—is peculiar to vision.

Nevertheless, the congenitally blind person can arrive at some notion of vision, however imperfect, through his experience of other people. This is illustrated in an example quoted by von Senden. A congenitally blind girl had deliberately gone to her governess in a dress that was too

small, and the latter had exclaimed about it as she had gone in through
the door, without laying a hand on her. This experience

> led to a complete transformation of my ideas. I admitted to myself that
> there was in fact a highly important difference of organisation between
> myself and other people; whereas I could make contact with them by
> touch and hearing, they were bound to me by an unknown sense,
> *which entirely surrounded me even from a distance, followed me
> about, penetrated through me and somehow held me in its power from
> morning to night* [italics added]. What a strange power this was, to
> which I was subjected against my will, without for my part being able
> to exercise it over anyone at all. It made me shy and uneasy to begin
> with. I felt envious about it. It seemed to raise an impenetrable screen
> between society and myself. I felt unwillingly compelled to regard
> myself as an exceptional being, that had, as it were, to hide itself in
> order to live.

It is interesting that the subject experienced the Other's look, which she
could only grasp through a kind of inference as an impingement and
intrusion on the privacy of the self—in a manner not unlike those
patients I described in Chapter 2. There was clearly the same difficulty in
integrating the Other's perception, the same struggle not to be taken over
by it. Perhaps once again it was the relative prematurity of the experience
that was traumatic, erupting, as it may have done, into a still merged-in
state of the self. Lack of vision may well impair and delay the separation-
individuation process.

   One of the things that all authors seem to agree about is the difficulty
that the congenitally blind subject has in forming a conception of objects
without the mediation of vision. Introspection suggests that in the normal
situation, tactile contact with an object, even with the eyes shut, provides
cues that arouse a visual image or schema of it. Operations upon the
object seem to be organized in relation to this visual schema; tactile cues
feed back data that are in some way subsumed within the visual structure,
allowing an orientation of self in relation to the object and possible
actions with it. The overriding organization of an object schema is thus
normally visual, the visual schema subsuming and subordinating a whole
array of possible operations upon the object within a totality that can be
conceived. The visual thus provides an envelope within which tactile/

motor operations can be organized. The congenitally blind person lacks
this visual envelope, which is very close to the *concept* of the object, and
can thus organize his relation to objects only within an envelope of time.
This must make it much harder to conceive of the object as a totality, as a
form that can be grasped.

The same kind of analysis can be applied to the space within which
objects are located. For the sighted, space is, from an experiential point
of view, essentially visual and can be conceived of only in visual terms.
Space *is* that extension beyond us that we can see (or imagine in visual
terms), within which objects can be *seen* to be located, and perceived all
at once, in relation to each other and ourselves. It *is* the visual envelope
that surrounds us, within which we orientate ourselves and anticipate our
future. The person who is congenitally blind lacks access to this immediately present organizing dimension for objects, just as he lacks that all-
at-once view that allows any individual object to be grasped as a whole
and conceived of.

The congenitally blind person's only distance modality is hearing;
while hearing carries speech, which ultimately becomes the most important means by which we stay in touch with each other, it lacks any
potential for providing that all-at-once perception of the coherence of
things which is central to the visual mode. It does not serve well the needs
of an infant struggling to integrate its primary perceptual data into those
constancies that are the basis of our idea of an object. For example, if we
try to imagine a congenitally blind infant trying to build up a "picture"[3]
of the world without the visual channel, we find him laboring under a
heavy handicap. The tactile ministrations of the mother will tend to be
experienced in a fragmentary way, lacking the binding together that a
continuous visual perception of the mother provides. While the clustering
of such tactile experiences will, in time, tend to provide some connections
and integrations within these islands of experience, the difficulties will
really become acute as soon as the tactile contact ceases. At that moment,
the infant will become dependent solely upon the auditory channel for
distance information about the object.

---

[3]The problems of the child who is blind are highlighted by the difficulties in describing a
nonvisual world. Language has been created by sighted individuals, hence the anomaly of
speaking of the blind infant's *picture* of the world. Such a child has to build up a *map* of the
world (another visual word) purely out of auditory, kinesthetic, and other somatic representations.

In order to grasp what this might mean for a baby who is blind we have to imagine the characteristics of a purely auditory organization of space. We can gain some idea of what such an organization might be like from the example of music. Its essential feature would be its sequential unfolding over time. Because of this it would force us to adopt a passive and waiting stance in relation to incoming data. Moreover, significant information would occur against a background of quiet or random noise, so that the total organization of "objects"—clusters of significant auditory data—within the auditory space would remain loose and lacking in coherence. Islands of integration, where rhythms and patterns of sound might become articulated, would be surrounded by large uncharted areas where the time span between events was too great for them to be linked together. The familiar object (in this case, the mother), the source of the expected rhythm or pattern of sound, could then easily be lost in this unformed, uncharted auditory space and might well seem not to exist between her successive appearances.

Although such nonintegration of separate occurrences is a part of all early experience, it seems likely that it poses more of a problem for those who are blind. The sighted have available from early on more continuous information about the object. Even when the object disappears from visible space, the place where the object was can still be seen; this might well provide a known point in space from which an active search for the object could begin. An auditory "space," spread out in time, would not permit of such active exploration. As a result, the child who is blind is not only more lost, but also loses the object more easily. On both counts, therefore, such a child is more at the mercy of the comings and goings of the mother than the sighted child and is less able to make active efforts to keep in touch with her.

As the blind child gets older, no doubt the mother will make more active efforts to keep in touch on the auditory channel. The child, too, will make vocalizations and speech to span the distance. Nevertheless, however much such compensations may foster the development and maintenance of attachment, they can never eradicate the basic phenomenological difference between a visual world that is present all at once and an auditory world that can only be built on succession. This difference between the spaces within which objects can be discovered and organized will, in the end, profoundly affect the way in which the self and its objects are structured.

In this chapter I have explored, albeit in an impressionistic way, the role of different sensory modalities, especially vision and touch, in the building of our first experiences and our first objects. I have also tried to sketch in how separation from the mother begins to open a gap in the fullness of that experience, a gap which is in part mediated by a new separation of vision and touch. I will show that this gap is momentous in its significance and is the space within which our human symbolic world is created. My detour into the world of the congenitally blind may not have been strictly necessary, but it served to underline the specific contributions of different sensory modalities to our experience of the world, and in particular, to emphasize the overwhelming importance of vision in synthesizing and integrating that experience into a unitary field.

5   The Space between Mother and Child

I am here staking a claim for an intermediate state between a baby's inability and his growing ability to recognise and accept reality. I am therefore studying the substance of illusion, that which is allowed to the infant, and which in adult life is inherent in art and religion, and yet becomes the hallmark of madness when an adult puts too powerful a claim on the credulity of others. . . .
        —D. W. Winnicott, *Playing and Reality*

When symbolism is employed, the infant is already distinguishing between fantasy and fact, between inner objects and external objects, between primary creativity and perception. But the term "transitional object" . . . gives room for the process of becoming able *to accept difference and similarity. I think there is use for a term for the root of symbolism in time, a term that describes the infant's journey from the purely subjective to objectivity; and it seems to me that the transitional object (piece of blanket, etc.) is what we see of this journey of progress towards experiencing.*
        —D. W. Winnicott, *Playing and Reality*

THE SPACE *BETWEEN* mother and child perhaps features more in Winnicott's writings than in those of any other British analyst. While the traditional analytic focus is on events within the baby, or within the individual, Winnicott shifted attention to mother *and* baby and what went on between them.

Like Mahler, whose work I referred to in the last chapter, Winnicott was concerned with that moment in psychological development when the primary mother–infant unity is beginning to separate into "mother" and "baby" in the infant's experience. Both writers provide us with an account of the psychological birth of the human infant; but whereas Mahler relates her findings back to classical ego psychology and metapsychology, Winnicott uses his to open up a new perspective in clinical theory.

Winnicott keeps far closer to experience and phenomenology than most analytic writers, so that we can feel our way into the baby or patient that he describes.

Perhaps because of this nearness to experience, Winnicott's work has a deceptive appearance of simplicity. In this chapter I want to tease out certain elements of his thought that have relevance to the overall theme of this book—in particular, those aspects that have to do with the development of symbols on the one hand, and the development of different modes of relating to external objects on the other. I include here the nature of the spaces within which objects and symbols are located. Considerations of space are centrally important in understanding Winnicott's work; they are also, as I hope to show, essential to an understanding of consciousness from an experiential point of view.

It is well known that Winnicott (1951) introduced the term *transitional* to designate a particular mode of relating to objects that he wished to discuss. The term drew attention to a moment of transition in development between subjective omnipotence and objective relating, between undifferentiated "oneness" and differentiated "twoness." *Transitional object* was the term he used to talk about an object that was neither wholly a part of the self (in the infant's experience), nor yet completely separate from the self; *transitional phenomena* was a more general term, referring to a whole group of activities, seemingly related to this very early moment in infant development. The term embraced the whole area of children's and adults' play, religion, artistic and other cultural endeavors—in short, all those activities in which the sustaining of illusion plays a central part.

Illusion is a term that has an important place in Winnicott's discussion of transitional phenomena, and like the transitional object itself, contains the idea of paradox—something both is and is not at the same time. In Winnicott's terms, we could possibly speak of something that lies between "is" and "is not." The transitional experience is based on illusion and paradox, and is not easy to speak of clearly.

I want to recapitulate something of what Winnicott says about this moment of separating and about transitional experience. The discussion is based on Winnicott's papers and essays on the subject, which are collected in *Playing and Reality* (1971).

In the beginning, the baby does not realize the mother as a separate object, "out there" and separate from himself; self and Other have as yet no experiential correlates. In Winnicott's account, this continuity between baby and mother, this state of being "merged in," has been possible because of the mother's adaptation to her baby. Her attunement has been such that no significant discrepancy existed between the baby's need and her response; an almost total fit has occurred between what the baby anticipated and what the mother provided. As a result, the baby could feel that it had created the object that had satisfied it (the breast), which had, in fact, been given by the mother. In this account, psychological separation begins to occur when the mother's responses become less well adapted; through this relative failure, there starts to be a discrepancy or gap in the baby's experience between what is needed or wanted or expected and what actually arrives.[1] There is no longer the illusion of creating that bit of the external world which the mother had put there at the right moment; there is now a gap of difference between the need and its fulfillment and between the baby and the mother. Continuity, as Winnicott says, has given way to contiguity.

Winnicott reflects on this moment "at the point of separation" of mother and baby and sees that, in the normal course of events, something happens which has the effect of plugging or sealing the incipient gap that is opening up. Maybe in the beginning, the thumb goes into the mouth, and it could be imagined that the baby was hallucinating the breast—a purely inner event. But Winnicott is interested in something that happens after that, which involves the baby using something that is not a part of its own body, but a bit of the outer world. Typically, it is a piece of blanket, which the baby seems to relate to as though it were the mother (or part of the mother) that it had lacked. Through this use of the piece of blanket, the separation that would have occurred, the space that would have opened up between mother and baby in the baby's experience, does not happen. There is only a potential space between them, not an actual one.

Winnicott then tries to describe what is happening when the baby takes this piece of blanket. The baby, he says, is faced with a "me" and a "not me," and a space of difference between them, as a result of this beginning separation; the piece of blanket is the baby's creative solution to the

---

[1]No doubt the baby's developing perceptual equipment will play its part here; as the child becomes able to discriminate in more detailed fashion, that which had previously seemed a good fit may no longer be so.

problem that this poses.[2] What the baby has done is to take a bit of this emerging "not me" world that reminds him of "mother"—a touch object, one that is soft and smells of body—and uses it in place of "mother." Through a creative fusion of part of the "me" (an image of the mother) with the emerging "not me" (the bit of blanket), a new subjective object has been formed that seems to perpetuate the unity with the mother that is being lost. If, at the very beginning, the baby could be said to have created the breast that the mother had put there, it can now be thought of as re-creating the breast that it wants and remembers, not just in fantasy, but through a *trans-forming* of emerging reality.

Winnicott sees in this a first step in symbol formation, for the object that is so formed, the transitional, or subjective, object, unites a subjective content and a bit of the external world (Greek: *sym ballo*, to throw together). But it is not yet a fully fledged symbol; the baby does not yet accept difference and similarity, which are based on a realization of

---

[2]Note that Winnicott does not talk about the baby's defense against separation anxiety—a type of statement that, although true, would have led him in the direction of pathology. Instead, he speaks of the baby's creativity, which leads him in the direction of adult creativity and hence thinking about normal development. This, I think, contrasts with the Kleinian account of symbol formation, which in certain respects is quite close to Winnicott's and to the line of thought that I am developing. For example, Segal (1986) writes: "Symbol formation is an activity of the ego attempting to deal with the anxieties stirred by its relation to the object and is generated primarily by the fear of bad objects and the fear of the loss or inaccessibility of good objects" (p. 52). This is quite similar to Winnicott's formulation. However, Segal emphasizes the defense aspect of the operation. In a way that is hard to define, this seems to color the whole subsequent direction of her account. It is not so much that I would disagree with what Segal says; indeed, I have considerable respect for her formulations, even though for me they are too tied in with a Kleinian metapsychology that I cannot really share. Rather, it is that her explanation seems to point all the time to that which is close to pathology and must therefore be superseded; while Winnicott's account somehow invites us to see something that is already, in a certain sense, a creative, developmental achievement. Winnicott's term *transitional* captures nicely that sense of moving forward; the Kleinian terms—*paranoid-schizoid* for the stage of development and *projective identification* for the defensive process that leads to this protosymbolic activity, the formation of a symbolic equation—somehow remind one of illness. I should perhaps make it clear that, in Segal's terms, the transitional object would be a symbolic equation. The symbolic equations "are hardly different from the original object . . . (they) are felt and treated as though they are *identical* with it" (p. 53). And again: "In the symbolic equation, the symbol substitute is felt to *be* the original object. The substitute's own properties are not recognised or admitted. The symbolic equation is used to deny the absence of the ideal object or to control a persecuting one. It belongs to the earliest stages of development" (p. 57).

separateness. On the contrary, it has forged an identity between blanket and mother and so perpetuates the union that is on the point of being lost. "The (transitional) object," Winnicott says, "is the symbol of the union of the baby and the mother" (p. 96). However, this way of putting things is misleading; the transitional object is not a true symbol, only a precursor. Winnicott knows this, for he says in his original paper: "It is true that the piece of blanket (or whatever it is) is symbolical of some part object, such as the breast. Nevertheless, the point of it is not its symbolical value so much as its actuality" (p. 6). So presumably, in the baby's feeling at that moment, the mother is still there. The cuddly blanket *is* the mother and can still be related to as though it is a part of the self.[3] This is the paradox of the transitional object, similar to the paradox of the sacrament of the Eucharist, which Winnicott in one place compares it to. It shares with symbolism a transference of meaning from one object to another, but the object transformed by this movement of meaning shares with reality a continuing quality of being real. The Eucharist, to a nonbeliever, is a *symbol* of the body and blood of Christ, but to a Roman Catholic it *is* the body and blood.

There is a similar problem of exposition when Winnicott talks of the baby's illusion in relation to the transitional experience. Does this illusion contain, for the baby, the apprehension of the mother's not being there as well as the feeling of her being there? I somehow doubt it and suspect that the experience of the baby, in that sense, is closer to delusion than illusion—until the state of not having the mother becomes so intense that reality reasserts itself. Illusion, as we normally understand the word, seems to me a far later development and one that always incorporates the apprehension of its own nonbeing. It can bring solace, yes, but only after the painful work of separation has taken place and been accepted.

I note in this context, that Winnicott himself saw transitional phenomena as lying on the threshold between sanity and madness (see quotation at beginning of this chapter.) The attribution of madness would depend on the circumstances and on the strength of the reality claim made for his experience by the individual. The more the individual asserts the *objective* reality of his (subjective) experience, the more likely he is to be

---

[3]Hanna Segal's term for this identity of symbol with object is *symbolic equation*. See footnote 2.

regarded as mad. The more content he is to limit his claim to the *subjective* realm, the better will that claim be tolerated. It comes back to a question of how much, and how forcefully, the individual or the infant is repudiating a shared objective reality in the assertion and preservation of his own subjective truth. I will pay further attention to such primitive or proto-symbolic mental activity when I come to consider the difference between metaphor and unconscious symbols in Chapter 10.[4]

POTENTIAL SPACE—THE EXPERIENCE OF MATERNAL PRESENCE

Until now, I have discussed the transitional object as a first step in symbolism—an object that is part of the emerging external world is transformed by the baby's early mental activity into something nearer to its heart's desire. I now want to discuss Winnicott's ideas about where this process takes place.

This "where" is an ambiguous term. On one level, Winnicott draws attention to a certain area of experience; at the same time, it is hard not to suppose that he is sometimes thinking about an actual physical space between the baby and the mother. We can speak, he says, of outer reality, a world of shared experience and meanings in which we all live, in which we all most of the time have to live. We can also speak of a world of inner reality, of thinking, fantasizing, and dreaming. But Winnicott wants to point us toward a third area of "experiencing," which lies in some sense between the other two. In the outer world, meanings are fixed and given

---

[4]The early symbol, whatever we might call it, is in reality Janus-faced. It is a primitive form, which on the one hand looks backward toward a re-creation of the missing object; on the other hand, it looks forward toward the later achievements of symbol formation. If we emphasize its object quality and its inability to include difference within its constitution, we perceive its defensive aspect. If we emphasize its pattern-recognition and pattern-using aspects, we are more likely to see its creative potential. It is this difference in emphasis that divides Segal and Winnicott (see footnote 2). When we concentrate on the persistence of or regression to primitive forms in adult life, we tend to adopt the language of pathology— illusion becomes delusion. When we perceive in the infantile process the seeds of adult possibility, we will talk in terms of creativity. Winnicott chooses to put the creative aspects first, the psychopathological second—in other words, the movement from transitional experience to art, religion, and culture before the assertions of madness. Segal's emphasis is the other way about—delusion, then artistic creativity.

and cannot be changed. In the inner world, they are fluid, subjective, and idiosyncratic. But in the transitional area, which can be thought of as being at the interface of the other two, there can be a dynamic interchange. External objects can be given a personal meaning by the subject in such a way that there is a realization of self in the world, an experience of the world as being in some degree malleable and transformable into something that the self wants it to be. This area, in which there can be a merging or intermingling of self with world, is for Winnicott the realm of creativity and the realm of illusion. In his view, it lies in direct continuity with the world of the infant, who transforms the piece of blanket into a continuing presence of the mother who is being lost.

Winnicott makes it plain that this third area is immensely variable between individuals, and the extent of its existence depends strongly on the kinds of experiences that the baby has had with the mother at the point of separating out from her. One baby creates a transitional object, another does not. One child can play easily, another with difficulty. One adult can be creative and participate in and enjoy the world of artistic and cultural activity; another adult seems quite unable to do so. What makes the difference is the way the actual mother is experienced by the baby at the time when she begins to be perceived as an objective object, no longer under its omnipotent control.

At one extreme, if the Other were a really "bad" mother who allowed her baby to get into intolerable states, separation would be experienced as catastrophic and absolute, and the only issue of importance would be survival. The objectively perceived world would be experienced as harsh and unyielding, and the space between the child and the mother it needed would seem an unbridgeable gulf. There would be no room here for that satisfied and unthreatened state in which "relaxed self-realization" (Winnicott's term, p. 108) might occur. The "actual space" between mother and child (to use another of Winnicott's terms) would be characterized by distance and the absence of the needed mother. (Winnicott does not spell it out in quite this way, but I think some such account is implicit in his writing.) In this environment a child could not play, but would be anxiously searching for or trying to cling to the mother; withdrawing into despairing, dejected, and hopeless states, or self-related states of auto-erotic activity; or frantically seeking alternative attachment figures (see, for example, Bowlby 1969).

In the more favorable situation that Winnicott describes in some detail, there is a "good enough mother" who continues to attend to her infant's needs in a responsive way. In this case, although separation actually proceeds, the *experience* of separation does not occur. In Winnicott's formulation there is no experienced space of separation, only a "potential space," which is filled with the infant's subjective objects. The first of these is, of course, the baby's transitional object; but as development proceeds, this first object gives way to all the objects of the child's play, and later to the subjective objects of art and religion. Winnicott is at pains to point out that the infant in this situation has developed a sense of trust in the mother's reliability as an actual object, and it is her continuing reliability as separation occurs that underpins its ability to keep alive the illusion of her presence during the times when she is actually not there.

Winnicott's position can be paraphrased as follows: The mother who has, in the earliest phase, been able to adapt in a nearly perfect way to the infant's needs has set the conditions within which the baby can feel it is able to create what it needs out of the real world. As separation begins, (as the mother adapts less totally), the gap between need and reality is bridged by the baby's creation of the transitional object. This sustains the illusion of the mother's presence through her absences. There is thus no loss of faith in the mother, who can still be "felt" even when she cannot be seen. The infant who moves into childhood from this position becomes a secure child whose world is horizoned by the mother's presence, and this child can play. Play itself helps to sustain the illusion of the mother's presence because it celebrates, and in a sense re-creates, the original creative interchange with the world that the mother had first made possible. Winnicott puts it thus:

> The baby's separating out of the world of objects from the self is achieved only through the absence of a space between, the *potential* space being filled in the way that I am describing.

> It could be said that with human beings there can be no separation, only a threat of separation; and the threat is maximally or minimally traumatic according to the experience of the first separatings.

> How, one may ask, does separation of subject and object, of baby and mother, seem in fact to happen, and to happen with profit to all concerned, and in the vast majority of cases? And this in spite of the impossibility of separation? (The paradox must be tolerated.)

The answer can be that in the baby's *experience* of life, actually in relation to the mother or mother-figure, there usually develops a degree of confidence in the mother's reliability. . . . Here, where there is trust and reliability is a potential space, one that can become an infinite area of separation, which the baby, child, adolescent, adult, may creatively fill with playing, which in time becomes the enjoyment of the cultural heritage.

The special feature of this place where play and cultural experience have a position is that *it depends for its existence on living experiences*, not on inherited tendencies. One baby is given sensitive management, here where the mother is separating out from the baby, so that the area for play is immense; and the next baby has so poor an experience at this phase of his or her development that there is but little opportunity for development except in terms of introversion and extroversion. The potential space in the latter case has no significance, because there was never a built-in sense of trust, matched with reliability, and therefore there was no relaxed self-realisation. [p. 108]

Winnicott's account contains a paradox that he seems to enjoy. The baby's differentiation of self from mother creates a space between them in which, essentially, the mother is *not*. Nevertheless, says Winnicott, the mother is there all the time in the baby's experience, given certain good enough conditions of mothering, and this is how it happens. It is not just a question of preserving and keeping alive a good internal object in memory, or in the internal world; instead, it involves the use of an external object other than the mother, which comes to embody what is good and loved about her. This transitional object continues to depend for its existence on a reliable and trustworthy mother, while helping to keep alive the inner mother and a sense of her actual presence.

There is a further point that I want to make in this brief examination of Winnicott's work. Winnicott stresses again and again that he is talking about something different from instinctual satisfaction. Transitional experience is not a substitute for that; indeed, it is not orgasmic or climactic in any way. Transitional experience is about remaining related to the mother when she is not there; Winnicott links this to a distinction that Fairbairn (1941) made between object seeking and satisfaction seeking. The baby engaged in transitional activity is object seeking, and although

Winnicott does not mention Bowlby, I think that what he is talking about is closely related to what Bowlby (1969) calls the "primary need for attachment." Play, in Bowlby's terms, is only possible when an infant is free of threats to its attachment; this echoes Winnicott who states that play can only occur in situations of trust that allow "relaxed self-realization." Instinctual arousal is a major threat to such states. Play can only occur when appetites are relatively quiescent.

SEPARATION AND THE GROWTH OF AWARENESS

It is apparent that Winnicott's work contributes to our understanding of how the self acquires structure. It is not about instincts and their vicissitudes, but about the origins of objects perceived as separate from the self, and the origin of the self in experience as separate from and dependent on an Other. It thus gives an account of the first great divide within experience between self and Other; and since, as I will show, this primary separation is a precondition for the development of symbols and consciousness, it provides a way of thinking about those developments as well.

The terms *subject*, *object*, *self*, and *consciousness* are, indeed, the major dramatis personae of this book. They form a cluster of closely interdependent ideas and all refer to phenomena that arise out of the process of mother–infant separation. Each is closely linked to the development of our use of symbols, and it could be argued that it is just this capacity to reflect the world symbolically that underpins all our most specifically human qualities. It was Pascal, in his *Pensées*, who called man *un roseau pensant*—a thinking reed—believing that it was this fragile quality of consciousness that differentiated him from all other creatures.[5]

In spite of the fact that these terms form a conceptual minefield, I want to look at each of them in turn. The root meaning of the term *object* is "something thrown or put in the way as an obstacle," which carries rather nicely the sense of a "reality" being discovered "out there" by the infant, as

---

[5]Suppose, said Pascal, that a man is being crushed by a great rock; he is gasping and is about to die. What is it that distinguishes this man from an animal in similar circumstances? The answer is that he *knows* that he is going to die; he is *conscious* of his imminent death.

something which does not conform to its wish or need. Such a "something" is just "there," and by its difference and nonadaptiveness threatens to hinder the realization of a primitive satisfaction. Winnicott's adaptive mother, as subjective object, is not yet an object in this sense; she is not yet "real" because she conforms exactly, or "well enough," to the infant's need or expectation.

The root meaning of *subject* is the converse of this. A subject is literally "one who is thrown under the Other," as in being a subject, or vassal, or as we say, "subject to" someone or something. The subject is under the power of the Other, a state of affairs the infant is bound to discover when it emerges from its state of primary undifferentiation. Being the Other's object carries something of this same sense; in a very extreme way it was this contingency that was the threat to the subject in Sartre's analysis of the "Look" (see Chapter 2). In Winnicott's terms, it is the ordinary mother's capacity *gradually* to become an object—by a "graduated failure" to adapt—that protects the child from the trauma of finding the object too suddenly. The mother screens the infant from too much reality. She does not allow the object suddenly to be "thrown or put in the way as an obstacle."

Moving now to the term *self*, the complexities deepen. Winnicott commented in *Playing and Reality* that the term *self* was larger than us and tended to use us; in this way, he avoided having to define it. To some extent, I have done the same, but a few notes on the term and my understanding of it may not go amiss. Sometimes I have used it interchangeably with the term *subject*—subject and object, self and other. However, I have also used it more specifically; for example, in Chapter 2 I spoke of the subjective self and the objective self as two phases of the self. My intention there was to differentiate between a sense of subjective integration and potency—a body-rooted experience of sensory aliveness antedating any experience of separateness and an objective perception of the self that can only be mediated by another's view. I highlighted this distinction by talking about the founding of the self, rooted in "good," confirmatory experience with the mother who is still a subjective object, and about the forming of the self, which can be thought of as the giving of external form to something that is already there. It is here in my account that vision takes primacy over other sensory modalities, since it is first and foremost through being seen that this objective form of the self arises. I see my self through the eyes of the Other.

This objective form of the self introduces the idea of self-consciousness—the self as an object of consciousness. The person operating as a subjective self is not self-conscious; he is unreflectively engaged with the world, lost in what he is doing. His consciousness is caught up with the objects that constitute his project. By contrast, the objective self is an object of consciousness—in this mode, I relate to myself as though I am the other, and see my "self" as though it is an object of the world (as a form and with a perspective provided by the Other). I may be forced to do this (as in the self-consciousness of shame),[6] or I may do so because I wish to "see" myself more clearly (as in the pursuit of insight and self-knowledge). In either case, the objective self implies a divided self, in contrast to the unitary subjective self of the person unreflectively engaged with the world. In self-consciousness, attention has been turned from the world on to the self, a move that is necessarily mediated by another consciousness, an Other's view.

This brings us to the last of these interrelated terms: *consciousness*. *Consciousness* is also a difficult term to talk about; like *self*, everyone thinks they understand it, but nobody can say what it means. Its Latin root has to do with "knowing something with another" (*con scio*), which seems to suggest the mediation of a social process in its constitution. If this is so, such a social dimension might be given by a knowing through the mediation of shared symbols (e.g., words) or through a mediation of the Other, as in shame.

One of the problems with the term *consciousness* is that its use spans a range of situations of varying complexity. On the simplest level, it refers to a basic state of awareness and responsiveness to the world—little more than an animal reactivity to surroundings. Normally, however, we use the term to refer to a more specifically human attribute—a symbolic awareness of things that imports meaning into our relation with the world, as Pascal observed. Into this definition we can easily incorporate the more

---

[6]Sartre's (1957, p. 259) well-known account of the person caught looking through the keyhole of a room at the events inside captures the distinction I am making. As the one who is looking and involved, he is unself-consciously engaged in what he is doing (subjective phase). As the one who suddenly finds that he, the looker, is being looked at, he becomes self-conscious and experiences himself as an object in the eyes of the Other. There is a dramatic shift of his consciousness from the world to his own self or, as I have said, from a subjective to an objective phase of the self. My subjectivity has become an object for the Other (see also Chapter 2).

specifically psychoanalytical meaning of the term *conscious*. The quality of a thing being conscious is given by its being able to be perceived within a nexus of available meanings; a thing is unconscious when it has become divorced from this nexus or has been incorporated into a different and distorting symbolic web (see Chapter 9). I use the term *consciousness* throughout as implying this knowing kind of awareness—a reflective grasp of objects, mediated through images or words, rather than a more direct and unmediated involvement with things themselves. In this sense, consciousness already implies a symbolic presentation of things, however primitive; it also implies at least a rudimentary perspective—a seeing of something in relation to other things and an ability to grasp what that relation means. It therefore implies some incipient organization of impressions, an understanding, be it ever so simple, of the object world.

If we think of consciousness in this way as a symbolically mediated awareness of things, the development of consciousness becomes only another aspect of our development of symbols. If the world of objects is given at first directly to our senses—above all to our eye, which organizes those objects within a visual space (see Chapter 4)—our consciousness of those objects is mediated by symbols that re-present the world to our inner eye within an inner space of "mind." The space of consciousness, within which those symbols can be manipulated and allowed to do their subtle work of representing, is thus the internalization of an originally external space within which the child related to actual objects.

This external space that is internalized has to be understood in terms of the space opening up between mother and child through their separation. We can in this way think of the space of the mind as partaking of the characteristics of this earlier space. Although, as we shall see, a person normally operates in several different symbolic modes according to circumstances, and thus can be thought of as operating in more than one symbolic space, the symbolic spaces that he is able to inhabit are likely to be colored by his experiences of earlier separation. If separation from the object, and separation of the pattern from the object, are essential elements of the process through which symbols are formed (see Chapters 6 and 14), the experience of that separation will imbue the person's symbols with a particular quality. At one extreme, perhaps the level we all occupy in dreams, separation is refused, and the symbol is related to as a reincarnation of the object, scarcely distinguishable from it. At the other extreme is the rigorous space of separated symbols that provide the power to envisage the world, but at the expense of expulsion from it.

I have already mentioned in the last chapter the importance of looking and holding off from objects in the development both of symbols and of this "looking space" (mind) within which they come to have their being. This is something to which I will return many times in later chapters, particularly in Chapter 14, but it is worth underlining here just how pervasive is this language of vision in talking about mental processes. In ordinary language we speak of the *mind's eye* and of *seeing* what the other person means. We talk of adopting a *point of view*, of obtaining *insight*, of thinking in a *clear* or muddled way. All of these ways of speaking refer us to an imagined visual space as the arena of our thoughts, as the place within which mind-objects can be imagined, located, and related to each other. In short, we can barely speak of consciousness without using such visual language. It is the eyes, and looking, that hold dominance over all other sensory modalities; the mind is above all a visual space. We can now see that it is the internalization of that visual space which first opened up between mother and child as the child became able to realize distance and separation and the possibility of the object being able to be lost, searched for, and found again within that space. It is the actual eyes that first seek out the patterns of the needed but missing object in the first looking space of separation; it is the eyes of the mind that will see through recollection or re-presentation, the pattern or the image of the object in the looking space of the mind.

The notion of searching for a missing object enables me to make one further point about consciousness and the genesis of symbols. I have been arguing that both are the outcome of developmental processes, in particular, the process of separation of the child from its original objects. It is unlikely that either can be regarded as a mere luxury that is added to our sensory equipment as separation proceeds. We have to think of both symbols and consciousness as having some practical value; we need to be able to understand not only how they arise, but what function they have in the infant's developing economy.

I want to introduce here the idea that consciousness may arise originally as a form of searching for a missing or absent object.

We can imagine a baby beginning to separate and perceive the "object-ness" of the mother. It becomes aware of a lack, a gap in experience. Something is missing from a previously experienced sense of completeness and well-being. The baby now searches for that which will relieve the feeling of lack, searches to reinstate the previous sense of wholeness. The transitional object is one outcome of this process; the baby, through a primitive symbolic act, creates an object of its own which sustains the illusion of maternal presence. Is this a primitive act of consciousness? The answer is yes, because it operates through a kind of symbolic mediation—the infant finds the missing pattern in another object. At the same time, the answer is no, because it obliterates the psychic space within which an awareness of the mother as an absent object could be sustained.

In this infant scenario, what is it the baby searches for, and what does it find? Probably the baby is searching for the mother, or the mother's breast or face. Maybe it does not matter at the moment to decide between these. What is in question is a certain pattern of sensory experience that the baby is looking for. If the mother reappears, the baby has found what it is looking for and all is well. If the mother remains absent—though not, says Winnicott, for too long—the stage is set for the baby to create a transitional object. The baby finds the searched-for pattern in something else—in the cuddly blanket or soft toy. It is as though the baby uses the sensory pattern (of the experience of the mother) that it has found in the new object to fill up the space that is left by the absent object.

We can next imagine a state of affairs in which, for whatever reason, the baby is beginning to sustain a sense of maternal lack and absence through a longer period of time. The "potential space" (where the mother is not but where her presence can be felt) has become an "actual space" that is experienced and felt as a painful gap to be tolerated. This baby, which has moved further on the path of symbol formation and consciousness, fills that separating space of absence, not with a re-creation or re-incarnation of the mother, but with an image or re-presentation of her. This re-presentation in-forms the gap of the mother's absence with a recollection and anticipation of her; but it does not obliterate the gap, and the feeling of her absence remains. The representation of the mother mediates a kind of knowledge of her, perhaps even an imagining of her whereabouts, which mitigates but does not get rid of the sense of separation. It enables her to be "kept in mind" until she returns.

At this stage, we have reached something approaching a fully fledged act of consciousness—an awareness of the object that recognizes its absence, mediated by an image that has been separated from the object. Such an image can be regarded as a representational symbol. In this case, the search for the object has led to knowledge about the absent object, not to the illusion of her re-creation or repossession. The full development of consciousness and the symbolic function requires an ever more complete acceptance of this fact of separateness—of the self *not* being that which it confronts and the symbol *not* being that which it symbolizes.

Consciousness, then, can be regarded as a form of searching for that which is missing; the primitive symbol is a finding of some part of that which is missing that sustains the infant in its continuing search for the whole. As development proceeds, the symbol, which has now become a separated pattern, becomes a tool to further the child's searching and finding in the real world. Only in the furthest reaches of symbolic development does the symbol become a means of representing the world in its entirety; even then, it finds its ultimate justification through its reference to the real world and the further orientation within that real world that it facilitates (see Chapter 14).

SEPARATION AND THE QUALITY OF CONSCIOUSNESS

We have seen that psychological separation of mother and infant brings about not only a first structuring of the world in terms of self and mother (Other); it creates a space between the mother and the infant in the infant's experience which is the rudimentary space of consciousness. For Winnicott, the transitional object is the infant's first attempt to deal with this space. While Winnicott makes the creative leap from this tiny beginning to the eventual flowering in the individual of cultural experience, he does not, in my view, spell out the momentousness of this first step for the development of "mind" and "consciousness." This may be because his primary focus was on play and the way in which the development of play depended on the presence and experience of a good enough mother during the stage of separating out. His primary concern was with a benign mothering, which prevented the experience of an "actual space," and with the transitional object, which is but a primitive way-stage on the path of symbol formation.

It can sometimes seem as though Winnicott believed the experience of an actual space of separation could be largely avoided if mothering were good enough. This may be part of an idealizing moment in Winnicott, which has sometimes been noted. In contrast to this, I shall develop a different view. I shall argue that the experience of separation as a painful absence is a necessary development in the growth of consciousness and symbolic usage. In this sense, the suffering of an "actual space" in which the object is absent can be seen as a precondition for the development of purely representational, as opposed to transitional, symbols. The trauma of absence, however, is not that of experiencing it per se; it is the experiencing of it precipitately and suddenly. I believe, paradoxically, this view can also be found in Winnicott. According to this view, no one can avoid being thrown into the harsh space of reality in some degree, but some people may be fortunate enough to be cushioned in their passage, and their symbolic capacities will reflect this more benign experience of development.

To illustrate this point, I want to juxtapose the theories of two very different individuals who already form, in a certain sense, the point and counterpoint of my argument. I refer, of course, to Winnicott and Sartre. Although it would be interesting, it would be beyond the scope of this book to compare the biographies of these two men. My intention is only to compare and contrast the tenor of certain of their formulations and to assume that these formulations bear witness to their own individual experiences in this area of separating out from the mother (see Chapter 17).

It does not take a profound reading of the work of Winnicott and Sartre to preceive that Winnicott's view of human nature is warmhearted and relatively optimistic, while Sartre's is fraught and angst-laden. Winnicott's focus is the child playing within the protective enclosure of the mother's love; Sartre's is that of alienated man, alone and without God, and tortured by the necessity of having to act in a world that is essentially absurd. Winnicott's Other is essentially benign, adaptive, and caring; Sartre's, as we have seen, is a threat to the very subjective being of the self and is essentially egocentric and persecutory. Winnicott's ideas on self-development move toward a confirming and reflecting face-to-face experience; Sartre's notions about the self move around the Look of the Other as a deadly and annihilating meeting. In short, Winnicott's platform for both living and theorizing is a state of relaxed self-realization; Sartre breathes and exudes an air of ontological fear.

For Sartre, like Adam, the birth of self-consciousness is a traumatic event. The Other, who makes me aware of my self, is like "a little particular crack in my universe," the word *crack* introducing the idea of an incipient break in something that was previously whole. Winnicott, as far as I am aware, does not specifically deal with the birth of self-consciousness, suggesting that for him it was scarcely an event at all, but perhaps something that was gradually negotiated, thanks to the sensitive handling of an adaptive mother.

When we look at the birth of consciousness, we find the same difference. In Winnicott we find a gentle and smiling account where spaces are not experienced and absences are not felt; in Sartre, we find a language of rupture and violence, of Nothingness inserted into the fullness of Being. It is true that in making these comparisons I am taking a certain philosophical license, for Sartre's purposes are philosophical while Winnicott's are psychological. It is also true that Sartre's terminology is idiosyncratic and at times difficult to follow. Nonetheless, I believe that the comparisons are valid in terms of the basic pulse and feel of the two texts. Sartre speaks of the For-Itself (very roughly, the conscious individual) arising out of the In-Itself (which we might equate to some aboriginal state of things before consciousness emerged).[7] Winnicott speaks of the infant self "separating out" from a state of being "merged in" with the mother—separating out into an ambience of care and love, playing in the carefree space that is still watched over by the mother. Sartre, by contrast, speaks of the For-Itself as "a lack," "a gap," "a fissure," "a nothingness coiled like a worm in the heart of Being"; "a fissure arising at the heart of the In-Itself." Surely this is Winnicott's actual space of separation, brought too suddenly to consciousness by an impinging or insufficiently adaptive mother.

We have then, two descriptions of what I am considering to be the same event—the birth of the self in individual development, and the ontological birth of consciousness in a world of plenitude and Being. The event is experienced in distinct, even antithetical, ways by these writers, and I would suggest that their contrasting views have been determined by each man's experience of that primal moment of psychological birth. For Winnicott, it is a moment of transition and potential growth; for Sartre, it is an inescapable trauma that throws us into the alien world of the Other.

---

[7]The In-Itself (*L'En-Soi*) and the For-Itself (*Le Pour-Soi*) are not experiential terms so much as terms with a place in Sartre's ontology. They have an interest from the present point of view, however, particularly the term *Pour-Soi*, which seems to emphasize the egocentricity of the individual that I have noted.

This account illustrates, I believe, that the quality of our consciousness, which must always relate to its objects across an empty space, will be determined by how the original space of separation from the first object, the mother, was experienced. It may have been just a potential space, as for Winnicott, with a real mother who made it feel as though there was no gap at all; or it may have been a "fissure," a "nothingness" in the heart of experience, as it was for Sartre, in which the mother's absence was felt as an abandonment. Whichever way it was (and there will be intermediate positions), it will be determinative, in one fell swoop, of our attitude toward the world, toward our selves, and toward symbols. For as Winnicott says poetically, and Sartre philosophically, consciousness, which arises from our primal separation, creates at one and the same moment the "I," the world, and the symbol that bridges their separation.

6   Symbol Formation

Not only the actual content of the symbol but the very way in which symbols are formed and used seems to reflect precisely the ego's state of development and its way of dealing with its objects.

—Hanna Segal, "Notes on Symbol Formation"

SIGNALS AND SYMBOLS

SYMBOL FORMATION AND the understanding of symbols occupy a crucial position in any attempt to make sense of emotional and psychological processes. Symbols are the means by which we communicate (both with ourselves and others), by which we make sense of anything, and by which we endow the world with personal significance.

At birth, we can neither understand nor use nor create symbols. All these things have to be achieved. We can approach symbols from this developmental perspective, asking how it is that we come to make that leap from relating to things to relating to meanings. We can also approach symbols from the other end, as it were. We can look at their fully fledged, formal characteristics, asking what a symbol is and how it achieves its function of expressing or conveying something. Both these approaches will tell us something that we want to know and will enlarge our understanding. They represent on the one hand, the standpoint of the adult world, which is situated in symbols, in "the Symbolic," as Lacan would say; on the other hand, the position of the baby, who is born into "the Symbolic," a world of meanings that starts to form him before he can have any idea what those meanings are.

My interest in this chapter is mainly with the developmental perspective, and I do not want to dwell at length on the purely formal characteristics of symbols.[1] In order to understand the issues of symbol development, however, it is necessary to have a clear idea of what, in a formal sense, a symbol is.

It is usual to distinguish between signals and symbols. A *signal* is indicative of something else in the perceptual field. It points to something that is happening, is about to happen, or has just happened. It operates within the same field as the objects it points to. For example, a footprint in the sand indicates that a man has recently walked there. Mares' tails in the sky indicate that it is going to rain. For a baby, we may suppose that the sound of the mother's voice comes to indicate that the mother will soon appear, or that the breast will arrive. Signals occupy the same order of events as the things they indicate.

Symbols, on the other hand, occupy a different order of things, the order of expression or meaning. They represent the order of events in a purely virtual, nonphysical space, which we can think of as mind or consciousness. Sometimes this space of meanings created by symbols is referred to as a semantic space, in order to contrast it with the physical space that it represents. So, for example, while these words exist as squiggles in the physical space of the page of this book, the things to which they refer exist, at this moment, only in a represented form in your mind. The ideas or concepts that the words refer to exist only in this virtual realm of expression. A symbol may be a word, a picture, a sound, or any other thing. What it is in itself is not important except in the capacity of being a vehicle for the meaning or the concept it conveys. In itself, it acquires a kind of transparency, so that we see through it to what is meant. As something related to in the objective mode, a word is just a sound or a few squiggles on the paper; but related to as a symbol, it is a *no-thing*, a transparency to the concept. It is important to note that the symbol does not refer directly to an object in the physical world but to the concept of that object, which is something that it arouses, and that we can hold, in our consciousness. The object in the physical world is related indirectly to the word through the concept.

This preamble gives some idea of what the child has to achieve in order to be able to use and grasp symbols, at least in their fully fledged form. It

---

[1]For an excellent short account of the formal characteristics of signals and symbols, I would refer the reader to Susanne Langer's *Philosophy in a New Key* (1942). A summary can also be found in Robert Hobson's *Forms of Feeling* (1985).

has to be able to give up the object (say the word) as something that is related to in the physical mode, as a sound, or as a noise, in order to get to the point from where it can be allowed to do something else—in other words, to convey something. The child has somehow to "hold off" from the object in the action mode in order for a space to be created within which the new function of the object can have room to happen. This space is, of course, the virtual space of meanings. We can imagine that this is not an easy process and will not be acquired all at once, or once and for all. Nevertheless, there is, I think, a sense in which the essential change of attitude in relation to the object has to be a discontinuous one—a kind of leap. Either you "see" it or you don't.

PSYCHOLOGICAL SEPARATION
AND SYMBOLIC AWARENESS

In the last chapter we began to look at one view of how the baby takes its first step in symbol formation. Winnicott described what he saw as the making of the child's first symbol, and I again take his account as a starting point.

According to Winnicott, this first symbol is the child's transitional object. We have already noted that this is indeed a kind of symbol because it brings together (from the Greek *sym-ballein*, to throw together) or unites a personal meaning with a new object; we have also noted that it is not yet a true symbol, but only a primitive early form, because it embodies or incarnates rather than represents. The baby has not yet achieved the capacity to separate a meaning from the body that contains it. In the case of the transitional object, the personal meaning is a particular experience of the mother (for example, the mother as soft, warm, and satisfying, having a particular feel and smell); the new object that is invested with this meaning is the baby's blanket, which is well suited to contain this fragment of rescued meaning on account of its own properties and associations.

We can talk about what has happened in a number of ways. Besides saying that the blanket has been invested with a new meaning, we could say that the blanket has become a vehicle for the new meaning, or contains the new meaning. We could also say that the baby has transferred something from the particular experience with the mother that is being lost to the blanket, and we could think of this as a *first transfer-ence*—rather like the transference of meanings that Freud noted in rela-tion to hysterical symptom formation. From the developmental point of view, we might say that the baby has made its first essay in *detachable* meanings; a meaning has apparently been detached from one object and attached to another. Or we might say that the baby has introjected a good experience of the mother and projected it into the blanket. Our choice of language will be determined both by our theoretical constructs and by what we want to say, and there will be endless arguing about which language will best fit the phenomena. I do not want to get caught up in a controversy between schools of thought on this point. I do, however, want to note that we have to be careful not to attribute to the baby processes that it is, as yet, incapable of achieving.

If we look at the relationship between the original object (the soft, warm mother or breast) and the new object (the soft blanket), we can see a similarity between the two which we suppose was felt by the baby. So we can infer that the baby is at least capable of matching one sensory pat-tern or gestalt with another, and that it is this matching that has enabled the transfer of meanings to take place. We can reasonably infer that this is a very early, perhaps even innate, capacity for perceiving an identity of perceptual gestalts in different settings. We can also see how this primi-tive function, which Langer (1942) called abstractive seeing, could be-come, through further refinement, the basis of a later manipulation of abstracted (i.e., disembodied) meanings (see Chapter 14).

I now want to look more closely at this apparent transfer of meaning from one object to another to see if we can glimpse more clearly what the baby is actually doing. As I have already noted, it might appear that a meaning has been detached from one object and attached to another; but this would imply the existence, at some stage of the process, of a detached (i.e., separated) meaning that could be held in some way in consciousness in a free-floating condition—in other words, something like a concept. Quite clearly, this could not be possible for a young child, let alone a baby, since it implies the existence of the very capacity to use symbols, which is still only *in statu nascendi* and has a long developmental path to follow. This illustrates the difficulty in talking about the process of symbol formation in ways that do not assume the existence of that which still has to be achieved. The baby at the stage we are discussing can still not tolerate separation and detachment from its objects; in an important sense, it is precisely that inability that the transitional object commemorates.

How is it, then, that the baby comes to be able to manipulate detached meanings? First there has to be a separation from the object, something that I have considered in detail in the last chapter. Next, there must be the disengagement from the object, which I noted in Chapter 4; this is the "holding off" from the object that allows the object to be looked at or contemplated in a way that is not anticipatory of immediate action with it.[2] This introduces the possibility of the object being conceived of, as an image within the space of separation from the object, rather than simply being perceived "out there" as a particular "something" in the object world. The word, or other symbol, can then be thought of as a new kind of object—a *tool* that can be used to *hold* or *convey* this *re-presentation* of the object (the image or concept of the object) within that *space of re-presentation* which we call the *mind*.

I think it is helpful to think of the process of separation/disengagement from the object as a progressively more difficult sequence of tasks that have to be fulfilled if the use of symbols is to progress. First of all, as we have seen, the baby begins to have a fleeting awareness of its separateness from the mother. As time goes on, there has to develop a tolerance of this awareness of separation, an ability to cope with the absence or unavailability of the object at least for a time, without occluding that awareness in one way or another. Eventually, there has to be a capacity to hold off from the object, without any prospect at all of imminently possessing it. Winnicott's transitional object marks a very early stage on this path of disengagement; for although, in a certain sense, it seems to imply some recognition of the mother's absence, it so effectively recreates an illusion of her presence that the experience of absence can be thought of as virtually wiped out.

It could be said that the ability to conceive of distance between an object

---

[2]The first separation from the object is something that is suffered—it happens to the infant as a result of the changing behavior of the object. We might say that the object first holds off from the infant. By disengagement from the object I mean to characterize a holding off by the infant from the object—an acceptance of the fact of difference and separation from the object and a tolerance of not being able to have and to hold the object in any immediate way. Disengagement reflects a state of affairs in which the infant relates to the object in the way in which the object first related to the infant.

and its meaning (concept) does, in fact, go pari passu with the ability to tolerate and accept distance between the self and the original object (the mother), and perhaps also with the ability to tolerate such distance and separation within the self.

If this is the case, we might expect to find that the way a person uses symbols, his capacity to detach or abstract a meaning from an object and maintain a psychic space for representation, will vary with his development along the path of separation-individuation. Obviously, this area of the capacity for abstraction and abstract thinking as opposed to concrete thinking is familiar to all who consider symbolic processes, and it is of great importance when we deal with borderline or psychotic individuals. Much has been written in this area, but it may be that this way of thinking about the development of symbol usage will help to clarify the nature of the problem with which the psychotic is struggling.

Putting the matter in its most simple form, we could say that the psychotic has failed to accept or cannot tolerate his separation from the object. The space of difference and separation from the object, which first of all allows the image of the absent object to be differentiated from the actual object, is repeatedly obliterated; in this way, the psychotic confuses the image with the actual object and makes believe that he possesses the object that in reality he is separated from. The comfort of this mode of functioning is, of course, offset by the terror that can then be caused to the psychotic by his apparently real objects. It is also offset by his impairments in thinking, for a psychotic person cannot properly differentiate an object of thought or feeling from a real object. Putting it differently, we could say that he confuses the different kinds of space within which the different kinds of objects exist; or perhaps more accurately we could say that he lacks any definitive space within which thought objects can be held, manipulated, and explored. He ignores the rules that open up and guarantee a symbolic world.

THE FLIGHT FROM SEPARATENESS

I want to illustrate these points with some examples from ordinary psychiatric practice. In the course of my work as a general psychiatrist, I see many people suffering from major psychotic illness. For the most part, there is little chance to become engaged in a dynamic way with such patients, the sheer pressure of work, and the setting itself, determining that the major effort will be on relief of symptoms. From time to time, however, a particular patient will begin to involve me in a different kind of way. Although the work that can be done is still very limited, it gives a fleeting glimpse of dynamic processes and a rich, if only transient, reward in the feeling of making contact with patients who are normally so out of touch.

The patients I am speaking of seem to be those with more transient psychotic illnesses. Between their breakdowns they are cut off and isolated individuals with extremely restricted lives, few social contacts apart from family, and a relative imperviousness to psychotherapeutic intervention. In each of the cases I am thinking of, the period of greater accessibility seemed to be at a time when the person was recovering from his psychotic illness but had not yet completely reinstated his rigid defenses.

I will try to explain the relevance of the following cases to the present discussion. Although each case highlights the issue in a slightly different way, all three individuals seemed to be hovering between delusion and insight—between an incarnated reality that commanded their belief and a represented reality, which they could see was a content of their own thoughts and feelings. In each case also, I thought that I could see a struggle in the person—not, as common sense might expect, to regain insight, but to cling to the delusion because of its comforting quality. For each individual the delusion was of a loved object that was claimed to be really there and communicating with them; whereas, for each of them, the painful reality that was being avoided was the reality of isolation, of feeling out of touch and unloved.

It struck me forcefully in these cases that not only was the delusional presence very similar to a comforting transitional object, but that what the person in each case was avoiding was the empty space (the actual space) of separation from the object within which a representational reality of the object could have come into existence. Such a space could not be tolerated, or only fleetingly so, with the result that the line of difference between the object and its representation could not be maintained.

CASE 1—MICHAEL

Michael is 30. He has had four or five admissions to a psychiatric hospital since he was 21, and on each admission he was acutely disturbed and floridly psychotic. He was behaving irrationally and acting upon his delusions, and he was completely lacking in insight.

His family was very disturbed. His father never came near the hospital and was reported by Michael to lead a solitary life in his own home. The father ate his meals separately and for long periods communicated with Michael's mother only through Michael. At other times, the father would ignore his son, which left Michael and his mother as the only ones who were in any communication with each other. Michael's mother struck me as being disturbed herself, and she talked in a rather chaotic and nonstop way, taking little notice of what the other person said. When Michael was first ill, she took a long time to accept that there was anything the matter with him, even though he was both behaving and talking in bizarre ways.

Michael's first breakdown occurred when he had been at college for only a short while. He had fallen in love with a fellow student called Marjorie, but while he may have been out with her on a few occasions, the relationship was, even then, more in his mind than in reality. It certainly did not develop, and when Michael gave up college, no contact was maintained. Marjorie, however, became an imaginary companion with whom he shared all his solitary life, and who occupied his thoughts to the exclusion of all else.

In his first breakdown, and indeed, in subsequent ones, Marjorie featured very strongly. Michael was, in fact, picked up by the police wandering in the buildings of the college where he had known her, though he now had no reason in reality, nor any right, to be there.

The girl featured very strongly in the content of his delusions as well. She had now changed from having been his imaginary companion to being his real wife, and his sister. They had children, and he had become at the same time a doctor of psychophysics, a doctor of philosophy, and every other kind of doctor. He treated both me and the nursing staff with utmost arrogance and contempt, attempting to annihilate us emotionally in a way that was reminiscent of Sartre's Other (see Chapter 2).

As he began to recover, the reality of these delusions began to diminish, and Marjorie again became the imaginary companion inside his head. He told me that he was deeply in love with her, that he shared all his thoughts with her as other people might with God, and that she would answer him in a voice that he could really hear. He dreaded the possibility of being without this experience because he felt that without it his life would be totally empty and meaningless.

I noted at the time: "As he talks about this constant fear, he creates a most abject picture, with his eyes full of tears, and I sensed something of the utter loneliness which he has somehow experienced. This must in some way have to do with the kind of upbringing he experienced at his parents' hands, because another part of his fantasy/delusion is that his parents are not his real parents and that he was brought up by a computer."

This pathetic, lonely, and frightened person that I briefly glimpsed became quickly concealed again behind his facade of impervious arrogance. For example, when I saw him the following week, he was not prepared to listen to anything I had to say, and when I asserted that in my view he was still ill he insisted that it must be I who was mad.

What I want to highlight here is the extreme imperviousness of the actual mother—like a computer, perhaps—who, one can surmise, would have found it difficult to adapt to her child's real needs. According to my basically Winnicottian position, psychological separation for this child would have been maximally traumatic, leading to a sense of abandonment and isolation that he still struggled with. He had tried to cope with this near total absence of an adaptive object (mother) by what I think Winnicott would have called introversion—a withdrawal from the world into an inner relationship with a self-created object who answered his every need (Marjorie).

At this stage of things, he could draw comfort from the illusion of contact which he had with Marjorie while still retaining, on some level, the knowledge that Marjorie was a comforting fantasy (i.e., a representational reality rather than an actual one). With the psychotic break, this knowledge seemed to disappear completely. He was married to Marjorie, and that was all there was to it. Illusion had given way to delusion. It is as though the tension of trying to maintain a representational space—which would also have been a space of longing, yearning, pain, and despair—had proved too much for him, and the inner "holding offs" from the object which guaranteed that space had given way.

It is interesting to try to relate this kind of phenomenon to Winnicott's theory of the transitional object. In a certain sense, the idea/experience of

Marjorie has many of the qualities of a transitional object. Like the baby, this patient had recognized in an external object a pattern of earlier good experience and had used this reincarnated pattern as an object under his own control. There was still a link, albeit a tenuous one, with a real object and a continuing knowledge about the absence of the object that was desired. With the tipping over into psychosis, the link with the real object all but disappears. Inner imagery takes over, and the attempt to forge a piece of the external world into a realization of desire disappears as well. There is instead a pseudo-realization of the image of the desired object through a total occlusion of the gap of separation and an annihilation of the "objectness" of the object.

CASE 2—ROGER

Roger is in his late twenties and has had numerous admissions to a psychiatric hospital over the past few years. As in the previous case, the admissions have been precipitated by major psychotic episodes, between which he is well in a psychiatric sense but leads a restricted and impoverished sort of existence in which he leans heavily on the support of his parents. He has no important current relationships.

Roger is teetering on the brink of a psychosis. He has been severely psychotic, overwhelmed by frightening paranoid experiences in which he felt his body and mind were being changed and controlled by a particular group of evil people who were actually people he had known in the past. Now he is superficially and precariously better. He stays voluntarily in the hospital and accepts medication. He joins in ordinary activities with other patients and says he feels much better, much calmer, and no longer persecuted. But as I engage with him, it becomes clear that inwardly he still clings to a psychotic perception of his experiences. He resists the designation of himself as ill and still feels that "Smith & Co.," as I have half-humorously termed his persecutors, were, in reality, doing things to him. He demonstrates to me the way the experience felt by making his arms hang down in an anthropoid fashion, with the fingers drawn out like claws. His hands had been "slimed," he said, and he had felt his hands were turning into claws like a demon's. He refers to the vividness of this experience and is clearly not ready to give up the idea that this was something that was really done to him in his body by some preternatural means.

During one particularly striking interview I tried to convey to him that I understood something of the intensity of his experience, saying something like: "It must have felt terrible"; but then I tried to help him draw the boundary of external reality more firmly around the experience. I said, "Suppose I were to say to you that this experience was like a dream from which you had not woken up. In a dream, which comes from your imagination, the experience is intensely real. You have no doubt at all that the dream events are really happening. You feel frightened; you try to run away; you know you are about to be killed. But then you wake up, and you know, even though your heart is pounding, that it was only a dream. Suppose that it was like this with Smith & Co.—like a dream going on while you were awake from which you could not 'wake up' because you were ill. What would you say to that?"

He said, "Do you mean 'ill' in quotation marks?" "No," I said, "ill in a real sense, precisely because you were muddled between something that was really happening and something that was like a dream." He responded equivocally, but I felt that he could, with a part of him, see what I meant and even agree with it; while there was another part that could not or would not give up the reality of the dream, and was perhaps even still immersed in it.

Maybe it was this other part that then started talking, opening up and letting me glimpse a much wider issue than whether or not Smith & Co. were *really* persecuting him. He made some references to the Bible—rather obscure ones that I didn't quite understand. I thought he was trying to find some underpinning for a plane of events that confused and frightened him, a plane of spiritual forces that produced real effects in the world.

Then he said: "You see, there was this girl." (He had talked about her before, several years ago.) "She was *very* beautiful. I don't just mean very beautiful; I mean *very beautiful*." I thought I half-knew what he meant—a falling-in-love kind of figure, a figure of his dreams; but I said little.

He went on to say that she was beautiful but heartless and cold; a "bitch" whom he had loved, but who "gave him the push" and would have nothing more to do with him.

I said: "So you lost her, and that hurt a lot."

He looked upset. *"Well, I haven't really lost her. She's still in my mind."*

I knew at that moment that he was avoiding the pain and I said, "You're fudging the issue, Roger. You *have* lost her. She's gone for good. And that really is painful."

At this his eyes filled with tears, and for a moment he seemed to acknowledge his pain and sadness.

"Yes," he said. "It is."

I don't recall exactly what happened after this, but he didn't stay with the pain for long.

"I think I can see now why you fudge the line between what is inside you and what is outside of you in the real world," I said. "It's because you can't stand the pain of losing her."

"No, it's not that," he protested.

Perhaps pressing my point too hard, I continued: "Well, I think it is. The girl in your mind is a memory, and a memory is a different thing from a real person. You confuse yourself if you say it's not. You blur the line between real and imaginary things, and then it backfires on you, like with Smith & Co."

This patient could not maintain the contact with his painful sense of loss. The case illustrates, in a way similar to the last one, how falling off the brink into psychosis seems to be a way of avoiding the painful fact of separation and the experience of real objects being unavailable. This avoidance of separation creates a situation where the person is used by his imagination rather than being able to use it. He refuses to *see* (and this might be a very important word) the separation and distance between himself and his object, between the object and its representation. As a result, he cannot represent the object to himself as a symbol and remains enmeshed with imaginary objects in a transitional space that has no definite boundary or location.

Roger had a better family than the patient in the first case, though, again, the father tended to be distant and uninvolved. This left him thoroughly enmeshed with his mother. Although a nice woman who communicated fairly straightforwardly, she seemed to have some difficulty in drawing and maintaining boundaries in a consistent and firm way. She appeared to alternate between an anxious overinvolvement with her son and a certain professional detachment. This seemed to recapitulate Roger's early experience of her as a working mother who was often unavailable—for example, when he came home from school—but at other times, oversolicitous and overinvolved.

CASE 3—SIMONE

Simone, a French woman, was living with a man whom she said she did not love; however, she felt herself to be deeply dependent upon him. He had "rescued" her from an unhappy situation in her own country, having met her in a bar, where she often sat talking to no one but evidently engaging in some nonverbal communication with those around her. Her rescuer was an Englishman on holiday who had brought her back with him to England. Neither knew the other very well, but he had installed her in his house as a mistress.

In her own country there had been frequent admissions to mental hospitals, though Simone did not regard herself as having ever been ill. She had been diagnosed as suffering from schizophrenia, but she felt that her family would put her away to get rid of her whenever she was a nuisance.

I was unable to get many details about Simone's background. My purpose here is to focus on a particular conversation I had with her, together with its immediate context.

Since living with her much older lover, history had begun to repeat itself. She had started frequenting pubs, and in the course of this she had "fallen in love with" a man whom she had seen there on a number of occasions but had never spoken to.

Perhaps one could say that she had seen in him the pattern of a lost but longed-for love object, who would provide her with that which her current relationship failed to offer. But rather than pursuing him and starting some relationship with him in reality—disillusioning as that might have been—she began to believe that he also loved her and communicated with her all the time. She became increasingly withdrawn, refused any longer to have any sexual relations with the man she was living with, and eventually moved out to a hotel, where she could enjoy her "relationship" with the "man of her dreams."

This situation was not viable; she had no money of her own and eventually moved back into her previous living arrangements. She was admitted to the hospital after deeply slashing her wrists and taking an overdose.

Simone told me that she had felt in despair and could not see any future for herself at all. Her despair seemed to lie in the partial realization that the (dream) man in the pub was not going to meet her need in reality, and she was therefore stuck with her actual man who did not seem to care for her at all.

When I tried to discuss with her the reality status of the man in the pub, she resisted my attempts to say that she had no evidence that he loved her. She argued: *"I know he does. He's in my mind all the time, and I feel so good when he is there."*

Although this case is sketchy on biographical and other data, it does seem possible to conclude that Simone's image in her mind of her love object was all that lay between her and a bleak despair (a place where the object was not). The actual object and the actual space of separation were desolate and intolerable, and she preferred to die rather than to suffer them. (She did eventually kill herself.) The comforting, near delusional object is again like a transitional object; but she progressively abandons the attempt to make some marriage between her dream and the real object, with the result that the image which first presented to her the form of her desire becomes fleshed out as the pseudo-realized object that will fulfill it. As in the other two cases, the space of absence in which her lack might have been felt and known is obliterated by the con-fusion of that space with the space of real objects in the real world.

CONVENTIONAL AND SELF-CREATED SYMBOLS

After these clinical illustrations, I want to return to one final feature of transitional phenomena, which will enable me to make an important distinction between different kinds of symbols. It is a distinction that therapists need to be aware of, as Winnicott often stressed.

In Winnicott's view, the transitional object could be thought of either as object (symbol) that the baby had created or as one that he had found.

In either case, it was a symbol-object that the baby had produced in answer to a felt need. It was the baby itself who had found the pattern that first of all re-created, and later re-presented, what it needed. This distinguished it clearly from a symbol produced by the Other, by someone else, from outside.

A self-created symbol of this kind is something new; it provides a container that fits the subjective content very closely, and answers the subjective (felt) need in the same way that the symbiotic mother had earlier answered and adapted to the baby's physical and emotional needs. Externally produced symbols, by contrast—those preexisting symbols of the cultural community, whether they be language, words, or other forms—lack this quality of adaptedness.[3] They are likely, therefore, to fit the self less well, and to entail an adaptation or molding of the self to the requirements of the Other, to external reality. In his later writings, Winnicott often stressed the need to wait for the patient to "find" the interpretation that was needed—in other words, to wait for the patient to create his own answering form. Winnicott likened an overzealous interpretation that he might feel inclined to make to indoctrination; it was the imposition of an external form. As such it might lead the patient even further from his own true subjectivity—quite the reverse of the avowed analytic aim.

SEPARATION AND THE REPRESENTATIONAL SPACE

Most psychoanalytic writings on symbol formation stress the relation between symbol formation and object loss. Only when the object is lost or given up in some way can the idea of the object, which is the basis of the symbol, begin to take shape. Winnicott's view is no exception: the first

---

[3]Such symbols offer a patterning of experience that is shared by others, containing patterns for the child's experience from out of an already existing stock of forms in the cultural community. The representation of experience so offered may not fit the individual so well as a personally tailored form, but it gains on the idiosyncratic symbol by drawing the pattern into a culture of shared experience, common to all. As I will show in the next chapter, these symbols are part of the world that exists outside the mother–infant dyad, which is, in a certain sense, the province of the father (see also Chapter 14).

step in symbol formation occurs at that moment when the mother is beginning to be perceived as separate by the baby, and thus when the baby is losing the sense of primal oneness with the mother that had existed until then. The primitive symbol that is formed, the transitional object, is both a memorial to the lost unity with the object and an attempt to reinstate it *in effigia*. Other writers stress the loss of the breast and weaning as the critical factor. For example, one of Bion's (1962) formulations was that a thought is a "no-breast." The idea of absence, of something missing that can be conceived of, imagined in the mind apart from the possibility of fulfillment with that object, thus becomes crucial in understanding what it is that creates the conditions within which a symbol can be formed. Lacan (quoted in Lemaire 1977) seems to make use of a similar notion: the critical factor of something missing is for him the child's recognition of the difference between the sexes—hence, of castration. It is somehow the father, or rather the Name-of-the-Father, who stands at the gateway to the Symbolic. The father is the castrator, the separator; he is also the one who forbids further carnal knowledge of the mother, the enforcer of the incest taboo. So he is the one who, in several ways, mediates the experience of loss to the child.

I have expressed some of my own thoughts on this subject in Chapter 4. What I was attempting there was not so much to suggest an alternative to this kind of formulation, as to shift the focus of attention from the earliest phases of separation from the object to the later stages of disengagement from it.

I was imagining the child, not so much emerging from the mother's arms and a primary relation to the breast, but a little later, crawling, taking its first few steps, in the midst of its "love affair with the world" (Greenacre 1957). All kinds of objects had become important and the child was feverishly exploring them. But in the midst of this, he begins to discover limits and boundaries imposed by the parents, which I formulated as a limiting of activity in relation to his objects: "You may look, but not do." I saw in this the beginnings of a separation between looking and doing, which itself seemed to introduce a bounding of the self and a gap or distance between the self and its objects. I argued that this was important in creating the conditions within which the visual perception of the object could begin to be separated out from immediate "doing" with it. I also had in mind Langer's (1953) notion of "unhinging from practical action," which she suggested, in her book *Feeling and Form*, was a necessary prerequisite for the perception of form, and thus for the aesthetic contemplation of objects.

The central idea I have been developing is thus that the limitation on action imposed by the parents—especially the father, in relation to action with the mother—creates a space within which first, the visual image, and later the idea of the object, can begin to be separated out from the object itself. Later still, the name of the object, the word, can be inserted into this space, as though the father were saying: "You can have this word, this name for the object, but not the object itself."[4] This is not to forget that for a long time the word may cling to the object just as the child before clung to his primary object; in this way, the word will at first be little more than one particular quality of the object through which it may be indicated. Only later may a wedge be driven into this clinging to keep the word and the object separate from one another.

Distance between word and thing or concept and thing, as between self and object, may be difficult to achieve and more difficult to sustain. It is doubtful how much any of us can manage this in a consistent way, as is evidenced by our relation to our theories and by our difficulty in sustaining the view that theories are constructs and not facts of the world (see Chapter 18).

THE FACIAL GESTALT AS PRECURSOR OF SYMBOL FORMATION

I want to end this chapter with an idea that will again bring the face to the center of attention. I have already mentioned in Chapter 5 Fairbairn's (1941) distinction between object seeking and satisfaction seeking, a distinction which highlighted a controversy in psychoanalytic theory between those who would derive the whole of psychic life from an instinctual relation to objects, and those who see evidence of primary

---

[4] I am trying to clarify here how it is that the intial space that is opened up between mother and child through their separation becomes more rigorously maintained and bounded as development proceeds. I am groping toward the idea that it is the father and his prohibitions that play a major role in this—an idea that I develop further in Chapter 7 and more specifically in relation to language and metaphor in subsequent chapters.

noninstinctual elements from the beginning.[5] Suttie's (1935) "primary need for the mother" would fall into the latter category, as would Bowlby's (1969) more carefully formulated "attachment." Winnicott's (1971) work on play would seem to place him also firmly in this group.

I myself find the Suttie/Bowlby/Winnicott view entirely persuasive. This being so, I have asked myself whether there may not be, in this developing area of symbols which leads on to communication, elements that themselves have a noninstinctual base. It is here that I have been struck by certain features of facial recognition—not just the very early recognition of the configuration of a human face, and later the specific configuration of the mother's face, but more particularly and especially the recognition of facial expressions (See Chapter 1).

The face is unique among the parts of the body in that it does not give its essential character to the sense of touch, even though the small child may explore it with his hands. (Actually, the voice, which also becomes a vehicle of communication, shares this characteristic of not being apprehensible in a bodily way.) What the face gives is a pattern, or sequence of patterns—a configuration or expression that can be grasped only through the eyes. In other words, all attempts to grasp the face as an object are doomed to failure. They will miss its essential characteristics.

A face is a centre of human expression, the transparent envelope of the attitudes and desires of others, *the place of manifestation* [italics added], the barely material support for a multitude of intentions. This is why it is impossible for us to treat a face or a body, even a dead body, like a thing. They are sacred entities, not the "givens of sight." [Merleau-Ponty 1965, p. 167]

The face is a "place of manifestation, the barely material support for a multitude of intentions. . . . It is impossible for us to treat a face . . . like a thing." I am struck by the similarity between the face and the symbol, especially the word. We could say of the word, too, that it is the "barely material support" for its meaning, or that it is meaning's "transparent envelope."

---

[5]In referring to instinctual and noninstinctual elements in behavior, I am talking about instincts in the usual psychoanalytic sense. Attachment behavior is in some sense instinctive, too, but in Bowlby's terms it is a *primary* organizer of behavior. Therefore, attachment is not secondary to, say, the satisfaction of an oral drive. I am aware that my usage may cause some confusion, but I think the sense of what I mean will be apparent from the text.

Here is another passage from Merleau-Ponty (1964a):

> When one goes from the order of events to the order of expression, one does not change the world; the same circumstances that were previously submitted to now become a signifying system. Hollowed out, worked from within, and finally freed from that weight upon us which makes them painful or wounding, they become transparent, even luminous. . . . [p. 64]

"Passing from the order of events to the order of expression"—from action to looking, from doing to contemplation; this is the essential leap of symbolism. "Hollowed out, worked from within . . . they become transparent, even luminous. . . ." Is that the face, expressing an inner state, or trans-*figured* with a smile of love or recognition? Or is it a word that suddenly means something?

> But then a miracle occurs. Through the manner in which it is contemplated, this simple sensory material takes on a new and varied life. . . . What it immediately is is thrust into the background by what it accomplishes with its mediation, by what it "means." [Cassirer 1953, p. 93]

We could say the same about this statement, too—*face* or *word?* "Through the manner in which it is contemplated, this simple sensory material takes on a new and varied life." Suddenly it *reveals* something. It passes "from the order of events to the order of expression."

Meaning emerges from the word, from language, in the same way that the expression emerges from the face: the face suddenly *means* "I love you" or "I recognize you" or "I'm pleased with you." The expression that shines through the face is the prototype of emergent meaning, occurring before language begins to draw the child into a cultural world of symbols. Could one say that the mother's face is the first experience the child has of that "miracle of transformation" that Cassirer talks about?

FACIAL EXPRESSION, VIRTUAL OBJECTS, AND COMMUNICATION

Psychoanalysis has concerned itself with the breast and the loss of the breast, and the way that this first loss or separation not only creates real objects (the Other experienced as Other), but "self" and "symbol" as well. The symbol is the re-presentation of the object that comes to *mean* the object, not just to point to it. This occurs when the relation to the object as object, that is, in action, is no longer possible, at least for a time.

It is clear, however, that from the beginning, the infant's relation to the face is significantly different from its relation to the breast. Characteristically, contact with the nipple elicits rooting and sucking behavior, while perception of the mother's face elicits smiling, babbling, and various other motor behaviors quite distinguishable from those occurring during feeding. The face is the focus of the earliest communicative behavior between mother and infant: the baby smiles at the mother's face, the mother smiles at the baby's face.

I can put this differently in a way that underlines a fundamental distinction. The breast is the object of the earliest *instinctual drives* (in the psychoanalytic sense). It is an object that gives itself physically, and in that sense allows the satisfaction of very early bodily needs. By contrast, the face as face (insofar as it is differentiated from the breast and elicits quite different responses) is not at all an object in the same sense. It gives itself visually, not through bodily contact, and from the beginning defies the physical incorporation that the breast allows. What is true of the face is even more true of the smile—it cannot be physically grasped by the child through hand or mouth, but can be received only by the eyes across a distance and then only evanescently. The smiling interaction is thus from the start a distance-spanning transaction, even though initially it will be experienced at the same time as the child is held, cuddled, or fed. There is an *essential distance* in relation to the smile that cannot be overcome.

From this point of view, the mother's smile is also the infant's first object that is not an object—the first experience of a "virtual object" that lies forever beyond the reach of tactile apprehension. It may be distorting Winnicott's usage to think of the mother's smile as the first transitional object, yet like the transitional object, it lies in some sense beyond a giving up of the mother as physical, tactile object, and points to a world that can only come into being in the space so created—a world *between* the mother and child, and spanned by their increasingly complex communications.

I am suggesting, therefore, that the mother's face, particularly her smile and facial expressions, occupies a very special place in the child's experience. From the beginning, spanning and allowing contact over distance, the face has an irreducible communicative significance. As pure visual form, it precludes the more primitive mode of tactile, bodily appropriation; thus, in some sense, it guarantees and points toward a space within which communication can develop. It is true, of course, that from a very early stage the vocal-auditory channel (the conversation of mother's talk and baby's babble) runs, as it were, a parallel course; it is also true that later on this vocal-auditory channel overtakes the visual, and indeed achieves a preeminence. (I mean when language develops and words become the primary vehicle of communication.) But it seems to me that the face and the expressions that pass over it nevertheless provide a kind of model for the later relation between words and meanings which has eventually to be grasped. In this sense, the facial expression, even though it is only vaguely apprehended, can be seen as a sort of protosymbol, paving the way for the more momentous later discovery that "all this noise (the spoken word) begins to mean something" (Merleau-Ponty 1964a, p. 40).

All of this would be entirely compatible with the view that there is a primary noninstinctual element in our constitution from the start, which links into the basic attachment propensity of the human species. It would not be surprising in such a view if the face, which plays such an important part in the development of attachment, were also to be important in the development of the symbolic function, and ultimately the communication that maintains attachment. There is much to suggest that the language function itself has a built-in biological basis, and it would be somehow surprising if the development of language depended solely on the attenuation of instinctual relations with objects for its development. My suggestion that the face and its expressions form a bridge or transition to the symbolic function and language, by providing an early model of emergent meanings, seems to me to find some justification in these thoughts.

7   The Role of the Father

So he drove out the man; and he placed at the east of the garden of Eden Cherubims, and a flaming sword which turned every way, to keep the way of the tree of life.

—Genesis 3:24

THE TIME HAS come for me to say something about the role of the father in the structuring of the self and the development of symbols. Up until now I have only considered the child's relationship to its mother, and in various ways, how developments in that relationship begin to create structure in the world and the self. I have been looking essentially at two-person relationships, as though the father had not yet existed.

From a psychological point of view, this has some truth, as I will show. Yet there has been, all along, an implicit third position in what I have been saying. When I wrote that I had been looking mainly at two-person relationships, where was "I" situated when I was looking? To put the matter in this way highlights the fact that there is a third position, that of the observer; it was from that external third position that I was observing the mother–infant pair and describing what I saw.

In this chapter, I want to suggest that this third position, that of the observer, is the place of the father, who is originally perceived by the infant as being the one who is outside the mother–infant pair (mommy-and-me). I will also argue that it is the definitive establishment of this third position within the experience of the child that guarantees the space for thought and representation, which I have so far considered as arising only as a gap or a space within the previously undifferentiated unity of the mother–infant dyad.

The reasons for making this claim will become clearer as my argument develops. Basically, they hinge on the fact that the observer position is essentially a looking position, created by the exclusion of the child from the space of the parental couple during the oedipal period. Up until then, looking had always been "anticipatory touching," moving over relatively freely into action and fulfillment with the object. But once the oedipal boundary is firmly drawn and the parental space established as an exclusion zone for the child, this passage from looking to doing is blocked. My argument is that this more radical divorce of looking from doing brings about the definitive separation of a looking space from a doing space in the child's mind. It is this looking space that is thus freed to develop into the space of representation and thought. I believe that this is the formulation I was reaching after in my earlier discussion of the topic in Chapter 4.

TWO-PERSON AND THREE-PERSON RELATIONSHIPS

If we start from the beginning, from the baby being totally unaware of a self–other distinction, it is apparent that the capacity to get outside of the self—in other words, to an observer position—is a major achievement. It was the first stage of this achievement that I considered in detail in Chapters 2 and 3. This first stage of getting outside of the self involved taking the position of the mother and looking back on the self through the mother's eyes. It consisted of "swapping places" within the first developing object relationship. What is now in question is more complex: it involves taking the position of the third person, the father, in the threesome and looking from his position at what the other two, mommy-and-me, are doing. Through this movement the baby comes to see itself in relation to mother through father's eyes. It is apparent, however, that this ability to identify with and accept the position of the third person lies at the end of a process, not at its beginning.

Psychoanalysis makes a major distinction between two-person and three-person relationships and in my view is right to do so. It started with three-person relationships and the discovery by Freud of the Oedipus conflict—the rivalry and hatred of the little boy toward the loved father who seemed to be in competition with him for the love and body of the mother. Only after this situation had been thoroughly worked over did psychoanalysis push back into the area of two-person relationships and all that had to do with the founding and development of the self and the beginnings of psychic life.

The issues I am considering in this chapter deal with three-person relationships, though what I say is in no way an attempt to summarize all that can be said about the Oedipus complex. As in earlier chapters, I am more interested in formal possibilities than in detailed issues of content, and it is the way in which the greater complexities of the three-person situation lead to more complex structures of psychological functioning that is my primary concern. Nevertheless, we cannot avoid at least a schematic look at some content issues.

INSIDE OR OUTSIDE—MATERNAL WARMTH OR EXPANDING VISION

First of all, the father appears on the scene. What we have to relate to here is the time when the father begins to be differentiated from the mother, seen as different from her. At first, he may well be experienced as just another mother—in other words, someone who will provide similar ministrations that will help to keep the illusion of oneness and nonseparation going.

As separation proceeds, the father will begin to be more clearly distinguished from the mother. He will be loved and hated for the different things he provides, the different ways he does things. He picks me up differently; he swings me around; he is more exciting. He is someone who is not always there like mother, but who comes and goes; but when he comes, he plays with me, perhaps in a different way from mother. He feels different, his voice is different, he tells me off more sharply, and so on. The details do not really matter—it is the *difference* that does.

Mahler and colleagues (1975) have pointed out from their work on separation/individuation that, as separation gets under way and the child becomes mobile, fathers begin to become more important. It is as though the father, as father, is found out there in the world that is beginning to be discovered. In this sense, we might think of the father as being, in the child's experience, more radically Other than the mother; the mother still has the aura of remembered oneness about her, an aura that still pulls and invites as something that might be returned to. The father is more clearly Other from the beginning.

So the father is found out there in the world as someone different from mother and other than self. He stands there over against "me and mother." I can lose mother and find him. In some fundamental sense, it seems to me, the father *is* the world, or stands *for* the world. I find him in the world, and he goes out into the world. He is like another pole to my experience, drawing me out from the comfort and security of my relationship with mother into an exploration of the world.

I believe that this is a powerful positive value of the pre-oedipal father for children of both sexes that is not sufficiently stressed in psychoanalytic writings. The father exerts a positive pull on the child, drawing him out from the regressive undertow of the maternal symbiosis. If he is absent, the child may fall back, enmeshed in a continuing state of quasi-fusion with the mother. This is one way that the father stands for a continuing progression and underpins the forward thrust of development. In Homer's *Odyssey*, Odysseus gets his men to strap him to the mast (the upright phallus) and plug his ears against the sweet siren voices so that he is not lured into their fatal, devouring embrace.

I cannot develop the theme of the absent father here, but I would stress that the father can also be absent by being absent as a father. He may be a weak father, himself not clearly separated from a dominating wife. He may, through his own needs, strive to be a mother to his child, depriving the child of difference and a star to steer by. It may also happen that a child who suffers a too sudden rupture of the maternal symbiosis—an actual rather than a potential space, in Winnicott's terms—may himself turn to the father as a substitute mother and strive to re-create with the father the lost fusional state. Again, the possibilities of the father *as father* are undermined, and the upholding of separateness and difference becomes precarious.

All of this, in my view, is something that happens on a pregenital level of relationship and is therefore prior to those events that form the substance of the Oedipus complex.[1] The girl who approaches her father

---

[1] I need to make some comment on the question of the difference between the sexes and how this relates to the difference between father and mother that I am talking about. I am not disputing that there comes a time when the bodily difference between the sexes and between father and mother become important. But I am suggesting that this bodily difference—the possession or nonpossession of a penis—becomes important at a relatively late stage of development; that before this there has evolved an important differentiation in the child's experience between father and mother based on quite other qualities and characteristics than the sexual. The sexual difference per se would seem more likely to act as a constellator of these previously perceived differences than as the prime cause of the discrimination.

from this base with an awakening sexual awareness may have difficulties in differentiating the wish for fusion from the more genital aims of sexual receptiveness. The boy who has related to the father in this fusional mode may have difficulty with passive homosexual longings. It is too threatening for him to stand up to the father and to tolerate the distance between himself and the father that the oedipal rivalry involves, as he still wants to be merged in with the father.

This is jumping ahead. What I intend to focus on is a particular moment in the child's developing perception of three-person relationships, which in a formal sense is the beginning of the oedipal situation.

Up until now, the child had related separately to the mother and the father. Both, in their different and differentiating ways, had existed for him alone. They were the two poles of his developing world, between which he moved. But now he sees them together. They are not interested in him, but only in each other. He has become the observer of them as a couple. He is now forced to take the position of the third person in the threesome, which was originally, from the baby's point of view, the father's, and to look at what the other two, the mother and father, are doing together.

Looking at what the other two are doing—this parental "intercourse" which the child sees is the core of the oedipal problem that has to be resolved. The child, who previously had enjoyed an apparently exclusive possession of the mother and later a different, though nearly exclusive, possession of the father, now realizes that he is left out. The parents do things together without him. I believe that this is a shattering blow to the infant's security—hence, his urgent attempts to break up the parental couple and reinstate his lost position. It is quite possible that initially, at least, such security considerations are of far greater importance than any supposed wish on the part of the child to usurp the parent of the opposite sex in a quasi-sexual way. In my view, it is the child's attachment to the mother that is being threatened.[2]

---

[2]That the parental "intercourse" from which the child is excluded is essentially the "primal scene," hallowed in analytic discourse, is to my mind somewhat doubtful. That eventually the fantasy of a sexual intercourse becomes important cannot be doubted, but it seems to me that an exclusive preoccupation with sexual content prevents consideration of other aspects of the situation that are at first more important. First among these is the fact of being excluded per se. From that point of view, it does not really matter what the parents

OEDIPAL RESOLUTION AND THE STRUCTURING OF MIND

The overcoming of the Oedipus complex is, according to psychoanalysis, a central task of psychological and emotional development. Freud's (1923, 1924) various accounts of the process hinge on his belief in the fundamentally sexual nature of its constitution. The little boy wishes to possess his mother in an erotic bodily way, and the father is a rival, an obstacle to this. The little girl has similar erotic desires for the father and wants to have his babies; the mother is her impediment and rival.

Freud postulated various processes that led to the dissolution or overcoming of the complex. These could be summarized as follows:

1. The waxing and waning of an innate developmental program. Freud did not seem to discuss this at great length.

2. The gradual attrition of the erotic desire for the loved parent through recurring frustrations and disappointments. The real situation leads gradually to a realization of the futility of the wish.

3. The threat of castration. Freud seemed to believe that there was some built-in phylogenetic engram of such a possibility. He also believed

---

are doing; the fact that they are doing anything at all together means that they are not doing something with me. They may be doing other things that by their nature exclude me, such as talking together. And they are probably doing things that seem to give them pleasure, from which I am also excluded. The actual realization of the fact of sexual intercourse, and eventually the realization that this is how babies are made, seems likely to be one that occurs at different ages according to circumstances; it is possible that it may not occur until relatively late in development and that it then constellates retrospectively all the other instances of exclusion from the parental couple under its aegis. Freud (Breuer and Freud 1895) himself made use of this kind of explanation in trying to account for the traumatic effects of sexual seduction in his early studies on hysteria. Later development fills in what could not be understood early on. This is a different way of looking at the matter from placing the sexual rivalry into the early era itself. What is certain is that the passage from two-person to three-person situations creates a problem of the excluded third, and what is likely is that the child's attempt to grapple with this problem begins well before the sexual issue becomes important. It is possible that psychoanalysis has been hampered by what I would call its phallocentric and later mammocentric views. If we take seriously the insights that Bowlby has given us through his work on attachment, it may be that we will have to begin rewriting such sacred articles as the Oedipus complex from the point of view of attachment theory. It would begin to make sense of what I am struggling to say if we saw the three-person situation as constituting a powerful threat to attachment, and the infant's reaction to the exclusion in terms of a wish and a need to reinstate that attachment. It is such considerations that are completely missing from ordinary psychoanalytic formulations.

that the various threats the child received from the parents—"We'll chop it off if you don't leave it alone"—played their part in influencing the little boy. But the most important factor was the child's recognition of the anatomical difference between the sexes—the fact that the little girl had an apparently missing member. For the little boy, this discovery meant that castration was a real possibility, not just an idle threat, so the prohibitions of the father now carried far greater weight.

Freud saw this realization of the "fact" of castration by the child as the critical factor. For the young boy, it was a devastating blow that rapidly led to an abandonment of the oedipal wish. For the young girl, it was less devastating—in a sense, the worst had happened already. Perhaps for her it was, after all, the nonrealization of her wish for a baby that was more important.

How does the child resolve this conflict between the wish for a (continuing) possession of the mother on the one hand, and the fear of castration by the father on the other? What is the resolution of the oedipal conflict in Freud's account? In simple terms, the child either gives up the oedipal wish or represses it.

What happens in the first case, when the conflict is successfully overcome? Freud turns for explanation to an idea he first formulated in *Mourning and Melancholia* (1917). Basically, it was the notion that when an object is lost, the object cathexis (the libidinal love for that object) is replaced by an identification with that object. In melancholia (depression) Freud believed he could see evidence that the (representation of the) loved object, which the melancholic patient had lost, was assimilated in some way into the ego. For example, when the depressed patient reproached himself so bitterly for supposed misdemeanors, Freud considered that he was actually reproaching the lost loved object for abandoning him. This was not at first apparent, because the loved object had been introjected into the ego. The patient had identified with the lost loved object, which had become, as a result, a part of the self.

In relation to the Oedipus complex, Freud (1923) tried to use the same explanation—the object that is lost as a libidinal object becomes an identification in the person's ego. But the explanation did not quite work. In the resolution of the oedipal conflict, the child gives up the parent of the opposite sex as libidinal object; in Freud's terms, there ought to be an identification with this opposite-sex parent. In fact, though, the identifications in the child's development seem to go the wrong way. The girl, as a rule, ends up identifying with her mother more than her father; the boy, as a rule, identifies more with his father than his mother.[3]

To resolve this discrepancy, Freud introduced the idea of the negative Oedipus complex. In both boys and girls, he said, there is a subsidiary, second component of the major complex which is like a shadow of it—the girl's libidinal love for her mother and the boy's libidinal love for his father. The dissolution of this total complex then gives rise to two

---

[3]Freud's attempt to talk himself out of this discrepancy is less than convincing—it suggests an effort to preserve a much loved idea rather than to look afresh at the facts in order to see what alternative idea they might suggest. The idea that object loss leads to identification is certainly a profound one; the question is whether or not it adequately accounts for the resolution of the Oedipus complex. The first relationship that both the boy and the girl have to "give up" is the powerful and exclusive attachment to the mother of the earliest years. If we take Freud's notion seriously, it suggests that the core of the ego or self in both the boy and the girl will be maternal; it would have to be later events that led to the boy child identifying with his father and the girl child with her mother. We then have to ask in what sense the boy child has to give up his father as a libidinal object, and it seems to me that what we come upon is the area in which the boy has related to the father in the early stages as a substitute mother. The father is not, in my view, a libidinal figure in his own right who promises instinctual satisfactions. The father as a homosexually gratifying object seems to me to depend on later confusions of identity and identification which are not the basis of normality. The situation with the young girl is somewhat different. Once genital sexuality becomes an important element of awareness, the girl may indeed long for her father in a libidinally gratifying way. Insofar as she has to give up such wishes, she loses an object for a second time. But this cannot really account, as Freud saw, for the predominantly female identification of the girl. In order to understand this, I think we have to look to a more social level of awareness. The young girl realizes that she is a female like her mother; she wants to be like her mother and do the things that she does, including perhaps having the father's babies. Similarly, the young boy realizes that he is a male like his father; he wants to be like his father and do the things that he does, including perhaps making babies with the mother. Both want to follow in the footsteps of the same-sex parent. But in the terms that I have been developing in this book, this is quite a different process from the earlier one of identification replacing object loss. That identification would be a means of closing the gap of separateness from a lost loved object, a means of reinstating a sense of lost fusional oneness. In this respect, it is similar to transitional phenomena that attempt to recreate the lost object in a new form (in this case, in the self). In Segal's terms the process would depend on a symbolic equation in which difference is repudiated. The later identifications, which I am suggesting are to be understood in terms of the social process, are not of this kind; they recognize and respect the sense of being different and separate from the loved object, and would be based on truly symbolic processes of wanting to be *like* father or mother but recognizing the impossibility of ever being them.

identifications for each sex, not one, and it is these two identifications that become a part of the child's ego.

> The broad general outcome of the sexual phase dominated by the Oedipus complex may, therefore, be taken to be the forming of a *precipitate in the ego, consisting of these two identifications in some way united with each other* [italics added]. This modification of the ego retains its special position; it confronts the other contents of the ego as an ego ideal or super-ego. [p. 34]

"A precipitate in the ego consisting of these two identifications in some way united with each other." Freud uses a chemical metaphor—the dis*solution* of the Oedipus complex causes a *precipitate* in the ego. Clearly Freud is struggling to explain something very important, and he is groping for a metaphor to catch his meaning. Something is deposited in the personality in a solid and permanent way as a result of the "dissolution." In being so "precipitated" or deposited, it undergoes a transformation. Under the threat of castration by the father, the child gives up a particular striving in relation to the mother. An old pattern of striving or relation—namely, for an exclusive bodily possession of the mother—is replaced by what Freud calls an aim-inhibited or sublimated pattern of relation, which settles for a more limited access to the mother.

> I have described elsewhere how this turning away from the Oedipus complex takes place. The object cathexes are given up and replaced by identifications. The authority of the father or parents is introjected into the ego, and there it forms the nucleus of the super-ego, which takes over the severity of the father and perpetuates the prohibition against incest, and so secures the ego from the return of the libidinal object-cathexis. The libidinal trends belonging to the Oedipus complex are in part desexualised and sublimated (a thing which probably happens with every transformation into an identification), and in part inhibited in their aim and changed into impulses of affection. [1924, pp. 176–177]

"The authority of the father . . . is introjected into the ego, and there . . . takes over the severity of the [actual] father and . . . the prohibition against incest. . . ." This is Freud's way of describing the inner change that comes from the resolution of the Oedipus complex. Is there any different way that we can describe the new inner structure that is formed as a result of the changed external relation to the parents? For this is a key question in this essay—in what way does the arrival of the father in the child's experience influence, and render more complex, the structuring of self and world?

I want to stress here that what is internalized by the child, what becomes a part of its functioning that was not there before, is something that first of all has been achieved in the real, external world. Something has been struggled with *in reality*; a conflict with the father for exclusive possession of the mother has been overcome. Because of his fear of the father's prohibiting, and because of his love for the father as well, the child has given up what he had previously striven for. The outcome is a new patterning of his relationship with both parents in reality.

This new patterning of relationships is one that grants to the parental couple their own bounded and privileged space from which the child is excluded in an absolute way. It is the space of parental "intercourse," whatever that might mean, within which the parents will interact alone. Through this new structuring of things, the child is, in effect, banished to a distance, from which he can only look and imagine, but not interfere.

It is clear that this space is both new and not new in the child's experience at the same time. The child has known before, as we have examined at length, a space within which the needed and longed-for object is not available, or not there. What he has not known is a space from which he is completely excluded, within which interactions occur that have nothing to do with him. We could say, therefore, that this new space is pure looking space, in relation to which the child can never be other than observer. The new pattern thus involves the acceptance of a quite different, more absolute kind of distance and boundary from any he has known before and, correlatively, a far more radical separation of self and Other.

I will return in a moment to what Freud says about the inner changes that stem from the dissolution of the Oedipus conflict, but first I want to complete my own argument.

I have tried to show in previous chapters, particularly through a discussion of Winnicott's work, how separation from the object introduces a gap or space into the infant's experience that becomes the space within which primitive symbols or representations of objects can be formed. Particularly in the last chapter, through a discussion of psychotic individuals, I drew attention to the precariousness of this space, and the relative ease with which its boundaries can give way under pressure from more "embodied" objects that seek to fill up and obliterate it.

What this new oedipal structuring of the earlier space provides, which was not there before, is a more radical underpinning, a more secure guarantee of its boundaries. It establishes a space, the boundaries of which must not be breached, a NO ENTRY space, within which objects can only be looked at or observed, but never touched. The strengthening of the "nondoing" constitution of this space is of vital importance; for, as I have shown in the last chapter, it is only within such a space of radical separation from the object that fully fledged, representational symbols, such as those of language, can arise.

I like to think of this developing space in experience as the space of the mind and to see the increasingly complex changes in the child's relation to external reality as being among its major formative influences. It is in this sense, therefore, that I see the resolution of the Oedipus complex, not only as a major social development, which it is, but also as a kingpin in the development of human consciousness.

INTROJECTION, IDENTIFICATION, AND THE PARENTAL COUPLE

I will return now to considering what Freud says about the new inner structures that arise from the dissolution of the Oedipus conflict. It is clear from the passage quoted earlier (1924, pp. 176–177) that Freud's emphasis was on the internalization of an external social reality into the ego. At the end of the oedipal period, the father's power and prohibitions have come to operate within the child—in other words, during his absence, not just when he is immediately there in reality. The father and the mother have both become a part of the ego, a new part that Freud termed the superego. This happens through introjection and/or identification, identification replacing the previous libidinal object cathexis.

Freud is considering here two different kinds of situations—first, where fear of the father and his threats and prohibitions predominate; second, where love of the father outweighs the hostility that is felt toward him. In the first case, as I understand it, the father becomes an object in the self that continues to have a kind of alien presence, hated by the child, but accommodated out of fear. Survival depends on conformity to his prohibitions, but there is no love and no closeness, something, perhaps, more like an identification with the aggressor.

In the second case, the father is deeply loved, and his structuring of the three-person situation will be more readily accepted. The child will feel: "I want to do this because I want to keep his love and affection." In this case, it seems to me, we can see in the identification something more than the introjection into the self of the Other. The identification seems, rather, to reinstate in the self a lost sense of earlier closeness or fusion—a closeness lost in reality through the fact that the parents had established their own space from which the child was excluded. I am reminded of Jesus' remark: "I and my Father are One."

There are two points to be noted here. First, the internalization of the father and the mother into the ego means that the Other's view (Chapter 2) has become part of the structure of every anticipation. Second, in so far as "I and my father are one," or "I and my mother are one"—in other words, insofar as I assume characteristics of either parent as "mine"—the distance and separation that had been developing between the child and its parents is reversed and a reinstatement of fusional closeness with the parent occurs. It is as though identification is the first and most basic mode in which a lost closeness with an object can be restored. There is a striking similarity between this process and the baby's creation of a transitional object. Both seem to be ways of mitigating a sense of loss and separation.

I will refer to one further aspect of Freud's account—the idea that the superego (which in Freud's view is formed out of the oedipal resolution)—consists of "these two identifications [father and mother] in some way united with each other." What did Freud mean by this? Obviously, it is difficult to say. He was developing a view of the ego as having an important synthesizing function, joining together and relating all the disparate data that came from the external world and the id. Whether "in some way united with each other" meant more than such a synthesis of identifications is hard to say.

As far as I am aware, Freud did not formulate the effect of this new structuring of the ego on the development of the symbolic function and consciousness, the aspect which, for my present purposes, I am most concerned with. But it may be that he was beginning to express something about the parental couple as such in his formulation—some representation in the ego of the couple who were now allowed to have their "intercourse," of whatever kind, free from interference by the child, in a space that had been created through the giving up of the Oedipus wish.

If this is so, then my own formulations about the progressive structuring of a psychic space (the mind) by the internalization of a developing social reality can be thought of as building on this idea.

SUBLIMATION AND REPRESSION—
THE IMPLICATIONS OF STRUCTURE

We have seen how a new inner psychic structure has been formed through the overcoming of a real conflict in relation to external objects and the creation of a new social structure in the external world. There is one final point that I want to explore in relation to Freud's text: What happens to the old psychic structure that is given up when the new is established?

This question is one whose answer has deep and far-reaching implications. It leads not only into the area of unconscious structures and motivations, but into issues concerning systemic change (in the systems theory sense) as well. Both of these are areas I will consider in detail in later chapters, but some of the issues are worth considering in a preliminary way at this point.

Freud had varying ideas about the fate of superseded psychic structures. In relation to the Oedipus conflict, he gives at least two answers. On the one hand, he argues that the old psychic structure is repressed and that it is the fear of the father that maintains this repression. In this case, the old structure may continue, in an unconscious way, to seek satisfaction, though its aims are not consciously acknowledged and it will not be integrated within the developing ego organization. On the other hand, Freud argues that if the old structure, the incestuous striving after the mother, is really given up, there is, in fact, nothing left to repress—the new structure has truly superseded the old.

I see no reason for denying the name of a "repression" to the ego's turning away from the Oedipus complex, although later repressions come about for the most part with the participation of the super-ego, which in this case is only just being formed. *But the process we have described is more than a repression. It is equivalent, if it is ideally carried out, to a destruction and an abolition of the complex.* We may plausibly assume that we have here come upon the borderline—never a very sharply drawn one—between the normal and the pathological. *If the ego has in fact not achieved much more than a repression of the complex, the latter persists in an unconscious state in the id and will manifest its pathogenic effect.* [1924, p. 177, italics added].

We see here a reciprocal relation between repression and sublimation, which is of great importance when we consider the question of ego structure or, as I would prefer to call it, the structure of the self. Where a new structure has developed from an older structure in such a way that the older structure has been abandoned or genuinely given up, the new structure has an autonomy and solidity about it that precludes the need for continuing parental constraints and prohibitions to keep its boundaries and limits in place. But where the old structure has been incompletely or reluctantly abandoned and is still sought after, the new structure can only be maintained by the continuing operation of parental constraints that resist attempts to undermine the new boundaries and distances the new structure requires. The old structure, which is banished from the new organization, continues, however, to exert psychological influence, albeit in unacknowledged ways. In Freud's language, it is "repressed" and continues to exist in the unconscious, or the id. In that sense, the unconscious is the realm of relatively primitive, untransformed structures that have never truly been given up, but continue to exercise influence in subtle, though disowned ways. The ego is the realm of transformed structures—that is, structures that have accepted the incorporation of limiting boundaries and distances that satisfy the requirements of social reality.[4]

Freud saw the dissolution of the Oedipus complex as a critical formative moment in the development of the ego. I believe that the conclusions that can be reached from an analysis of that process can be the basis for trying to clarify what we mean by ego or self. The ego, in Freud's terms, can be seen as a more or less coherently organized schema of relations between the "I" and the world. This schema has been gradually built up through an adaptation to lived reality during development. It is a complex structure of anticipations and expectations that reflects the social

---

[4]To speak in terms of structures and boundaries is another way of thinking about Freud's reality principle.

and nonsocial realities that the person has lived through. It is a "precipitate" of experience that has had to be taken into account, sometimes reluctantly, sometimes willingly.

The examples discussed here indicate that the growth of more complex structures of experience involves the insertion of boundaries and limits into a previously impulse-driven relation to objects that regarded only the goal as important. Some of these boundaries may be given by the structure of the world and have had to be learned through discovering them, perhaps painfully, in the course of exploration. But in relation to the human, social world, such boundaries have been set in myriad ways by the parents, who have tried to shape or form their child's behavior to fit an expected pattern of social interaction. The extent to which such boundaries are stable is probably determined by the degree to which they have been accepted in some fundamental way. Where they still require underpinning by parental sanctions they can be looked upon as precarious and always in danger of breaking down, especially under the pressure of more primitive impulsive upsurges. Willing or unwilling acceptance of the limits is a key issue; the balance of love and hatred toward the enforcer of limits is another. There is also the question of autonomous rewards. Every new structure brings new possibilities and new potential achievements, as well as the sacrifice of some previous goal; much will depend on the balance of these gains and losses. Speech and thought are examples of developmental achievements where the rewards of the achievement are incommensurable with the step that must be taken to bring it about.

All that I have said here about the growth of more complex structures from simpler ones applies equally to that peculiar and tantalizing human development—the emergence of consciousness, symbolic understanding, and mind. I have sketched a way of thinking about this development that is based on the child's gradually increasing ability to relate to objects in more complex ways, ways that can tolerate the insertion of ever more restricting boundaries and distances into a previously untrammeled access. The possibilities for only partial or unwilling acceptance of the rules and limits is as great in this area as it is in relation to any other developmental task, as is the persistence of more primitive modes of functioning. It is in trying to understand just what these rules and limits are that we will arrive at a clearer understanding of humanity's symbolic life in all its forms.

Is it possible to summarize the role that the father plays in facilitating the development of psychic structure? I think in a general way it is. In the beginning there is only the mother. The father is there supporting the mother, but the baby doesn't know this. The father may be there as a substitute mother, but then he is only a kind of stopgap in mothering and not really there in his own right. As the gap of separation begins to open up between mother and child, the child begins to discover the mother as Other, and the world is found "out there" in all its amazing and compelling variety. "Out there" is where the father is found, in the world and a part of the world. He draws the child out into a distance from the mother, counteracting the regressive pull of the so recently vacated womb of symbiosis. He helps to guarantee the space in which the world can be discovered and explored. But then comes the oedipal moment, in which the child seems to have lost both parents—who exist for each other, but not for him. He is separated from them by a cruel space and has to learn what may be the hardest lesson of his life: to allow the parents to keep that space without hindrance from himself. He has to learn to "look and not do" in relation to the parental couple. If Freud is right, this space is guarded by the jealous and possessive father who upholds its boundary with a castrating phallus, like the flaming sword of the Cherubim. It is an absolute boundary, the barrier against incest. Levi-Strauss has argued that this barrier, the taboo on incest, is the underpinning of all culture, and it may be that this is just. As I will try to show in the next chapter, the achievements that created this parental space are the same as those achievements that make room for the Word and for language. This is my understanding of Lacan's assertion (quoted in Lemaire 1977) that the father, the Name-of-the-Father, stands at the entry to the Symbolic Order.

8   **Language and Thinking**

The limits of my language are the limits of my world.
    —Ludwig Wittgenstein, *Tractatus Logico-philosophicus*

My spoken words surprise me myself and teach me my thoughts.
    —Maurice Merleau-Ponty, "On the Phenomenon of Language"

LANGUAGE AS DEVELOPMENTAL ACHIEVEMENT

THROUGH EACH CHAPTER thus far I have extended my account of those developments that seem to underpin the use of symbols and language. Whether they are essential steps or merely facilitators of the process is difficult to be sure, but it seems likely that without them a mature use of language would be impossible.[1] What appears more certain is the formal sense in which such achievements create the conditions within which the leap into language can occur.

---

[1]The ability to learn a language seems to be innate in the human species and to have a critical phase, during which the environment must provide favorable conditions if it is to develop (Lenneberg 1967). In this it is like many other biological processes. Such a notion is central to Winnicott's work—one of his books is called *The Maturational Processes and the Facilitating Environment* (1965). Bowlby (1969) has talked in a similar way about attachment, as have Mahler and colleagues (1975) about separation-individuation. In each case, a process with an apparently innate thrust is facilitated or impeded by the environment, and the final result is significantly shaped by that interaction. In relation to language, it is probably the "babbling" stage of sound production that is the critical phase for language acquisition, such sound production being the necessary building material out of which words can be shaped through example and imitation. Words, of course, are acquired before they can be used in a fully symbolic way. Initially they may be just imitative sounds; then almost certainly they become sounds that in some general way adhere to objects or situations—a word is the name of something. Later words may be used to exercise magical control over objects or to manipulate other people in relation to objects. Only finally does the symbolic function of words arise. It is primarily this development that I am interested in in this chapter.

I talk about the leap into language because the capacity to use language in a symbolic as opposed to a signal fashion (see Chapter 6) is, in a certain sense, an all-at-once phenomenon. Perceiving that a word *means* something rather than *is* something is a phenomenon that either happens or it does not. Like any radical shift in perspective, or transition from one systemic organization of phenomena to another, it is difficult to conceive of in-between stages: either you "see" it or you don't. Such seeing involves a shift, as Merleau-Ponty (1964a, p. 64) said, "from the order of events to the order of expression." The new relation to objects is governed by a different set of rules. The particular sound, the word, is no longer just a noise; nor is it something that is used to indicate, a verbal pointing (signal function); nor is it an object with which to manipulate others in the social field to do things for or to one (again, a signal function). It has come to stand for the thing, to be a means of representing it to oneself in the mind or to others through speech, even when the thing itself is no longer present (symbolic function).

The best account I know of this phenomenon, quoted so often because it was put so well, is Helen Keller's (1902) description of her "discovery" of language. Keller had been blind, deaf, and mute from the age of nineteen months, when she had contracted a serious illness. Attempts had been made to teach her a sign language, but she failed to grasp the essential symbolic function of the signs she had been taught. She experienced them as little more than a meaningless finger play. Then one day, she went out for a walk with her teacher, Anne Sullivan, and the leap into language occurred:

She [Sullivan] brought me my hat, and I knew I was going out into the warm sunshine. [hat = signal] This thought, if a wordless sensation can be called a thought, made me hop and skip with pleasure. [It is, in fact, more like an immediate anticipation than a thought—a reaction to the signal *hat*.]

We walked down the path to the well-house, attracted by the fragrance of the honeysuckle with which it was covered. Someone was drawing water and my teacher placed my hand under the spout. [World of immediate sensory experience.] As the cool stream gushed over my hand she spelled into the other the word *water*, first slowly, then rapidly. I stood still, my whole attention fixed upon the motion of her fingers. Suddenly I felt a misty consciousness as of something forgotten—a thrill of returning thought; and somehow the mystery of language was revealed to me. [The dawning of the symbolic. We might wonder, though, whether the sense of dim remembrance might not hark back to the child of nineteen months who may just have been beginning to grasp the idea of the symbolic in an embryonic way.] I knew then that w-a-t-e-r meant the wonderful cool something that was flowing over my hand. That living word awakened my soul, gave it light, hope, joy, set it free! . . . [The word is a new kind of object that operates in a completely new kind of space. It opens up a completely new world.]

I left the well-house eager to learn. Everything had a name, and each name gave birth to a new thought. As we returned to the house, every object which I touched seemed to quiver with life. That was because I saw everything with the strange new sight that had come to me. [pp. 23–24]

This passage illustrates the way in which the word, an object that cannot itself be touched or handled, is made to become a tool through which the idea of an actual object can be held in the mind, brought into relation with other ideas, and conveyed to another person. The precondition of this leap is that an attitude of "doing" in relation to the object shall have been given up, in order to make room for the *idea* of the object, which can be entertained within the mind and contemplated.[2] Correlatively, a space shall have been created between the subject and the object (a mindspace), within which the subtle doing of words can take place.

In the following chapters I want to draw together the structural developments that make this achievement of language possible and to look at various aspects of language use, particularly those that may throw more light on the nature of consciousness. Psychoanalysis is "The Talking Cure," and I am certainly not the first to have thought that the boundary

---

[2]I have chosen these words carefully. *Entertain* means literally "to hold among." *Contemplate* means: (1) "To look at with continued attention; gaze upon; observe." (2) "To view mentally, to meditate upon, ponder, study." The first word conveys something of the sense of holding objects in some relationship with each other, which I will be stressing as an essential feature of thought (Chapter 11). The second word bridges nicely the functions of looking and thinking, a bridge which, according to my argument, is taken in the development of the symbolic function. The *templum* of *contemplate* refers to "an open space for observation; a temple."

between what can be spoken and what cannot be spoken may be another way of talking about the boundary between consciousness and unconsciousness. Language and consciousness will be the main topic of the next chapter; but before tackling that difficult question, I want to approach language from the perspective I have already mapped—namely, from the more general direction of the developing symbolic function within the child's early object relationships.

LANGUAGE AND THE SHAPING OF EXPERIENCE

Language exists before the individual. The child is born into language and a world that is structured according to language.[3] From the beginning, the child is "shaped" by language and its meanings, and it suffers those meanings and begins to respond to them before it can know what they are. For that knowledge to be possible, language must be acquired; it is the key that unlocks the human world. Without it the child would not gain access into that world except in a very rudimentary way.

Language is originally the province of the Other. The word is the gift—or the imposition of the Other, depending on how you see it. Spoken language arises in the space between mother and child, father and child, and also in the space between the parents. As a tool of the Other, it forms an interface with the emerging self. This it does in two ways: it abuts the child's experience of the external world, of things; and it makes contact with the developing inner world of imagery and feelings. There are, then, really two interfaces: one where the word defines and delimits external objects and relations with these objects; the other where the word gains entry into the self, marking or not marking, naming or not naming elements in the shifting flux of experience.

In both cases, the word is prescriptive of vision and attention. It points to what shall be seen.[4] A name is like a face, a kind of identity. *That which has no name in some sense does not exist.* In the new "reality" created by language, there is no place for the thing that has no word to represent it.

---

[3]This way of putting things comes from Lacan.
[4]This is the sense in which language is a tool of the Other.

I feel sure it was some such idea as this which Freud was struggling with in his varying attempts to define the nature of consciousness, as for example in his *Note upon the Mystic Writing Pad* (1925). He seemed to state more clearly there than in other places the idea of a double transcription, one of which was fleeting, the other more permanent. The fleeting, "surface" transcription was, like consciousness, a quality that could be added or taken away. The deeper engraving was one that remained, even though invisible, corresponding in some way to the unconscious registration of memories. I do not want to try to unravel the complexities of Freud's thoughts in this area, linked, as they were, with continuing efforts, never completely abandoned, to think in a neurophysiological and anatomical way about mental phenomena. What can be said, however, is that for Freud, the quality of consciousness seemed to reside in the bringing of an inner representation of an object into a relation with language—linking it with a "word presentation." That which was not linked with a word presentation was not conscious. It might be enacted or lived or even dreamed, but it could not be spoken about or thought about. The counterpart of the word presentation on the unconscious level was the "thing presentation." Thing presentations were mute.

The world, and the infant's experience of it—the world of things and thing presentations—is there before language comes to structure it. This is the counterpoint to my first assertion that language exists before the individual. If, however, we think of language as something that is superimposed on some earlier "stuff" or *prima materia* of experience, we may be better able to understand how it is that there can be things which people are not conscious of. This notion is quite distinct from any notion of a dynamic unconscious or of defense mechanisms. Things are unconscious because they have not been marked with a linguistic marker, a word, so they cannot be represented to others or to self. *There is a failure of coincidence between a represented reality (the linguistic one) and an actual state of affairs—that which is inscribed in some way in the body and in feelings.* The question of dynamics enters in when we start to ask why there is a mismatching between the two orders—the order of expression and the order of events. Is the mismatching merely a mistake, or is it in some sense deliberate or motivated?

It is this mismatching that, since Freud, any serious attempt to understand another person has to take into account; and it is this gap or difference between what is represented and what is lived that is the point of entry of much psychotherapeutic endeavor. It was this difference that led Freud to many of his insights about unconscious mental processes, and it is this gap that we, too, must question if we are to understand any better the threshold between conscious "seeing" and the "unthought known"—to borrow a phrase from Christopher Bollas (1987). I will return to the whole question of consciousness later, but I want to sketch here an overview of the terrain that may serve as an orientation in an area where it is very easy to get lost.

THE SPACE FOR LANGUAGE

In Chapter 1, and again in Chapter 4, I spoke about those experiences that cumulatively "founded" the self, creating as a background to everything else a sense of basic trust in the Other and in the world. In Chapters 2 and 3, I explored an alternative scenario, one in which the "founding" was not secure enough (or should I say not "good enough"?) and seemed to collapse under the impact of the Other's view. The phenomenology of that experience highlighted a certain interaction between something which came from the other person—a view, or a visual image of "me" from "out there"—and a more bodily rooted, subjective experience of self from "in here." There was a deep sense of separation from the object within this experience, a gap across which I myself could see this image of me. It now seems that this image of me from "out there" is a symbolic form; it is a re-presentation of myself from the other person, which fills my awareness, but at the same time offers me, or forces upon me, a self-consciousness mediated both by the Other and by a form that is "not-me" even while it is me. As Sartre has indicated, although robbed of my subjectivity, I *am* this guilty object that the Other sees.

This lived dislocation of the self highlighted the separation between an experience of myself (*prima materia*) and a view of myself (symbolic form); but in so doing, it opened the way to looking at the development of consciousness (symbolically mediated awareness) as arising out of the primal separation of self and object, which had created the space between (Chapter 5).

The "space between" was the space in which the object was not, and therefore the space within which the image of the object could first be

experienced as separate from the object itself—in other words, representing it rather than indicating it or re-creating it. In this way, I had
inadvertently approached the whole question of consciousness and symbol formation through a back door—by examining first the development
of self-consciousness and working from there to the earlier development
of consciousness.

It now seems that there is a sequence. The first difference, the mother's
failure to be what the infant anticipated, creates the first gap in experience and begins to establish the mother as objective object rather than
as part of the self. This difference or gap is also the precondition of
forming an image of the object that represents it—in other words, it is a
precondition of symbol formation.[5] As development proceeds, the space
of separation from the object becomes the space of symbols whose function may lie anywhere between a re-creating of the object and a representing of it. The more complete the infant's tolerance of separation, the
more representational the symbol can be; until, with the development
and eventual resolution of the three-person oedipal situation, the representational space is freed from the object sufficiently to become a space of
pure representation. As I argued in Chapter 7, this comes about through
a firming up of the boundaries of the parental space, from which the child
is absolutely excluded by the father. The father's prohibitions make
the oedipal space a space of absolute separation from the body of the
mother.

Self-consciousness arises after this. It does not make sense to think of a
self-consciousness that does not travel this circuit of otherness. It may,
however, arise within the two-person or the three-person situation. The
impetus toward self-consciousness must surely lie in the fact that the
Other regards us, and eventually we have to take account of this. We *have*
to take into ourselves this view of the Other because it is this view that
determines our whole fate as dependent beings.

It follows from what I have said that the earlier in the separating
process that self-consciousness is forced upon us, the more primitive will
be the symbolic function that tries to assimilate it. Where the symbolic
function is still transitional, the Other's view will be difficult or impossi-

---

[5]Because the precondition of symbol formation proper is that the symbol is *not* the object;
or, as Korzybski (1941) indicated, the map is *not* the territory.

ble to keep at a distance, and will be more likely to usurp or take over the self.

The symbolic image of the self that is mediated by the other person thus completes a circle of development. First, the infant differentiates from the object (the mother) the image of that object and so begins to learn what a symbol is; then that object gives back to the baby an image or symbol of its own self.

The first move gives the baby two things—its mother as an object and its mother as an image, which lies in the space of differentiation from its mother. The second move, this time objectifying the self rather than the mother, gives the child a sense of its self as an object and also an image of its self that is potentially separate from the self as object, but that can very easily be experienced as constituting the self in its objective essence (e.g., "bad," ugly, helpful, devious, and so on).

We can think of this second move as introducing a gap into the self that is phenomenologically similar to the first gap in experience between self and object. If we think of the first gap as the gap of consciousness, then we could say that the second is the gap of self-consciousness. *It is only where there is a gap that there can be symbols and circulations of symbols.*

I now want to add language to this schema. Language spans the gap of separation from the object, through communication, but it can only be used and understood so long as the experiental gap (differentiation in its literal sense) is maintained. It exists only within the precarious gap for meanings that difference and separation from the object guarantee. Language brings the separated object closer, but it never will bring us, of itself, the actual object. It will glance off the invisible barrier that separates it from the object and will defy all attempts to possess the object through it.

THE MIRACLE OF LANGUAGE—A CHILD'S VIEW

What is language, and where does it come from? This must be the question that at some point every child, and perhaps every human being, asks. Mythology has its answers, and so do philosophy, linguistics, psychology, and so on. But the simplest answer is that it comes from the Other. In the child's experience it is the Other—the mother, the father, other people—who brings words to the child. At first these words are mere noises, sounds. Then they seem to have shapes and faces that are given them by things—their own physiognomy. Then they acquire a magical power to control other people and to bring things to them. Only gradually and much later do they come to "mean," to symbolize. Only as the object is given up and a space made for the word does the word come to stand for the thing. The Other gives the word into the space of absence, the space of not having, the space of pure looking. In a very fundamental sense, the word is the reward for abstinence.[6]

Language, of course, seems to exist out there, separate from us. It is, in a very real way, a part of the object world. But it does not belong to anybody and cannot be possessed by anybody. There is not a limited supply of it. It is not an object at all. It has to become nothing, a no-thing, before it will "mean," before it will light up the world for us and enable us to share the world and our experience with others. It is a very strange object indeed.

It was given to our parents just as it was to us. And to their parents and to their parents and so on and so on. It seems to have existed forever and ever. And yet it comes to exist within us. We think through language. We see through language. We hear through language. We know ourselves through language. We may wonder if it is possible to see anything apart from language. What would the world look like if you could see it apart from language, apart from this filter that structures everything? The world is the world according to language. That, anyway, is sometimes how it seems.

We say something, and that is how it *is*. We *believe* the word. We *believe* our theory. The concept *is* the thing. The map *is* the territory. The line of difference begins to disappear. The space for meaning is very hard to keep open. Separateness from the object is hard to tolerate. We believe what we say. We believe what we tell ourselves. Reality doesn't matter. We don't want to know about it.

But we do. We have to know about it, have to find a way of getting back to it. So we put aside words, ideas, concepts, jargon, beliefs, institutionalized doctrines. We try to look afresh at the things themselves. Yet how do we tell ourselves what we can see, and how do we share our *re-visions* with others? It can only be with words.

---

[6]Compare this with the analytic rule of abstinence. I explore this further in Chapter 16.

I had not intended to speak about language in this way, with a kind of childish wondering. But perhaps it is a way of conveying something of the wonder and amazingness of language. Perhaps it may help one to look past the words about language at the miracle of language itself. The miracle that Helen Keller felt when she "discovered" language. Perhaps, too, the idiom helps to show or present some of the themes I will develop in more discursive form in later chapters. It is, after all, only a convention that we have to be scholarly.

THE NATURE OF THINKING—A PERSONAL VIEW

I will have more to say about the relation between language and reality later. Here I want to approach the question of language from a different perspective: What is it that we are doing when we are thinking? This is a huge topic, but I will consider it in a personal and introspective way in order to bring out certain elements that seem important.

1. When we are thinking, we are not doing anything at all with concrete objects in the physical world, in physical space. We are doing something with psychic objects in some sort of psychic space.

2. We often talk of this psychic space as in our minds, because first, it is quite clearly not outside of us; second, there is a sense in which the objects of our attention do sometimes feel as though they are somewhere inside us, though not necessarily in our heads. I have already pressed the claim that this space of thought is, in a certain sense, the space that divided us from our original objects—the space of separation from the mother, and beyond that, the space of "no touch" and "no entry" that divided us from the parental couple.

3. The objects of our attention in thinking may be dimly sensed forms, which we apprehend somewhere in the depths of our bodies. For myself, I have a sense of such forms somewhere in my chest, definitely above the solar plexus. If and where other people experience such sensations I do not know.

4. When we are thinking, we are trying to *grasp* something, *groping* toward some clearer sense of what must be described. *Groping* and *grasping*—these are tactile words, suggesting that we are, in our imagination, trying to *take hold of* objects and *feel out* their forms and relationships.

5. We are also *looking*, trying to see something (vision). Sometimes there is a sense of strain, as though we are trying to see something that is hidden, *peering* through the dark or into the distance. Sometimes there is a sense of looking too hard, not allowing the feel of the thing to guide us.

6. I am assuming here a vague sense of direction—we have a sense of what we are trying to discover, an overall bearing on what we are trying to *formu*late. If we could put it (see it) more clearly, we would have formulated it already—it would have entered the "universe of things said."

7. We are *searching*, but we are not searching empty-handed. There is a partly verbal notion that locates a general area for us; and there are perhaps a few phrases that have occurred to us that seem to pinpoint some aspect of what we are trying to say more clearly. We will recognize what it is that we are trying to find when we find it. (This idea of thinking as a searching links directly with the idea I have already put forward in Chapter 5 that consciousness is originally a form of searching for the lost object.)

8. We have *tools*, and these are words (the tools that have been given to us by the Other to help us). It is as though we hover over the field of almost palpable objects with words; and somehow, at a certain moment, the words, and the thing we are trying to give form to, resonate, and we know that we have a correspondence or fit. It seems as though we have to match a whole array of quasi-physical forms and impressions with linguistic forms, and we must go on trying to do this until there is a sense of recognition, capture, or equivalence.

9. Thinking can occur in sleep, or at least when we are half asleep. The example of Kekulé dreaming the solution to the benzene ring formula is a well-known example. When I am writing a paper and have struggled unsuccessfully in the evening, I may have a sense of writing going on in my sleep, and awake in the morning with the knowledge of how I can continue. Perhaps sleep reduces the element of too much trying that can interfere with more spontaneous processes of exploration and matching.

10. All of this is a way of saying that we can know things intuitively, feel them, half know them, but we have to *determine* to know them more clearly before we can see them. We have to approach the task like mountaineers. We have to equip ourselves with the relevant tools, with words, put ourselves into the right frame of mind, and finally test out the terrain in a practical way—put pen to paper and see how far we can get.

Perhaps this trying, this *determination to know*, is the central thing. It is certainly very important in psychotherapy. If we want to know what it is that is stirring in us, striving for expression, we have to find a way of speaking it. We have to reach for it, go toward it, lie in wait for it, make raids on the inarticulate, as T. S. Eliot said[7]—but always with language. We have to answer with language, with the word, the need that we feel. There is a "speechless want," as Merleau-Ponty (1964b) put it, that "gives itself a body and *knows itself* by looking for an equivalent in the system of available significations" (i.e., in language).

First we *sense* there is something there, then we *grope* around it and toward it; finally, perhaps, if we are fortunate, we *grasp* it. And we grasp it with language, which at last enables us to *see* it—but not *have* it. So it is that we use this gift of the Other to speak those things that "stir in our middles," as Robert Hobson (1985) said, which would otherwise remain mute and unformed. We give birth to ourselves through language.

I hope I am not laboring the point too much if I say again that there are rigorous conditions attached to this process. The object itself can never be possessed, only known. However much we may reach out with our hands or peer with our eyes, we never actually take hold of the object except with words. The words reveal the object in the clearest possible way, but they do not give it to us.

This knowledge through words is, I would suggest, the reward for what we have given up. There is an angel with a flaming sword standing guard over the garden we have lost forever. If we tried to break the rules, the whole structure would collapse. All of its delicate boundaries and spaces would vanish, and we would be thrown into a psychotic chaos where words are things and would have lost their power to guide or reveal.

Yet there is a kind of consolation. Winnicott has described how the baby who is on the point of losing the symbiotic mother closes the gap with a symbol of unity—the first symbol, the transitional object. With language, too, one can see a similar consolation in the process by which word and thing seem to refind each other like the two halves of the Greek *symbolon*.[8]

---

[7]The whole process of struggling to find words for feelings is beautifully put by T. S. Eliot (1944) in "East Coker" (*Four Quartets*), section V, lines 1–18.

[8]The word *symbol* is derived from the Greek *symbolon*. For the Greeks, the *symbolon* was a means of identification between two members of a religious group. It consisted of the two halves of a broken object that could be fitted back together again.

THE RELATIONSHIP BETWEEN WORD AND SELF

I have tried to demonstrate that the linguistic process has two parts—a part that comes from the Other (the word) and a part that comes from the person using the language (the idea or the concept of the thing). In linguistics these two elements are often called the signifier and the signified; and this usage has been adopted by some psychoanalysts, notably Lacan. What I am saying may have been indirectly influenced by his ideas, but not in any close or definite way.

The use of language in relation to ordinary things and objects in the world is not a matter that I want to dwell on further at the moment. What is more interesting is the situation where the object to be signified is a part of the self. This is the situation I have been concerned with in this chapter.

The two parts of the linguistic process in this case are the word, which comes from the outside, from the Other; and something that comes from the inside, the "speechless want" of Merleau-Ponty, which is a part of the self and is looking for a form.

However, it is only in the original sense that the word comes from the Other. Once language has been acquired, the operation of language is a self-contained process. It is I myself who try to find the words for what I want to say. What is it, then, that determines the way in which we use language? Why will one person fumble about in a clumsy way with words, grasping at the first word that comes to mind, irrespective of the fit or accuracy, while another person will use language creatively, with a freshness and accuracy of fit that conveys vividly the needed meaning?

There is probably a whole chapter of psychological development that could be written here; but I want to draw attention to the possibility that exists in this situation for a want, "the speechless want," to be met well or badly. At one end of the spectrum, there is the near-perfect-fit type of situation, in which the word is like Winnicott's subjective object—it meets the need in such a way that the person could feel he had created the word for himself. At the other end is the word that hardly links up with the felt need at all.

I think we could guess that the creative word is in direct descent from the symbiotic mother who closely adapted to her child's needs; as though the child, in its use of language, has tried to re-create that lost sense of oneness with the mother. In this case we might speak of a maternally adapted word or a maternally adapted symbol. In the second case, we might have to suppose that the child had abandoned all attempt to re-create the lost state—at least in respect to language—with the result that the self remains unspoken, the need for expression unmet. Language here does not look after the self.

LANGUAGE AS HELPER OR DEPRIVER

Language has the possibility of creating the illusion of oneness through the perfectly fitting word. It looks after the self, goes toward the self to put into words what the self wants. Or, it sits over against the self as an alien power, depriving the self of its "kingdom of touch," and is accepted only begrudgingly as something to be spoken to keep the "aggressor" at bay.

That is one way of putting it—though it gives too much autonomy to language. It is true that, in a sense, we are made and formed by language, constrained within its web of preordained meanings; but it is also true that we use language, and approach what has not yet been said with language in order to say it.

I want to say that these two attitudes of the person toward language reflect two attitudes of the original Other toward the self. We are probably speaking of the mother. Where the original Other was experienced as adaptive and helpful, language, the word, is felt to be adaptive and helpful, too. It is experienced as a gift from the Other that can be used by the self to enable its needs to be expressed. Where the attitude of the original Other was not felt to be adaptive and helpful, language is experienced as alien to the self, not a fitting vehicle for self-expression. The self will turn away from it and not experience it as a helpful tool that will further the self's aims. This may be particularly so when language has been used to distance the self—to set the self "out there" as an object of critical regard, far from the touch of the empathic mother (see Chapters 2 and 3).

THE LOOKING AND TOUCHING OF THINKING

In discussing thinking and the person's own attitude toward the unspoken in themselves, I have emphasized the looking aspect and the fact that the object cannot be touched. Nevertheless, I have indicated that there is a touching and a holding and a grasping in thought, although it is of necessity of a subtle and immaterial kind.

What is the relationship, then, between looking and touching in thought? I believe that looking remains the dominant mode, since there is, in the foundation of thought, an essential distance and separation from the object that has to be maintained for thought to be possible. Thinking takes place, after all, in the space that has been established by the development of separation and distance from the object, by that primal fall that is the essence of our human condition. That essential distance we have seen to be the precondition of the existence of the virtual objects of thought.

This does not mean, however, that a more identificatory mode of relating to the object cannot be a part of thought. Looking, approaching, feeling, grasping, seeing—does that mean standing back again? Perhaps at some point in the sequence also becoming, entering into the object, merging—knowledge through identity? But if I *become* the object, where is there now room for any thought at all? Has not the space of thought once again collapsed into the fullness of being?

I believe the answer is no, for it is a given of experience that such an identificatory mode of knowing objects is possible. To describe what is happening, however, is a different matter. What is in question is the thin, fine line of difference. To know an object, or myself, or another person through identification is quite different (and in some sense, the difference *is* the thin, fine line) from *being* an object, or myself, or another person, or at least believing that I am those objects. So if I am to know by identification, there must be a sense in which I take with me, into the identification, the thin, fine line of difference, of separation, that preserves for me the objectness of the Other and a space for thought.

This area of empathy and identification is one that is very familiar to analysts and therapists, and much has been written about it. It may be that I have little to add. The usual view would be that we save ourselves from being swallowed up in the identification by continuing to observe (i.e., to look across a distance). In this case, the part of us that merges with the Other is only a part of the self. The other part maintains the distance, the otherness of the Other and the space for thought in between, by maintaining a looking or observing position. The observing part, like Odysseus strapped to the mast (is this the oedipal Father with his castrating phallus?), remains in executive charge, while the merging part (the part that harks back to an earlier mode of being with the mother) is allowed a moment of resurrection. In this account, it is the coexistence of imaginative looking and identification (being) that preserves the structure of separateness and the possibility of thought.

Perhaps this is the whole story, though we might wonder if the part of us that in imagination becomes the object ever really loses the sense of separateness from the object. Is it not, after all, an illusion, like the illusion of oneness in the perfect fit between word and thought? For the whole process is taking place in a world of thought, in a mediated world of consciousness, and we are not in reality entering into the other person or object or part of ourselves at all. We are not in reality touching or being touched, though we feel these things in a shadowy way in the illusory world that we have created. We are relating to images and representations in a thought world, and to the relationship between them, not to objects in the real world. This account would bring us back again to a much more radical underpinning of the process of thought in the deepest part of our being—where distance and separation and the Law of the Father have staked out once and for all a space of separation from, and nonpossession of, the mother.

If this is so, then the processes of thought, established in this ground, can be thought of as giving us a double illusion of oneness. When we move toward the object of our thought with our psychic eyes and hands, we are allowed the illusion of a momentary possession; where word meets the first representation of thought in maternally adapted fit, there is a second illusion—of the two, once separated, again becoming one.

LANGUAGE AND EXPERIENCE— AN ESSENTIAL DISJUNCTION

Language, in some fundamental sense, is a representative of the Other in the self; yet it becomes so much a part of ourselves that we often feel that a person is characterized by the way he speaks or writes. It becomes the major means that we have of representing to ourselves or to others our understanding of the world or ourselves; and equally, it becomes the major means through which others will give back to us their view of us, which in turn will reshape and re-form us. It is able to do this by offering a vast and complex array of symbols, which constitutes a lexicon of the world and what it is about. Language is like a map of the world and experience; we are able to locate our experience within this vast symbolic structure once we have learned its rules and how to use it. It is a system of conceptual correspondences that reflects the real world, and it becomes capable of providing us with a mediated representation or image of whatever we meet in the world.

But this account is only part of the truth. There is an unbridgeable gulf between the actual world of things, including the world of our feelings and experiences, and this re-presented world (the same gulf or gap that created the possibility of their being a representation at all). The symbolically mediated representation of the world that language enables us to speak is always approximate, often incomplete, and sometimes falsifying. It is limited by both the constraints of the instrument which is language, and by the will and intention of the person who is representing. This introduces the possibility, indeed the probability, that much of our primary experience will go unmarked and therefore unnoted; or that it will be seriously misrepresented in ways that are determined by our inclinations and needs.

I believe it was Lacan, who haunts my thought without my ever being able properly to engage with him, who spoke of this essential mismatching between the represented world and the actual world as a "slippage" between the signifier and the signified. It is this slippage or mismatching that leads us to the unconscious, to that which in these terms has not been or will not be spoken. This in turn leads me to the topic I will tackle more fully in the next chapter—the relation of language to consciousness, and the nature of the boundary between that which is conscious and that which is unconscious.

9 Language and Consciousness

It was often when Freud came to a problem belonging to the theory of consciousness that he broke off his discussion. The most notable example of this was the missing chapter(s) of the proposed book on metapsychology.
—John Forrester, *Language and the Origins of Psycho-Analysis*

IN CHAPTER 5 I laid out the elements of my own views about consciousness; in this chapter I want to present some of Freud's thoughts on the matter and to engage in a dialogue with him. It is clear to me that Freud saw that consciousness was inextricably bound up with language and speaking, but I argue that, in the end, he endangered this insight because of his need to describe the mind as a machine.

Freud's definitive metapsychological paper on consciousness was never published. The editors of the standard edition of Freud's writings talk of it as "lost" (1915c, pp. 191–192 footnotes); I cannot help wondering if the real reason may not have been continuing difficulties with the topic, which are to some extent in evidence in his published writings. The above quotation from Forrester (1980) seems to imply a similar thought.

In Freud's earlier writings, up to *The Ego and the Id* (1923), the conscious-unconscious dichotomy was one of the cornerstones of psychoanalysis. Making the unconscious conscious was, in a real sense, the essence of psychoanalytic treatment. Nevertheless, the attempt to formalize his data in a systematic way into systems Cs, Pcs, and Ucs caused him quite a few problems, largely because it did not coincide exactly with another major dimension in terms of which he wanted to organize his findings. This was the dimension of reality adaptedness–instinctual gratification: the coming to terms with reality that gradually modified the original instinctual aims; bringing them, through attenuation and incorporation, into ever more complex structures, into a modus vivendi, if not harmony, with the real world. Interestingly, this "giving up" of the instinctual relation to objects also came to be seen as an essential dimension of the analytic treatment, where it was in the field of the transference that the battle was particularly hard-fought (Freud 1915a).

In *The Ego and the Id* (1923), Freud finally reorganized his data along new lines that cut across the conscious-unconscious distinction, giving primacy to the instinctual striving–reality adaptedness dimension. However, even in that work, his ambivalence about the matter is forcefully expressed. Having put all the reasons for favoring the new organization of the material, he then writes: "Nevertheless . . . the property of being conscious or not is in the last resort our one beacon of light in the darkness of depth psychology" (1923, p. 18).

The equation that Freud wanted, but which would not quite work, was to be able to put all unmodified, instinctual derivatives, all that had to be "repressed," into the unconscious system, and all that had been "reality adapted," modified to take account of reality, into the conscious system. He found, however, that things which apparently had the hallmark of such reality adaptedness were not always conscious, or even "capable of becoming conscious"; also, to a lesser extent, that things which "should" have been unconscious were not always so.

There was another question in which Freud had always been deeply interested—namely, the question of what was stored in the different systems of the mind and in what form. What distinguished what was stored in the system unconscious (Ucs) from what was stored in the system preconscious (Pcs)? And what about the conscious system (Cs)? This seemed to be quite different. If it were a storage system like the others, it should soon be full. But it was not; things were conscious only in a temporary and reversible way—consciousness seemed to be a reversible quality that could be attached to things and unattached again.

It was this reversible quality of consciousness that led Freud to consider the role of language. Perhaps the transience of consciousness consisted of the attachment and subsequent disengagement of word presentation and thing presentation. Freud at least in part rejected this idea, concluding instead that such an attachment to a word presentation rendered the thing presentation "*capable* of becoming conscious"—in other words, it gave it a place in the system Pcs rather than in the system Cs.

Freud sought the explanation of consciousness elsewhere. Consciousness, he suggested, was a perceptual attention, which he termed (because of his love of describing processes in energic terms) hypercathexis. Something became conscious, partly through this extra attention that it got, but not without the involvement of word presentations.

It seems that Freud saw two steps: first, there was the step by which that which was unconscious was made preconscious; then there was the further step by which the preconscious was made conscious.

We now seem to know all at once what the difference is between a conscious and an unconscious presentation. The two are not, as we supposed, different registrations of the same content in different psychical localities, nor yet different functional states of cathexes in the same locality; but the conscious presentation comprises the presentation of the thing plus the presentation of the word belonging to it, while the unconscious presentation is the presentation of the thing alone. The system Ucs contains the thing-cathexes of the objects, the first and true object-cathexes; the system Pcs comes about by this thing presentation being hypercathected through being linked with the word presentations corresponding to it. [1915c, p. 202]

But a little later on, apparently contradicting himself, he writes:

As we can see, being linked with word presentations is not yet the same thing as becoming conscious, but only makes it possible to become so; it is therefore characteristic of the system Pcs and that system alone. [1915c, p. 203]

In *The Ego and the Id* (1923) he writes in a similar vein:

The question, "How does a thing become conscious?" would thus be more advantageously stated: "How does a thing become preconscious?" And the answer would be through being connected with the word presentation corresponding to it. [p. 20]

A word presentation is a memory of a word that has been heard—in other words, it was once a conscious perception. This leads Freud to the idea that "dawns on him like a new discovery" (1923, p. 20), that only something that has once been a conscious perception can become conscious again. So becoming conscious involves somehow acquiring a perceptual status. Inner things, apart from feelings, about which Freud makes an exception, must therefore make themselves into perceptions in order to become conscious.

The part played by word presentations now becomes perfectly clear. By their interposition, internal thought processes are made into perceptions. . . . When a hypercathexis of the process of thinking takes place, thoughts are *actually* perceived as if they came from without—and are consequently held to be true. [1923, p. 23]

The implication is that thinking can occur through some interaction of these combined word and thing presentations on its own, but it becomes conscious when the process of thinking is hypercathected.

What exactly is this hypercathexis of thinking, and where does it come from? Freud is hardly clear on this point. However, he does make one attempt to define it in *The Unconscious* (1915c):

. . . the act of becoming conscious is dependent on the attention of the preconscious being turned in certain directions. [p. 192]

Unfortunately, according to the editors of the standard edition, this phrase is ambiguous. Literally, it translates as: "We learn in addition that becoming conscious is restricted by certain directions of its attention," and they comment:

The "its" almost certainly refers to the Pcs. This rather obscure sentence would probably be clearer if we possessed the lost paper on consciousness. The gap here is particularly tantalising, as it seems likely that the reference is to a discussion on the function of "attention," a subject on which Freud's later writings throw very little light. [1915c, p. 192 footnote]

The editors give several quotes, mainly from *The Interpretation of Dreams* (1900), where attention is mentioned: "Becoming conscious is connected with the application of a particular psychical function, that of 'attention'" (p. 593). And again, "The system Pcs not merely bars access to consciousness, it also . . . has at its disposal for distribution a mobile cathectic energy, a part of which is familiar to us in the form of attention" (p. 615).

What does all this add up to? I have to confess to finding this rather mechanical account of consciousness less than fully illuminating. It seems to me that it brings us hard up against the difficulties that arise from thinking about psychological phenomena in terms that mix phenomenological and physical/biological frames of reference. Psychological phenomena that imply a person or an agent are mixed in with terms more appropriate to biology or physics, with the result that one feels thoroughly confused. For example, consciousness itself is a psychological attribute, and the giving or withholding of attention would seem to be something that a person or part of a person does—there is an agent who looks at or attends to something. A distribution of cathectic energy, however, would seem to be something that occurs in accordance with forces and laws in a biological or physical system. If Freud thinks that attention and perception are important in explaining consciousness—and he does seem to—then we ought to concentrate on what kind of perceptual attention we give to inner things to make them conscious, in other words, to know them. If this attention involves looking at or listening to ourselves as though we are other (i.e., as object of our own perception), then we ought to ask how it is possible that we can come to do this. This refers us, as I have tried to show in previous chapters, to such developments as taking the role of the Other toward ourselves with vision or with language, and knowing ourselves (i.e., becoming conscious of ourselves) in this mediated way. Instead of talking about the "distribution of a mobile cathectic energy," we might better consider how attention to ourselves is motivated, and how we either want to know—and turn toward the unknown with language to try and speak it—or want to turn away, and try not to see, withholding the illuminating power of words from things.

This is not to detract from the almost unbelievable range of Freud's discoveries, which he mapped with the best means available to him nearly a century ago. It is, rather, to suggest that we look more closely at what he says, to disentangle those areas that are truly illuminating from those in which he may have been "duped by his own metaphors" (Turbayne 1962).

SHORTCOMINGS OF FREUD'S MODELS

I think one of the problems inherent in the topographical models Freud gave us is that they encourage a view of the mind as divided into levels or areas that occupy a continuous space. No doubt this division made many important discoveries possible. For example, it helped to clarify the radical differences between unconscious and conscious mental processes (primary and secondary processes); it enabled the concept of boundaries between different parts of the mind to be formulated, with the attendant ideas of communication or noncommunication across them and the related notions of psychological defense. It also introduced, or formalized, the idea of boundary crossings requiring transformations of content to render content compatible with the new system. Where it led Freud astray, and where I believe it continues to mislead us, is in regard to the nature of consciousness.

In the area of consciousness that we are discussing, Freud failed, in my view, to perceive the radical discontinuity between the "I" who is conscious (of something) and the "me" that I am conscious of. They are separated as subject and object, and, as I have tried to show, their separation is critical and, in a sense, formative of consciousness. It is in the space between them that, through the word and the "look" of the Other, self-knowledge is able to arise. I believe that Freud made a fundamental phenomenological mistake, being misled by his model and by his never having fully abandoned the wish to explain psychological phenomena in terms of the more basic sciences.

Phenomenologically, knowledge about myself exists in a different space from both the space within which I act, instinctively or otherwise, in the world and the inner representation of that action space which unconsciously guides my behavior in relation to objects of the world. Consciousness (knowledge) of myself exists in a virtual, could I say a conceptual, space. My unconscious "knowledge" of the world and my unconscious intentions and aims in relation to objects are "written" in quite a different place—engraved in my body as templates for action, and not separated from me by any distance at all.

Bearing in mind these criticisms, I now want to examine more closely the borders between the systems in Freud's account in order to understand the movements of content between the systems and the processes that Freud postulated as governing these. I will focus particularly on the relation of the content to language, and the factors of hypercathexis and attention, both of which Freud regarded as important in determining the quality of being conscious.

> We may say that in general a psychical act goes through two phases as regards its state, between which is interposed a kind of testing (censorship). In the first phase, the psychical act is unconscious and belongs to the system Ucs; if, on testing, it is rejected by the censorship, it is not

allowed to pass into the second phase; it is then said to be "repressed" and must remain unconscious. If, however, it passes this testing, it enters the second phase and thenceforth belongs to the second system, which we will call the system Cs. But the fact that it belongs to that system does not yet unequivocally determine its relation to consciousness. It is not yet conscious, but it is certainly *capable of becoming conscious* . . . that is, it can now, given certain conditions, become an object of consciousness without any special resistance. In consideration of this capacity for becoming conscious we also call the system Cs the "preconscious." [1915c, p. 173]

In this quote Freud seems to be examining the transition between the systems in a sort of time dimension—the *Vorstellung*, or representation of the object, goes through phases: it presents itself, the censor "looks" at it, and it can either pass to the second phase or not, depending on its "appearance." But a little later, Freud seems to be thinking spatially, or at least considering whether a change in location or a change over time is the more appropriate way to look at the problem.

When a psychical act . . . an idea (a *Vorstellung*) . . . is transposed from the system Ucs into the system Cs (or Pcs), are we to suppose that this transposition involves a fresh record—as it were, a second registration—of the idea in question, which may thus be situated as well in a fresh psychical locality, and alongside of which the original unconscious registration continues to exist? Or are we rather to believe that the transposition consists in a change in the state of the idea, a change involving the same material and occurring in the same locality? [1915c, p. 174]

In his further discussion Freud highlights the fact that telling someone what the unconscious idea is does not "remove the repression nor undo its effects. . . . But now the patient has in actual fact the same idea in two forms in different places in his mental apparatus" (p. 175). He has the "word"—the analyst's word; and he also has the unconscious *Vorstellung* "as it was in its earlier form." But ". . . actually there is no lifting of the repression until the conscious idea, after the resistances have been overcome, has entered into connection with the unconscious memory trace. It is only through the making conscious of the latter itself that success is achieved" (p. 175). So the critical thing is the analyst's word actually connecting up with the thing that is repressed and unconscious. Only then does the unconscious *really* become conscious. Toward the end of the same paper is the quote that I gave earlier, wherein Freud states that the conscious presentation is the word presentation plus the thing presentation belonging to it, while the unconscious presentation is the presentation of the thing alone.

In spite of some ambiguities in Freud's account, I think it is possible to find justification for the view that a person becomes truly conscious of something that was previously unconscious when the speaking of the thing—be it feeling, experience, or idea—is allowed to come into the closest possible contact with the thing (presentation) itself. The speaking may be my own speaking or the speaking of another; but in order for the linkage to take place, I have to allow the words into myself (take them to heart, perhaps), to "touch" the emergent inner something. Alternatively, I might say that I have to be able to allow both the words and the inner thing to come together in the special space that exists between the "I" and the "me" or between myself and the other person, the space where symbols are formed. For the process is clearly not just a question of expressing something, as in the early abreactive idea. Equally clearly, it is not just a saying of something, which, as Freud indicated, would be empty words. It is a coming together of an inner something and an outer form, a refinding (by each other) of the two halves (of the *symbolon*), as in symbol formation, to make a new kind of object—an affective object. This is not just an object of thought nor yet an object of feeling, but something that is formed of them both, and that is to be contemplated with both thought and feeling. The ingredients of this new object are an impulsive-emotional "something," which has accepted that it is "not to be" in action, in reality; and a word that has wanted to know, to find what its real meaning is. The place of this meeting—is it Cs or Pcs? Or is it somewhere that is neither inside nor outside, as Winnicott has suggested and Freud knew clinically all along—a place between, that is inside and outside at the same time?

CONSCIOUSNESS AS A LOOKING SPACE

There may be room here for a parallel, perhaps supplementary, account that makes more direct use of the idea of consciousness as a looking space and a searching (see Chapter 5). Freud says that if the patient is told what his unconscious idea is, it will not make any difference to him. The patient has insight, but not an insight that produces change. From this he concludes that a repression is lifted only when the word and the thing presentations are in the same place and connected with each other. Having the two presentations in different places does not help. So far, so good, except that Freud seems already to have committed himself to the idea of the mind as a continuous space with compartments. The point I am arguing is that it is phenomenologically false to think of the mind in this way; it is nearer to experience to think of the mind as occupying a virtual realm within the divided subject, with an "I" who is either trying or not trying to "see" what is "there"—in the "me" on the other side of the divide. The "me" may also be trying to hide, because of its fear of the bringer of words (originally the parent, but now the analyst) and its fear of being seen in the light of those words. Insight and the lifting of the repression occur only when the looking is allowed to see and the looked at allows itself to be seen.

If Freud had pursued the dual registration theory, I do not think it would have solved his problem, as he would still have been stuck with that part of his theory which thought of the mind as a continuous space with barriers across it. In order to get to the position that I am recommending, he would have had to insert a distance into his model, an actual space of separation between the thing presentation and the word. Perhaps then he would have been able to think of the boundary between the Cs and the Ucs as a space across which two people—originally the parent and the child—were facing each other. From this point of view, the discontinuity between Cs and Ucs is the internalization of an originally perceived interpersonal space, an internalized interface, across which the subject looks at himself through the eyes of the Other. The state of consciousness, according to this view, depends on events in the relationship that exists between two subjects—a way of speaking that finds a ready extension to the therapeutic relationship.

PSYCHOLOGICAL DEFENSE AS
INTER- (INTRA-)PERSONAL ACTION

Attention is given in the attitude of the person who is attending, not in the supposed extra bit of energy with which a content is invested that makes it noticeable. The attitude of trying to get to know my feeling self with words, the extra attention that I give, is the hypercathexis in which Freud very nearly obscured the phenomenology of consciousness. I turn toward myself in a certain way—with empathy, with looking, with listening, and above all with words—that, in my view, is the hypercathexis which facilitates the transformation of becoming conscious. What then of repression?

> The essence of repression lies simply in turning something away, and keeping it at a distance from the conscious. [1915b, p. 147]

If consciousness arises when the attention is turned toward the self, and the self allows itself to be touched and seen, is not repression the turning of a part of the self away from that attention? And who does the turning away? Is it the bringer of words who turns the self away? Or does the self turn away from the bringer of words? These are the questions that should be asked about repression. If we stay with Freud, however, we get drawn again into the misleading intricacies of a machine:

> We have arrived at the conclusion that repression is essentially a process affecting ideas on the border between the systems Ucs and Pcs (Cs), and we can now make a fresh attempt to describe the process in greater detail. It must be a matter of a *withdrawal* of cathexis; but the question is, in which system does the withdrawal take place and to which system does the cathexis that is withdrawn belong? . . . [1915c, p. 180]

Freud reaches the conclusion that there are two sorts of repression—a primal repression and a repression proper. Primal repression involves an anticathexis, "by means of which the system Pcs protects itself from the pressure upon it of the unconscious idea" (1915c, p. 181). In repression proper, there is in addition a withdrawal of cathexis by the Pcs from the idea that is pressing to become conscious. "It is very possible that it is precisely the cathexis which is withdrawn from the idea that is used for anticathexis" (p. 181). In other words, in the beginning, before any idea has become conscious, there is a primal repression that involves a "pushing away" energy, a repelling energy, in the Pcs against the "offending" idea. Once the idea has been repelled, it is, as it were, put out of action, disabled, by having its energy taken away from it. This same energy is then used to push it away even harder.

Again, I think we have to ask ourselves whether a real understanding of what is happening is furthered by this kind of theorizing. Freud's account creates an impression of processes that operate independently of motives and intentions. For the most part they seem like impersonal or mechanical processes, not processes that originated in forms of personal action and reaction, which I believe them in fact to be.[1] It is true that repression may be automatic and unconscious, but so is much unconscious behavior. That does not mean the absence of a personal motivation, only a disavowal of it. I want to return to my earlier questions about who might be turning away from whom in repression.

Recall for a moment the phobic scenario I sketched in Chapter 2. There was someone, myself, raging against a controlling and constricting object, at a distance from, and unrecognized by, the one I loved. I saw myself there through the eyes of the Other as this awful, nearly subhuman sort of creature. But I, as the person with phobic anxiety, cannot see that this scenario portrays myself in a rage and threatened with loss of love. I merely see an incomprehensible and terrifying situation from which I flee. If I, the analyst, now go toward this bit of the self portrayed in the symptom with words, there is no doubt the patient will turn me away. My words will not touch him (resistance). He protects that bit of himself from my words, even as he no doubt protects me from the self that is disguised and in hiding. Fear is pervasive. *The self that is in hiding (repressed) fears me as the bringer of words, because those words will reveal (make conscious—show to me and to him) the very thing that threatened the rupture in the relationship with the original loved object. My words threaten a recurrence of that event, of that original turning away and original banishment.*

The intrapsychic processes of consciousness and repression can thus be seen in object-relational or quasi-personal terms as antithetical moments of an original interpersonal relationship. Self-consciousness involves

---

[1]There is obviously some similarity between these ideas and those put forward by Roy Schafer in *A New Language for Psychoanalysis* (1976). However, it would take me too far from my overall task to explore this further.

being seen, and consciousness in this sense involves being seen and accepted by that Other on whom we originally depended. Consciousness implies closeness and relationship. Repression, by contrast, implies distance; it involves the banishment and hiding of those parts of myself that I believe will threaten the continuing acceptance and love of that Other on whom I depend. That "aboriginal" Other (1915c, p. 195), which is myself, for example, is my image to that Other (at least as I envisage it), with which I remind myself that I must never be that raging person (who I now disown) again. But there is not only the relation to me, the analyst, as the bringer of words to be considered. There is my own relationship, as the patient, to this thing inside me that is even now aroused to express itself (within the vicissitudes of my current relationships or, more pressingly, within the transference). I turn away from this Other, which is (but which must not be) myself, in fear and horror. There is no way that I could approach such a terrifying object with words to understand it. Indeed, if I were to use words at all, it would only be to repeat the banishing words of the mother who originally could not cope with me— "Get thee hence!" And so this unloved self is banished to the "not-me" part of the original separation, a part of the world that, in consequence, I have to avoid.

This account, and I expect there could be others, illustrates that we *can* talk about repression, and perhaps even projection, without resorting to mechanical or pseudoscientific models. We can use a human, interpersonal language, which, in my view, illuminates the problem we are dealing with far better than the mechanical model that is supposed to explain it. The mechanical language in fact dehumanizes the person and makes him into a thing; in doing this it seems to collude indirectly with the dehumanizing processes through which the person originally took flight from, and tried to disown, his own sentient self. In using such a language, we are also, of course, colluding indirectly with the original Other who was unable to stay with the raging infant in a containing, human way.

This conclusion is paradoxical, because it was Freud who went such a long way toward rescuing from their exile the distorted and banished elements of the human person that he found disguised in the phenomena of mental illness and gave them, as it were, a human face. His wrapping them up again in such a "scientific" parcel may in part reflect his own ambivalence about what he was doing. Breuer literally ran away from

Anna O. when she became too hot to handle, and it was only when Freud was able to hold up to what had happened the distancing mask of the transference that Breuer could be persuaded to put his name to the joint project on hysteria (Szasz 1963, see Chapter 13). Freud was a lot braver than that, but perhaps he, too, had a need to protect himself from too much reality and needed to distance himself in order to go on exploring.

10 Language and Metaphor

There's a cool web of language winds us in . . .
—Robert Graves, "The Cool Web"

WORDS AND THINGS

THE KNOWN WORLD is defined and fixed by language—a word for this and a word for that. Word refers to thing; the thing is named and recognized by the word—a reciprocal relationship of familiarity. The world is known and defined: complete, in some sense, with everything named. If I point to anything, you can tell me what it is—everything has a name. Words define relations, too, so in the end, the whole structure of the world is given in language; there is a system of complete correspondences. That, anyway, is the myth—the myth of the familiar established order of things that will not change and will go on forever and ever. Language has tamed the world, made it known, and keeps it in its place.

But language also constricts—it leaves things out. What you see and what I see may not be quite the same thing. And there may be things that neither of us can see:

There's a cool web of language winds us in . . .

It prescribes what will exist and it limits our vision, even as it separates us from our primary sensual relation with the world. We come to see what we can say, rather than saying what we can see. We forget that language is only a map—perhaps no one ever told us. We take the map for the territory.

This is the world that we are born into—the linguistic world: the world according to language. As Lacan says, we are born into language. And so we are taught the world, and what to see in the world, and who we are, by the word.

But what happens if we can see or feel more than the word describes . . . or prescribes? That is the question that every single person has to answer.

World is crazier and more of it than we think, . . .

says Louis MacNeice.

The poet's answer is to try and *say* it, to give expression to that excess of world, or self, over language.

Here is the time for the Tellable, *here* is its home.
Speak and proclaim . . . ,

cries Rilke, passionately *saying* what he can see and feel. The poet often speaks of that which in some way is excluded by language, and this is why poetry is sometimes seen as subversive—it threatens the established order of things that language has laid down. The poet is a seer, a visionary. He creates a rift in the linguistic order of the world, points to something that has been left out, and reminds us that the raw, untamed world is still there, threatening always to break through the "cool web" of words.

How does the poet achieve this saying and this pointing to the things that lie beyond language? Above all, through metaphor—which, of course, is why metaphor is sometimes associated purely with poetry. Clearly, it is not my intention to discourse on poetry, but to point to the fact that we are all, to some extent, poets; at least we all have to choose whether we will see (and feel) what is said, or say what we see (and feel). And if we decide to say what we see—that in our experience which is not given by the available words of language—then we may, like the poet, turn to metaphor.

The interest and excitement of metaphor probably lies in the fact that it *is* subversive, that it allows us, in Winnicott's sense, to create the world afresh for ourselves. We reverse the previous order and undo the prescriptive primacy of language. With metaphor, we make a new symbol: we bring the word into a new connection with sensory lived experience, so that the word vibrates with this renewed contact with the world and ourselves. Metaphor enables us to redefine the world in *our* way, taking account of what *we* see and what *we* feel to be important.

Poetry is not, of course, the only way of seeing afresh. All the arts achieve this in different ways. But there is also scientific seeing and scientific discovery to take into account, and this is relevant here, as many would see our activity as therapists and analysts as having at least a scientific dimension. Whether as artists or scientists, the question is a crucial one in our work. Do we see only what language, analytic theory, defines (prescribes?); or do we say what we see, even if it does not agree with theory? It seems a simple question, with only one possible answer—we would all shout at once that we would say what we see. And yet this is not what happens. The dialectic between the new vision and the established order is far more complex. The world view, the theory, any linguistically established order, becomes interwoven with the fabric of the self—*is*, in some sense, the self—and is defended, individually and collectively, against the new which threatens it with change. So the new vision, expressed in a new metaphor, is always a problem for both bearer and receiver. We have only to look at the history of the psychoanalytic movement from its beginning, with Freud's burgeoning new metaphors, through the period of institutionalization of his ideas into an established and defended order of things to see this illustrated (see Chapter 18, pp. 323–325).

METAPHOR AS EXPLORATION

Metaphor, then, is the linguistic tool of the explorer. It is through metaphor that the explorer describes the unknown. There is no word for the unknown, so something has to be found that will bring this new something into a relation with what is already known. The unknown is "the thing without a name," so it has to be named by linking it to something else that is already named. "Metaphor," says Aristotle, "consists in giving the thing a name that belongs to something else." It is, to use Aristotle's word, a "transference," and like *transference*, *metaphor* means literally a carrying across of something from one location to another.[1]

---

[1] *Transference* is a direct Latin translation of the Greek *metaphor*: *meta-* (of place, order, condition, or nature) corresponding to the Latin *trans-*; *ferein* (to carry). Hence, both words have the same sense of carrying something across from one place to another.

How, then, can I lay hold of this new thing? There is nothing that matches it exactly. How can I convey what it is—its meaning? All I can do is bring it into some close relation with something else that is known and named and to which it has an analogical or iconic resemblance, and see if a meaning that fits the new thing can be generated from this relationship and carried across to the new thing from the old. The result is a change in the word; the old word is used in a new way.[2]

I will look more closely at the structure of metaphor and how it achieves this function later. Here I want to stress that even in talking about metaphor and what it does, or about the nature of thought, as I tried to do in Chapter 6, it is hard to avoid speaking metaphorically. I automatically reach for words that belong to some different context in order to convey the meaning I need. "Reach" itself is metaphorical; a "tool" . . . "to hold" . . . a meaning and "convey" it elsewhere—all these are terms from a context of concrete relations with objects which I have adopted and put to use in a different context, in the hope that they will illuminate what is going on in that new context.

In *Philosophy in a New Key* (1942), Susanne Langer discussed the possibility that all general words in language have a metaphorical origin. She quotes Wegener, who described words as "faded metaphors" that had lost contact with their plastic referents through repeated usage, and Mallarmé, who described the word as "the worn coin placed silently in my hand." According to Wegener, all words start life with some concrete referent in sensory, practical experience; gradually through metaphor their meaning is extended. For example, in the phrase "the fire flares up," "flares up" refers to a concrete situation; but in "the king's anger flares up" there is a metaphorical extension of meaning. We have somehow to grasp what is the relevance of the first context to the second in order to get the meaning. Once "metaphorized," the term can be used in more general situations by further extension—a riot or a noise flares up, for example, and we may then cease to be aware of the original connotation to do with fire. In each successive extension of meaning, the distance

---

[2]In this adaptive relation of word to thing, we can see a revival of the infant's earlier relation to the adaptive mother. The word becomes what the object needs it to be, rather than the more usual relation of the word imposing its pattern on the object world.

from the original concrete meaning is increased, and it is only then by an act of imagination that we can revive that original meaning.

Metaphor, says Langer, is the law of growth of every semantic—I quote from memory. It is the means by which language is made to embrace a multimillion things. Or, we could say, the means by which the boundaries of the unknown are gradually pushed back. Some metaphors will merely assimilate the unknown to the already known; in this sense, they tame the unknown. But it can happen that a powerful new metaphor will overthrow the old order and demand a whole reorganization of the way we see things. It is against this kind of upheaval that established orders defend themselves (Kuhn 1962).

Metaphor is scarcely the deliberate process that "reaching for a tool" might suggest. It is, rather, the way that language has of answering my "speechless want"—of giving me the thing that I am trying to say. The less that thing is known, the more chance there is that language will find a metaphorical way of saying it. And when we come to the expression of inner things and feelings, things that cannot be seen, metaphor is the only linguistic way of giving them form. For this reason, if for no other, a study of metaphor should be on the syllabus of study for all psychotherapists.

THE DIFFERENCE BETWEEN METAPHOR AND SYMBOL

Word and flesh; visual knowledge and carnal knowledge; seeing and doing; looking and touching. Somehow metaphor has to do with the relationship between these oppositions. Nowhere in language is the relationship between sensually perceived things and their meaning closer, and much may be learned by questioning what this relationship is. "In the beginning was the Word . . . and the Word was made flesh and dwelt among us . . ." (John 1:1,14). In metaphor, the word *almost* becomes flesh—or is it that the flesh becomes word? But the critical term is *almost*. Metaphor brings us closer, sometimes very close, to our sensory experience, our carnal knowledge; but it never loses the thin, fine line that separates us from that experience and never deserts the world of meaning that arose through the original giving up of that sensory experience. It creates the illusion of being in contact with that world of experience, but the thin, fine line of separation from it never disappears.

What is the difference, then, between a metaphor and a symbol,[3] that rich heralder of unconscious meanings that seems to be striving for expression in dreams and psychological symptoms?

We could say that metaphor is a structure of words that, through bringing us into contact with sensuous images, enables us to conceive of a meaning that we have sensed. It gives form, and almost flesh, to a meaning that we have already discerned; but it stands firmly in language and in the "universe of things said"—in a semantic space, where the only doing is the doing of imagined bodies.

A symbol, by contrast, whether in dream or in psychological symptom (see the phobic symptom described in Chapters 2 and 3), embodies a meaning that has yet to be discovered and conceived of, and still exists in the carnal mode. It is still one with the flesh of action and doing, and has not yet subjected itself to the refiner's fire of separation and giving up. It knows only the physical, bodily mode—whether flight, as of the phobic patient from his phobic object; or dream, where the dream object (symbol) evokes terror or desire.[4] The symbol is a meaning still embedded in the flesh of desire and its consummation, "mythically bound and fettered," as Cassirer (1946) said. The symbol has the power of the real and *uses us*—even though it is *imaginary*, it is not *imagined*. Metaphor has power, too, but *we use it* for our own purposes of conceiving and enlarging our understanding.

It has taken me a long time to appreciate this difference between metaphor and symbol, though from the beginning I felt that the difference was crucial and that formulation of it would open up a whole world of understanding. It would highlight, in Freud's terms, the difference

---

[3]There is a problem here with the word *symbol* that has to be tolerated. In linguistics and semiology the symbol is the higher development—the full realization of the conceptual reference rather than the object reference of the word (sign). The unconscious symbol, the symbol of dream and psychological symptom, has not yet reached that level of development, though metaphor has. It is lived, avoided, striven after in the action mode and is not yet a signifier or symbol in the linguistic sense. It only acquires this status after its transformation to metaphor.

[4]In dream, there *is* a doing, and the doing, although imaginary, is not imagined. It is a *frustrated* doing that has become a hallucination, not a *conceived of* doing that is imagined. As such, it is still enmeshed with our flesh and blood, and moves or involves us with the terror or pleasure of immediate action, not with the distanced and empathic emotion of a mediated presentation.

between ego and id, between conscious and unconscious; and it would clarify the nature of that essential work of therapy that Freud (1933) so clearly understood:

"... Where id was, there ego shall be." [p. 80]
Where symbol was, there metaphor shall be.

TRANSFORMATIONS: FROM LIVED MEANING TO REPRESENTATIONAL FORM

In *Self and Others* (1961) Laing described a patient who for a long time intrigued me. Her utterance, as she recovered from her puerperal psychosis, seemed to crystallize the essential moment of transformation that I wanted to understand. As she came out of her "twilight state," in which she had suffered terrible hypochondriacal delusions, she began to make connections between her symptoms and events in her life that began to render her symptoms more intelligible. After a further period during which this developing insight was consolidated, she was finally well, once again living in the real world rather than her nightmare world of dreamlike symbols. At this point, she summarized her experience in this way: "I seem to have been living in a *metaphorical* state. I wove a tapestry of symbols and have been living in it." This statement stuck in my mind, and for a long time it misled me into thinking of the unconscious symbol as a kind of metaphor. It only gradually dawned on me that this was illusory and obscured the subtle processes of transformation that we need to understand. The illusion that the unconscious symbol is a kind of metaphor stems from the way that we, as therapists, relate to the patient's symbols. Because *we* can see the missing elements of context that make bridges to the symbol, we anticipate the transformation that has not yet occurred in the patient. *We can see what the symbol might mean, so for us it is a metaphor. But the patient is still living "in" the symbol, and so it is still part of his reality.* Only when the patient himself can see and feel in his mind's eye the missing contexts, linking them with the symbol, can there truly be a metaphor, a structure of thought that yields a meaning.

I must explain here how meaning is always related to context. *Meaning* is a relational term. We know what the meaning of something is when we can see how it is related to other things. The more relationships a thing has, the richer its meaning. An unconscious symbol often seems meaningless because it is isolated from its proper context of relationships. Freud showed very clearly that the transposition of a symbol from its own to an alien context of relationships was one way of making it unrecognizable, of disguising it; discovering its proper context was an important part of discovering its meaning. The whole method of free association depends on this, as does Freud's own method of dream analysis. The "true" context of the dream symbol had to be found by listening to the patient's associations to that symbol.

Nevertheless, it is misleading to talk of the unconscious symbol as having meaning in the same way in which we talk of a word having a meaning. The meaning of a word is a concept—an idea that has been disengaged and separated from any actual context of physical relationships between things. It has been abstracted from such concrete relationships and now exists in a virtual, semantic space, which is the space of thought or language. There the relations of the actual objects can be recreated in schematic form through the mediation of a language, and the meaning of the word is given by its relationships within that system of correspondence that we call language. Where the unconscious symbol is concerned, the relational meaning is still embodied in the concrete situation. The person does not "see" it, but lives it in his body, or his actions, unknowingly. Meaning channels the person's behavior and feelings, but he himself does not realize what that meaning is. Unconscious meaning is not only meaning that cannot be thought or spoken; it is meaning that is still lived and enacted as real.

I am reminded here, by way of a clinical vignette, of a patient whom I once heard discussed at a case conference. He was a lad in his teens, who because of learning difficulties and disturbed behavior was requiring the services of a teacher in his own home. Many of the details of the case escape me, but I remember that the teacher's impression (he was a man) was of a very overinvolved relationship with the mother, and a father who seemed to have been distant or absent, as he scarcely featured in the story at all. One of the things which made teaching a problem was the boy's extreme degree of restlessness. But this did not just take the form of fidgeting or being unable to sit still. The teacher described vividly how the boy would charge repeatedly from one end of the room to the other, often banging himself on the walls of the room as though he were trying to get out.

As I listened to this story, certain things seemed to come together into a meaningful whole. In other words, I thought I was able to put the story together in a way that created a context within which the boy's behavior made some kind of sense.[5] The story of the overinvolved mother and the weak or absent father reminded me of the dangers of an unopposed relationship with the mother—the kind of thing I was sketching in Chapter 7. I was also reminded of phobic patients, who often seem to have a similar family constellation, and how the claustrophobic patient feels trapped in enclosed spaces and feels the need to get out. I then began to see this boy as dashing himself against the boundaries of the room in an attempt to escape from a situation he could not name but lived as constricting and stifling. I saw him as enmeshed with his mother, but enacting this predicament in relation to the room in the presence of his teacher.

It would be easy to say that this behavior symbolized and enacted the intrapsychic and, in some degree, the real situation with the boy's mother. In some ways this might be true. But it would not be true to say that he was living in a metaphorical mode; and it would not be true to say that the boy was telling us about his predicament. It might be true to say that he was enacting his predicament, but again, not in the sense of a dramatic *mise-en-scène*, which he intended to portray. I am contending that the boy was living and suffering a psychological situation he could neither name nor know about; he was expressing the feelings it engendered in him in a symbolically displaced but real way. Symbolic processes can be seen to be at work, but they are symbols that the patient is used by, not symbols he can use for any purpose at all, let alone for the purposes of communication. They have more in common with the infant's transitional object than with the symbol that can be used to convey a state of affairs. Once again, I found myself speculating about the state of this boy's separation from his objects.

The process of transformation of unconscious lived meaning (symbol) to consciously grasped meaning (metaphor and thought) involves more than just seeing the symbol in its proper context of relationships. It means a certain giving up of the lived relation to the symbol, a certain acceptance of its nonreal status—in other words, an existential as well as

---

[5]Whether I was right or not in my interpretation is another matter, compare Spence (1982).

a cognitive change. It means a movement from *living in* the symbol to *being outside* of it; from perceiving the symbol as a real limit of the world to perceiving it as a subjective structure, a part of the self.

This transformation necessarily involves a substitution of looking for doing. It involves a positional shift, a change of perspective (quite literally) in relation to one's own self. "Myself in a particular relation to someone or something" is now to be viewed from somewhere else; in practical terms, that means from the position of a third person. The requirement for this transformation is a change of location—seeing myself as Other—and a substitution of imagined doing for living and attempted doing in the real world. The most likely way of achieving this is by taking the position of the previously excluded third party in a three-person relationship (see Chapter 7).

This raises again the whole question of the oedipal situation and its relation to thought. It also recalls the original separating out from the primal object, the mother, as the ground condition for the development of an objectifying consciousness. Moving into the position of the Other implies an acceptance, willing or otherwise, of the fact of separateness and distance from the first object. In turn, the three-person relationship, in which the self is excluded from the couple, is the structure that guarantees a space within which imagined relationships, the basis of thinking, can occur.

Seeing the matter in this way highlights the clinical relevance of the example I have been discussing. If the father is absent as a psychological force, it not only will render more difficult the process of getting free from the mother and the regressive pull of that relationship; it will also jeopardize the associated development of mind and symbol formation. Symbols will remain poorly differentiated from their objects and will still have more of the characteristics of objects that invite actions rather than of images that convey knowledge.

I want to return to the example of Laing's patient, who came to see that she had been living in a metaphorical mode. We can now see that this is precisely what she had *not* been doing; she had been living within her tapestry of unconscious symbols in the mode of the real. The distinction over which I am laboring is not a matter of pedantry or splitting hairs; for the "hair line" I am talking about is the thin, fine line that is constitutive of consciousness—the thin, fine line of difference and separation that makes thought possible. As Bateson (1979) said in another, though related context: "It is the difference that makes the difference."

Separation and difference were two things that Laing's patient found difficult to tolerate. Perhaps this is one reason why she was suffering from a puerperal illness. She could not tolerate the separation of birth. But according to her own later understanding, she had not coped well with previous separations either—notably, from her father and brother, who were both dead. She eventually came to realize that the awful feelings she had experienced in her body, which had made her believe she was dying of a terrible illness, were things that she had seen and felt (through identification) in her father and brother during their last illnesses. During her own illness, she was one with them without knowing it.

To take but one example: The patient felt that her tongue was paralyzed and twisted. She did not realize during her own illness that this was one of her father's symptoms when he had had a stroke. So instead of grieving the father (allowing separation and loss), she became one with him and suffered his twisted tongue in her own body. Presumably the pain of parting from him was too great, and she could not allow the separation to occur. She could not allow there to be a space between her and him. Since there was no space and no thin, fine line of difference, there could be no grief, because there was no space in which the symbols of her grief, in the sense of metaphors, might be formed. Instead of being able to sob something about feeling torn apart, or allowing her face to be twisted with the grief she could not put into words, she suffered instead an unknown feeling (her tongue felt twisted in her mouth). This was the price she paid for not being able to let go of objects, not being able to think.

I want to finish this section by quoting again from Merleau-Ponty (1964a):

> When one goes from the order of events to the order of expression, one does not change the world; the same circumstances that were previously submitted to now become a signifying system. Hollowed out, worked from within, and finally freed from that weight upon us that makes them painful or wounding, they become transparent, even luminous. . . . [p. 64]

How does this happen? How does this hollowing out occur? Merleau-Ponty's poetic formulation seems here to make contact with my own attempts at more discursive description. Hollowed out—allowing the space of separation; the "solid" unconscious symbol becomes the "hollow" metaphor with its space for meaning, the empty space that allows room for the word.

METAPHOR, SYMBOL, AND COMMUNICATION

At first sight, an unconscious symbol seems like a *forme fruste* of metaphor, and metaphor merely a further development of unconscious symbol. The symbol conceals because it is divorced from its natural context; the metaphor reveals because the contexts are plain to see. Like the change from unconscious to preconscious in Freud's account, the transition can be understood as a small addition. There it was the addition of a word presentation to a thing presentation. Here it is the addition of a missing context. I tried to show in Chapter 9 that such a view was misleading and tended to conceal the radical discontinuity between what is conscious and what is unconscious. I believe I have demonstrated in my discussion of metaphor and symbol that a similar danger of misunderstanding the phenomena exists, and with it the danger of glossing over those vast steps of developmental history that are assumed in the capacity to move from one kind of structure to the other. Before I end this chapter, I want to make one final differentiation between metaphor and unconscious symbol. I will focus the discussion on this question: Is the unconscious symbol a communication?

In a rather unthinking way, I have always tended to believe that it is. How often have we not heard supervisors or colleagues, or even ourselves, saying: "I think the patient is trying to tell you . . . that they feel this, or they feel that; that they are angry with you, want to be loved by you, fed by you, and so on. The implication is that the patient is trying to communicate but is afraid, for some reason, to do so in direct fashion. The communication is therefore distorted, disguised, broken up, and scattered in all the ways that are familiar to us since *The Interpretation of Dreams*. There is no doubt that it can seem like that, just as it can seem that the patient's unconscious symbol is a type of metaphor. But I think it is possible to doubt it for the same reasons.

A metaphor is an instrument of communication. It is a verbal form that presents images showing what something is like. Its intention is to show, reveal, point. It is a presentational symbol, in Langer's terms (see Chapter 14). It locates an experience or perception in such a way as to facilitate our imagining it. It says: "Feel your way into that and you will have an idea what I am talking about." It does not offer us anything that we can touch or taste or smell or get our teeth into. At most it offers us food for thought. But it touches us with the idea of these things, arousing memory, perhaps nostalgia, but not desire. "Hollowed out, worked from within"—the function of metaphor is communication, not consummation, and the recollection of sensory experience is harnessed in the service of this.

An unconscious symbol is quite different from this. We could say, for example, that a patient is trying to hide and not express his anger—but *express* is the operative word, referring to being, not knowing. The problem is an anger that seeks consummation, which will not be put out or extinguished, yet it must not be shown. And so, as in dream, it finds a devious route to consummation, in the body of the symbol. In the dream, as Freud showed, there is a *mise-en-scène* of what cannot be allowed to happen in reality, an attempt at realization akin to hallucination. The dream or symptom is not a communication, but a kind of enactment in defiance of the reality principle, or of the Other, whichever your prefer.[6]

---

[6]We could ask, as Winnicott did of the transitional object, which is the more important—the objectness of the (primitive) symbolic object or the fact that it symbolizes something. Obviously, both are important to the baby. But I do not think it would make much sense to say that the baby who was relating to its blanket was communicating something to the mother. Even so, the mother might see and understand that her baby was contented and was managing to cope better without her through its use of the blanket. This is something the sensitive mother might see without being told.

If we shift the ground a bit, we might ask what is the situation when the baby cries. Is the baby communicating, or is it merely expressing something, its distress, which the mother then responds to? This is a more difficult question, because it does seem that the cry is a primitive form of nonverbal communication that is biologically determined and matches an inbuilt tendency in the mother to respond. It might be argued that the primitive symbolic enactment of an inner state had something in common with a cry. If it has, we still have to contend with the fact that the symbolic enactment is not direct. It has suffered a displacement, based, we might suppose, on the knowledge (or do I mean on some dim, half-realized anticipation?) that the mother would not respond kindly if she knew that it was she who was the cause of the distress (the anger, for example). This might make the communication into a kind of strangled cry. Maybe. There are many uncertainties here that are difficult to formulate. What is important in the present context is not to lose sight of the fact of difference and the way in which a symbolic enactment is different from a fully fledged symbolic communication.

So the symbol that presses into the known from the unknown is made of quite different stuff from that which approaches the unknown from the known. It is not a *forme fruste* of knowledge, but an attempt, within the confines of the person, to do what cannot be done in the real world. It is more like a *forme fruste* of action—a detour, as Freud often said, around the obstacle of the Other. So the "solid" symbol embodies this continued striving, after the Other has turned away.

11 Metaphor and Structure

I think that one of the means to meaning in this art is a certain relationship of images: what might be called a coupling of images, though the coupling may include more images than two. One image is established by words which make it sensuous and vivid to the eyes or ears or touch—to any of the senses. Another image is put beside it. And a meaning appears which is neither the meaning of one image nor the meaning of the other nor even the sum of both but a consequence of both—a consequence of both in their conjunction, in their relation to each other.

—Archibald MacLeish, *Poetry and Experience*

IN THE LAST chapter I discussed the transformations that an unconscious symbol must go through before it could be regarded as a metaphor. Indirectly this was a way of describing the structure of a metaphor. However, I now want to focus more directly on the structure of metaphor, as I believe it can be regarded as a paradigm of what might be called an ego-integrated structure, perhaps even of ego structure itself. Much of what I am saying here I first tried to express in my paper on metaphor (Wright 1976), though perhaps the accent and emphasis are now different.

I will take as my starting point a line of poetry I have already quoted from Robert Graves's poem "The Cool Web":

> There's a cool web of language winds us in . . .

There are at least two metaphors here, if not three, though the idea generated by each integrates into an overall idea generated by the line as a whole. The overall sense of the poem is that, as we grow through and out of childhood, we gradually lose touch with the rich immediacy of our first experience of the world, which becomes attenuated and distanced by language.

The two metaphors in this line of poetry seem to be

1   a cool web of language
2   language winds us in

Looking more closely, however, we can see that the first metaphor is really two condensed metaphors: "cool web" and "language is a (cool) web." Through this example we can look more closely at how a metaphor achieves its function of generating an idea.

Reading the line slowly, we move through the images that each metaphor arouses, in the way that Archibald MacLeish so well described in his *Poetry and Experience*.

cool . . . web . . . language . . . winds . . . us in.

The sentence is a clear one; a statement is being made about language and what it does to us. Each sensory image, with its own aura of associations, adds to the message. I could write the line differently, including some of my own aura of associations:

cool . . . . web . . . . winds us in.

emotionally cool   spider's web   playing a fish

no passion or   catching and   winding sheets
sensuality   killing

quietly and   spider entwining   corpses and
without fuss, etc.   its prey, etc.   death, etc.

All these chains of associations are made to work together around a central idea; in turn, the whole operation is held in place by the syntactical structure of language—subject, verb, object, and so on. This syntactical structure is really a set of rules, determining the kinds of relationship that must exist between the ideas or the concepts to which the words refer. The freedom of the images to be what they want, or more accurately, what we might want them to be, is subordinated to an external constraint which dictates what part they *must* play in an overall linguistic task. In this way, we finish, not with a salad[1] of superimposed, condensed images, as might be the case in a dream; but with a central idea illuminated by a nexus of reverberating images, which, nevertheless, are clearly anchored and related to each other within the semantic space of the line.

These meanings could be paraphrased discursively as follows: Language, which is unobtrusively given to us by the Other, quietly pulls us in like a fish from our original freedoms, or traps us within its meanings like the spider does the fly in its web. This slowly kills something alive and passionate in us and separates us from a more immediate relationship with the world and ourselves. This process is like being wrapped up and poisoned by the spider in its silken thread, or being wound up in winding sheets like a corpse.

Obviously, all the associations are personal and will not be exactly the same for everyone. In addition, associations will lead into deeper areas of the psyche, where the imagery can draw on more primitive energies that are not accessible to consciousness. I would suppose, nevertheless, that there would be a certain communality between my associations and those of the poet and my own and those of others, so that a genuine communication would be deemed to have taken place. This issue, however, is incidental to the main point—that the metaphors stir such associations in us without having to be fully aroused. The metaphor plays upon our organization of personal associations and recollections, causing them to resonate and interact, giving the line a vividness and force that take us by surprise.

A further point is worth making. In its actual form, the line is simple, clear, and firm; it is as though in its form, and in its "cool" relation to underlying images, it illustrates or presents the very idea it expresses. It "winds in" the images; but that which has been wound in, within our own depths, is made to stir and resonate. We are made to recollect what we once knew directly and immediately.

The metaphor refers us to images that we recollect, recall, contemplate—not to images that anticipate a future relation with an object. This distinction is important. The images are about once having had, not

---

[1]It was Eugen Bleuler (1911) who coined the term *word salad* to describe certain forms of schizophrenic speech.

being about to have—there is an essential distance and separation from what is imagined.

I will summarize what I have said so far. Metaphor poses a linguistic task, and that task is circumscribed by certain clearly defined rules that have to be followed. The task of metaphor involves using sensual and evocative imagery, but that imagery is not allowed free rein. In the first place, the images have to reveal something about the central idea that the linguistic structure presents. Second, the sensual images are not allowed to function as anticipatory images, which would indicate an action frame; they must be content with recollection, with the remembrance of things past. I will now take just one of these metaphors and look at it in a more formal way to illustrate what I am describing. I will consider the metaphor "Language is a web."

How do we know that this is a metaphor? If we were schizophrenic, we probably would not know; we would be confused by it and start talking about webs and spiders and all the other associations on a concrete level of actual relationship with objects. We would not understand the task that the metaphor posed. Presumably we would either be ignoring or failing to properly understand the rules that defined the metaphor task. If we are not psychotic, we know that the metaphor is a metaphor because it makes no literal sense. It actually is more or less nonsense. Language is *not* a web. But the context—the fact that it is in a text that is otherwise meaningful, our trust in the speaker or writer that he is not trying to deceive us—all this points to a meaning that is to be found. We know that the speaker or writer of the phrase intended a meaning. We understand that there is a task, provided by speaker, language, and context, that this conjunction of objects will make sense on the level of meaning. The image of the web *must* in some way illuminate what language is, and we intuitively, if not explicitly, understand the rules that will enable us to complete the task.

By what process, then, do we envisage the connection between the two terms of the metaphor? I think that in some way we stand back and look at the two objects presented—"language" and "web"—and ask ourselves: "What is the *relevance* of these two objects to each other?" We then have to imagine these terms, these two objects, interacting with each other until they produce something that makes sense on the level of meaning. We have to look at them, feel our way into them in imagination until we can see how they inform one another, and what it is that their interaction will produce. In a formal way, the task is similar to a riddle or a joke; we know that there is an answer, and we have to allow the apparently disparate elements to interact until something new, that is both obvious and surprising and common to both, is born out of their juxtaposition.

It is crucial for the success of this linguistic task that we do not approach these two objects on the concrete level of things, nor in terms of what at this moment is relevant to us—to our wishes, needs, or intentions. We have to concern ourselves only with the relevance of the two terms to each other, as they exist in their own particular contexts and in their interaction.

If we fulfill these limiting requirements of the situation, what happens? Of course, in a flash, a new meaning is born from the interaction of images—the idea that language is a kind of net that catches us up and separates us from our primary sensual awareness of the world and ourselves.

In a formal sense, this situation of understanding a metaphor has the same characteristics as the oedipal situation—albeit an oedipal situation that has been successfully overcome. (I have already made this link in Chapter 7.) In each case, I am the observer of two objects interacting in their own bounded space. They are doing something, with each other or to each other, that is independent of me and my concerns, and I have to allow them to do this and not interfere. Something will be produced from their interaction which I can relate to and make use of, providing I observe the basic rules of the situation. The parental intercourse that produces a baby is not difficult to "see" once you have "seen" it, nor is the meaning of a metaphor once you have learned how the system works at a higher level. But the difficult thing, developmentally, is to allow the process to happen.

We cannot escape from metaphor. Even when I am talking about the structure of metaphor in this way, I am presenting a further metaphor—the idea that metaphor is an "intercourse" of images. At the same time I am suggesting something much more basic than this: *I am saying that the capacity to use language and to think about thought objects and their relationship with each other is founded on that overcoming of the Oedipus complex which occupies such a central place in psychoanalytic theory. Only when the child can tolerate his separation from the parental couple, and can bear to contemplate their intercourse without him, has the ground been established on which metaphor and thought in general can flourish.*

The Law of the Father, the incest taboo, establishes and guarantees this space for thought, for the contemplation of objects in relationship. But the possibility of symbolization, in the linguistic sense, depends, as we have seen, on an earlier development—namely, all that has to do with the first bounding and separating out of the self from the maternal symbiosis, the tolerance of separation from the mother, and the inter-position and maintenance of distance from her. The ground rules of thought (and the understanding of metaphor) include this maintenance of an irreducible gap between self and object and between object and object; any loss of that gap or failure to properly achieve it will lead to the collapse of thought, because there is no longer any space within which thought can occur.

That space for symbolization and thought first arises in the area between the mother and child after their primary separation, at a time when there is sufficient satisfaction of needs for the object to be recol-lected and contemplated rather than sought after. I like to think that perhaps the object that is recollected rather than sought after is the mother who has been related to across a distance in a noninstinctual/ attachment way. It would be her face, with its patterned gestalts of expressive meaning, that might be prominent in such a recollection. As I suggested in Chapter 6, this could be the precursor of the kind of pattern recognition that is so essential to thinking and symbolization.

Lest it be thought that my description of metaphor as an intercourse of images is purely a flight of my own fancy, I want to refer the reader to the Archibald MacLeish quote at the beginning of this chapter. Note his words—a "coupling" of images; a meaning appearing that is "a conse-quence of both in their conjunction, in their relation to each other."

I will complete this section by summarizing the structure of metaphor:

1. Metaphor is a linguistic structure that presents and contains within a single boundary discrete sensory images. The function of the structure is to generate a specific symbolic meaning through the interaction of these images.

2. The boundary of the structure is given by the grammatical-linguistic form of the metaphor and the intention toward meaning of the speaker or listener. It can be seen as a set of rules governing either the behavior of the objects within the structure or the relationship of the observer to the objects within the structure. Or again, the boundary can be seen as a kind

of work task[2] imposed on the objects within the structure—a demand that they create a new meaning through their interaction, as required by the total context.

3. The speaker or listener is rigorously excluded from active involvement with the images. He has to maintain distance from them and must not regard them as inviting any action on his part. Insofar as he enters imaginatively into the life of the coupled images, there must be no fusion with those images or loss of boundary between him and them.

4. The imagined objects within the boundary will not be allowed to fuse with each other. Although interacting, they must remain separate.

5. If all the rules are followed and the boundary conditions fulfilled, then the structure will provide what the user of language needs. It will generate the searched for meaning. Any breakdown of these conditions will lead to a breakdown of function. Children have to learn the necessary rules before the structure will work for them,[3] schizophrenics disregard or fail to understand the rules, and lose the capacity to use metaphor.

AUTONOMY AND CONSTRAINT
IN STRUCTURE FORMATION

I now want to look more closely at what might be called the dynamic of metaphor. In every metaphor there is a certain tension. The sensual

---

[2]The idea of the work task is one I assimilated during my years at the Tavistock Clinic. It stems from the work of Bion (1959b) and extends readily to thinking about any kind of system (see Chapter 12). Bion suggested that we think of any group as having a work task as its primary function. But this primary task could be undermined by subtle and unconscious processes that substituted alternative but unstated goals for the group's activity. These subverting goals of the group were generated out of the emotional needs of the group members and led to what Bion called "basic assumption groups." These were groups dominated by some unconscious aim or goal that was quite different from the primary work task of the group. The activity in any group, according to Bion, had to be understood as a resultant of the tension between the primary work task and the basic assumption aim that was dominating the group at any particular time. If we think of a metaphor in these terms, we have to suppose that the work task, its linguistic aim, is very much in the ascendancy; but even here, more primitive aims may be seeking satisfaction, as may be seen in the choice of metaphor, the particular image chosen, and so on.
[3]"Learning the necessary rules" means, from a slightly different point of view, mastering the necessary developmental steps.

images of the metaphor pull the user toward the bodily experienced world, the world of action; the demand or need for meaning pulls the user in the opposite direction, toward the abstract, semantic space of language, the world of reflection and thought. The life of the metaphor seems to depend on this straddling of two worlds, and the meaning of the metaphor is an instantaneous creation that seems to spark from between the two sensory images, like a flash of lightning, into the symbolic space which has been prepared and maintained for it. The generation of this spark depends, as I have tried to show, on all the different "holding offs" from actual, concrete involvements that the sensuous parts of the metaphor seem to propose. Certainly, from a developmental point of view, one can imagine that such capabilities and "holding offs" are not easily won. During the time of their formation, the constraining boundaries of the structure must continue to be very important. In their origin, these are the actual demands and injunctions of the parents—for example, that the child may look but not do—but these are then internalized and, within the self, will guarantee the incipient new organization or structure that will make the new achievement possible.

One can imagine a certain moment in this structuring when everything is in place, but the new function has not yet occurred. At this moment, we can think of the structure as poised for a solution; alternative outcomes of the tensions in the structure are blocked off through parental constraints, and, in a sense, there is now only one possible outcome waiting to be found—the transcendent function of meaning. Now suddenly, it is discovered; the flash has occurred. But perhaps most important of all is the effect this discovery of meaning has on the stability of the now reorganized structure with its newly emerged function. The structure, which before was unstable and held in place by external constraints, has now found a new stability, reorganized, and held in place from within, by the superordinating power of the emergent function. The process may be compared to a horse being led to a jump in such a way that the only way on is over. Once the jump has been made, the freedom of the other side is its own reward. I would remind you again of Helen Keller's description of her "discovery" of language (quoted in Chapter 8). *The solution that is found itself becomes the reward and at the same time the stabilizer of the new organization or configuration.* Once this has happened, it would seem likely that the boundary rules of the structure become less important in maintaining the new system. They were necessary to bring about the transformation, but the new structure has a degree of inbuilt autonomy and stability provided by the positive feedback that achievement of the new goal brings.

This model allows us to consider the regressive possibilities that are inherent in the structure of a metaphor. Regression to a more concrete resolution of the tension in the structure implies a giving way of some of the boundary conditions. For example, a weakening of the external boundary constraint—of the demand for meaning, or of the "holding off" rules—would lead to the incipient new organization falling apart. The images are no longer part of a work task, which through their conjunction would have created the meaning of the metaphor; they are now freed to function independently, and probably at a concrete level, as anticipatory representations of physical objects or as symbolic equations (Segal 1986) of primary objects. On the other hand, if the external constraint holds but the internal boundary, preventing fusion of separate objects, weakens, then the images may condense to form composite dreamlike images.

This dynamic view provides a way of thinking about the borderline individual, in whom a hold on the symbolic function may be precarious, and the frankly schizophrenic patient who has become thought disordered and unable to symbolize or "metaphorize" at all consistently. In such patients we can at least ask whether there may not be a failure of some kind in the governing boundary conditions of linguistic and prelinguistic structures. Reminding ourselves that these boundary conditions are the limiting parental injunctions that make the development of all such structures possible, we might be led to look more closely at the ways in which parents of schizophrenic and normal children stake out and keep in place these first boundaries[4]—not to mention the ways that children react to, rebel against, attack, or accept such boundaries, and the ways that parents respond to these child reactions. To emphasize the way in which a particular symptom (in this case, a type of psychotic thought disorder) might be the outcome of earlier parental failure in boundary setting and maintenance would be in keeping with a modern trend in psychoanalytic thought that sees ego defects as resulting from environ-

---

[4]I think here of Lidz and colleagues' (1957) work on the families of schizophrenics, where a failure to preserve the normal generational and sexual boundaries was a common finding.

mental failure.[5] But it would also be in keeping with the thinking of that ingenious and creative theorizer, Gregory Bateson (Bateson et al. 1956), who formulated the double-bind hypothesis of schizophrenia some forty years ago.

Structure is a term that has recurred throughout this book, and it could be said that each chapter is about some aspect of psychological structure. From a certain point of view, psychological growth *is* the development of increasingly complex structure.

> ". . . Where id was, there ego shall be." [Freud 1933, p. 80]
> *Where formlessness was, there structure shall be.*

It could be argued that ego *is* structure or organization. Structure and organization are centrally important in differentiating ego from id, and Freud himself wrote in *The Ego and the Id*: "We have formed the idea that in each individual there is a coherent organisation of mental processes; and we call this his *ego*" (S.E. 19, p. 17). Metaphor, as I have shown, is differentiated from unconscious symbol by a more complex structure, and one of my reasons for focusing on metaphor is that it begins to highlight those structural features that distinguish higher psychological processes from more primitive ones.

In one sense, what I have been doing is to approach Freud's notion of primary and secondary processes from a different angle—from the point

---

[5]This approach, which emphasizes a failure in boundary conditions and boundary setting in psychotic thinking, would be in contrast to Bion's (1959a) approach in his paper "Attacks on linking." Bion saw the problem of psychotic thinking as arising in the patient's intolerance of any linking function, linking being related to early linking relations between objects—infant and breast, penis and vagina, mother and father, and so on. This, in keeping with much psychoanalytic thinking, places the problem firmly in the behavior of the patient rather than in that of his object. Opposition between perspectives of this kind is not, however, essential, and this could be a case in which environmental and individual perspectives could be complementary. Such a synthesis would not be Bion's, but if we saw the linkages the infant/patient attacked as being the linkages that make thought possible (its boundary conditions), and if we saw these as originating in a parental function of rule-making and boundary-setting, we could see the patient as wanting to attack such constraints if they proved to be too frustrating or even intolerable. The outcome of such attacks (with which we can probably all feel some empathy) would then depend on the relative strengths of the "holding" boundary function (as internalized) and of the attack itself (conceived also in intrapsychic terms).

of view of object relations. Another way of approaching the same distinction has been to define the transformational rules that govern the passage from primary to secondary process functioning. My attempt to clarify what is happening in such a transition has been facilitated by a systems theory type of language; in addition, metaphor has provided a paradigm of a system that, while clearly standing in secondary process, nevertheless remains nearer to primary process than ordinary discursive language.

In the next chapter, I will summarize some of the features common to any kind of structure or system. While this could be seen as an unnecessarily abstract digression from the twin themes of self and symbol formation, it may, in the end, help to clarify certain characteristics of both self and symbol that are normally overlooked when we speak in our traditional psychoanalytic ways. In order to see how higher processes and structures develop from simpler ones, we have to understand, in a *formal way*, what a structure actually is.

12 Structure and Organization

Nobody, to my knowledge, knows anything about secondary process. But it is ordinarily assumed that everybody knows everything about it. . . .
—Gregory Bateson

THE STRUCTURED AND THE UNSTRUCTURED

IN THIS CHAPTER I want to bring together a number of different ideas that hinge on the notion of structure. For a long time, psychoanalytic thought tended to ignore the importance of structure, and although with such trends as ego psychology and self psychology this is no longer completely true, there is still, in my view, a tendency to pass over structural issues in favor of a more content-oriented approach.

I am talking here about *structure* in the ordinary sense of the word, the sense in which its meaning can pass over very easily into the more precise usage of general systems theory (von Bertalanffy 1968). I am not talking about structural theory, which is a more narrow usage but one with which psychoanalysts are very familiar. Structural theory in this sense is a specifically psychoanalytical notion that refers to Freud's tripartite theory of the mind, which was ushered in with *The Ego and the Id* (1923).

To illustrate what I mean: It is the psychoanalyst's preoccupation with content at the expense of structure that would lead him to gloss over the difference between a metaphor and an unconscious symbol—the very difference I was at pains to clarify in the last chapter. Such an analyst, for example, would focus on the content of a metaphor and would treat it in exactly the same way as a dream symbol. Content analysis leads, in this way, to an elision of structural differences; structures of quite different complexity, from quite different modes of experience, become equally reduced to supposedly root structures of a more primitive kind. I am not completely against such a method of analysis for certain purposes, but the danger is that it will lead to an overly simplistic picture of the mind. The fact is that structural differences may convey as much information about an individual, and about human development, as any consideration of content, and about certain processes they will be far more informative.

The whole thrust of this book so far has been toward structure at the expense of content—toward how "self" and "world" begin to be structured in the baby's experience and how symbols and a consciousness of things begin to arise through a structuring of previously undifferentiated experience. This exploration has thrown up a number of key ideas that illuminate the notion of structure in different ways. Insofar as they illuminate what structuring involves, they also, at least implicitly, have begun to illuminate what it means in human psychological development for things to remain unstructured, or less complexly structured. In this chapter I want to bring these ideas together—to structure them—and to see whether such a closer juxtaposing and mutual informing will throw any new light on this difficult area of thought.

If we take the view that psychological development involves progressively more complex structuring of experience and behavior, we quite quickly get to the point Freud addressed in his early theories: What happens to those aspects of a person's experience or behavior that somehow escape this structuring process?

Although Freud did not specifically emphasize the importance of structuring in psychological development, his formulations seem to imply it. The system Ucs was the domain of relatively primitive (unstructured) impulses (instinctual derivatives) that had not been subject to the workings of the reality principle. It lacked the organization and coherence of conscious mental processes and was characterized by a blind pleasure seeking that did not take account of the object or the multiplicity of limiting demands constituting reality. Reality was seen primarily in terms of the constraints it imposed on more primitive impulses and their expression.

The same considerations about organization and conforming to the demands of reality were apparent in Freud's later account of the mind, where the opposition was now between ego and id. The ego was that part of the mind that had been modified by contact with external reality; the id was the realm of all that was primitive and had not been so modified.

The concepts of primary process and secondary process were Freud's attempt to formulate just how different was the functioning of the two systems. The Ucs and the id functioned according to primitive laws of primary process—time and place did not impinge in this primitive domain, and objects were free to condense and recombine in ways that were untrammeled by any normal regard for differentiated boundaries. The pleasure principle held sway. By contrast, functions and activities under the control of the ego took due account of the normal dimensions of reality. The laws of secondary process were basically those of reality.

My own attempt to conceptualize what is involved in the structuring process of development is a way of approaching the same problem that Freud was grappling with. But rather than assume, as Freud to some extent did, that we all know what "reality" is, I have tried to question that concept in various ways, teasing out in the process various elements to be thought about separately.

There are three main strands that I want to bring together under the notion of structure. The first comes from systems theory (von Bertalannfy 1968). How does systems theory help us to think about structures—of which the whole of reality is built up? And how, if at all, can we relate this apparently quite different way of thinking about things back to more psychological ideas? This is an approach I have already begun to sketch in the last chapter, where I suggested that a metaphor could be looked at as a more complex system or structure that had developed from simpler ones by accepting certain limiting conditions. In this case, the limiting conditions turned out to be the rules of engagement with objects which the child had come to accept. So here was a first bridge between the impersonal language of systems theory and a more psychological language of personal interaction.

The second idea builds on a notion that I have taken from Winnicott, but crystallized in a quotation from Rilke: "Where *you* are a place arises" (see Footnote 2, p. 33). Rilke, of course, was talking about his beloved, but I have transposed the quotation to the realm of the mother with her child. I have tried to think about the child's first structuring of the world as occurring within that space that is presided over by the mother, both in the sense that it is facilitated by her and that it is her view which will determine what is included and what is excluded from the child's reality. It is her likes and dislikes, her wishes and fears—in short, all her reactions, spoken and unspoken—that will determine the child's view of the world.

In this sense, we could say that reality is not only the place where mother is; it is also the place mother decides. It is the mother's view and, of course, later, the father's, that structures the child's behavior, self, and view of the world. Does it follow from this that reality is what the mother says it is? That the self is what the mother says it is? Or does the child also have its own structuring vision, its own symbolizing consciousness in the space where the object is not?

I move from here to thinking about the domain of the unconscious as "the place where mother is not." Playing on Freud's conception of the unconscious as a place where time and space are ignored, I think of the unconscious as a "no place"—to which no structuring consciousness has access, neither that of the mother nor that of the child.

The third strand concerns the notion of fit, which I see as fundamental to any understanding of our psychological organization. It is related to another idea that is equally fundamental—the notion of difference, of not fitting. Both ideas have already featured frequently in what I have been saying. But in the present context, I explore how they can be related to the idea of structure. Within a structure, everything has to fit with everything else. That which does not fit is excluded from the structure. However, the notions of fit and difference take us back to the very beginning—to the infant's first relation with its mother, and the question of whether her ministrations fitted or did not fit with what the infant needed or expected.

In this chapter I do not speak very much about language. This is not because I think that language is unimportant in the structuring of the child's self and world. What I have written in previous chapters should make that clear. The reason for the omission is partly the fact that it is not possible to speak of everything at once. But beyond that is the attempt that I have been making throughout to get to a place before language was so explicitly important. This is the place where vision and touch begin to separate, where things can be seen but not touched. So I try to link the thoughts that spring from this area of my concerns with the basic dichotomy between the structured and unstructured parts of the person that has exercised psychoanalysis since its beginnings.

STRUCTURE, CONFORMITY, AND CONSTRAINT

Perhaps I should begin the difficult task I have set myself by saying what I mean when I use the terms *structure* and *system*. There is no doubt that they are related terms and can sometimes be used almost interchangeably. Perhaps, though, because of systems theory connotations, the term *system* seems to have the more dynamic emphasis, *structure* the more static one. Etymologically, the term *structure* comes from the Latin *struere*, to build. It thus comes to refer to the way in which something is put together, the way in which its parts are mutually interconnected. *System* comes from the Greek *sustema*, set together, hence an organized whole. In this sense it seems little different from *structure*, but perhaps it acquired its more dynamic emphasis from its early connection with astronomy—for example, the planetary system with the planets moving according to certain laws. In my usage, I try, but do not always succeed, to use *system* when I want to emphasize the dynamic aspect.

We already have, then, the notions of things being mutually interrelated, built together as part of a larger whole, of organization, and perhaps also the notion of functional interdependence. It is not far from here to the idea of fit.

The term *fit* implies a relationship between parts: one part, usually the smaller, must fit with, or into, another part, usually the larger. On the physical level, we may think of actual shapes that fit together. But in more complex structures, we think in terms of principles of organization—the smaller part must fit in with, obey, or conform to the principles of organization of the larger structure of which it is a part. The concept of deviance highlights this fact. The deviant is the *misfit*, the one who does not fit into society or the family, who does not conform to the principles of organization, the rules, according to which that society or family runs itself. The fact of deviance highlights the rule or organizational principle that is being challenged.

Being part of a structure or system operates as a constraint on anyone or anything that is within it. By virtue of being a part of the structure or system, freedom of operation of the component part is limited. This is true whether we are considering the operation of a physical, biological, psychological, or social system. General systems theory provides a way of talking about systems wherever they occur. It is constructed at a sufficient level of abstraction that enables it to see beyond the content of any particular system to those features common to all systems. It seems to me that ideas borrowed from this theory provide the best perspective within which to organize the more formal aspects of functioning of psychological systems. However, while we can usefully consider aspects of psychoanalytic theory in the light of systems theory, at the same time, we have to remind ourselves that there can be a psychoanalysis of systems theory— of systems and structures—that can illuminate systems theory itself. Each point of view "sees" things that the other cannot.

Every structure or system has a function, and it is organized in such a way as to make that function possible. The constraint on each component part of the system is therefore in the service of a function. Something is to be done, or produced, or achieved by the system, and each component part of the system has a part function that contributes to the overall function of the system.

The science of physiology, for example, is now largely the study of such systems. Detailed theories and descriptions exist of how such systems work—the circulatory system, whose function is to circulate the blood throughout the body; the locomotor system, which serves the function of movement; the immune system, which combats infection; and so on. With increasing knowledge, it has become ever more apparent that the system must be the unit of consideration at whatever level we choose to look. Systems within systems, hierarchically organized—this is the way in which higher systems are formed. Thus, for example, we can regard the cell as a living system. But the cell itself is composed of myriad other systems, harnessed in the overall service of the particular cell's function. The cell wall, which is the boundary of the cell system, turns out to be a miniature system itself, whose function is to maintain the constancy of the internal environment of the cell, and so on. And the cell is a part of a tissue that has a function in a particular organ, which itself has a function in the overall economy of the organism. Hierarchies of systems; hierarchies of functions.

We could make a similar analysis of a large social organization such as an institution; indeed, this is one prevalent way of thinking about institutions and their operation. Again, we would see some overall function or functions of the institution, and we would be able to describe hierarchically arranged subsystems within the institution that fulfilled (through specific work tasks) a part function which contributed to the overall aim or function. Institutions are now often analyzed in terms of how well their structures serve the overall aims of the institution (Trist and Emery 1970). Sometimes it can become apparent that hidden functions or aims are undermining the institution's aims and even subverting its structure, rather in the way that hidden unconscious aims can undermine the consciously espoused aims of the personality (Menzies-Lyth 1989) or that basic assumption activities can undermine the work task of a group (Bion 1959b; see also Chapter 11, note 2).

My aim is not to elaborate in detail on specific instances of the systems way of thinking, but rather to illustrate the ubiquity of systems and the general similarity of their features in whichever setting the system is situated.

SYSTEMS, THEORIES, AND THE NEED FOR COHERENCE

In a system everything fits together. There is an exact correspondence between what the system needs and what the element of the system provides. This recalls the state of affairs of the preseparation infant, whose mother provides exactly what the child needs, at exactly the right moment. Is this purely a chance similarity? Or is there some connection between these widely disparate phenomena? Could it be that our love of systems, our need to see everything as related to everything else and having its exact place, is the heir to that moment when we first sensed that reality, the objective object, was *not* exactly what we needed? If this were so, we would have to say that all our views of reality, all our theories about the world, were at least in their formal characteristics determined by our need to celebrate and remember a time when reality seemed to be related to *us* in this entirely fitting way. We would have to see these theories about the world, which we create in the gap of difference between the real object and our recollection of it, as being there to comfort us against the possibility of chaos; and we would have to wonder whether the whole structuring tendency of our consciousness did not arise out of our initial need to reassure ourselves about this first gap in mothering.

I will address these questions more than once in the remainder of this book, but I want here to reemphasize the position I have reached that consciousness is, first of all, an awareness of a gap between a needed or expected experience and an actual one. It becomes a searching of the gap for the object that is needed; and finally, it becomes a means of symbolically realizing within the gap (i.e., thinking about and recollecting) the object that is needed. It is in this way that our consciousness can be thought of as a structuring vision that sees the pattern of things and thereby becomes the means through which our whole experience of the world and ourselves is organized. This brings us closer to Freud's system Pcs and ego, and offers a way of looking at structure and organization, the principal defining characteristics of these systems.

THE UNCONSCIOUS AS A "NO PLACE"

This account of things leaves out one important idea—the sense in which, in a dynamic way, the content of consciousness is determined by considerations of a different kind of fit. I am referring here to the idea I have already expressed that the mother's view determines how the child structures its view of self and object worlds. Only that which fits with the mother's expectations is allowed a place. That which will not fit is excluded. Where will that excluded content go and what will become of it?

It would be logical to consider that the excluded content would have to inhabit a different kind of place, which we could think of as the place of the unconscious. I want, however, to suggest a different idea and to think of the unconscious (the unstructured) as a "no place." I believe that this is a useful way of thinking about the unconscious and about Freud's concept of primary process. It is also a way of trying to relate Freud's impersonal mechanisms, systems, and processes more clearly to the experiential realities, past and present, in which they have their origin.

Suppose, then, that the unconscious is a "no place," a kind of nowhere, because it has no structural dimensions of space and time. We can ask why there is this lack of structuring and we can give at least two answers. We can pursue the idea that the unconscious content (whatever that is) has been refused access to the place of structuring (i.e., to consciousness), which is overlooked by the mother.[1] We can also say that the unconscious content is that content which has refused to be structured. The first idea points to the mother determining what shall and shall not be a part of the world; the second idea refers us implicitly to the child, who refuses to accept the rules and limitations that being part of a structure of the world necessitates. In Freud's terms, it means a nonacceptance of the reality

---

[1]It could be said that in Freud's topography the superego overlooks the ego.

principle; in my terms, it means a nonacceptance of what the mother sees and ultimately what she says.

Logic seems to require that we speak of the unconscious as "containing" all those elements that will not fit into the body of larger integrated structures (the preconscious or ego). But this lands us in a contradiction: to speak of the unconscious as a container is, in a very important sense, a contradiction in terms; for what we are talking about is precisely that which has not been able to be contained within the mother's orbit. "Being contained" implies being contained in a place or a space, being "looked after" by the mother. I am suggesting that the unconscious is not a place; it is a "no place"—a dumping ground or dustbin for *refuse* (that which has been refused).

I think it can be seen that the unconscious is, in many ways, the opposite of that place pointed to in the line: "Where *you* are a place arises." It is the "no place" where the mother is not; it is the "outer darkness," outside of the circle of her light and love, where nothing can be seen and things cannot, therefore, be related to each other within the field of (her) vision. It is an abode of banished and uncontained elements, of terrifying presences with no place in which to be.

It should be clear that I am trying to combine two different thoughts. First is the idea that consciousness is a place where the mother is present or available, and a place *because* the mother is present and available. Correlatively, the unconscious is a domain that lies outside the orbit of the mother's presence (vision) and influence. It is an unthinkable domain where the mother is not; and it is such a "no place" precisely because the mother is not there.

The second thought comes from a different frame of reference. It is the idea that consciousness operates as a structuring vision within a space of structures, while the unconscious lacks structure, and in this sense cannot be thought of as a space at all.

The linking idea is the thought that the seeking and finding and structuring activities of consciousness—in other words, the child's exploring and linking together of the patterns of the world to make structures—can *only* happen within the orbit of the mother's presence and influence. This is true whether we think of Winnicott's view that the child can play only when there is no experienced actual space of separation from the mother, or if we think of the mother as offering ready-made symbolic structures (e.g., words) to "contain" elements of the child's experience. Whichever way we think, it is the mother's presence that makes there be a place within which a structuring of the world can occur; as a result of this, the space in which we can *see* how everything is joined together is this very place, the space of consciousness.

The unconscious is not a place, because it is not blessed with the mother's presence. The contents of the unconscious are those that were unacceptable to the mother. They have not been able, for whatever reason, to be contained within the space of her presence nor within the symbolic garment she weaves about her child. It is because they have not been accessible to the structuring vision of consciousness that the unconscious is not structured.

The dichotomy Cs–Ucs in this way becomes the dichotomy between the space where the mother is and the space where she is not.

I have been thinking throughout this section of the mother's presence in a relatively nonspecific way. I have been guided by such general notions as Winnicott's "facilitating mother," Bowlby's "attachment," and Suttie's "primary need for the mother." This has led me to speak in a very general way about the mother's presence and of consciousness as being within the orbit of the mother's presence and influence. At the same time, I have alluded to the structuring function of the mother, the way in which she determines the child's reality and offers to the child containing structures for some, but not all, of his experience. I have been aware, as I write, of a certain ambivalence toward this idea, feeling that it was giving too much power to the mother in determining the child's view of the world; and something in me wanted to protest and say: "What about the child's own structuring of reality? What about the child's play? What about the ideas the child forms for himself about the nature of things and the world?"

I now think that this wish on my part to curtail the power of the mother has prevented me from making explicit something that has all along been implicit in my argument. This is the idea that the power of the mother to structure her child's consciousness of things resides in the fact that the child himself needs the mother to see everything that he does. The child needs the mother to confirm his actions and later his thoughts; in order to do this, they have to take place within the orbit of her presence and influence, where she can see them. In other words, I have underplayed the visual, "seeing" nature of the maternal presence, and

failed to spell out sufficiently that it is the mother's structuring *vision* that
first structures the child's vision (consciousness) of the world.

I can try to trace the development of this need of the child to be seen. It
seems obvious that, in the beginning, the mother's presence and influence
must be linked with the possibility of the child's being able to see where
the mother is. Being conscious of her presence means being able to see
her (and perhaps hear her). But at a certain point in time, the child
becomes aware that the mother can see him and what he does. Everything
takes place within her view; the fact that the mother sees all that the child
does becomes a means of confirming the validity of those things, their
goodness, even their actuality: "If she can see it, too, then it is real"—the
beginnings of consensual validation. I am reminded here of George
Berkeley's view that the world existed only in the mind of God. His
phrase *Esse est percipi*, "To be is to be perceived," captures very well the
power of being seen to validate our sense of personal reality.

If we accept this linkage of the maternal space with what the mother
can see, then it could be thought that, initially, *the dichotomy between
what is conscious and what is unconscious might depend on the mother's
seeing*. All that which she can see, recognize, and later name becomes
part of the larger structure of the child's conscious awareness. Each thing
that she cannot see—either because she ignores it, or refuses to acknowledge it, or because the child does not allow her to see it—becomes an
isolated, unstructured element in the developing domain of the unconscious. According to this view, consciousness in the child is linked indis-
solubly to the mother—it is coterminous with that which can be integrated within *her* structuring vision.

These thoughts can now make some contact with questions of language. While the mother's structuring or containment can certainly be
prior to language, since it presupposes an acceptance or encouragement
which may be purely nonverbal, the naming of something can only occur
through language. And it is the naming of something, as we saw in
Chapter 9, that above all seems to be important in drawing an object out
from the thing world of experience into the quite different universe of
things said. It is the name that facilitates the separation of the idea or
concept of something from the thing itself and allows it to be referred to
and shared with others in the space where the object is not. And it is the
name of something that also facilitates its being drawn into a linguistic
universe in which everything is structured and everything has its place. As

Helen Keller observed (see Chapter 8), it is the name that enables everything to be seen "with a strange new sight," a new kind of vision.

SEEING AND NOT SEEING— THE CONSCIOUS–UNCONSCIOUS DICHOTOMY

To speak of consciousness seems always to refer us back to vision and seeing. To be conscious of something is to be able to "see" it, and to "see" where it fits in with everything else. I want to examine this Cs–Ucs dichotomy in terms of vision.

If we take the notion of conscious seeing seriously, the equivalence of not seeing with unconsciousness takes on a new meaning: the domain of the unconscious can be thought of as somewhere outside of seeing, an "outer darkness"; it invites the idea that the unconscious is a blind man's space (see Chapter 4). It is somewhere, but it cannot be experienced as a space at all. It has extension, but that extension is deprived of the organizing power of vision. It is a gap, a cliff to nothingness at the edge of the world, a darkness, where the light peters out. It is a darkness, where first the light of the mother's face goes out, and after that the light of her understanding.

In this "no place" nothing is related clearly to anything else. Unconscious elements are unstructured and uncontained. They are isolated and not related to each other in consistent or coherent ways; they lack structural organization. *Something is there, but we do not know what it is. If there is no sight, we are thrown back into a world of touch and other proprioceptive sensory modalities with their tendency toward all or none operation.* Our "knowledge" of such things is carnal, immediate, evanescent: all or none; something touches me or it does not. There is contact or there is nothing. Recognition and affinity in such a world would be based on patterns that were felt and sensed, not on patterns that were seen: homologies of texture and bodily sensations, rhythms and patterns of sound, rather than the clearly differentiated outlines of visually perceived external form.

Since the rules governing structures have not been accepted, felt affinities pass directly to primitive identification and fusion; none of the "holding offs" that would lead to comparison and recognition of differences apply. The power of vision to insert distance and promote differentiation is excluded. To recognize an object is once again to fuse with it.

This world—of fluid and indistinct boundaries; of momentary combinations and recombinations; of like piling on like in confused images; of identities, not similarities—is, it seems to me, the world of dreams that Freud described. It is a prestructural world, a world that has not yet accepted, or has once again refused, the rules that make structures and ordering possible. It is a world that refuses the primacy of vision,[2] a world in which condensation and displacement, not comparison, are the order of the day. Recognition leads to union (or more accurately, reunion) with the object, not to relationship with it and greater knowledge of it; the pleasure principle, not the reality principle, holds sway.

STRUCTURING VISION AND APPROPRIATIVE LOOKING

There is one snag to this argument. If dreams are the main embodiment of the unstructured, uncontained elements of this "blind" domain, how is it that dreams are so often visual—indeed, vision seems to be their dominant sensory modality? How is it possible to speak of a blind man's world, when all about us in dreams are vivid images and colors?

This would seem to be a serious blow to any attempt to equate consciousness and vision, unconsciousness and blindness. It seems that the metaphor of the blind man's world is leading us astray, even though it seems to tell us something about the domain of the unconscious.

I believe the answer to this apparent contradiction lies in the different ways in which vision can be used. In the dream, vision is part of a total and immediate apprehension of the world, where we are immersed in an unreflective doing and experiencing of things—a sensually involved experience, where vision has only the degree of dominance that it has in such unreflective living in our ordinary lives. There are no barriers between seeing and doing, between the wish and its consummation; or if there are,

---

[2]According to my argument, the primacy of vision precedes the primacy of the symbolic (in the sense of fully fledged representational symbols). As development proceeds, the verbal-symbolic comes to overlay and almost obscure the visual roots of consciousness, and we come to equate consciousness with verbal apprehension. Although such an equation has an approximate truth and may be pragmatically useful, it obscures all the earlier developments that paved the way for verbal-symbolic apprehension and makes it difficult for us to relate to forms of consciousness other than the verbal (see Chapter 14).

they seem to be the barriers and obstructions of the sensually perceived world, not the proddings of conscience or the wider implications of what we are doing. Similarly, in dream, we seem to move from one structure of experience to another, without knowing how the transition was made. The experiential structures activated in dreams seem to be separate modules of experience that are not related in any way. This brings us once more to the disjointedness of unconscious elements, or at least of those elements that have not been exposed to the organizing power of conscious vision.

If this is so, it is not so much a question of whether one system is characterized by vision and another by touch; it is more a question of the way in which vision is being used in each case. Is it being used merely as a leading modality to take the person to the object of his desire? Or is it being used in an essentially distanced way, providing a field for observation, a perspective, within which all the elements in the field can be related to all the others?

In the first case, vision is serving the goal of consummation with the object in actuality. In the second case, consummation with the object has been abandoned in the interests of knowing more about the object, what it is doing and where it is—in other words, in the interests of a more perspectival view of the object field. Such an organizing vision seems to imply a shift from primitive and egocentric goal-seeking behavior to a more complex aim in which understanding the activities of the object in its own nexus of relationships has at least temporarily become more important than trying to obtain immediate fulfillment with the object.

It was this developmental shift that I was describing in Chapter 4. I spoke of it as the separating of "looking" from "doing," the insertion of a boundary into a previously untrammeled relationship with the object in such a way as to create a space between the subject and the object within which the image of the object could be entertained. I described how this first purely visual space, to which "doing" had no access, could be seen as a prerequisite for symbol formation and therefore a first stage in the development of mind. In later chapters I went on to show that this representational space became gradually strengthened through the oedipal period and finally held in place by the insertion of the oedipal father's prohibitions against possession of the body of the mother. I argued that a part of the mind became guaranteed in this way as a purely observational space, a space for thought.

It is this purely observational space, in which a structure that is independent of the self can be viewed and understood from the outside, that provides the arena for conscious mental activity. It is a space of fully separated symbols whose function is purely representational. This carefully guarded space offers to the subject a purely observational and symbolically mediated vision that can perceive an entire field of objects and relate them to one another, not just to the self; it includes the capacity to move out of one's own position to the position of a third person, in order to be able to view the structure of which one is a part from the outside. It thus enables the subject to move in imagination from within a structure to outside of it, and to see a single structure from many different viewpoints. It is this ability to maintain an objective view, together with the ability to move in imagination from the position of one observer to that of another—to obtain multiple views of a particular field—that underpins the synthesizing, structuring function of consciousness (see Chapter 13).

If I have in some measure resolved one contradiction into which my argument has led me, by indicating how it is that the unconscious is relatively blind and fragmented, I seem to have created a second contradiction by describing the space of structuring vision and clearly interrelated forms as standing in the shadow of the Father. For until this point, I had been talking of a space that was the province of the mother, a place of maternal presence, and it was her care and containing, her vision, her looking after what the child was doing, that allowed there to be any structuring of things at all. Have I now changed my ground completely and decided that, after all, the space of consciousness is a space made possible by the father?

To resolve this issue in any satisfactory way would take me beyond what is possible within the purview of this chapter. I believe, however, that the contradiction is not as serious as it might appear; it arises from thinking about the conscious mind as a single space, standing in some way against an ill-defined and murky region of unconscious elements. That model seems to force a view of consciousness that is fixed and cannot vary. If that is so, then the answer may lie in finding a more dynamic way of thinking about consciousness that gives scope for different modes of being conscious and aware of things operating at different times and serving different functions. This could make room for a variety of conscious spaces or systems fulfilling different functions according to circumstances, and would dispose of the more static view which seems to force one into making a fixed choice between alternative descriptions. I must, however, leave further elaboration of this question until another chapter (see Chapter 14), as I still have something to say about the basic constitution of a system.

SYSTEM, REALITY, AND CONSCIOUSNESS

Within systems theory, the system is the basic unit of reality. Reality is made up of systems within systems within systems . . . , and understanding reality necessitates understanding what are the basic elements that go to make up a system.

Systems theory, however, is only a theory, an attempt to symbolically reflect reality, and as such can be seen as part of the human attempt to understand the world.

Perhaps the most difficult part of such a process of understanding is to come to terms with the complete separateness and independence of reality from us, and the complete separateness and independence of reality from our theories. It does not conform with our wishes or our theories as the adaptive mother did, and in its being it is oblivious to our existence.

The ability to conceive of reality in this way—as composed of objects that interact and form systems independent of us—links, I believe, to the oedipal achievement of being able to tolerate two objects, the parents, in interaction within their own bounded space, in a way that absolutely excludes the child who now has only an observer status.

I have already established that consciousness, at least in its most highly developed and structuring form, derives from this same achievement. It is thus, in effect, one and the same development that constitutes, on the one hand, an observational consciousness, and on the other, what we might reasonably think of as the basic unit of reality-reflecting thought—a system.

I want to describe a very simple system. In Figure 12–1 the shaded areas represent objects, the connecting arrows the interaction of these objects. The surrounding line represents the boundary of the structure. The nonshaded area within the boundary is the space within which the interaction is occurring; the arrow leading from the system, marked (f),

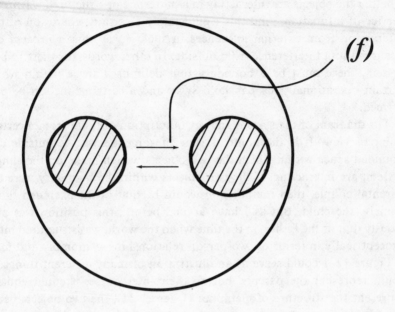

Figure 12-1. Essential elements of a system.

indicates the function or purpose of the structure. Within the structure, including the boundary line, the operational rules or the principles of organization of the system hold sway. The boundary is the limit of the system and anything outside of that is not under its control.

We might make a tentative definition of a system:

A system is an interaction of two or more objects within a bounded space in the service of a function.

If we imagine one object on its own, this is not a system. There is no interaction serving a function.[3] What if we imagine two objects interact-

---

[3]It might be asked: What of the human being on his own? Isn't the human being a system? The answer is no if we think of the person in isolation. There is only a system if we think of two or more people interacting within an organization, however informal that might be. It

ing? Is that a system? The answer is that it may be; but this depends on whether the objects are interacting in a patterned or structured way in the service of a function. And this would imply a certain separation of this interaction from external influences in such a way that a process can occur without interference from outside. In other words, for there to be a system, there must be a boundary that delimits a space within which certain operational rules can hold sway and a certain function be performed.

The diagram of the system and my description of it are from a certain point of view. It is the point of view of someone who is outside this bounded space within which the two objects, which make up the simple system, are interacting. If the two objects within the boundary were the parental couple, then the position would be that of the excluded third, namely, the child. But as I have argued before, this position was previously that of the father, in the time when the world was structured more egocentrically in terms of two-person relationships—"mommy and me."

Figure 12–1 could serve as an illustration of many different things. It could represent the parents' having their intercourse; it could equally represent the structure of metaphor (Chapter 11), the two objects being the two images interacting to produce a meaning. I believe that the diagram represents the simplest system that can be imagined, and in that sense it can be regarded as the basic building block of thought that has to be grasped before a person can begin to build up any picture at all of a world independent of the self.

The parts of a system are all interrelated. The boundary marks the limit of the system. It demarcates or delimits it from what is outside. It protects the system from "nonconforming" outside influences, and it marks out an area of constraint within which the activity of component objects is constrained by certain operational rules to ensure the fulfillment of a function. It may also prevent those component objects from leaving the field. (Examples of system boundaries are the cell membrane,

---

might be just two people talking on the street who could be regarded as forming a system for the duration of their conversation. The isolated person, however, can be regarded as a psychological system if we look *into* him—we can then consider interacting parts of his mind as forming a system (e.g., internal objects interacting within an inner space). Similarly, if we think of his physical parts or biochemical parts, we again have a multiplicity of functions and a multiplicity of systems.

the analytic setting, the marriage contract, and the boundary between consciousness and unconsciousness.)

The objects within a system are constrained by those operational rules that ensure the function, the laws of the system, and they accept that constraint. A nonconforming object will be extruded by the system, or the function of the system will have to change in order to include it. (Examples of objects in a system are the cell nucleus, mitochondria, and ribosomes within the cell; the patient and the analyst in the analytic setting; the partners in a marriage; and symbolic objects in the space of consciousness.)

The space of the system is harder to define, but one can think of it as the container of all the component parts that go to make up the system. It allows room for the ordered operations of the system relatively free from outside interference. (Examples here are the interior of the cell, the analytic hour and space, the spatiotemporal envelope of the marital interaction, and the "space" of consciousness.)

All of this is quite abstract but absolutely fundamental. These are the ground rules of systemic organization, whether of ego, self, society, family, marriage, business operation, or of the biological system of the cell. They are also the ground rules of the metaphor system, described in the last chapter, of language as a set of conceptual markers, and of thought as a system of symbols reflecting reality.

Finally, as I have pointed out, they are the ground rules that mark the resolution of the Oedipus complex, and this is a fact of fundamental importance. The parental couple, interacting in their own shared and exclusive space with its containing boundary, is the first external system that the child must recognize, and therefore forms the basis for the recognition of all later systems.

PSYCHOLOGICAL DEVELOPMENT AND SYSTEMIC COMPLEXITY

From a systems point of view, psychological development has two major thrusts: the first is the development of ever more complex structures and systems from simpler ones; the second, a developing awareness of such structures, in particular, those structures in which the self is a participant.

These two lines correspond very roughly to Freud's notions about the development of ego from id, on the one hand, and of consciousness from unconsciousness, on the other. Both developments also correspond, in some degree, with Freud's related ideas about the change from primary process to secondary process functioning, and from pleasure principle to reality principle or reality adaptedness. In various ways, this book attempts to clarify the nature of these transformations and the means to their achievement. I have already indicated how Freud's objective and mechanistic terminology might be translated into a language that would state more clearly the interpersonal and object-relational framework of mind. But I think one can also see that Freud knew more than he was able to express within the constraints of his mechanistic language.

The development of complex structures from simpler ones is a matter that Freud was always concerned with; I think he understood clearly the issues that were involved, even though he lacked the conceptual tools to formulate his views in a way that was satisfactory. His espousal of instinct as the basic unit of analysis made it difficult for him to grasp the profound changes in function that can be brought about by an increase in structural complexity; and the notion of emergent function, a function that is completely new, arising purely from an increased complexity of organization, was perhaps difficult for him to entertain. It was easier to see the old structure within the new than to see something radically new arising from the old.

However, one part of Freud's work that got close to systems theory was libido theory, with its idea of component sexual instincts (oral, anal, phallic) that each dominated behavior in succession. In the genital organization of the libido, all component instincts were gathered into a new system with a new superordinating function. In systems theory language, the component instincts no longer operated as isolated structures, but were integrated into a larger structure. The original functions of the earlier structures were now subordinated to the hierarchical dominance of the genital function. Insofar as they found expression in the new structure, the earlier aims were curtailed and constrained, for example, as foreplay to the sexual act. They no longer had unbridled expression. Similarly, the genital organization implied an acceptance of the wishes and needs of the other person in the relationship, so that the structure of genital organization further constrained the purely egocentric functioning of the component instincts.

The example provides a glimpse of how a simpler structure is incorporated into a larger structure with loss of its autonomy and increased constraints on its functioning. Its previously free expression is subordinated to the function of a larger structure, which is hierarchically superior to the part structure and exercises a control function on it.

I believe it could be demonstrated that this is a major principle of psychological growth, as it is of biological growth, and that if we wish to imagine what ego is, we have to think of it in this way—as a structure that becomes increasingly complex and hierarchical, with every step in growth and complexity bringing about a further subordination and constraint of earlier structures and functions and the emergence of new functions. Whereas biological growth tends to occur through the unfolding of a genetically programed sequence of events, psychological growth almost certainly is less programed, and thus more subject to the shaping of an interpersonal and social environment. The systemic organization of the self and the coherent organization of behavioral patterns into an interrelated whole owe more to the social expectations and applied constraints of parents and family than to any autonomous process. With the development of the self there is always the possibility of system forming and structure building not occurring, or miscarrying in some way, through the failure of the rule-making function on which social as opposed to biological systems depend. Obviously, it was this aspect of psychological development that Freud was trying to express in his writings about the superego.

Another well-known piece of psychoanalytic theory that can be thought of in a systems way is the Kleinian concept of development from paranoid-schizoid to depressive positions. These can be thought of as two organizations or structurings of psychological function; in normal development, the earlier paranoid-schizoid organization would evolve into the depressive position. The paranoid-schizoid organization involves simpler structures of part objects or split objects that function relatively independently of each other and are, indeed, kept apart in a defensive way. The depressive organization is a more integrated structure in which part objects and part functions come together in a larger structure centered on the whole object. This brings about a curtailment of the earlier part object expressions (e.g., in relation to aggression) with the recognition that the attacked object is the same as the one that is loved. Guilt, concern, and reparation are new functions that emerge from the new organization. They can be thought of as the new controlling functions of the structure,

aggression, for example, no longer being unbridled, because of its consequences. Here again, though, the development in question cannot be
thought of as innately programed and automatic. Its achievement depends on the quality of mothering that is provided, not only on the
continuity and consistency of the mother's being there, but on her capacity to "hold" or "contain" her infant's impulsive expressions.

One very important question that is implicit in my whole project is the
part that language plays in the development of psychological systems.
There is no doubt that in the beginning, and for quite some time during
early development, the infant has no understanding of what language
means or expresses. The growth into being able to understand and use
language is probably the most important systemic development that the
child has to make. It seems to be clear from this point of view that the
first systems the child becomes a part of are purely behavioral (e.g.,
systems of interaction with the mother). The rules of engagement that
shape these systems are purely implicit. In this sense, early development
would seem to be uncontaminated by, and uninvolved with, language.
Nevertheless, a closer look suggests that this is not strictly true. This is
because the world in which the mother is living is through and through a
human, and therefore a linguistically shaped, world; everything that the
mother does, and the way she does it, is shaped by human reasons that
can, in principle, be expressed in words. The forms into which the child is
being behaviorally rather than linguistically inducted are thus forms that
are part of the linguistically described reality that is the human world. I
think that this is perhaps the sense of Lacan's assertion that the child is
born into language. The patterns that shape him may be behavioral, but
they themselves are rooted in the forms of language.

Learning to symbolize means learning to stand off from the object that
we were engaged with in order to "see" it and hence come to know it
better. It is what we can "see" that we can "put into" words. The rules of
engagement for symbolizing are quite different from those for doing, and
when we are symbolizing, we are part of a quite different system from
that which we are in when we are doing. I have tried to make these
differences explicit, especially in the last two chapters. Symbolizing and
thinking require that the person be outside the structure they are symbolizing and thinking about, though inevitably they would then be situated
within another structure. But whether we are engaged within a lived
structure or are reflecting upon (i.e., thinking about) that structure from

somewhere else, the basic ground rules of system and structure have in each case to be followed. In both cases, separation, distance, and limiting boundaries have to be upheld. Their inviolateness is the condition of reality-integrated action, just as it is of reality-reflecting thought.

SYMBOLIC SYSTEMS: TRANSITIONAL COMFORT OR "OBJECTIVE" REFLECTION?

I will finish this chapter with some further reflections on the notion of fit. I have spoken of the necessity of an element to "fit in" with the rules of a structure if it is to be a functional part of it and also of the way that structures fit together to make larger and hierarchically organized wholes. I want now to say that both reality and the self are organized in this way; when we speak of either, we are referring to this situation in which everything is integrated into a state of affairs and has its place. Wittgenstein (1922) said that the world was the totality of "facts," the totality of everything that was "the case." I think by this he did not mean the "noumenal" reality of Kant that we can never actually know. He was referring to a much more human construction: the reality within which we live.

A feature of this human reality is that it aspires to the quality of a seamless garment—everything will be related to everything else, and there will be no gaps in the structure at all. Everything has a place, and everything "fits in"; everything has a name, and everything can be explained. It is language that enables us to make such structures, in which the coherence of the symbolic order covers over the gaps—the unpredictability and capriciousness of raw experience. Language gives us symbolic markers for things in the world and enables us to more than half-believe that the coherence we find in reality or the self is the coherence of the thing-in-itself, not merely the coherence of its symbolic representation.

The coherent system which language creates is the fiction with which we paste over the cracks in the underlying structure—that, anyway, is the danger. I am talking about theories, ideologies, religions, self-images, and worldviews. The thing that does not "fit" with the system is a serious problem; it is a threat to the system and as such must be disposed of. Suppression, repression, expulsion, nonrecognition, covering up, pretense:

the mechanisms of disposal are similar wherever the problem occurs. The system is more important than the individual deviant, the misfit, or the exception, because security depends on the system's continuance. It is better to destroy the evidence than to turn the system on its head.

What is this deep insecurity which makes the system more important than the individual or the deviant instance? To answer this we have to go back to the very beginning and recall a different kind of "fit." This is the area of Winnicott's adaptive mother, who was able to make reality be what the infant needed: her "breast"—her actual breast, no doubt, but also her holding, smiling, caring, cooing, and talking—as well as her face and voice and smell, all of this had just the right "shape," just the right configuration, and was given in just the right moment to be what the baby wanted. In this way, the baby could feel that its own want or lack had created the answering reality. *There was no gap, no discrepancy, no rift in the mother–infant continuum.* Surely this state of total coincidence between wanting and finding must be the image of all later security?

As time goes on, a developing gap between need and satisfaction marks the beginning of separateness and, in some primitive sense, of separation anxiety. But in the favorable situation that Winnicott describes, the gap in experience, the gap of "no mother," is never too large for the infant to tolerate. Anxiety is calmed and the gap in experience is healed by the mother's real presence and through the creation of the transitional object (see Chapter 5).

Where the situation is less favorable, there will develop an actual space or gap in experience as separation proceeds. There will be times when the mother cannot be "felt," and that, in Winnicott's terms, is really the first catastrophe, whose recurrence is always feared. When Winnicott says to the anxious patient that the catastrophe has already happened, he is talking about this primal catastrophe when the gap became too big; as a result there was a gap in the continuity of being, a hiatus that could not be bridged. I think it is this gap, in the space where the mother is with the infant, that opens the window to some unseeable and unthinkable place of outer darkness, which is not a "place," and where the mother is not. It is the glimpse of this window that makes the baby reach for its cuddly blanket and the adult to reach for his seamless symbolic garments that he has forged for himself to keep the terrors away. The seamless symbolic garment closes off the gap of discrepancy, and everything once again is known and predictable and in place.

I am once again talking about theories, ideologies, religions, self-images, and worldviews, which define a "place," a state of affairs, in which the self and the mother can be clearly seen to be related. The crack in that state of affairs, through which the person had glimpsed himself as lost and without the mother and surrounded by terrifying "presences," is the crack that is opened up by the first separation from the mother and closed over in varying degrees by developing symbolic activity. In its highest development, symbolic activity can be used to know about this crack in the fullness of being and to look beyond it to see what is there. In its very constitution, such symbolic activity implies a capacity to stand back and *see* and thus a certain tolerance for separation. It was this kind of knowing and looking to which Freud aspired and which in considerable measure he achieved. The problem, however, of a symbolic garment such as Freud's theory, which originally enabled there to be *an extension of seeing and knowing*, is that it can become, through a kind of regression and loss of distance and separation, the transitional mantle that hides the crack from us, *a means of not knowing and not seeing and a vehicle of reassurance*. All our images of self and world have this same potential.

It is a lack of fit that starts the first process of separation going, and yet the notion of fit becomes central in the processes of thought, in the finding of words to fit our thoughts and of theories to fit our facts. We can only understand reality at all in terms of things fitting or not fitting with each other, as perhaps my discussion of structure and systems in this chapter illustrates. It is as though the perfect fit that we once experienced becomes a most treasured possession that we may still use in the symbolic world of thought. *We refind in thought the perfect fit that we have lost in reality*.

The dynamic of this process, however, includes the possibility of regression, and it is not always obvious when this is happening. Regression to concrete thinking is sometimes obvious, as when it leads to psychotic thought disorder. It can be much more subtle and hard to detect when the loss of distinction between symbol and thing symbolized occurs in relation to theory. When this happens, there is a reification of theory: the concept or the idea is related to as though it were a concrete and indisputable reality, the thing-in-itself, not just a way of seeing it. The crack, the discrepancy, is closed (see p. 322).

This reification of theory is probably something that happens all the time. It may occur in some individuals more than others, and will tend to occur in each of us when our tolerance for separation from the object decreases. At those times, the separated symbol again becomes a transitional object, and the urge to see and know is replaced by the need to refind the certainty and security of the object we have lost. Reality-*reflecting* thought then becomes reality-*creating* illusion.

We have to recall that the creation of the transitional object is the baby's response to this incipient intrusion of reality. So, in the adult case, the comforting pattern is retained in preference to the obtruding difference. When this happens, the thought object, the piece of theory, becomes an experiential substitute for the real object that is no longer available. The new reality, which does not fit, is avoided by clinging to the old pattern and wiping out the difference. In this way, knowledge is sacrificed to experiential continuity, and the position of the self within a familiar structure of experience is not disturbed.

It may be that knowledge about a structure can only be obtained when there is a change in that structure, or more importantly, in our experience of it.[4] Unchanging operation of a structure or system, and of the self that

---

[4]If we want to think biologically—and there certainly is a sense in which our theories should be compatible with biological thinking—we might try to link these issues of sameness and difference with a very well-known strand of biological thought. For at least one hundred years, the "constancy of the internal environment" (Claude Bernard) has been a mainstay of physiological thinking. Any change in the internal environment of the organism is reacted to in such a way as to reduce the difference and return the state of affairs toward that which existed before. This internal homeostasis is regarded as essential to the functioning of the organism and is really only an earlier way of talking of something that we might describe using a more systems type of language. It is a feature of systems that they operate within more or less tight constraints; indeed, as I have tried to show, the system can be defined by the constraints that it places on its component parts, which are interacting in the service of a function.

When we look at the external environment of the organism, we find a similar tendency toward constancy, though one that is not necessarily mediated in the same way. What we see here are behavioral systems that are adapted to a certain environment; if the environment changes, the first reaction of the organism is likely to be one of threat. Certainly if we think of the mammals, we can perceive an attempt to locate and identify the change or difference in the environment, as a preliminary to dealing with it. For example, a sound might provoke an orientating response, alertness, searching for the source of the sound, followed by some variety of fight-or-flight reaction. We can think here in terms of the preservation of the organism, but we can also think about what has happened as an attempt to keep the environment in a harmonious and fitting state with the organism. The intruding visitor is driven out or destroyed, so that a status quo *ante* is reinstated.

If we think of the human situation, we are speaking mainly of the social environment. In this case, the familiar expected environment to which the human being is adapted is that

is a part of that system, results only in an unreflective perpetuation of a state of affairs. When there is a change in the system, or in the self as a part of that system, a gap of difference is introduced into awareness, which stimulates panic or provokes curiosity, depending on the security of the person who is involved. This gap, in a certain sense, recreates the original gap of separation from the object; it raises anew the question of whether the gap is to be sealed over, or whether that new piece of the objective world that is announcing its presence in this way is going to be discovered.

The answer to this question depends on whether the objectively perceived world is felt to be manageable or not, and it seems reasonable to suppose that this depends on how the original gap in experience was handled. Where curiosity prevails, exploration follows; exploration involves looking at the object from many different angles. In relation to human realities, this tends to mean looking at the same thing through the eyes of different people. This capacity is certainly not one we are born with; it can scarcely be thought to occur before a clear sense of self and other is established. As I indicated in Chapter 2, I believe it can occur well before language has become the major means of knowing another's view, but the acquisition of language will greatly enlarge its scope. Seeing through the eyes of the other person means not only hearing what he says but, more basically, putting ourselves in imagination in his place and trying to see what he can see.

In the next chapter I will explore in more detail what this movement from self to other involves and how we relate to what we see through the other's eyes. It will involve yet again trying to understand the way in which we use the other's view in both structure-building and structure-denying operations, and in particular how it enables us to enlarge our self-awareness and our vision of the world.

---

which has been patterned by past experience. The pattern here is a part of the self, the implicit or assumptive world, the representational world, that represents (social) reality to the individual. When actual contemporary reality deviates from this representational reality, then the issue becomes one of systemic constancy versus systemic change. The system in question is the person's "map" of the world. If that were to be acknowledged to be faulty, there would be a sense of confusion and panic. Therefore, the tendency is to cling to the representational reality rather than to acknowledge the actual discrepancy. The person does this by blocking out the discrepant evidence and continuing to believe that reality is what he needs it to be.

13 Position and View

Then felt I like some watcher of the skies
When a new planet swims into his ken;
Or like stout Cortez when with eagle eyes
He star'd at the Pacific—and all his men
Look'd at each other with a wild surmise—
Silent, upon a peak in Darien.
—John Keats, "On First Looking into Chapman's Homer"

WHEN THE FIRST astronauts were shot into space, they may not have been fully prepared for the far-reaching and lasting effects the experience would have on them. They were expecting, perhaps, to find something completely new. What I think they did not anticipate was that their most lasting impressions would have to do with seeing something very familiar in a new way.

Some of their experiences were summarized by Kevin Kelley (1988) in *The Home Planet—Images and Reflections of Earth from Space Explorers.* In his introduction, Kelley writes: "Many astronauts and cosmonauts, upon returning from their missions, report changes that are powerful and life-transforming, whole-life changes they attribute to the simple experience of looking back at our home planet from the remoteness of space." He goes on: "*Space offers us a chance to see our world with new eyes* [italics added], a perspective that may have great significance for the planet for all of the future."

Summarizing his own experiences of interviewing so many astronauts, sharing their experiences, and seeing so many images of space that the missions had brought back, Kelley writes: "Something has happened to me in the making of this book. . . . *The context of my reality has broadened* [italics added]." He goes on to speak of his new sense of the earth's fragile existence and its place in the solar system, the galaxy, and the universe.

What is common to many of the astronauts' accounts is a new perception of the earth as a whole; it is no longer limitless, vast, and invulnerable, but small, bounded, fragile, and located in a much larger context. For example, James Irwin, one of the earliest space travelers, writes: "That beautiful, warm living object looked so fragile, so delicate that if you touched it with a finger it would crumble and fall apart. Seeing this has to change a man. . . ." Many astronauts also echoed the view of a Saudi Arabian space traveler, who spoke of his experiences circling the planet in this way: "The first day or so we all pointed to our countries. The third or fourth day we were pointing to continents. By the fifth day we were aware of only one Earth."

The importance of this dramatic example lies not only in the changed view of our planet Earth that it has helped to foster, but in the way it graphically illustrates how a changed position in relation to an object, giving a different view and perspective of it, has far-reaching emotional and cognitive repercussions.

If for planet Earth we substitute the mother of the small child, and if for that point in space from which a view can be obtained we substitute the position of the father, who lies outside the mother–infant pair, we come to the *first* moment in our experience of such a transforming and transformative vision. This is the moment, in a schematic sense, when the infant is first able to move in imagination to the position of the third person in a triangular relationship, and to glimpse his earlier lived relationship from the outside.

The importance of this move for the development of the child's consciousness and its capacity to form and use symbols is very great. It is a move that, once mastered, becomes a major tool of our thinking and symbolizing, the primary means through which we come to be aware of ourselves as objects with a particular place in the world. In this chapter I want to explore this transforming development of consciousness in a variety of ways—not only in terms of its initial occurrence in the move from a two-person to a three-person organization of experience, but also in its more formal characteristics as a structure of our adult consciousness.

GETTING OUTSIDE OF THE SELF

The child living within a dyadic relationship with the mother is immersed in its immediacy. The mother is the limit and horizon of the child's world, the bringer of satisfactions and the imposer of limits that have to be accepted or fought. The mother is the first *object*, in the literal as well as the psychoanalytic sense of the word, and the child's relation to the mother is similar to that of the inhabitants of earth to the planet—she is immensely important but is taken for granted, except when she is not there.

How does the child get outside this two-person structure of which he is a part in such a way that he can begin to apprehend its nature? In a formal sense, there is only one way—by moving to the position of the third person in a three-person relationship. The child now stands where the father stands and sees his previous world through the father's eyes. Just as the astronaut looked back at the earth and saw the planet as a whole, so the child can now look back in imagination at himself and the mother and perceive a new kind of unity, "mommy-and-me," with the new external vision that the father provides.

How the child gets to that position is not my immediate concern. The necessity of accepting an excluded position in the oedipal triangle probably plays an important part; the love of the father and being drawn by this from out of an exclusive involvement with the mother surely also play their part. What concerns me at the moment is to define the formal changes that this move brings about. I can best describe these changes by a series of numbered points:

1. The child's earlier *lived* structure has become a *looked-at* structure. Doing and having have given way to looking.
2. The earlier lived structure, of which the child was a part, is now bounded and seen as a whole. The external vision of the third position has given it an "outside," an external boundary.
3. By the same vision, it has acquired a place within a new organization of objects. The structure "mommy-and-me" is now just one object within a larger organization of objects. For the astronaut, the earth was, first of all, the background for all his activities—his family, his house, his country, his home. Through a new and

totalizing[1] external vision it becomes "the planet," in which personal concerns and projects shrink into a larger perspective. It is the planet we all share, the world which must be looked after, the world that revolves in space and is part of the solar system, the galaxy, and the universe.

4. To all intents and purposes, this new vision of the object has created a new and more complex object. It is also a more complete object. The new view shows the earth as a system of interdependent parts in which all are related to all; likewise, the child has now to see himself as part of an interdependent unit with the mother, where what he does affects what the mother does as much as the other way about.

5. It is fundamentally important to realize that what is mediated by this changed position is nothing more nor less than a new *view*—it is entirely a matter of "seeing." The change of seeing may lead to a change of doing, but this is secondary. The system formed by the new seeing lies beyond the reach of touch; it is in the mind, although it reflects what is there in the world. The astronaut cannot touch the fragile earth that he sees from space. He can only talk about it and allow the lasting vision of it in his mind to alter what he does on the earth and to the earth. Similarly, the child cannot do anything with or to the new structure of the world—himself and mother as an interactive unit—that he has glimpsed through the father's eyes. He can only allow it to affect the way he relates to his mother.

6. It can be seen that the move to the outside of an earlier lived structure relativizes the position of the subject. Within the dyadic, lived structure, the subject experiences himself as the center of the world; the world (the mother) being either taken for granted or loved and hated by turns, according to the degree to which she satisfies or frustrates. The move to the outside decenters the subject. The subject is now one among others, no more and no less important than them; things no longer revolve around him alone.

---

[1]A favorite term of Sartre. The earlier dyadic parts are seen from the new viewpoint as part of a larger totality. In the *Critique of Dialectical Reason* (1976), Sartre writes: "The unity of a dyad can be realised only within a totalisation performed from outside by a third party" (p. 115).

I am not suggesting that the infant comes suddenly to such a reorganization of his experience, and it is certainly the case that many people acquire such a view of themselves only in small degrees or not at all. What I am stressing are the formal consequences of such a change of view for ourselves, for our consciousness of things, and for the objects with which we live.

THE MOVE FROM TWO-PERSON
TO THREE-PERSON PERSPECTIVE

Marital therapy provides a good illustration of the move from a two-person perspective to that of a third person. The couple who are quarreling can almost always be seen to be operating within a dyadic perspective. Each partner sees only what the other person is doing and not what he or she has done. One person attacks the other for insensitivity or lack of accommodation to some felt need: "I got angry because you let me down, were critical, greedy, demanding," and so on. The other partner says: "I only did that because you did some other thing that hurt me, let me down," and so on. Each can only see the other as the cause of what happened; the row was always started by the other person, and there is no solution to this mutual recrimination from within the dyad.

The marital therapist is in the position of the third party, the observer, who is able to perceive the behavior of each protagonist within a wider frame of reference. The therapist has a totalizing, or systematizing, view and from his position can present a view of the dispute that enables each of the parties to see the clash within a different and wider view. The third-person perspective, in whatever terms it may be couched, will see the *interdependence* of the couple's behavior—the sense in which the behavior of one partner belongs with the behavior of the other within a circular or interlocking system that has no real beginning or end. It is this view that may enable each partner to modify his or her response—the critical factor being whether each partner can hold off from dyadic attack and counterattack long enough to enable the larger view of the situation, a triadic structuring from outside, to be seriously entertained.

It is important to note that in relation to the couple, the therapist occupies this crucial third-person position. Even though he may be attacked by each in turn, just as they attacked each other before, he has to keep open the possibility of three-person structuring and to protect the space within which this could happen from all the various assaults and seductions that may attempt to destroy it. Ultimately, this third position can be traced back to the father, who originally provided a position external to the mother–infant dyad.

FROM LIVING TO LOOKING: THE EXPERIENCE OF PERSPECTIVAL SHIFT

I now want to take you in a more immediate way through a moment of transition of the kind I have been talking about. I want you to feel the sudden shift from one view to another. I want you to imagine a dream.

> You are running through a thick forest. Someone is after you. You can feel his footsteps behind you, closing in on you. You are running for your life. If only you can get to a certain place, you will be safe. But will you make it? He is almost upon you, and you turn to strike him with the stick you are carrying. Suddenly there is a loud noise . . . and you wake up. Your heart is pounding, and you still feel the terror and suspense. Perhaps as you woke you just heard yourself trying to cry out, or felt your arm trying to hit out at your assailant. Gradually you are aware of relief as the dim outlines of your bedroom swim into view. . . . *It was only a dream.*

Consider what has happened. Just a moment before you were in a terrifying world of violent action, and you were totally involved, bodily and emotionally. You were aroused for fight or flight and your adrenaline was surging. Nothing could have been more real . . . *but it was only a dream.* Now you lie in your own bed and reach for a glass of water. "Thank God! This is reality."

Two worlds, two "realities," two different structures of experience; a curious transition between them—waking up. In the twinkling of an eye, or rather in the opening of an eye, you have moved from one to the other. Each was fully involving, but there was an important difference between those involvements. When you were in the dream, you were not aware of any waking world at all; but now you are awake and firmly located in the real world, with all its familiar landmarks. You can still recall the dream, but now you are distanced from it and can put it in its place—*it was only a dream.*

Only a little while before, the dream scenario, as *present* experience, was the world that encompassed you; but now the dream, as *recollected* experience, is just one small structure that takes its place within that larger structure of reality which you now recognize and inhabit.

MATERNAL PRESENCE AND THE CONTAINMENT OF ANXIETY

Waking from a dream is a dramatic example of moving from inside a lived, experiential structure into another structure outside of the first. First we live an experience from the inside, then we view it from the outside as a more distanced and contained object—the dream. In this way, the raw and frightening experience of the dream is contained, by bounding it with the concept "dream" and anchoring it in our real world of known and named objects. By defining the experience as a dream, it becomes a bearable part of the structure of the real world—it acquires a place and a location in the scheme of things. The dream as an object has, in fact, been created by viewing a block of experience in a particular way from the outside.

Although we cannot so clearly see the third position here, the experience has all the characteristics of a shift from a two-person to a three-person perspective. The experience within the dream is immediate; we are involved in a passionate and bodily way; we are doing, not looking, except in order to do. The experience of recollecting the dream, and managing to contain it, is one of looking at the dream with a structuring vision, which has more to do with knowing and locating than doing. The astronaut somehow knows the earth for the first time when he sees it from space and locates it as a discrete object in the universe; there is a similar sense in which we move from living in to knowing when we awake sufficiently to "see" that we have been dreaming.

I want you now to imagine something else—a young child having a nightmare. The actual scenario of the dream does not matter.

The child wakes screaming. The mother runs to the child, picks it up, holds it, and comforts it: "Hush! Hush! There! There! There's nothing to be frightened about. Mommy's here. *It was only a dream.*" The child's experience must be a bit like our own in the first example—relief, which comes with recognition of the familiar, real world, and the real, familiar mother driving the terrors away. The mother's presence and words put the terrors in their place—"There, there! It was only a dream."

As in the first example, there are two worlds, two different structures of experience, and waking up—the transition between them. But there are important differences from this point on. The child needs more than just waking up to reinstate the structure of the real world. He needs the mother's actual presence, her voice, her words—framing the experience, containing the uncontainable: "*It was only a dream.*" The dream is something that has a recognizable place in *mother's* experience, and mother is not frightened of it. Later, perhaps, the child will become able to dispense with the actual mother, taking the mother's role and telling himself: "There's nothing to be frightened about . . . it's only a dream."

THE MOTHER'S VIEW—THE BEGINNINGS
OF SYMBOLIC CONTAINMENT

While the adult already has a systematized view of reality in which the dream can find its place, the child lacks any such all-embracing schema and therefore depends on the mother to provide one; the mother provides both immediate reassurance and safety in face of the unknown and unfamiliar, and at the same time helps the child to build up a map or schema of reality that will eventually make it more independent of her. The mother offers both herself, as immediately reassuring presence, and the word *dream*, as a building block for "reality." Gradually the child will learn to use the word *dream* to contain the raw experience and build it into a fabric of "reality," to which, at the moment, only the mother holds the key.

In this way, that which was first experienced by the child as a capricious and terrifying irruption into the world of the known and familiar, totally overthrowing its normal structure and coherence, becomes, through the mother's ministrations, assimilated to that familiar world.

Is it possible to relate what has happened here to the earlier example? How can we relate the child's transition from dream to reality to what happened in the adult case? And how, if at all, is all this related to the transition from a two-person to a three-person perspective which seemed to explain things in that instance?

The child we are talking about still lives within a two-person relationship with the mother. He has not yet achieved the structuring vision of the third position. This means many things; but what is important here is the fact that the child has not yet acquired a coherent structure of reality, which comes from being able to stand outside an experience and see what it is and how it fits in with everything else. The child is therefore totally dependent on the actual mother to reassure and on her structured view of reality, which she can bring to bear on his experience. Her structured view of things is the equivalent of our own adult view of reality that swings into place when we ourselves wake up from a dream. It is the third-person view that we bring to bear on our own relatively unstructured two-person experience.

In this example, the mother is the second person in the two-person experience of the child, and she carries with her the third-person structuring view of reality which in time the child will build up for himself. At this point, the most important thing that calms the child is undoubtedly the mother. But the words she offers to the child—"It's only a dream"—begin to provide a needed symbolic container and marker for his experience that contains the seed of his own future reality structure. It may be that at this moment her words are still more of a comfort than a source of knowledge. They are still a part of "mother" and "what she knows." But we can imagine that gradually, over time, these isolated words of the mother will begin to cohere into an intelligible structure of things that the child can begin to use for itself.

FROM DYADIC CERTAINTY TO TRIADIC RELATIVISM

It is clear from this example that the child we are considering, a child who has not yet fully separated from the mother, is totally dependent on her, both as the actual pivot of his world and also as the one who has a view of the world within which all his experience can be contained. This seems to be one important meaning of the idea of containment[2]—if the mother knows what the child's experience is and can give it a name, then the child can feel that the experience has a place within the mother's world, and therefore is a part of the order of things. In this sense, the mother's view is constitutive of the child's world or reality.

Against this backdrop of the mother's world-creating vision, we have to imagine a place for the child's own explorations and discoveries. It may well be significant that the example I have chosen to illustrate describes a child who is afraid and turning to the mother for security. But this is only one side of the child's experience—what happens, we might ask, when the child feels safer and able to play, to explore the world for himself?

Within the protective confines of the two-person relationship, we know that the child moves between exploration and return, referencing back to the mother for approval or "refueling," to use Mahler's term, and returning to base when the unknown becomes too threatening. In this rhythm of reaching out and back, the child's discoveries are real enough, but they remain subordinated to the primacy of the mother's view and the necessity that the child feels to have them confirmed by her.

Within the orbit of the two-person relationship, the child cannot reach a position from which the absoluteness of the mother can in any way be questioned or relativized. She remains the ultimate support of everything, and, in that sense, her views are absolute and cannot be questioned. Just as the unwitting voyager on the spaceship Earth cannot begin to dream of the possibility that the planet is anything but a vast, solid, and inexhaust-

---

[2]*Containment* is a term that arises naturally out of the language I am using, and I allow it to suggest nuances of meaning as it will. I have already considered some implications of the idea of containment in the previous chapter. However, the term also has a place within a more specific psychoanalytic discourse and particularly owes its position there to Bion (1962b). Bion's usage is linked to the Kleinian notion of "projective identification." The infant projects its uncontainable distress into the mother, who processes it through her "reverie" and makes it more manageable. The infant then reintrojects the transformed feeling (object) and is now able to contain it. In time the infant also introjects into itself the maternal containing process and thus becomes able to do for itself what the mother originally did. It is certainly true that what I am talking about has something in common with what Bion is talking about, but the processes and mechanisms that Bion assumes seem to me to alienate what is essentially an intuitively understandable process. The result is a danger of mechanizing the mind yet again, just as Freud did before. I do not wish to get caught up in that process; indeed, it is part of my intention to demechanize the mind and to render its activities understandable in terms of ordinary human interactions.

ible arena for his very important activities, and just as he cannot begin to imagine this earth as a fragile and limited planet that needs his care and consideration unless he is shown this fact by the astronaut, so the child cannot, within the dyadic relationship itself, begin to reach a position from which the mother and her views can be relativized and seen in perspective. It is only by the radical separation from the mother that can come about through "taking off" into the position of the third person, the father, that the all-embracing power of the dyadic Other can begin to be reduced.

The space explorer has the courage to leave the earth to see what he can find. Separation from Mother Earth and from the view within her holding arms is somehow tolerated. Looking back from space, there is a different view that the astronaut discovers for himself. So it may be also with the child. For a long time the child needs to live within, and be contained by, the mother's view. But he cannot begin to form his own view until he has been able to move out of her envisioning orbit and see her and her view as themselves circumscribed and occupying but one part of a larger whole. This brings us back to the father and his third position, whence this view can first be obtained.

I can now take this question one stage further in a way that will link it to the different ways of structuring the world that coexist in every individual. The child's own structuring of the world is from the beginning largely nonverbal. What the child "knows" about the world he has discovered in his body and knows in his body. In the language of Chapter 4, it is carnal knowledge. The structure of reality that the mother imparts to the child, however, moves very quickly into the verbal mode. It is her words that structure the world and tell the child what things are and where they fit together. The child still may explore and "know" with his body, but the mother knows best, because she knows in words, and from the child's point of view, she knows everything. The primacy of the word over experience and preverbal knowing begins at a very early age.

THE MOTHER'S VIEW: STRUCTURING VISION OR BANISHING DENIAL

We cannot think of this process of structuring of reality without at the same time thinking of its obverse—the process of turning something away from the world of structure. For while the mother helps the child contain the overwhelming experience of the dream, she simultaneously turns away its actual contents. It is as though the mother's words throw a circle around the contents of the dream, defusing their dangerous power to be real, but at the same time banishing them from any need to be structured. The word *dream* excludes and occludes those contents and banishes them into an unstructured limbo. The implicit instructions the mother gives to the child with the word *dream* are to pay no attention to its contents and to forget them. They are in the same category as "silly, unreal fears," and the effect of her communication is *to turn the child's attention away from the dream, and equally to turn the contents of the dream away from the child.*

Containment here has a double edge, which may not be entirely typical. A whole block of experience is named, and in that way allowed a place in the order of things; at the same time, the contents of that block, the dream experience itself, is refused structuring. The dream contents are not named or allowed a place within the mother's (or child's) established order of things, but are shooed away as being too disruptive and disturbing.

We may well consider that these implicit instructions to pay no attention to the dream contents are part of the process through which repression is first mediated. For just as the mother mediates to the child that which is to become part of the structure of reality—that which is to be recognized and named—so also does her mediation determine that which is not to be named, not to be recognized, not to be accorded a place in the order of things. Freud wrote: "The essence of repression lies simply in turning something away, and keeping it at a distance from the conscious" (1915b, p. 147).

At this dyadic stage of things, the mother's view, on which the child depends, has both a structure-building and structure-denying face. Which face is turned toward the child's experience depends on the mother and what she is able to accept within her purview. This in turn will depend on whether she feels comfortable and relaxed about what the child is doing or whether she is getting anxious and uptight about him.

The child, for his part, pursues his exploratory, largely nonverbal, structure building of "world according to self" within that circumscribing orbit of the mother's vision. As we have seen, this can only take place in those situations where the child feels safe and unthreatened and able to make use of his own resources—but even there it remains subject and subordinated to the mother's vision and words.

We have glimpsed, then, how the child begins to acquire his sense of reality. There is a constant interplay between mother and child, each contributing to the structure. But because of the child's total dependence on the mother, the mother's view will, in the end, carry greater weight. Where the mother's increasingly verbal view is unopposed, the child's more fragile view of reality—largely nonverbal and self-discovered—will be in danger of being submerged.[3] What saves the child from this danger is the third position of the father. This enables the child to move out of the absolutism of the two-person situation and see not only himself as decentered, but the previously all-powerful mother in a more relative light.

TRANSFERENCE AS RE-VISIONED REALITY

The outside position, the position of the third person, is extremely important in understanding what goes on in therapy. This is something I will discuss more fully in Chapter 16. Here I will indicate how crucial is that notion in understanding the concept of transference.

It is the shift to the third position that quite literally creates the transference as something that can be perceived and known. I have already mentioned Thomas Szasz's (1963) account of the use Freud made of the concept of transference in trying to help Breuer come to terms with his experiences with Anna O. (see Chapter 9). I will now discuss that example more fully, as it demonstrates so well the point I am making about the formative significance of the third position and its importance in creating a larger view.

According to Szasz, Breuer had been frightened off any further involvement in the development of psychoanalysis by Anna O.'s sudden expression of passionate feelings for him and her hysterical pregnancy at the end of treatment. It was apparent to Breuer that Anna O. had fallen

---

[3]There is a sense in which the contents of the dream, in the example I have given, can be thought of as the child's own two-person and nonverbal structurings of things. It is these that become excluded from the mother's verbal structuring in the way I have described.

in love with him, and he did not want to have anything more to do with a treatment that could have such dire consequences. Some years later, however, Freud wanted Breuer to assist in the writing of *Studies in Hysteria*, and Breuer was still reluctant to be involved. According to Szasz, Freud then explained to Breuer his ideas about the transference, and indicated that what Anna O. had demonstrated was not quite what he, Breuer, had thought. Anna O. only thought she was in love with Breuer; what she was really demonstrating was the phenomenon of transference. The relationship with Breuer and his care and attention had, according to this view, revived traces of an earlier relationship—that of Anna O. with her own father. So she was not really in love with Breuer; she was reliving, in relation to Breuer, her long-buried feelings for her father. This explanation was evidently helpful, as Breuer agreed to some degree of collaboration on the book.

Szasz describes this as the use of the concept of transference as a defense—perhaps a necessary defense for the analyst. It shields him, putting him at a distance from the raw and passionate feelings of the patient. In this sense, Freud's use of *transference* was similar to the mother's use of *dream*. Freud put Breuer's frightening experiences with Anna O. at a distance with the concept of transference; the mother chased away the frightening experience of the nightmare with the concept of dream.

But there is also an important difference. Whereas the concept of dream, as used by the mother, acted to turn away the contents of the dream and encouraged their forgetting, Freud's concept of transference placed the phenomenon (Anna O.'s passionate expression of love) in a new context that invited further exploration. From Breuer's point of view, Freud's mediation provided not just a shift to the position of the third person, and thus a sharing of Freud's containing external view of what had happened; it also brought about a shift of context, whereby the phenomenon was removed from the "here and now" context of reality and placed in a developmental, "past" context, within which it would make a different, less frightening kind of sense. Freud's intervention thus illuminated that which it contained, in contrast to the mother's intervention, which banished the contents of the child's dream to a limbo of unstructured forms.[4] Freud's intervention potentially enlarged Breuer's

---

[4]By *unstructured* I mean lacking the third-person transformation.

reality, at the same time as it reassured him by containing in a new way that which had earlier been so threatening to him.

What I want to highlight in this example is not so much the way in which Freud's interpretation diminished Breuer's anxiety and enabled him to contemplate that which before had been too frightening; this is certainly important and probably something that happens in every therapy. Rather, I want to emphasize the formal aspects of the maneuver—the shift from a two-person to a three-person frame of reference. Breuer had found himself in a two-person action frame with Anna O., which was not the one he had intended. It was a contemporary, "real" structure, and one which compromised him. Freud entered the scene as the third person with a different view—the view of Anna O. as repeating, transferring some unfulfilled longing from time past, enacting a past structure in the present situation. This enabled Breuer to move from the two-person action frame into a three-person looking frame. By moving to Freud's position, identifying with him, and seeing through his eyes, through his view, Breuer was enabled to see something about his interaction with Anna O. that he had not been able to see before. He could get outside of his immediate experience, because Freud had given him a place to stand and a view to see with. Anna O.'s and his earlier "reality" in this way became a "transference."

This position, from which a re-visioning of reality can take place, is a very powerful one. John Padel (1985), in his essay "Ego in current thinking," also emphasizes, though in a somewhat different way from me, the importance of vision in the child's organization of his experience from different perspectives—in other words, from the position of significant Others. Padel refers in this context to Archimedes, who is said to have exclaimed: "Give me a place to stand and I will move the earth!" I have tried to show that the place where the third person, the father, stands does indeed give the subject a perceptual leverage almost as powerful as that which Archimedes, in a different sense, envisaged.

The difference between the mother–child dream example and the Freud–Breuer–Anna O. example is perhaps worth emphasizing in another way to highlight the difference between two-person and three-person structuring. In the two-person example, the mother draws the child's experience into the holding of her view. Although she gives the child a word, which will one day lock into his own growing structure of reality, what mainly helps him to recover his sense of location and security is her holding presence. The word may be important as a talis-man, as that which conveys that the mother does indeed have a place for the experience; but the word does not yet convey understanding—it does not show the child the place of the dream in the order of things or even the child's own relation to his dream.

In the three-person situation, the order of importance would seem to be reversed. It may have been important to Breuer that Freud was able to contain emotionally what he, Breuer, was unable to handle; what was much more important was that Freud could provide a new vision of the phenomenon which Breuer could understand and use to alter his own view of reality. The two-person situation provides maternal holding and containment within a preexisting view of the mother; the three-person situation provides knowledge and understanding—in other words, a sym-bolic view that will alter and enlarge an already existing view within the subject.[5]

SEEING ONE'S OWN SELF

We have seen how the child turns to the mother in the face of the unknown or threatening and looks to her to provide a structure that will contain the new experience—at least when anxiety is uppermost. Correla-tively, we can imagine how the child who is not anxious or threatened may seek to explore this unknown in order to find out what it is for himself.

---

[5]The whole process of structuring and containing is fundamentally important in therapy. The therapist may "hold" and "contain" just by being there (like the mother), but the importance of the cognitive aspect should not be underestimated. It is this aspect in particular that I consider in this chapter. The therapist's interpretation offers a containing and organizing structure for the patient's previously unrecognized strivings and feelings; it will be critical for the result of therapy whether these containing structures the therapist provides are treated in two-person or three-person terms by the patient. The "two-person patient" will try to take refuge in the analyst's structure, just as the child did in the mother's word *dream*. The analyst provides a new containing home for the patient's self, and the patient is converted to his analyst's view. The "three-person patient" will feel himself to be more separate from the analyst's word, and he may thus be able to relate to it in a more critical and optional way. The analyst's word is here something that may be used or not, as the case may be, to help build up a structure of one's own, and it can be repudiated—if the analyst will allow this.

There is, however, one situation in which the child can only obtain the structuring he needs from the other person. This is in the creation of that structure of reflections, which I have referred to earlier as the objective self. The reason for this is intrinsic rather than contingent: we cannot exist as social beings without a clear sense of an objective self; *yet in order to see ourselves as an object, either in isolation or in relation to another person, we must, of necessity, first put ourselves outside of ourselves and observe ourselves from somewhere else.* Just as we cannot see our own faces unless we look in a mirror, so we cannot properly see our self except through the eyes of another person. To requote from Sartre: "If I am to conceive of even one of my properties in the objective mode, then the Other is already given" (1957, p. 270). And again: "That subject's presence, without intermediary, is the necessary condition of all thought which I would attempt to form concerning myself" (1957, p. 271).

Depending on our stage of development, this move to the Other's position may be dyadic or triadic, and once again we can see how this organization will determine both the quality of the self-image and our relationship to it. Where the organization is predominantly dyadic, the move to the Other will also be dyadic. The image of ourselves from this perspective will partake of the absolutism of the two-person mode, and it will be difficult to maintain separateness from it. This is the image mediated by the Gorgon, by the Other that Sartre describes in his account of the "Look." It freezes the recipient's subjectivity—the subject becomes no more and no less than what the Other sees. The image does not mediate knowledge, but it shows me how I am. It is not a view of myself for me to consider but an exhibition of my very essence. This may be an utterly bad self that I must never be, or it may be a wonderful self that all will adore.

The move to the position of the third person is potentially more transforming. It mediates something that is closer to knowledge, a new vision of myself that may radically alter my conception of where I stand in the world. Although this view may diminish and relativize my status, making me more aware of my real position among others, it does not totally define me, nor make me so utterly into an object as does the dyadic view. I can still maintain a sense of myself as a separate subject; and although I may feel small and uncomfortable, or in an opposite sense, proud of myself and the way I look, I am still something more than and different from this particular image that has been put before me.

The image that the Other mediates to me is in each case a symbol of the self that comes from the Other; but as such, it will be imbued with the quality of those symbols that the person is currently using. If the person's organization is predominantly two-person, the symbol will be relatively primitive and poorly differentiated from the object. If the organization is three-person, the symbol will be more representational and separate.

How we experience the Other's view is determined by the level of development we have reached. So also is our capacity to move to the position of another person. The child who is still enmeshed with the mother may not manage to move from his own view at all. The child who is beginning to walk the path of separation may begin to be able to explore how things look from where the mother is. When the child becomes more secure in his separateness, he may then negotiate the passage to the third position and try to see how the world, and himself, looks from there.

Both the Other's view and the Other's position can be used in different ways, depending on whether confidence or anxiety is uppermost. The confident child may seek out an alternative view to his own with which to experiment—"Here is a new pattern of things to be tried on for fit." An insecure child, with a poorly organized view of his own, may seek out the Other's view as a place of refuge—"Can I hide in here, within the containment of your view?" His own view will then be submerged.

Similarly, a child may be pushed into a position for which he is not yet ready (the "dislocation" of Chapter 2), or he may seek out a position because it provides a new vantage point from which to explore the world. "How does the world look from where Father is?"—that is the confident child who is ready to move away from the mother and can do so without too much fear. "What is this bleak place in which I find myself with no mother?"—that is the question of the child who has been ejected from a still needed and sought after symbiosis. Position and view are two sides of the same coin.

Freedom to move to more and more positions seems to be the essence of an exploring consciousness; clinging to a single view is the recourse of someone who is frightened to leave home base. Each new position gives a new vision; each new vision throws a new pattern on reality; each new pattern relativizes the previous ones. Enlargement of vision does not, therefore, depend on widening the angle of our original view. *It depends on being able to move to different positions to obtain new perspectives.*

Breadth of vision results from a multiplicity of perspectives, not from a single view that will try to eradicate all others.

Each new step from within a structure of experience to outside of it—in other words, to someone else's position or view—totalizes the more limited views of whoever is within that structure. Such a totalizing view may be wider and embrace more of reality, but it has no license to be totalitarian or to invalidate those earlier views. For although limited, those earlier views may yet see things that the larger, more abstracted vision has left out. Seeing "eternity in a grain of sand" has its own kind of truth that has to go on being asserted, even in the face of the grand system. The grand system, the totalizing view, which claims to see everything from some privileged vantage point, may be an irresistible temptation; but at the end of the day it is the flexibility of multiple perspectives that will reveal more of reality to us.

Being able to see through different eyes relativizes the perspective. No longer is there the certainty of one "truth"—truth disappears in the multiplicity of perspectives which all say something different. Whether we experience this loss of "truth" and enlargement of perspective as a gain or a loss will depend on our earlier experience of the more simplistic, more absolute (two-person) world. If it was the security we most valued, it will be felt as a loss; if we experienced the original world as confining, we may experience the loss of absolutes as a liberation.

In this three-person, and larger, social world, what becomes of the idea of an objective view? I think it is clear that there is no longer any place for it. All views are *situated*, to use a term of Sartre, and all views are limited and biased by this very fact.

If we think for a moment in a structural or systems way, we can easily see that, *within* any social system, there is no such place as an "objective" position—in other words, no position can describe the "truth" of the system. No view is privileged or has preeminence over any other. All are relative and describe a limited perspective.

Outside of the system concerned, however, there do exist one or more privileged positions. They are privileged *because* they are outside and therefore allow that particular system to be viewed as a whole. The subject within the system can certainly aspire to such a position, but only through identification with a particular Other who is outside the system.

In relation to that system, this Other may claim that his view is objective. But it is not really so. All that can be said of it is that it has the whole system as its object and can see the relation between its parts in a way that is not possible from within the system. In a similar way, this external Other may be able to see how the system as a whole relates to other systems within the field. Such a systematizing view has great value, as I have been arguing, but it tends to conceal the limitations of such an apparently Olympian perspective. For even though we escape from a system in this way, we inevitably take up a position within some other system, since it is not possible to take a stand in a void. The view we take from the outside is inevitably bound and limited by its very situation. It is always somewhere and is always the view of someone.

If there is no truly objective position, all we can hope for is to realize this and to relativize our views as much as possible. The greatest danger of any situated position is that it will claim to be the "truth." Such absolutism strives to suppress all relative views that exist both within the system and outside of it, often using the prerogatives of power, while regressing to the egocentricity of our first omnipotent view. This attempt to monopolize the truth will be familiar to anyone who works within an institution.

The notion of relative truth—what George Kelly (1955) called constructive alternativism—must not be confused with a blurring of boundaries and absence of structure. Structures, with their clearly defined, maintained, and defended boundaries, are an essential part of the way we experience the world and an essential part of our social and psychological organization. But the usefulness of boundaries is a different matter from their truth, and usefulness is not only a matter of opinion, depending on our situated view; it is a matter that changes over time, both developmentally and historically. A young child may need absolute boundaries, which an older child will find stultifying and will have to knock down; a particular theoretical formulation is bound, in the nature of things, to outlive its usefulness, because it is situated in a larger sociocultural structure that will change over time.

THE THIRD POSITION AND THE OBJECTIVE SELF

This analysis of positional shifts of consciousness—looking from the position of various Others—enables us to see how behavioral (looking out) structures and reflexive (looking back) structures interweave and feed upon each other in the development of the self.

If we consider the situation of the mother and infant, we can see that at first there is only a developing behavioral structure, a patterning of interaction within a behavioral unit. (I am talking from the baby's point of view.) The mother can be thought of as the *horizon* of the infant's world, a world of action and reaction. Then the father starts to become important as a figure in his own right, but the child is still functioning in a closed, even if more complex, behavioral system. A new complexity is introduced by the baby's realization of the otherness of the Other, since there is now, in principle, the possibility of the infant swapping places in the behavioral unit and a developing conception of roles. Taking the role of the Other in a dyad increases the complexity of the field into which the infant behaves, and introduces the possibility of a shift from purely egocentric to more allocentric behavior.

We might conceive of the next step in development as being brought about by the infant's realization of the Other's view in a dyad (Chapters 2 and 3), as it introduces an imaginary element (the Other's image of me) into the behavioral system.[6] Presumably, up until then the child would have been responding to a purely behavioral feedback.

---

[6]In an unpublished paper ("On developing the capacity to symbolise") Peter Hobson (1988) argued that the infant's gradually developing awareness that the mother has a view of every situation that is different from his own is a critical point in the growth of his capacity to use symbols. It could be that this is so, but it begs the question as to how the child begins to be able to conceive of the other person having a view at all. It seems much more likely that the child first begins to be able to differentiate a view of an object from the object itself within his own experience. From that base he begins to grasp the notion of the other person having a view that is different from his own. I could put this slightly differently: the view of the other person clearly has a built-in separateness about it. But will this separateness be realized unless there is already beginning to be an awareness of differences which has come about in another way? My own preference has been to see the unhinging or dislocation of image from object as occurring, first of all, in the infant's own experience with the object through what I have called limitation of access to the object. Only when that has reached a certain level (in other words, when separateness is already beginning to be a fact), will the child begin to appreciate the more radical separateness of a view from another person. Hobson at least realizes that there is a problem to be explained here, and I am sympathetic to his approach, which considers both vision and object relations as playing an important role in the development of symbols. But I think he is probably getting things the wrong way around and is explaining one sort of separateness in experience (the separation of symbol from object) by another sort of separateness (separation of Other's view from self's view),

But it is the next step that is the critical one. Taking the position of the third person makes possible the first envisagement of a simple structure, as defined in the last chapter (the parental couple), and taking the view of the third person makes possible for the first time an appreciation of the subject's position within an interactive behavioral system. All this will lead to an increased complexity on a behavioral level; but in addition, the child's behavior will be increasingly controlled by a cognitive (symbolic) map of the social field, which can only be built up through positional shifts of the kind that I have outlined.

I have spoken in previous chapters about the relation between seeing and understanding, between looking and the development of mind, symbols, and consciousness. *Position*, like *view*, is a word that has been incorporated into this language of mental activity—people talk about having changed their position on something when they have changed what they think about it, or have changed their view.

Together with looking, the Other's view (the Other's looking) has been a twin theme running, in different ways, through almost every chapter of this book. The realization that the other person has a view that is different from our own is a major achievement in development, and its effects may be truly Copernican in proportion. This is not to say that the discovery of the Other's view is always sudden and traumatic, in the way that I describe in Chapters 2 and 3; but even when it is gradual, its transforming effect on the consciousness of the individual is momentous.

In this chapter, I have concentrated on the dramatic change in the child's awareness that is brought about by its ability to move in imagination into the position of the third person. This is part of the change from a dyadic to a triadic organization of experience, which includes an altered view of both self and reality, and a growing capacity to form and use representational symbols. It can also be thought of as completing a line of development of consciousness. In its earliest beginnings, consciousness is little more than a searching and scanning of the perceptual field for patterns of the mother. It then progresses through the separation of

---

when in fact both of these depend on the same earlier development that makes it possible to *conceive of* anything at all. It seems to me that when the infant appears to be influenced in its behavior by the mother's *view* of the situation, it is responding to behavioral cues, not to a realization of the mother's view as a protosymbol.

looking from doing in experience, and the creation of an inner looking space within which patterns of the mother that are separate from her can begin to be entertained. Finally, it becomes, in the three-person phase, a means of scanning both the perceptual field and the inner field of mind with these separated symbolic patterns, which in their essence are the now-disembodied patterns of earlier experience with objects. The ability to move in experience and imagination to the position of the third person, who is outside of the structure that is being lived, provides a vast extension of consciousness by making available a position and view that lie beyond our own immediately lived perspective. This first move, which can be so difficult to make but which is so liberating in its effects, is capable of an almost infinite extension if we care to use it.

In the next chapter, I will summarize and draw together the changes in our appreciation and use of symbols that parallel this development of consciousness. Inevitably this will involve some repetition, but it will also allow for further development of certain key ideas.

14   Pattern and Object

In the silence of primary consciousness can be seen appearing not only what words, but also what things mean: the core of primary meaning round which the acts of naming and expression take shape.

—Maurice Merleau-Ponty

I N THIS CHAPTER I will draw together and elaborate on the story of symbol formation, which I have approached from many different directions in earlier chapters. What I present is a recapitulation, involving repetition but also development and extension. In the second part of the chapter, in particular, I explore the impact of language on our earlier, preverbal symbolic experience.

I refer to the *story* of symbol formation, because we can never know how the earliest processes of psychological development actually occur. All we can do is weave stories—quasi-scientific myths—about that earliest era, and in that way create a prehistory that is in some degree believable.

The story of symbol formation is the story of the infant's changing relationship to those patterns he forms out of the flux of his experience with objects. Patterns are the "shapes," the constancies and recurrences that we abstract from our primary sensual experience of the world, and they form the basis of all future symbolic usage. We cannot understand either the formation or the usage of symbols unless we understand something of the infant's first experience of patterns and its gradually evolving relationship to them.

The ability to mark and recognize patterns must be among the most basic capacities of the human infant. Probably an innate process, it may be already present in intrauterine life and is certainly operative very soon after birth. Without such a capacity, there would be no possibility of marking or differentiating experience at all and no possibility of organizing an experiential world. Both the refinding of patterns that are wanted and the repudiation of patterns that are alien or unwanted depend on this fundamental ability.

Langer (1942) used the term *abstractive seeing* to describe this basic human potential for recognizing form or pattern in a sensory field. Also, Daniel Stern (1985), in *The Interpersonal World of the Infant*, summarized experimental data that suggest infants as young as two to three weeks old have a capacity to recognize perceptual patterns in a number of sensory modalities, and even to transfer such pattern recognition from one modality to another.

Apart from such evidence, we know from earlier research into facial recognition (summarized by Bowlby 1969) that from the age of about six weeks the infant is beginning to learn and respond to the pattern of the human face. Although at first the facial pattern that elicits the smiling response is rudimentary, the required pattern becomes increasingly complex and specific, until, when the stranger response is established at around eight months, the mother's face is clearly differentiated from that of anyone else.

By this age, we can be sure that the infant has learned, and can differentiate, a complex and highly specific pattern—the mother's face—and can determine whether or not any actual object conforms to it. What is true of the face can reasonably be assumed to apply to other primary objects in the infant's experience. Patterns of experience with these objects will be built up gradually, forming patterns of expectation against which the pattern of ongoing experience will be matched.

At this stage, the patterns that the infant learns and recognizes will be (from our point of view) perceptual patterns, marking constancies and recurrences in the external and internal environments. We can think of the infant as already, in a primitive way, scanning the environment with patterns, searching for patterns it wants, and obtaining a sense of closure or satisfaction when a pattern is recognized and found.

Perhaps the origin of the pattern is not yet an issue; all that matters is the fact that it matches a remembered pattern. It is basic to Winnicott's formulations, for example, that in the beginning the infant is not concerned with the source of a satisfying pattern. The mother's adaptive provision presents the pattern that is searched for, and this delays the experience of "otherness"—the experience of reality as different from the wanted pattern. In this way, reality does not impinge on the baby's experience, which must, like a seamless garment of interdigitating "want" and "satisfaction," be all of a piece, without a break. Only as the fact of separateness impinges, only as the mother adapts less completely to her baby's need, will the pattern of the mother begin to be truly wanted (lacked), and thus be experienced as "out there" and beyond the infant's grasp or reach.

From this point on, psychological development consists of the insertion of increasingly complex and ever more firmly maintained gaps or separations into the originally unitary fabric of experience. Just as the development of the infant proceeds through a gradual, but increasingly definitive, separating out of infant and mother from an undifferentiated matrix of experience—the "merged in" state—so the development of symbols seems to follow a similar path of separation. The pattern by which the object was first of all recognized becomes gradually loosened from its attachment to the object and eventually becomes a symbol, or signifier, through which the object can be represented. In the further stages of symbolic usage, the separated pattern becomes a form in its own right that may be used to signify relationships in contexts distinct from the original one, as we find, for example, in play or metaphor. *The pattern of the object and the object itself can thus be thought of as separating from each other in a way that parallels the separation of the infant from its mother.* What originally inhered in the object, as part of the object (the patterned object), comes to inhere in the subject as a form (pattern or symbol) the subject can use for his own purposes of signifying.

What is in question in this separation of pattern from object is not, of course, some process that is independent of the infant. *The separating out of the pattern must depend on the infant's altering relation to the object.* The question we have to answer is how the infant comes to appreciate that the pattern of the object is something which can be conceived of apart from the object; or putting it differently—what alterations in the relation of the infant to the object might facilitate the insertion of a difference, or a gap, between these two previously inseparable experiences of the object? I will try to summarize the position I have reached.

Although initially I was looking for some single factor to account for this separation, I have come to realize that there are probably a series of factors that can facilitate the process. At different times, different factors will be more important; I have come to think of the process as a cumulative one, with each new factor strengthening and extending an earlier stage of the process. The separation of pattern and object, of "symbol" and "reality," is at best a precarious one, never finally established, and easily reverting to earlier stages of the process.

Winnicott's account of the transitional object leans on what is probably the earliest and most fundamental element in the process—the failure of reality to conform to a patterned expectation, formed through earlier experience with the object. This failure of reality to conform drives a first rift into the previously unitary experience of the object. The object part of a previously unseparated patterned object—or pattern-object—is missing, introducing a gap or space between the pattern and the object.

In the case of the transitional object, the pattern turns up in another object over which the baby has control, no doubt diminishing the sense of separation between expected pattern and absent object. But as separation from the object begins to be better tolerated, we can imagine that the searched-for pattern itself becomes heightened as a subjective experience, in proportion as it is not real-ized in the actual object. The nonconforming or absent object, the new emerging reality, begins to be located beyond the reach of the infant, somewhere in the outside world. The extreme instance of this would be the situation that is central to Kleinian formulations—the outright loss of the object, as for example, the loss of the breast in weaning. The real breast is gone; the pattern of experience with the breast remains. The pattern of experience is in this way disconnected from the real object, becoming a pattern within the subject rather than a pattern without. It is in this sense that Bion (1962a) has spoken about the word as a "no-breast," meaning, I think, that the word, or the concept, of "breast" comes to fill the place of the absent object—the place in experience where there is no actual breast.

As a shorthand, summarizing a whole complex line of development, this makes a lot of sense. As a total account of what happens, it leaves out too many in-between stages. It does not explain sufficiently how the separation of pattern from object actually takes place. For example, Winnicott's account of the transitional object describes a situation where a mini-loss of the object has provoked a search for the missing object; but the search results in a refinding of the wanted pattern in another object. Surely this demonstrates that loss of the object on its own does not guarantee a separation of pattern from object into a purely subjective realm. A subjective realm, as such, does not yet exist. It will only be constituted when the missing pattern finds a place to be that is apart from the real world. In this case, the search continues in the real world for the missing pattern until another object has been found. Mourning, or as Freud said, "the verdict of reality that the object no longer exists" (1917, p. 255), is still a long way from here.

It is for this reason that I have looked for other elements that might help the infant to move through the following sequence: *perceiving* a pattern that announces the object (e.g., the actual appearance of the mother's face or breast); *recollecting* a pattern, in the gap between wanting and having, which *anticipates* a repeated experience with the object (e.g., a remembered image of the mother's face or breast); recollecting a pattern that *recalls* the missing object without so clearly anticipating it; and finally, recollecting a pattern that merely *stands for*, or *represents*, the object, in a way which seems no longer to anticipate "having" it at all.

Of these four points, all but the last stand within an anticipatory time frame in relation to action. The first point anticipates the object in an immediate sense; the second anticipates the object very soon; the third still anticipates the object, but can cope with a longer delay. Only the fourth seems to have escaped from the bondage to time and need, and does not seem to imply any expectation of reunion with the object at all. It is easy to see from this why Segal, for example, places such emphasis on the mourning and giving up of the object in her account of symbol formation. Only when the actual object can be given up completely can there be something that approaches pure representation.[1]

I have tried to approach the question of symbol formation from a somewhat different angle. Whereas Segal and Bion seem to assume object loss as a fact and use this to explain the separation of symbolic pattern from object, I have tried to examine various ways in which such object loss may come about, as it seemed possible that the actual process of

---

[1]The problem I have with Segal's (1986) account of symbol formation is not this aspect, which relates the capacity for representational symbols to object loss. That kind of formulation is not all that dissimilar to some aspects of my own account. The part that troubles me is the link of symbol formation to a more specifically Kleinian perspective. Through this, representational symbol formation is linked to the infant's achieving of a depressive organization (a realization that its attack has damaged or harmed a loved and needed object). Symbol formation is then, if I understand Segal correctly, given a reparative significance, perhaps through the capacity of the symbol to make new links with the damaged object.

losing the object—the way in which the object came to be given up—
could tell us something more about the way in which the symbol became
disengaged from the object.

I have put considerable emphasis on what might be called the curtailment of access to the object, as this was something that could be thought
of as gradual and cumulative (cf. Winnicott's notion of graduated maternal failure). A previously untrammeled relation to the object, a situation
of free and unlimited access, becomes structured by the insertion of
various (parental) limits. As a result, the infant is made to hold off from
the object in a variety of ways, to accept a distance of time or place or
access in relation to the object.

These limits would be imposed in innumerable ways. Although at first
almost entirely behavioral and nonverbal, their spirit and effect can
perhaps be partially captured by the injunction "You may look but not
do!" in relation to the object (see Chapter 4).

The "not do," or equally "not have," is fundamentally important
because it requires that the infant holds off from the object to some
degree. This holding off creates a space of "not doing," of "not having,"
between the infant and the object, in which the infant is obliged to relate
to the object across a distance. The importance of this idea is that it
introduces the possibility of losing an object without actually losing it.[2]
The object is lost to "having," but not to "seeing." Indeed, insofar as the
infant is now obliged to stand off from the object, at a distance, the
distance senses will begin to achieve far greater importance in relation to
the object than the earlier contact senses. The object, separated by a
distance, can be explored and related to visually, for example, without
this experience being immediately superseded by a far more compelling
and engrossing touching and having of the object that would once again
immerse the infant in bodily and proprioceptive perceptions.

It can be seen that limitation of access to the object begins, in this way,
to introduce a disjunction between looking and having or doing, and
correlatively, between the visual image of the object and more proprioceptive patterns of experience with it. Looking, which had at first flowed
freely into action and was anticipatory of it, begins to be experienced as

---

[2]Perhaps I should make quite clear that I do not subscribe to the Kleinian idea that the
object that is unavailable is necessarily experienced as having been destroyed or damaged by
the infant.

unhinged from action, and the image of the object begins to become a substitute for its possession.

The importance of this idea for thinking about the origin of mind and thought should now be clearer. We can think of the holding off process as creating a looking frame, as opposed to a having or doing frame, within which the image of the object can be contemplated. In this way, we can start to link the idea of not having the object with symbol formation through the intermediate idea of being able to have or know an object visually, which has been lost, for example, to the tactile sense.

It is here that the face may have a particular importance, providing a model of an object that can be apprehended only by the visual sense (see Chapter 6). The mother's face, as a pattern or gestalt the infant can recognize, can only be grasped visually, and not at all through touching or holding. Perhaps partly through the mediation of this experience, the infant might begin to be able to experience the visual image of the object as a kind of "face" of the object, yielding a form that can only be obtained through this particular kind of holding off. It is interesting in this context to consider the term *facet* to describe a delimited aspect of the sur-*face* of an object.

As a result of holding off from the object, the infant now has a looking space, within which visual forms or images of the object begin to acquire preeminence. We can regard this looking space as an early stage of what will later become the mind. As the visual image of the object becomes separated from action with it, the possibility increases of the image acquiring a representational function. Unlike the earlier touch and proprioceptive patterns of experience with the object (which we can glimpse in the transitional object), the visual image has a degree of separation from the object built into it. It is not an image or memory of possession of the object—which might be expected to revive that experience in a vivid and bodily way—but an image of an object that is already separate and "over there." At best (from the baby's point of view), it anticipates a reduction of distance from the object; at worst, it may mark a gap that will be bridged only with difficulty or not at all.

We can now see how the imposition of a limit on the infant's access to the object might create the basic conditions for a representational space that we have been looking for. We have a space that is a "nondoing" or "looking space" and an image of the object that has begun to be unhinged or separated from the anticipation of action with it. We can also begin to see why we come to conceive of our minds in such a predominantly visual way (see Chapter 5). It is because vision, as our major distance sense, plays a predominant part in creating our first representational symbols and the space within which they can be contemplated.

There are two further points to make in this recapitulation: the first concerns language and the word; the second concerns the passage from two-person to three-person experience.

I have emphasized in previous chapters the fact that the word comes from the Other; in this sense, it is part of the object world that exists apart from the child and "out there." The point I wish to make is this: unlike either a proprioceptive pattern of experience with the object or a visual image of it, the word is not *like* the object at all. Its relationship to the object has to be slowly learned—we have to learn to talk. This external origin of the word, together with its complete difference from the image of the object, must be very important in establishing and maintaining the word as a pure representation of the object. It fosters the process of separation of image and object that has already started, drawing the image, one might say, away from the object it portrays, away from the "thing world" of action and doing, toward a realm of pure meaning. In this, the word can be said to repeat a function of the father, which I sketched in Chapter 7. Just as the father facilitates the separation of the child from the mother–infant symbiosis, drawing the child out into the object world, so the word facilitates the separation of the image of the object from the object itself, drawing it toward a purely representational space of "looking" and "not having."

Although this touches on the part the third person, the father, plays in the development of purely representational symbols, there is one further point to be made before I embark on a discussion of that topic. This concerns the relation between words and the infant's earlier preverbal representations of objects. Just as separation from the mother does not occur in one fell swoop but gradually, so the separation of image from object must be a gradual affair. I have already discussed how the first "holding offs" imposed by the parents begin to create a looking space—a first rudimentary space of thought; and equally, how the visual image, formed by standing off from the object, would be the first tool of that primitive thought. We cannot suppose that the word suddenly enters this new looking space and forthwith operates as a separate and separating symbol. It is more likely that the word is first related to in a way similar to the visual image; it will partake of the characteristics of this early looking space and, like the visual image, be experienced as a "face" or *facet* of the object, albeit a peculiarly useful facet by which it can be manipulated and handled. Only later would it come to be drawn by the rest of language, of which it is a part, into the quite different and separate verbal space of language.

We can now move on to discuss the part that three-person relationships play in the development of symbols. So far, we have considered only the realm of two-person relationships, and how a primitive symbolizing process gets under way in such a context. I have tried to establish how, within this two-person situation, a space of relative separation from the object begins to be achieved, a space of primitive mind and thought. I characterized this as a looking space, but I indicated that it is a precarious achievement, always in danger of slipping from representation toward possession. What is it, then, that is so different about the three-person situation, and why is it important for symbol formation?

I will summarize the arguments already made in Chapter 7 and reiterated in the last chapter. The importance of the third person, the father, is that he is from the beginning outside the mother–infant pair. Because of this, he can draw the child out from the mother–infant matrix into a wider world of more complex relationships. Because of this, he provides a place for the infant to stand, from where the infant can begin to see both himself and his mother as part of a wider context. But perhaps most important of all is the oedipal aspect of this three-person situation. Because the father lays claim to an exclusive possession of the mother for certain periods of time—an exclusive possession in which the infant cannot share—he obliges the child to come to terms with being the one who is absolutely excluded from access to the mother. I have argued that this exclusion places the child in the position of the observer—the one who can look, but never have. It is this not-to-be-questioned, or absolute, boundary, placing on the child an inescapable position as observer, that is of fundamental importance in understanding the development of a purely representational space and a purely representational symbol.

Within the two-person setting the space of looking was insecure. There was no guarantee of its boundaries, and there always existed the possibility that looking could still be anticipatory touching—it could still pass over into possession of the object. With the oedipal exclusion, this looking space becomes established on much firmer foundations. The road to possession and fusion is closed and the closure is guaranteed by the father. As the story of Adam and Eve puts it, entry to the Garden is closed forever and is guarded by cherubim with flaming swords.

This is the space that psychological development prepares for the words of language—a space of radical looking and of separation from the mother that is guaranteed by the father. While language may develop in many different psychological settings, I believe that its use as a purely representational instrument will depend on the strength of the oedipal boundary. I am reminded here of work by Lidz and colleagues (1957) on the families of schizophrenic patients, which seemed to show that, almost invariably in such families, there was a weakness or defect in this boundary, with skewed relationships between the parents that opened the door for incestuous fantasies and enactments. It is interesting to wonder whether such boundary failures may not be part of the process through which the door to symbolic regression and fusional thinking is also opened (see Chapter 11, p. 181).

PLAY—FROM INCARNATION TO REPRESENTATION

So far in this chapter I have presented a story of symbol formation within a developmental context. I have constructed an account that seeks to link directly the growing separateness and distinctness of the symbol—its developing representational potential—to the increasing capacity of the infant to hold off and separate from the primary object, the mother. In this, I have not only made use of the idea of increasing distance from the object; I have linked this idea of increasing distance with a progressive shifting of the dominant sensory modalities the infant uses to relate to the object.

My analysis has emphasized the importance of the shift from a two-person to a three-person frame of reference in creating the conditions for a purely representational function. This has again drawn attention to the importance of the father, the third person outside the mother–infant pair, in promoting and eventually guaranteeing the separation of the infant from its primary merged-in state with the mother. It has underscored his integral link with the acquisition of language—as the one who is outside, he is linked with the word, that major vehicle of representation which can only be comprehended when the body of the word, the word as object, can be given up.

It is the move from nonverbal to verbal apprehension of the world that I want to address in the last part of this chapter. But before I can do this, I must retrace the path of symbolic development and underscore the changing function of the pattern of the object in the infant's experience during that development.

So long as the pattern of the object is experienced as inseparable from the object, any representation of the object by the pattern is impossible. The pattern *is* the object, and the infant is at the mercy of the appearance and disappearance, the availability or unavailability, of the actual object. The pattern *is* reality itself, which is sought after, waited for, or possessed. This presumably is the original state of affairs for the infant, who recognized those patterns that heralded the arrival of the object or the satisfaction.

If we move from here to the stage of the transitional object, which marks an early stage of subject–object differentiation, we find that the pattern of the object has achieved a *limited* independence from the original object, the mother, but is still firmly bound by its object status. The new object provides a vehicle for the old pattern—it re-presents it— but this re-presentation is in the form of an object that is still a part of the infant's real world. The original pattern, with all its immediacy of proprioceptive experience, still inheres in this new object just as firmly as the pattern originally inhered in the experience with the first object. In this sense, the transitional object is like a holy relic—a relic of the first adaptive mother and a holding on to that which is on the point of being lost.

As we move on through the two-person stage, we find the gradually more disengaged patterns of objects, which I have discussed earlier. I have suggested that these patterns show a gradual shift from proprioceptive (especially touch) to distance receptor (especially vision) mode; I have also argued that with this shift of sensory mode toward vision, there begins to be a degree of separation possible between the pattern and the object. No doubt at first, the visual image the infant has of the mother has as much of an object status as the transitional object. The image of the mother's face, for example, might be held in the mind and babbled to, just as the earlier tactile memory of the mother was held between mouth and hand as a means of keeping "in touch" with her in her absence. However, as separation advances and the capacity to tolerate absence becomes a fact, so a visual image of the object might begin to disengage from the object, not just as a precursor of, or substitute for, experience with the actual object, but as a form in its own right. Only when this occurs does the representational function of the image begin to take precedence over the direct object-reference or reincarnational function of the image.

This is the development that we see in play, which lies further along the path of symbol formation than the moment of the transitional object. Winnicott has bracketed together play and transitional experience, and this may have obscured the differences between the play object and the transitional object itself. That difference is profound and critical and lies in the degree to which the pattern in the object is felt to be separate and separable from a single object. In the transitional object, the pattern inheres in that single object and in no other (except the original one); in play, by contrast, the pattern is freely transferable from object to object. Both the earlier and the later process make use of idiosyncratic pattern formation; but in the latter case, the child has made the transition from re-presentation or reincarnation of pattern as an actual object to a more mobile representation of one object by another. When this occurs, the pattern has begun to be liberated from the object.

Such a liberation of the significant pattern or image from its attachment to any particular object has dramatic consequences for the infant. Instead of indicating the approach or the presence of the object within a framework of immediately lived relations with things, the liberated image becomes a means of comparing objects, of recognizing similarity and difference between them. *That which before had marked a very particular pattern of the infant's object world has now become a measure—a subjective, symbolic yardstick—of that world.* Not only is the pattern now under the infant's control—possessed, just as it was in the transitional object—it can now be used by the infant as a means of exploring and "knowing" his world. It can be tried on for fit on any object the infant wants—an operation that yields a primitive form of knowledge of the object rather than merely its recognition and possession. The earlier subjective discrimination of one particular object has thus become a discriminating tool in terms of which the object world (reality) may be ordered.

It is this new freedom of subjective patterns and discriminations from attachment to any particular object that characterizes play and makes it a genuinely symbolic activity. In the transitional object, there is still a fixity of relation between the infant's subjective discrimination (pattern) and one actual object—the piece of blanket. It is the most treasured possession, indispensable in the way the earlier adaptive mother was felt to be. In play, this fixity has been swept away. The subjective pattern, freed from its state of fusion with a single object, is literally like a new toy. There is a rush of experimentation, of trying out the pattern in different settings, of organizing and reorganizing the world in the light of its newfound symbolic power. Play, therefore, celebrates not only the merged-in, adaptive mother who is beginning to be lost; it celebrates even more the growing ability to separate from that mother, and to explore the space of the real world which is opened up by that separation, with the symbols that begin to be formed when that separation can be tolerated.

This freeing of the connection between pattern and object has opened the way for the pattern to be used by the infant in a different way. Before this came about, the infant who wanted the pattern was at the mercy of the object that carried it; we could say that the infant was used by, or subject to, that object—he was *in bondage to the object world* and to the vagaries of the actual object. *The freeing of the pattern frees the child from this bondage. He possesses the pattern, and can now use it for his own purposes.*

Putting the matter in this way enables us to see the continuity in symbolic development, which is nothing other than the changing relation of the infant to the pattern perceived in the object and the changing use to which this pattern is put. In the transitional object, the crucial first step of separating the pattern from the original object, the mother, has been achieved; the infant now can use this pattern to perpetuate an original maternal function of comfort, of maternal presence. With the development of play, the infant's use of the pattern changes. As a more separate and mobile instrument, it becomes a tool for exploring other objects, for disclosing their nature and discovering their possible uses and potential.

In the last section of this chapter, we have to look forward from this moment to the acquisition of language, which can be thought of as a later and more sophisticated development of the symbolic function. In doing this, there are several questions to be addressed. First, we need to ask whether this further development introduces any new change of function into the symbolic process, and if it does, what effects this has on the previously developed symbolic function of nonverbal forms. Second, we have to ask how the relation of the child to these same nonverbal forms is changed by the acquisition of language. And third, we have to ask what the relation is between the new symbolic forms of language and the earlier preverbal forms that constituted the child's first symbolic relation with the world.

DISCURSIVE AND PRESENTATIONAL SYMBOLS

In *Language and Myth* (1946), Cassirer discussed a prevalent tendency in thinking about man's use of symbols, to take discursive language as the model and norm for all other symbolic activity. He showed how misleading this can be, resulting in an attempt to understand all nonverbal symbolic forms in terms of language. This idea was vigorously taken up by Susanne Langer in *Philosophy in a New Key* (1942), in which she argued for a reinstatement of nonverbal symbolic forms into the arena of serious philosophical inquiry. What she had in mind, and what she sketched out in this book, was an antidote to positivist philosophy. Arguing against the view that philosophy could do little more than chase its own linguistic tail, she seemed, with breathtaking freshness, to open the door to far wider vistas of meaning. For example, against the positivists, who had suggested that any analysis of artistic creation was beyond the pale of sensible discourse—the artistic product being little more than an emotional grunt or cry—she proffered the view that all forms of art could be seen as sophisticated *symbolic* creations presenting a detailed and precise *formulation* of the patterns of human experience and feeling. Artistic creation was a mode of symbolic activity, which had its own rules and coherences that were just as rigorous as but quite different from those of language and served quite different purposes. Its aim was to present the patterns of our emotional and experiential life in an evocative and sensual way. Its motive was not primarily to present ideas or propositions, which was the role of language, but to *show*, to body forth, the nature of those patterns that we live. To emphasize the showing or presentational aspect of such symbolic activity, Langer termed this kind of formulation *presentational symbolism*. This contrasted with the *discursive symbolism* of language, which conveyed relations and discriminations in the world of objects through an agreed set of conventional symbols (words), which merely referred to, but did not iconically (i.e., imagistically) present, that which they symbolized.

Langer made the point that presentational symbolism was far richer in its detail than discursive symbolism and able to reproduce that which it conveyed for our senses to apprehend. Discursive symbolism, in contrast, conveyed much less information but located referents in relation to other things in a clearer, less ambiguous way. It allowed things to be comprehended (i.e., thought about), but at the expense of considerable loss of richness and detail. Langer compared the painting of a portrait with the description of a face to highlight this distinction, and the subtle nuances of feeling that could be apprehended through a piece of music with the relatively external descriptions of such feelings that could be furnished by language. Music, for example, might convey directly what sadness or longing was like; words could only sketch in the experience in a far more rudimentary way.

Langer's thesis provides a means of approaching the relationship between verbal and nonverbal symbols. Both presentational (iconic) and discursive (usually verbal) symbols may refer to nonverbal referents (patterns and discriminations of objects); but while the presentational symbol presents directly, in an iconic way, the nonverbal pattern of the subject's experience, the discursive symbol (e.g., the word) refers to that nonverbal discrimination indirectly. Language talks *about* those things we have experienced; art shows forth the patterns directly. If language refers to that which it talks about (the patterns of our experience), art *objectifies* those patterns by re-creating them in another form.

The directness of the presentational symbol, its immediacy, must not be confused, however, with the immediacy of a pattern that is lived. The symptomatic enactment of an unconscious pattern (see Chapter 10) is quite different from an artistic presentation. The difference spans a whole era of symbolic development. The unconscious pattern unfolds within the painful involvements of an actual life; the artistic pattern is a mediated presentation, symbolically portrayed, a representation of life.

Insofar as the artistic presentation gives form to a nonverbal pattern of our experience, it looks back to the transitional object, which recreates in another object the wanted (subjective) pattern of experience with the mother. At the same time—and this is what differentiates it—it looks forward to the separated symbol that exists in its own right and can be used as a means of "knowing" the world or the self. In this respect, the art object is closer to the object of play: it objectifies and makes available to the subject the forms of his inner life.

If one might easily confuse the art object with the child's first primitive symbols, there is a further pitfall that lies in wait for the unwary. This is the trap that Cassirer indicated of seeing all symbolic forms in the model of language. We might easily suppose that the primary function of the presentational symbol was communication. I have already suggested, and want to underline here, that this is not the case. It is true that art may aspire to sharing and communication, but I believe this to be a secondary development. The primary motive of art is much more personal. It provides a means of self-exploration and discovery for the artist—a need he has to fulfill beyond any subsequent communication to others of what he has achieved. It is as though the nonverbal pattern of experience, in itself mute and evanescent, moves toward symbolization in a presentational form, almost, we could say, as a means of knowing itself. It is an objectification that serves the needs of the subject to grasp, and make available to himself, that which he has sensed and wants to preserve and perhaps to use. It is a means of preserving and holding on to something of personal value rather than a means of saying something to another. But just because it is a showing and an objectification, it renders visible a pattern of the subject's inner life; this pattern can be seen and experienced, and indeed valued and appreciated, by another as a secondary affair.

It may seem a great distance from the child's first steps in symbolic realization to the process of artistic creation. But what I am approaching is the idea that the purpose or function of the subject's first preverbal discriminations of the object world (just as of the art object) is not primarily communication to others, but something far more self-contained. It is a purpose that has to do with maintaining a sense of continuity of self and object, a purpose of becoming oriented in the world and eventually of exploring and taming the unknown. Finding the familiar in the unfamiliar by the transference and matching of patterns can be thought of ultimately as a process of "maternalizing" the world—extending the maternal presence, through a refinding of the original maternal pattern in other objects, and thus re-creating a home in which to dwell.

This whole process of early pattern grasping and primitive symbol formation takes place in the orbit of the mother and is a function of two-person experience. The mother is still the pivot of the infant's world, and if she is not there, her presence has to be sustained. If she disappears, she has to be found again, and the infant's patterns facilitate these needs for continuity. Without the mother (or her pattern), there is no "place" to be.

In such a two-person ambience, radical separation from the mother has still not taken place. Separation is quickly followed by reunion; losing is followed by refinding. The separated pattern, which spans the gaps, need never last for long; reunion in the flesh is never far away. Wanting, of course, resurrects a craving for the actual object; the pattern as independent form thus has a brief and precarious existence. Winnicott has called these first symbolic patterns transitional symbols, emphasizing the fact that they lie between fusion and separateness in the infant's experience of its mother. I like to think of them as *maternal symbols*, emphasizing their continuing closeness to the maternal body and the fact that it is the mother who constellates their appearance.

It is these two-person patterns, moving back and forth between symbol and object status, that lie at the core of the person's self. They provide the support and foundation of that self, remaining forever the most cherished, the most "treasured possession" (Winnicott 1951).

PREVERBAL PATTERNS AND COMMUNICATION

In attempting to understand the nature of the child's first preverbal symbolic patterns, we have reached the following position. Such patterns have an evolving function in the child's experience and relation to the world, but through all their changes, they remain self-contained and self-orientated. They do not look toward the Other, they do not look across the gap of separation; instead, they enable the child to deal better with that separation, and they look after the self in its growing state of aloneness.

We will see that it is the purpose of words to bridge the gap and to send messages to that Other who is no longer a part of the self. But before considering this further, we might ask two things: How does communication take place in a two-person, preverbal world? And what is that communication which might be possible, and to which art perhaps aspires, that seems in some way to bridge between subjects without the use of words?

The first question is relatively easy to answer. Infant and mother are in nearly constant communication, but this communication does not use words. It takes the form of the cry, the smile, and the tantrum; the touch, the holding, and the tone of voice. Communication is interaction or affective demonstration, a showing of distress or pleasure and a responding to this in the action mode. The mother reads these signs through her attunement and responds to the baby's situation. The baby's first symbol patterns play no part in the process; they are not communicating symbols. Those first maternal symbols are not there to convey anything to anyone; they exist for the child himself, not for the mother. The gap that separates the mother and infant is spanned communicatively by the visual or auditory gesture, not by a showing of symbolic patterns. These exist for the infant himself, as sustaining and supporting structures when the mother is not available.

The second question is more problematic. The playing child is self-absorbed yet may wish to show the mother what he is doing. The artist is also self-absorbed. Creation is normally a private matter, yet there may be a wish to share in some deep way what one has achieved. Recognition and understanding are both part of what the artist might wish for. Yet the artist does not *say*, even though he has words. It may be that he does not say because it cannot be said in words. Words, as we will see, are a singularly poor vehicle for conveying to others our deepest selves—those "thoughts that do often lie too deep for tears." As Walt Whitman said: "I, too, am untranslatable; I sound my barbaric yawp over the roofs of the world. . . ." Despite the difficulty, however, there is a sense in which we know what he means. There is a sense in which deep answers to deep, through or around the words.

We can see this as the point at which the nonverbal symbol is stretched to embrace a communicative function, or as the point at which words are twisted by an underlying need to make them say that which is normally beyond their scope. The nonverbal symbol here has forced the words to conform to its shape and purpose—to *present* a vision. But this hides the fact that the nonverbal symbol is itself mute, and it reverses the "normal" relation in which words impose their forms and limits on what can be said. In poetic metaphor, the words correspond to the objectifying medium of the plastic arts and are drawn into a form that reveals a nonverbal pattern. The nonverbal pattern that is thus objectified is not, however, following the rules of discursive thought. It presents a personal or idiosyncratic image for those who have eyes to see or ears to hear. This objective form (Langer's presentational symbol) operates by creating a resonating echo within another subject. My "barbaric yawp" creates a sympathetic and resonating response in you by arousing in you the latent patterns I have idiosyncratically expressed. There has been *a resonating recognition of iconic patterns of experience*, made possible through the mediation of an external form that embodied in some analogical way the primary pattern.

THE RELATIONSHIP BETWEEN VERBAL AND PREVERBAL PATTERNS

We have considered the evolution (and limits) of preverbal pattern-symbols within the orbit of the two-person, mother–child relationship. It is against this that we have to consider the advent of language. This represents a radically new departure in the development of symbolic processes, because language and the word are part of a preexisting structure of symbols which themselves are part of the world of the Other.

Until this time, the development of symbols was entirely self-contained, the infant forming his own patterned perception of the world and using these preverbal patterns to make sense of his expanding reality. The major question we have to ask is how this addition of language affects the infant's earlier symbolic activity. Does language facilitate the child's own symbol-making and pattern-realizing activity? Or does it overlay it by offering a compelling alternative means of making sense of the world, with the added lure that it provides an almost unlimited means of communicating about that world with others?

The answer to these alternatives is not either/or; it is certainly complex, defying formulation within any neat package. All that I can hope to achieve in the last part of this chapter is to highlight the complexity of verbal-preverbal relations and to underline the Janus face of the word, which is both revelatory and vision constricting.

I have argued that development prepares for language a particular psychological space (the three-person space), one which has been shored up against the regressive pressures of the two-person situation by the instatement of the oedipal father. This space is one from which the child is excluded. There is no longer unrestricted possession of the mother's body; exclusion, and looking from outside of the action frame, have taken the place of physical repossession of the loved patterns. Within this space, the separated looking pattern of the original object, freed from its objectness, is linked with the word the Other brings. The word, from outside, thus becomes the instrument by which inner patterns can be talked about. This completes a process that had started earlier in the two-person setting, in which inner patterns, which were themselves beginning to be freed from the original object by standing back and looking, had become, through embodiment in external objects, the means of manipulating and exploring a larger world of objects (as in play).

Language, however, almost certainly makes its first appearance in development before the dynamics of the oedipal situation are resolved. It first enters the two-person setting, with its less complete sense of separateness and its far greater potential for regression to a preseparation state. In this setting, the word will not function as a truly representational symbol, but will have a more transitional status, being experienced as an aspect of the object. Just as the pattern of the object in this stage is not yet securely separated from the object, so the word will be imbued with quasi-object characteristics. In the same way that a person's name forms part of the core of his identity, so the word will enter into the constitution of the object and seem to be inseparable from it.

It may not be too fanciful to think of the word as standing over against the patterned object, with the pattern of the object, as potentially independent form or concept, standing between them. This form is drawn, now toward the word and a signifying existence free of the object, now toward the object and a continuing existence in the realm of things. It is as though the new relation of word and pattern-object repeats the earlier struggle of the infant with his primary objects—whether to move toward the father from out of the maternal symbiosis, or whether to give way to the regressive lure and sink back into fusion with the mother. In this new version of an old struggle, the word stands as a representative of the father, drawing the pattern into a separate existence—or at least into a new relation with a very different object, the word—separating it out from the original object and preventing it from falling back.

If we take such an image seriously, we could begin to sketch a sequence. We could think of the child as first taking a step back from the object and looking to see what he could see, before again collapsing the distance through bodily contact. Next, we could think of the mother herself as placing limits on the infant's freedom of access to her, reducing and attenuating the frequency and intensity of her nurturing. Then we could think of the father holding the child, holding him off from the mother in a distanced position, and saying to the child: "Look at what you can see from here! There is Mommy over there!" Finally, and only after he had helped to establish this distanced looking position, would the father close off the route of return to the mother once and for all. Only then would the child be left to dream about the space that had become a "no entry" area, free to look into its forbidden darkness and perceive (create) the forms (patterns, symbols, images) of a parental intercourse.

We might also wonder if we, too, cannot see in that looking space of the mind a pale reflection of such an intercourse. For in the space that is created by exclusion from the maternal object, is it not possible to discern word and pattern *interpenetrating* each other in the creation of meaning?

Throughout this sequence we can see the demand, or expectation, or invitation of the father to move away from the primary object—the demand for meaning and symbolic representation—struggling with the continuing wish of the child to regain possession of the actual object in a concrete way.

What I have been describing is a state of affairs in which the word, which is ultimately the gift of the father, becomes the vehicle of a preexisting pattern of experience with the object, which in the beginning was nothing other than the mother. The word finally frees the pattern from its bondage to the original object, thereby creating a signifying form.

In Freud's terms, we might say that the word presentation (the representative of the father) has been brought into the closest possible connection (intercourse) with the thing presentation (the representative of the mother), marking and fixing for consciousness the earlier discrimination. But what this also achieves is a communicable form. That which before was mute and unsayable, existing only as a presentation to the subject (as an inner preverbal discrimination of the object), has become a form that can be spoken, a form that can begin to bridge the gap of separation, which in a fundamental sense was constitutive of that very form. The word is given to the child by the Other across the gap that separates; only when that gap can be maintained can the word be used, as a word, to convey across the gap in the other direction some personal and subjective meaning. It is the gap that makes possible the word (as a signifier), but it is the word that makes possible the bridging of the gap.

As we have seen, there was an earlier presentational mode (Langer 1942), in which the child could mark for himself the sensory discriminations and patterns of objects he had noticed and wanted to hold on to. This involved embodying or refinding the pattern that had been experienced in some other object. Only the embodiment of the pattern in the word, however, can enable it to be communicated to another; for only the word can provide an object that means the same to all, and only language can enable such objects to be joined together into messages about things that are relatively clear and unambiguous in their reference.

LANGUAGE, COMMUNICATION, AND THE SELF

So far, I have been assuming that the word exists to serve the needs of the subject to express his inner patterns (his wants) and simply provides the vehicle for this to occur. That this is only half of a dialectical relationship between language and the self I will now consider. I have already indicated that language, at least in its discursive form, is more likely to impose on the self the patterns of the Other than to give form to the patterns of the self.

It may seem too obvious to state that the primary function of words is communication, but it highlights the radical difference that exists between words and earlier preverbal symbols. Communication, as the symbolic exchange of information between subjects, is a new function that comes into experience with the development of words. This is not to deny the existence of an earlier and relatively crude communication (expression) of affect through nonverbal means from the very earliest period. But just as the primary function of the maternal, preverbal symbol is to serve the self—providing comfort and maternal presence in the absence of the object, and later providing a tool for exploring and rendering familiar (maternalizing) the world—so we can think of the word as serving the needs of the Other, or, at the very least, as mediating events at the boundary with the Other. If there were no Other, as from the baby's point of view there was not in the beginning, there would be no need for words. The need for words arises when separateness becomes a fact. Words reduce the isolation, span the gulf, make things and experience shareable, and make possible the coordination and planning of activities between separate subjects. That the communicative function of words is primary can scarcely be doubted. The enormous potential of words for enabling thought is a later, though equally momentous, development that comes from internalizing the originally external processes of speech. (We talk to ourselves, we talk to the Other in our minds, and so on.)

Once they have been discovered, words have their first existence in the child's experience at this interface with the Other, and from the start establish a simple sharing and communication between mother and child. They are founded in separation and serve the needs of separated subjects. If the father is one of the principal instruments of separation from the mother, words are born under the sign of the father.

But if words enable the child to get something across to the Other (its patterns, its wants), from the start they also enable the Other to get something across to the child. They are not only a way for the child to express its wants and needs to the Other, but also a means for the Other to assert needs in relation to the child. In the merged-in state, the mother effaced her needs in the interest of the baby; she molded reality to the child's needs. Now she can begin to reassert her needs, introducing a reality that is not infinitely malleable and tolerant but expectant of some adaptation on the part of the child.

We could say, therefore, that communication is inextricably linked with the exerting of influence one upon another. It is in its essence a two-way process, and the word gains from this its essentially ambiguous or two-faced character. Communication not only serves the needs of the child to express his patterned wants to the Other; it also serves the needs of the Other to impose patterns on the child and its experience from the outside.

From the child's point of view, the word will call to the Other, tell the Other what is the matter, relate a need or a wish or a fear across the gap. It removes the guesswork, and it may improve the adaptation of the Other to the self's needs, once those needs have become more complex and difficult for the Other to discern. Again, from the child's point of view, the word is the key that gives access to the world of the Other. As Helen Keller said, it gives "a strange new sight"—everything now has a name and a place in the order of things that language reveals. For the child, this "knowing," which the mother can communicate in words—her revealed reality—contains and frames his experience. Through her web of words, the mother creates a place for the child's fears and hopes, and makes them manageable (see Chapter 13). The structure of the known, that which the mother embraces in her view, begins gradually to replace the mother's actual presence as a means of sustenance and support. The unknown and the inexplicable would, in that sense, be equivalent to a gap in the mother's all-embracing knowing.

From the parental side, whether or not the parent is aware of the fact, this same process is a means of inducting the child into the larger cultural world into which he must eventually be integrated. Each word that is given is a mediator of this world, a hook that will draw him into the Gordian knot. It is a hidden snare that enables the knot of culture to be tied around the child without his knowing it. Just as in relation to a theory, every single concept is "theory-laden" and implies the rest of the theory, so for the child, every word carries in principle the rest of the culture in its train. The child may enter the world "trailing clouds of glory," as Wordsworth said, but every word that he learns trails the rest of the culture behind it. Even as the child seeks to discover what the mother can tell about the world, the child is being drawn into that world, which, in its very constitution, is the world of the Other, not the world of the self.

There is thus a tension in the origin of language in our experience that continues to follow it throughout our lives. The huge advantage that language brings—facilitating communication between separate subjects, enabling thought and a detailed communication with oneself about the world and experience—tends to obscure the disadvantages, the snags to the subject it entails. It takes the subject away from his own (nonverbal) experience of the world, and overlays it with structures that are mediated through language and hence by the Other. Language creates for us the world according to the Other, and by drawing us into that world gives the Other the power to phrase every aspect of our experience. In this way we are translated by language into something that is different from that which we have experienced ourselves to be. This is not only because the categories of language are the categories of the Other to which we constantly fit our experience; it is also because the pressures and expectations, the attributions and assertions of the Other are mediated to us through language by those on whom we depend. I will return to this topic more fully in the next chapter, when I again discuss the self and the dialectic between the subject and the Other in its constitution.

From this point of view, Walt Whitman's cry, "I, too, am untranslatable . . ." is a claim to reassert the validity of that which has been left out of the process of linguistic acculturation; a claim to be heard, with one's "barbaric yawp," which "speaks" of things that language has not spoken. It is an attempt to retrieve the nonverbal kingdom from the clutches of language (from the Other). To *explain*, in other words, to set out in the linguistic categories, the words of the Other was, to Spencer Brown (1969), ". . . to take a view away from its prime reality or royalty, or to gain knowledge and lose the kingdom." Walt Whitman, and perhaps all artists and poets, are thus engaged in a *project of retrieval*—an attempt to regain from the Other that which has been overlain by language and thus lost by not being spoken.

I will show that retrieval is also, in various ways, the project of therapy. For psychoanalysis, the unspoken is very nearly synonymous with the unconscious, since bringing the word presentation into connection with the thing presentation—speaking what has not been spoken—was, in Freud's formulations, a central part of becoming conscious. This unspoken was, for the most part, that which *must* not be spoken, that which was denied access to the word, because it must not be acknowledged. If we think in these developmental terms, the unspoken may well be more extensive than the realm of the repressed. It is brought into being not only through a desire that it be not known, but by the process of induction into language itself, whereby the earlier self-orientated world of preverbal forms is overlain and submerged by the later acquired world of linguistic forms—in Graves's phrase, the cool web of language winding us in.

METAPHORICAL PATTERNS AND INNER STATES

We do not know what the origin of language in the human race was, but it seems likely that it first arose in relation to that part of our experience that is most easily shared—in other words, in relation to a world that we can see and hear and touch, where the idea of a common referent is easy to understand. In the development of language in the child it is just this area of *things* that the child first approaches with words—namely, an experience of objects shared with the mother.

In this sense, words, which probably first arose in the space between subjects as a means of pointing to and sharing objects, have evolved as the most fitting and accurate tools with which to communicate and to think about reality. Operating in the most "objective" part of our minds—in that space where we are most clearly differentiated from the object (the oedipally guaranteed space of separation)—words serve us well by allowing us to talk about those objects that are most "objective" and "out there." With them we can create models and representations of those objects that compose reality, and through these creations we can coordinate and plan our activities in a shared social world. This does not mean that there is an exact equivalence between the verbal representations we share and the object world we wish to share; nor does it mean that a particular verbal creation of this sort means exactly the same to one party as it does to the other. But precisely because we live in a world of shared physical and social objects, the match is often good enough, and when we speak we can have a clear sense of the other person's having understood the import of what we want to say. It is true that even here, the word confines our vision and channels our perception (see Chapter 10), but this is not too serious a problem in everyday discourse.

It is quite a different matter when we come to feelings and inner states. In this case, words are relatively inefficient vehicles of meaning. That which we are trying to express is not clearly given and visible, and we have to grope around our meaning with metaphorical patterns of words that we hope will capture something of the sense and form of what we want to say. Words have to be bent to accommodate this type of situation. That to which I refer is available only to me. I have to hope that you might have a similar referent in your experience; and rather than pointing through the word, which appeals directly to your experience of an object, I have to paint pictures with words, conjure up analogical images that in some way may force upon you the experience I am speaking about. Words exist for basic emotional states, but beyond that, feelings and emotions are an uncharted territory that can only be captured by metaphorical pattern making.

This metaphorical pattern making is thus the only verbal way we have of communicating about and sharing feelings. But in this process we see language moving away from its normal and discursive mode and assuming a more presentational form (in Susanne Langer's sense). Language, here, has assumed a maternal mode to become the servant of the inner pattern that "needs" to be objectified; like the first maternal reality, it has to allow itself to be molded by the need of the inner pattern for expression. This maternal mode of language reverses the original and constituting paternal mode, which depicted a world of already ordained and delimited categories (the objects of reality) to which the subject had to submit.

This reversal, however, in no way abandons the constitution of the word as a representational instrument, which we have seen is related to a paternal separating function that lifts the pattern out from the matrix of the object and guarantees a space for meaning.[3] It merely revives a maternal function of looking after the self, obliging the word once again to serve the inner needs of the subject rather than the civilizing and societal needs of the object and the exigencies of the external world. In this way, language helps to create a form for the self within the larger world of shared social reality. It retrieves the self from its unspoken limbo, giving it a maternally fitting "place" and a habitation in which to dwell.

---

[3]The father can be thought of as having a separating function in more ways than one. In Chapter 7 I sketched a view of the father as an important facilitator of separation-individuation, a view I believe is shared by Mahler and colleagues (1975). Within the oedipal setting the father can be seen as threatening the separation of castration, as well as removing the child more radically from the mother by staking his claim to the parental space. But within the context of symbol formation I have argued that he is the guarantor of the space of symbolic meanings, and I have suggested that the word can be thought of as a paternal representative in the life of the child. In terms of the symbolic process itself, the word becomes the organizer of meanings, helping to fix them within the symbolic space and hindering their being drawn back into the world of objects. In this sense, the word can be thought of as drawing the pattern of the object (the child's first preverbal discrimination of it) from its primary attachment to the object into its new function of meaning through an attachment to the word.

It was Malcolm Pines, in a personal communication many years ago, who first drew my attention to the etymology of the words *pattern* and *matrix*. *Matrix* comes from the Latin *matrix*, womb; it is closely related to the word *mater*, mother. In English usage it has a variety of meanings, all to do with the idea of a maternal origin or root; but more generally it means a place or medium in which something is bred, produced, or developed. It can also mean an embedding or enclosing mass, which links the idea of matrix to the original pattern-object to which the child relates. *Pattern* comes from the Latin *pater*, father, via the French *patron*. In a general way it is a reverse meaning of *matrix*. It is something already formed, as for example, the mold in foundry work. It is the design or shape that can serve as a model, a plan or design from which something can be made. In its most abstract sense it comes to mean something that is typical or archetypal—in other words, something that displays the essential form of some class or other.

I think we can say, then, that *matrix* is a term that refers directly to maternal origins, to original or basic material, which becomes formed into something more differentiated and patterned through contact with some paternal agency or principle. In the creation story, the Spirit of God moved upon the face of the waters. The "Spirit of God" is the paternal or patterning influence that forms, designs, and separates; the "waters" are the primitive maternal substance out of which all things come.

15 Self and Symbol

The individual enters as such into his experience only as an object, not as a subject; and he can enter as an object only on the basis of social relations and interactions, only by means of his experiential transactions with other individuals in an organised social environment. . . . He becomes an object to himself only by taking the attitudes of other individuals towards himself. . . . The self, as that which can be an object to itself, is essentially a social structure. . . . It is impossible to conceive of a self arising outside of social experience. . . .

—George Herbert Mead

When I draw I'm in oblivion. I don't see what I've done because I can't see my own face—I don't know what I look like.

—A schizophrenic patient

THE SELF IN PSYCHOLOGICAL THEORY

FREUD'S TOPOGRAPHY OF the mind had no place for the self. The ego, which might at first glance seem synonymous with the self, was a theoretical construct with a quite definite meaning and a place within a specific theoretical model. It was not an experiential entity, but a theoretical construct; partly conscious, partly unconscious, it was situated at the interface of the id with the external world, processing information from that world through the perceptual organs. As "that part of the id which has been modified by the direct influence of the external world" (1923, p. 25), its function was to control behavior and somehow accommodate the conflicting demands of instinct (the "aboriginal" id), of internalized parental representations (the superego), and of reality itself.

It might be said that Freud's ego was at the center of a drama, but the drama portrayed was not on the level of experience; it was a drama between parts of a model, which, although closer to the stuff of experience than some of his theoretical constructions, was nevertheless still at several removes from it.

In contrast to Freud, some of the early dissident psychoanalysts paid more attention to the self. Adler, for example, made it a central notion in his attempts to formulate the often unconscious overarching goal that gave coherence to a person's life. It was an integrating concept, and even though not immediately experiential it was close to the fabric of which lives are made. It gave coherence to a person's disparate activities; it was a pattern that ran through them like a melody of his own creation. For Jung, too, the Self—this time with a capital *S*—was an important term. Like Adler's term, it had a final and integrative aspect that made of it a goal rather than an actuality. The Self was that which might come into being when all the work of individuation and integration had been achieved. It was a new organization of all the earlier parts of the person, prefiguring some of Erikson's thoughts about ego identity as the integrator of earlier identifications. Like the term *identity*, the Self stood for an integration of parts, a totality that could be sensed and sought after, even if not experienced directly. Once again, then, Jung's term pointed toward personal experience rather than alienated theory.

It is only over the past thirty years or so that the concept of self has found its way into mainstream psychoanalytic discourse. Although there is still no general agreement as to how the word should be defined, and some would spurn its use for this reason, there is a growing view that the term has some clinical usefulness. Not surprisingly, the term *self* is central to the work of the self psychologists (Kohut [1971] being their chief exponent), and in their work it has acquired some technical definitions that would not necessarily be accepted by other schools of thought. Other writers have used the term more freely and in a way that is closer to experience. Laing, for example, writing from within a phenomenological frame of reference, popularized the term through his book *The Divided Self* (1960), where he spoke of the "true and the false self" of schizoid individuals. Winnicott (1958) has used a similar terminology, though perhaps with different meaning, speaking of false self-functioning based on compliance with the Other rather than on creative interchange between self and Other. He also used the term more generally, for example, in the notion of the baby's "seeing the self in the mother's face" or of "having a self into which to retreat for relaxation" (Winnicott 1967, p. 117).

There is no doubt that the looser, more experience-laden usage of the last two writers has found an immediate echo in many people. The self and its state or condition is an idea that seems to appeal to something in ordinary experience, and to write about it seems to bring psychology back from the alienation of theory and into contact again with people and their actual lives. The self is a given of experience, while the ego is not.

While psychoanalysis has been encumbered by nineteenth-century pseudoscientific concepts, psychology has been in the thrall of behaviorism and its even greater "scientific" rigidity. But psychology, too, had its marginal figures who refused to submit their personal vision to a totalitarian orthodoxy; once again, it is on this fringe that the idea of the self has seemed to flourish.[1] In particular, it was central to the formulations of the symbolic interactionists, Mead (1934) and Cooley (1902). Much later, George Kelly (1955), with his personal construct theory, could be seen as carrying on some aspects of the same vision; and from quite a different direction—though still from the camp of nonbehaviorist, nonpsychoanalytical psychology—Carl Rogers (1961) made the self a central concern in his writings on nondirective counseling. The psychiatrist Harry Stack Sullivan (1953) might be seen as falling between these psychologically derived theories of the self and the fringe psychoanalytical theories of Adler and Jung. Working mainly with schizophrenics, Sullivan developed his own interpersonal theory of psychiatry, which laid much emphasis on the vicissitudes of the social in development, and made the "self-system" the center of his theoretical edifice.

It is perhaps the very vagueness of the term *self* that frightens off serious theoreticians; it may also be that same vagueness, combined with the closeness to people's concerns and feelings, that makes the term redolent with meaning and draws others to it. Winnicott wrote that the term *self* is larger than us and uses us. But precisely because of that power to enthrall us, the term presents a challenge to unravel its contents.

---

[1] It may be those whose self has been (and is) most threatened by a totalitarian Other who have been most concerned about finding a place for the self in theory that will guarantee its ongoing integrity. It may also be those same people who have most rebelled against the hegemony of orthodoxy.

It has not been my purpose in this book to engage in detailed conceptual analysis; for the most part, I theorize *within* the term *self* and do not try to take apart its ambiguity. Nevertheless, my discussions may help to clarify some aspects of what we mean when we use the term *self* to refer to something in our experience.

The idea that the self arises as an *object* in experience and that this process is essentially *social* in nature are two themes which my own work shares with that of George Herbert Mead. Mead's (1934, 1956) position is put very clearly and succinctly in the quotations at the beginning of this chapter. The self is essentially a social structure and cannot be conceived of outside the social matrix within which it develops. It is impossible to imagine a self arising in isolation. To understand the individual, and in particular to understand the individual as a self, we have to start with society and see how being a part of that society generates an experience of self. We cannot start the other way around and assume a self, then put selves or individuals together and try to understand society. Society has to be seen as primary and the self as derivative; the self requires something from the societal and social for its very formation and constitution. The social and the Other are already there in the very heart of the self-experience.

To think in this way is to say something that is not so very different from Winnicott (1958) when he writes: "There is no such thing as a baby" (p. 99). We cannot think of the baby as existing in isolation; we have to think of "baby-and-mother," of the baby being born into an already existing social and family matrix. Only gradually does the baby differentiate the mother from within this early matrix of experience, and only as that happens can there begin to be any sense of being "self" at all. Before this, there may have been an experience of potency and plenitude and well-being, but not yet an experience of self.

To have a vague sense of being different from, separated from, distinct from the Other, is still only a very early stage in the process of becoming a self. Becoming aware of the self as an object is a later development, though which aspect of the social process is most important in bringing this about is not a matter of universal agreement. Mead stressed the importance of two things: first, language, because, he said, it is only through language that I can affect myself and the other person simultaneously, and thus be recipient (object) of my own act (speech); second, taking the role of the Other toward myself, because only through this can social development progress. Only when interaction becomes a "conversation of gestures," in which each can be simultaneously self and other, can it be said to be truly social.

For Mead, the unit to be understood is the social act, often likened by him to a complex game in which each has to be able to present to himself the "attitudes" of all the others. The type of awareness of self that this presupposes, however, is not as clear as it at first appears. The self that is realized is not primarily an object of reflective awareness, but rather a realization of oneself as both agent and object in a social game. But this realization never comes fully into the limelight; it is a fleeting and fluid background realization, moving as fast as the game of baseball through which Mead illustrates the process he has in mind.

My own emphasis, especially in Chapters 2 to 4, has been somewhat different. It is not so much the ability to take multiple roles in a complex "game" that I have been concerned with but a very special instance of this, namely, *the ability to see oneself through the eyes of the Other*. The visual channel apparently is not one with which Mead concerned himself, yet in my view it is centrally important in understanding any more sustained and reflective awareness we have of ourselves as objects. Whether we concern ourselves with the relatively sudden and even shocking irruptions of self-awareness that constitute the experiences of embarrassment, pride, and shame, or whether we consider any more sustained attempts we might make to know ourselves better or to see ourselves more clearly, we have, as I have argued, to presuppose a capacity to see oneself as a visual object from the position of the other person.

REFLECTIONS IN A SOCIAL MIRROR

In the last chapter I emphasized the role of vision, the prime distance sense, in facilitating the separation in experience of the pattern of an object from the object itself, and thus the development of symbols. Because of distance, the child could begin to separate out the visual pattern of the object from the experience of actually having or possessing the object, so that the visual image became something that could be entertained in the mind apart from the anticipation of an immediate tactile, "having" experience. I have considered this process to be a gradual one, the separation of visual pattern from object only becoming definitive when the child is finally cut off from the mother by the oedipal father and obliged to occupy the third or looking position in relation to the parental couple. In the ideal case, this increasingly separate pattern of the object would then be linked with the word, which comes from the Other, marking the discrimination and drawing it into a space of representation and communication.

In all the earlier stages of this process, the child's pattern of the object would have been drawn from his own experience. This would have ensured a continuity and congruity between the child's experience of the object and the pattern-symbol of the object that he subsequently formed. Only with the transition to verbal forms does there come to be a potential disjunction between the word, which comes from the Other, and the preverbal pattern, which comes from the child's own experience.

When we now consider the process by which symbols of the self might be formed, we have to confront the fact that the object (his own self) the child has to grasp symbolically is not one which he can get hold of or envisage in any direct way. It is true that the child has access to his own feeling states and may sense their patterns and rhythms. But such apprehensions of his own subjectivity are, at best, likely to be fragmentary and evanescent; inevitably, they will lack the organization and integration that is given by the visual dimension (see Chapter 12). Barring the use of mirrors, the child cannot see himself directly; even when he does see himself in reflection, he sees only the exterior of his own body and not his subjectivity.

How is it, then, that the child arrives at a sense of himself, not just as an object, but as a subjective and social being? Surely it is through the eyes of the other person who mediates to the child views of who he is. First, he becomes aware that he lives in a world of "being seen by the Other"; through this, he begins to realize that every act, every movement of his being, has at the same time another and external dimension. While this soon becomes a dimension that the child can imagine, he first experiences it directly through the Other's reactions to everything that he does. The image of the child that the Other conveys back to him becomes, in this way, the form through which he grasps himself and comes to know himself.

We can now see what a difference there is between this process and the earlier process of forming symbols of objects. While in that process there was a continuity between pattern-symbol and experience with the object, in relation to patterns of the self there is an *essential* disjunction. The pattern that characterizes the self, the form, which for the first time allows the self to be grasped in a more total way, arises in the experience of the Other, not in that of the subject. It comes from outside the subject and partakes of the subjectivity of the Other. It is this piece of the Other's subjectivity that creates and constitutes the self as an object for the child.

There is a sense, therefore, in which we can say the following: if the child's own looking plays a constitutive part in forming the first symbols of primary objects, it is the looking of the Other that plays a similarly formative role in the development of symbols of the self. If this is so, precisely because of the indirect nature of the process, we would have to admit that the child's capacity to form symbols of the self might always be more limited than, and lagging behind, its capacity to form symbols of primary objects.

It may be that this is the point where we have to look again at Lacan's ideas about the mirror stage of development (see Chapter 1). It will be recalled that Lacan gave a peculiar importance to that moment when the infant first discovered its own reflection in the mirror. For Lacan, this seems to have been a critical moment that determined the whole subsequent course of the child's development. The reason for this lay precisely in the disjunction that existed in the infant's experience between his bodily experience of himself as clumsy and unintegrated, unable to perform the motor acts he desired, and the visual image of himself, yielded by the mirror, of formal completeness and perfection. The mirror gave to the infant an image of his own self that belied his incomplete experience. And precisely because of the seductive completeness of the image, the infant incorporated this image as the first objectification of his own self. In Lacan's view, the first experience of the self is thus based on lies and deception, and the pursuit of such lies and the continuing attempt to be that which the image reveals becomes the hallmark of personal development. For Lacan, any subsequent objectification of the self that the person believes in—and I take it that he would include the images of the self that come from the Other—is also a lie, interposed between that person and his own subjective "truth."

I have to say that I am not a Lacanian. I find Lacan difficult to read and understand, and am not even sure that what I am presenting is an accurate portrayal of this aspect of his work. When I started my own work on the disjunction between a lived experience and the visual image of that experience to the Other (Chapters 2 and 3), I was not at all familiar with Lacan's work. As my own theory has become clearer, however, I have come to think that the problems I am trying to elucidate are probably not so different from those that concerned Lacan. I might now be getting to the point where I could understand Lacan better, but I still do not know whether I would agree with him. I still do not know, for example, what to make of his "mirror stage," in the literal sense that he describes it. Are actual mirror reflections really of crucial importance in determining our whole development? Or is this merely one of those instances in which the mirror and its reflection provide for us a model or metaphor of relations between ourselves and others—a relation that is harder to grasp, precisely because it takes place in the realm of the imaginary? (I am not using the term *imaginary* here with any particular reference to Lacan.)

In spite of these doubts, I do believe that the reflections we get back from the other person are of fundamental importance in understanding certain aspects of development, particularly those that concern the development of the self. The self that we know, and love or hate, is the self that is reflected back to us by the mirror of the Other—whether that reflection is a real or imagined image. We need, therefore, to examine that reflection in more detail in order to determine its characteristics.

Once again, we can start with symbol formation in relation to primary objects, as this enables us to see something about the process, which we can then extend and modify in relation to symbols of the self.

We have already seen that the use of a symbol seems to vary according to the stage of development that we are considering. In the very beginning, the pattern of the object is experienced as part of the object itself. It heralds the approach and actual presence of the object. A little later, the pattern-symbol, as in the early transitional object, seems to have a substitutive function, the reincarnated pattern of the object serving to preserve a sense of still possessing an object that has become unavailable. Next we can think of the pattern-symbol (still the transitional object) as a stopgap, reducing the sense of separation from and wanting of an object that is nevertheless "known" to be absent. At this stage we can think of the transitional object as a *center of indwelling presence*; the new object provides a *habitation* for the presence of the missing object—like an icon, it preserves and nourishes an experience of communion in absence.

Later, the more separate pattern-symbol becomes a means of exploring the world, a practical means of measuring or "knowing" objects by charting their likeness or difference, by seeing how well any new object fits with the pattern of an earlier one. Finally, with the advent of the word, the symbol becomes a means of sharing and communicating between separated subjects, a means of pointing to or evoking objects in experience that are not necessarily present to either party.

We can now ask what is the use to the child of those symbol-patterns of the self that are reflected back to him by the significant others in his life. Can we perceive, in relation to those patterns, any similar evolution of function?

What is immediately clear is that these reflections, or "reflected appraisals" (Cooley 1902), are not made by the parent in a disinterested way. They are the substance of the parents' response to the child's behavior, and as such they have a prescriptive or command aspect that the child cannot ignore. They are far from neutral reflections, and they indicate to the child whether his behavior is acceptable or unacceptable, whether he is good or bad, and whether he continues to be loved or has at least temporarily fallen from grace.

Such reflections are thus indicators of parental mood and intention as much as they are patterns that define the self. Insofar as they do provide an "objective" (i.e., external) view of the self, they furnish images of a self that the child must strive to become and others that must never again be. What they fail to provide in any degree is a fitting image of the self as it might be objectified in its subjectivity (if that were possible)—in other words, if it were to be described as "other," but within its own framework of intention, experience, and desire. Although the self-image that is offered may go beyond the pure externals of behavior and penetrate the realm of subjective intention and ideation, the image of that subjectivity is inevitably distorted by the parental desire to control. The parental wish to curb "bad" aggression, for example, will very likely prevent an understanding of the child's legitimate desire to stand up for himself against oppression and attack; likewise, the child's exploratory wish to discover some aspect of the world may never come to be seen through the attributions of badness that greet its consequences. The parental symbol marking the child's behavior may thus paradoxically have the effect of banishing and excluding the subjective intention that gave it birth. In turn, in the child's attempt to remain within a loving parental containment, the parental definition of the self may be embraced, even at the cost of sacrificing and disowning a portion of subjectivity.

In relation to the object world, the symbol (word) brought by the Other may, with reasonable good fortune, come to express some part of the child's earlier subjective discrimination of it. In relation to the self, because of the parental desire to control and mold the child, this outcome is far less likely. The external parental symbol becomes a pattern that is *imposed* on subjectivity, not a pattern that gives form to it.

In considering pattern-symbols in relation to the object world, we saw that the symbol changed its function as development progressed. It is more difficult to describe such a sequence in relation to the self, perhaps because the process is so dominated by the dissonance between parental symbols and the child's subjective strivings. What can be described, however, is the varying relation of the child to such parentally formed images.

We have seen that the earliest pattern-symbols are virtually indistinguishable from the object itself—pattern and object are one. So, too, we might suppose that at this primitive level, the parental symbol of the self will utterly define it so that the child will feel himself to be nothing other than that which the parent has depicted. Here there is no room for separateness and disengagement from the symbol, no room for taking up an attitude in relation to this self—symbol and self are one (see Chapter 13).

At a later stage, we find the transitional object, with its indwelling presence, providing a habitation for the absent mother, and thus a continuing maternal place for the baby to be. We can likewise think of the self in these terms, as providing a maternally guaranteed place in which the child can feel "at home"—a maternal container within which he can feel accepted and loved.[2]

Finally, we can think of parental symbols of the self as being patterns that can be tried on for fit. In this sense, they are patterns by which the self can be discovered, just as the object world can be discovered through the trying on of patterns of earlier objects. Implicit in this stage is the

---

[2]That which cannot be allowed (contained) within the self has no "place" to be—it exists in the "no place" of the unconscious (see Chapter 12).

possibility of rejecting one pattern and finding another—the possibility of recognizing similarity and difference between pattern and self, and the realization of the ultimate separateness between the two. This also implies, of course, the possibility of standing apart from that pattern which is the guarantee of continuing parental love, and a capacity to stand alone and risk parental disapproval.

Mead discussed the formation of the self within an ongoing process of social interaction. His self was a self in interaction, and he wanted to describe how the socialization of the individual within that process led to the incorporation of the attitudes and roles of others within the core of the person. My own aim has been to clarify the genesis of an objective self—of a self that is an object for the subject's own consciousness.

It should be clear that I do not regard this objective self as created *de novo*, but through an interaction of the child's subjectivity and behavior with the view or reflection of first the mother and later the father. The forming of this objective self can be thought of as a process of bringing pattern and definition to a previously lived and unreflected subjectivity—a process of *symbolizing*, in however primitive a sense, that which the subject already is. It is a process of self-realization, a process of drawing out defining symbolic patterns from a previously lived reality.

INDWELLING AND KNOWING

It is clear from what I am saying that the self, the objective self, is a structure of symbols. It is also apparent that the symbols that constitute this self may share the characteristics of any stage of symbolic development, from the most primitive to the most separated and representational. I have concentrated thus far on those symbols that originate in the pattern-forming symbolic function of the other person and their fate within the subject who is exposed to them. What we now have to ask is whether this mode of symbolizing or apprehending the self is the only means available to us of grasping, in some objective mode, our own subjectivity.

It is helpful here to think in terms of the distinction between two-person and three-person modes of functioning, which I characterized in the last chapter. Within the two-person mode, the child is embedded in his own subjectivity. An appropriate model might be that of the playing child, whose life unfolds within the orbit of the mother. In that situation, the mother is taken for granted, and while she provides the support and the horizon of the child's world, the child is, in a certain sense, "lost" in what he is doing. His major aim is exploring the world, and through the processes I have outlined, he will begin to form primitive patterns and symbols of that world. The most basic condition for forming such patterns and symbols of objects is, as we have seen, the "holding off" or "standing off" from the object, which allows the pattern to be seen.

If we ask whether the *self* enters into experience in this two-person setting, the answer must be equivocal. The basic condition for forming the first pattern-symbols of objects—namely, standing back from them— is not, for the most part, fulfilled. The only possibility of this occurring would be in the dire circumstance of the mother's rejection and disapproval creating a crisis in the otherwise unbroken fabric of subjective involvement. In this circumstance we would find an enforced and sudden rupture of oneness with the mother, and a first experience of being an object in the eyes of the mother, similar to that which I have outlined as characterizing the phobic experience. What is formed in that circumstance is almost certainly an image of the self through the eyes of the Other, but one which utterly objectifies the self (the "Look" of the Gorgon) in a primitive object-symbol.

Apart from this primitive irruption of "self as object" into the two-person setting, we have to think of the child as immersed in the object world. There will be loved and hated patterns of objects, and perhaps correlative patterns of feeling—patterns of excitement, satisfaction, tranquility, frustration, or anger; and rhythms of searching-finding, wanting-having, separation-togetherness. All of these patterns pertain to the self, just as the transitional object pertains to the emerging self as much as to the emerging and missing mother. These patterns of feeling will have no visual aspect, however; insofar as they acquire any independence of immediate experience, it seems probable that this could only be through an *embodied* existence of some kind, similar to the transitional object. We can think of such primitive patterns of subjectivity as existing only within some new object or image, which resonates in an iconic way with the original pattern or object. Such a transference of patterns does not yet embrace the fact of separateness, nor does it comprehend the reality of a pattern that can be seen yet not possessed.

All of this suggests that in the two-person mode, the self cannot yet be known, though it may, in some relatively inchoate way, begin to be embodied in primitive symbolic form. Such symbols, however, have more to do with being and having than with knowing; more to do with the preservation of a containing, maternal environment than with mapping and orientation within a social world. What is important in the two-person mode is to have a self in which to *dwell*, or "a self into which to retreat for relaxation" (Winnicott 1967, p. 117). Self-knowledge is a more ascetic achievement that belongs to the three-person setting.

If being able to dwell within a symbolic structure can be thought of as the salient feature of the two-person mode, being outside of the symbol and thus able to use it as a measure of the world is the principal characteristic of the three-person mode. Only when the child can vacate a lived relation to an object is he able to use the pattern of that relation as a means of knowing about other relations. As we will see in the next chapter, this distinction is vital in understanding what we are trying to do when we interpret the transference. The uninterpreted transference is a form of living within the pattern or symbol, a means of perpetuating a relationship with the original object that has been lost. Interpreting the transference is a means of moving the person out of the lived relationship to an external position where the pattern can be seen and disengaged from the lived structure to create a representational symbol.

In relation to the self, it is only from the third position, the position that is outside of the lived structure, that the self can be known. It is the third position that offers the possibility of knowledge about the self, of knowing about the patterns that have characterized the previously lived relations of the subject. These symbolic forms provide a map of the self, a representation of the person as a subject within a nexus of past relationships that renders his behavior and feelings within a present nexus of relationships more comprehensible.

THE PARADOX OF SELF-KNOWLEDGE

We are left with something of an enigma. We have found that it is only from a position external to the self, in other words, from the position of a third person, that the self can be grasped and understood in any coherent and comprehensive way. Only from that position can the patterns of subjectivity be lifted into a purely representational frame; only within that representational frame—which originally was the frame of an organized visual space and later the frame of language—can those patterns be organized in a coherent way that reflects the structures of reality (the way the self really is) rather than those of desire (the way I would like myself to be or the way someone else would like my self to be). At the same time, we seem to have established the impossibility of such a coherent self being created, except in a partial and distorted way. Within the confines of personal development, the position of the third person is powerful and prescriptive. It is biased by personal need and the necessity of socializing the child and curbing certain kinds of behavior. This tendency of socialization to emphasize appearance and behavior contributes to an exclusion of personal subjectivity (I mean by this the personal vision, intention, and motivation of the child) from the process of objectifying or symbolizing the self. All of this leads to a structure of self-images that is incomplete and often poorly congruent with the totality of the person's subjectivity.

It is true that the child may, to some degree, be able to disengage himself from the perspectives of actual mother and father and adopt the perspective of less biased or more liberal-minded Others. In this way, new symbols of the self might be formed. It is also true that the person may be able to adopt toward his own subjectivity, his own thoughts and feelings and half-sensed intentions, the perspective of such an Other and thus begin to extend the process of symbolization into the heart of his own experience. Nevertheless, there are powerful factors working against such an easy solution. Such is the strength of the early socialization process that people remain lumbered with the attitudes and reactions of those early figures, perpetuating, below the level of awareness, earlier images of the self and earlier exclusions of forbidden modes of being.

This is the arena within which therapy has to operate. We will see in the next chapter that, in a sense different from Balint's (1952), therapy can be thought of as "a new beginning." Therapy presents a renewed opportunity for symbolizing and knowing the patient's subjective self; but as a new Other, the therapist has to struggle with the old patterns and attributions the patient would cast upon him. These patterns themselves have to be lifted to the level of signifying symbols before the patient can allow a new patterning of his subjective self to begin. Paradoxically, these old patterns are part of the very subjectivity that is in question.

16 Therapy and the Self

For him (the physician), remembering in the old manner—reproduction in the psychical field—is the aim to which he adheres, even though he knows that such an aim cannot be achieved in the new technique. He is prepared for a perpetual struggle with his patient to keep in the psychical sphere all the impulses which his patient would like to direct into the motor sphere; and he celebrates it as a triumph for the treatment if he can bring it about that something that the patient wishes to discharge in action is disposed of through the work of remembering.
—Sigmund Freud, "Remembering, Repeating and Working-Through"

And yet it is quite out of the question for the analyst to give way [to the woman's demands for love]. However highly he may prize love, he must prize even more highly the opportunity for helping the patient over a decisive stage of her life. She has to learn from him to overcome the pleasure principle, to give up satisfaction that lies to hand but is socially not acceptable, in favour of a more distant one which is psychologically and socially unimpeachable. To achieve this overcoming, she has to be led through the primal period of her mental development, and on that path she has to acquire the extra piece of mental freedom which distinguishes conscious mental activity—in the systemic sense—from unconscious.
—Sigmund Freud, "Observations on Transference Love"

This glimpse of the baby's and child's seeing the self in the mother's face and afterwards in a mirror, gives a way of looking at analysis and the psychotherapeutic task. Psychotherapy is not making clever and apt interpretations; by and large it is a long-term giving back to the patient what the patient brings. It is a complex derivative of the face that reflects what is there to be seen. I like to think of my work this way, and to think that if I do this work well enough the patient will find his or her own self, and will be able to exist and to feel real. Feeling real is more than existing; it is finding a way to exist as oneself, and to relate to objects as oneself, and to have a self into which to retreat for relaxation
—D. W. Winnicott, *Playing and Reality*

It is good to remember always that playing itself is a therapy. . . . Psychotherapy of a deep-going kind may be done without interpretative work.
—D. W. Winnicott, *Playing and Reality*

THESE TWO PAIRS of quotations span fifty years and two poles of therapeutic technique—Freud, with a high moral tone, exhorting to a struggle and an overcoming; Winnicott, with a sort of lyrical tenderness, watching over a playing child. They provide a point and counterpoint in analysis between two styles and two visions, and neither ever wins the day completely. Freud, it seems to me, stands for the father with his forbidding and prohibitions; Winnicott stands for the mother and her caring, nurturing, and loving. Freud is the mediator of the reality principle to which the child must adapt; Winnicott is the protector of a kinder, more lenient space, which keeps that reality to some extent at bay. Winnicott is only the latest in a series of "maternal" therapists who have periodically dared to stand up to the father and state an alternative position. Ferenczi and Balint spring to mind as two important earlier representatives of this standpoint.

Two points of view, two theories, perhaps two autobiographies—I develop the idea of theory as autobiography in the next chapter. My purpose here is to highlight two models of therapy and to explore some of their theoretical implications.

When I was a trainee at the Tavistock Clinic twenty years ago, the prevalent model of therapy was work. People talked of the therapeutic *task*, the *working* alliance, *working through*. As in Freud's quotation, therapy was a *struggle* with the patient and his *resistances*; there were *battles to be fought out* in the transference and *triumphs* to be won. It was like a field of war, with *strategies* and *moves* and obstacles to be *overcome*. This was the paternal model of therapy, stemming from Freud, the stern father, who insisted that mother be given up. The idea of therapy as play has irrupted since then, perhaps largely due to the publication of Winnicott's book *Playing and Reality* in 1971.

Winnicott's ideas have become extremely popular among some analysts, and it is difficult to get back to the sense of surprise and excitement that his new metaphors engendered. Like all much used ideas, they are in danger of losing their force and becoming clichéd—everybody now knows what Winnicott meant by "transitional object," "potential space," and "play," and every therapist now plays with the patient, and so on.

Throughout this book I have repeatedly returned to these ideas of Winnicott, questioning them and trying to tease out their hidden implications. They have formed the support for much of what I have written about symbol formation, but I have tried to demonstrate the need to go beyond a Winnicottian position and reinstate the father in the process. I have argued that the development of fully fledged symbols requires moving out of the two-person, maternal matrix and into the more distanced third position of the father from which the pattern of things can be clearly seen. In this chapter I want to relate these ideas on symbol formation more specifically to the therapy situation. I will show how both maternal and paternal modes are necessary in therapy and how both contribute to the genesis of those symbolic forms of the self that therapy creates. In the genesis of such symbolic forms, there may be times when a therapist needs to function almost entirely in the maternal mode; but equally, there are others in which the toughness of Freud's struggle and overcoming is the most important factor.

FORMING AND RE-FORMING IN THERAPY

There are many ways in which we can think about therapy, and each will highlight its own particular aspects of the process. In this chapter I will not attempt to be comprehensive. I will limit myself to relating key ideas from earlier chapters to the therapy situation, building particularly on the idea of maternal and paternal functions and the part these play in the symbolic process.

Patients come to therapy for many reasons, but within the framework I have sketched we can think of them as coming because something has gone wrong with a process of forming. The external form, the image of the self, in some way does not fit the inner substance. The person may be *overformed*—he may have conformed too much to the external image from the Other; or he may be *underformed*—there is too little containment of impulsive expressions. Many patients are *deformed*—there is simply too great a discrepancy between the external form provided by the Other and the inner, subjective self. From this point of view, every person, every patient, is a "compromise formation," as Freud said of the neurotic symptom—a compromise between the forms imposed by the Other and the inner forms or patterns of the self.

What we have to confront in this context is that therapy involves a renewal of this process of forming. It involves the possibility of finding new forms that will better fit the sentient, subjective self. But it also involves a new showing, a new exposure of the self, and a new formative looking. The hope, as I have said, is to find a more fitting form for the self—one that more accurately contains its heterogeneous and often conflicting parts. The fear is a repetition of that earlier trauma of being seen, a fear which perpetuates the hiding and self-deception that has hindered the realization of the person's potential. Interpretation is a formative looking that is both wanted and feared.

Therapy provides the space within which such new forms or symbols of the self may be created. It also provides the vantage point of the Other, the third position, from which such a re-view or re-vision may take place. But in its attempt to re-view things in a more loving fashion, and in its search for more fitting and "sympathetic" images of the self, it has to confront and come to terms with all those more frightening images of the self which the Look of the Other has created, and which stand as memorials to a subjectivity that has been banished into hiding. It has to see beyond those terrifying images that are now inserted between the subject and his own sentient aliveness.

MATERNAL AND PATERNAL MODES IN THERAPY

I want to return to the quotations at the beginning of this chapter. Therapy is not only a looking at and a being seen through interpretation. Winnicott reminds us that psychotherapy of a deep-going kind may be done without interpretive work.

The later Winnicott seemed to shy away from interpretation. He would write down his interpretations rather than give them to his patient. Interpretation, he thought, might take away the patient's own creative forming of things for himself. Rather than taking interpretation as the core of therapy, he thought of his work as a reflecting process, "a long-term giving back to the patient what the patient brings . . . a complex derivative of the face that reflects what is there to be seen." Here is a view of therapy reminiscent of Carl Rogers's (1961) nondirective counseling—empathic reflection, putting into words the half-spoken feeling, sharing in a stumbling attempt to phrase or pattern experience. This is a maternal view of therapy, linking to the infant's early experience of the mother who mirrored and confirmed its spontaneous expressions and conformed reality to the infant's needs.

Most of Winnicott's writings about therapy bring us back to some aspect of these maternal functions: holding, reflecting, being there, facilitating, enabling, and surviving; providing the conditions within which growing, developing, and exploring can take place. The maternal stance posits faith in the background process. Things will happen if you wait. The moment will come when something more specific is needed, but then the answer will be found: the patterned need will find for itself (almost) the patterned answer. Maybe the patient will find the pattern (interpretation) for himself. Or maybe the mother-therapist will supply some part of it or help it to be there at the right time.

This is a warm and reassuring view of therapy and human nature. But often, I think, it lies nearer the end of a therapeutic process than the beginning. It comes after the fears and the hectic strivings have been laid to rest. "Relaxed self-realization" is rather like enlightenment; it can only happen when you stop trying and struggling, when you stop being afraid, when you can learn to trust. Maybe it can only happen after the struggle and after a great deal of interpretation.

This brings us back to Freud's paternal stance: his struggle with the patient "to keep in the psychical sphere all the impulses which his patient would like to direct into the motor sphere. . . . [The patient] has to . . . overcome the pleasure principle . . . give up the satisfaction which lies to hand. . . . it is quite out of the question for the analyst to give way [to the patient's demands for love]."

Here is quite a different scenario. Stern, ascetic, morally elevated—the therapist is struggling with his patient. We might wonder whether the battle is just with the *patient's* impulses; certainly there are instincts and impulses and a struggle against them. The therapist is confronted with a turbulent world of arousal and conflict, far from "the seashore of endless worlds [where] children play" (Tagore quoted in Winnicott 1971, p. 95).

Do these two scenarios portray two different therapeutic styles and two different kinds of therapist? Or do they reveal a polarity of therapeutic possibilities, both of which might inhabit, at different times, the same therapeutic space? Both alternatives may, in fact, be true. Freud and Winnicott do indeed seem to be radically different in both temperament and style. At the same time, it is apparent that the tasks and problems that each is grappling with in the therapy situation are quite different, and both tasks could be faced by any therapist at different times.

In terms of personality, Freud's stance is predominantly paternal—the struggle with the father is at the center of both his personality and his therapeutic formulations. Winnicott, on the other hand, is more evidently maternal; it would seem that a maternal identification is central to both his personality and his conceptualization of therapy.

In terms of task, each is confronting a quite different situation. Freud has a patient who is not interested in knowing or symbolizing. She is trying to usurp the unique function of the therapeutic space, which Freud is struggling to maintain. In the last resort she is struggling against the radical gap between herself and the therapist, which Freud is trying to keep open—the gap within which symbols of the self are (to be) formed.

Winnicott's patient, by contrast, is not struggling in this way, but is happy to explore and pattern things within the protective orbit of the analyst-mother. Within this maternal space some kinds of symbols are being formed and used, and instinctual striving is not a problem or a threat. Unlike Freud's patient, Winnicott's is not satisfaction seeking, but instead is relating to self and object in a noninstinctual, pattern-matching way. The patient is making no attempt to possess the therapist in an appetitive way, nor to obliterate the gap that separates her from this holding and containing maternal object.

It is true that the gap between patient and therapist is quite different in the two cases. Freud is asserting a space of radical separation and radical otherness; Winnicott is tolerating, even fostering, a space in which separation is a fact but not an experience. Each has his reasons that are, in part, determined by the behavior of the patient. But we would also be entitled to ask how much the behavior of the patient was determined by the differing behaviors and expectations of the two therapists.

What I am suggesting, then, is that different modes of therapist behavior are appropriate in different circumstances; equally, different modes of therapist behavior will foster different therapeutic possibilities and perhaps different modes of symbolizing. Over and above this, however, it remains true that therapy offers a space for forming and symbolizing, not a space for action. Where the patient does seek action and consummation, a battle has to be fought. The action element has to be given up before the structure can be transformed into a form or symbol of the self. Where the patient is already forming, no battle is required. In the end, we have to know when to stand firm and struggle and when to watch over and allow.

THE THERAPEUTIC SPACE AND SYMBOL FORMATION

I now want to examine further the idea that therapy offers a space for forming, and creating symbols of the self.

In "Remembering, Repeating and Working-Through" (1914), which I quoted from at the beginning of this chapter, Freud discusses how long-repressed material from the patient's past comes to be repeated in the analysis. The aim of analysis, Freud says, is to remember; but this is precisely what the patient cannot do. Instead of remembering, he repeats. And repetition urges toward action, not toward observing and saying, which is the basic analytic requirement. The analytic "rule," impossible, of course, to fulfill, is to *say* everything that passes through awareness. If the patient were able to remember, he might well say what he can remember. He might, in other words, be able to symbolize. But because he cannot remember, he can only repeat: he acts out this patterned piece of his past life.

Freud's use of the word *remember* is highly metaphorical. What the patient cannot remember is inscribed and patterned into his feelings and expectations; it has never been symbolized at all. The exhortation to remember is thus an attempt to get the patient to symbolize that which he has never before symbolized but only enacted. As Freud said in a much earlier publication, it is a question of "thoughts which never came about, which merely had a *possibility* of existing, so that the treatment would lie in the accomplishment of a psychical act which did not take place at the time" (1895, p. 300).

In order to achieve this saying or symbolizing of what has never been put into words, the patient has to "stand off" from what he feels and what he wants to do—to contain it rather than enact it; to experience it rather than express it; to reflect upon it rather than reject it. All of this is a way of saying that he has to learn to "hold" something in his mind that would rather express itself directly, in order that he may explore and investigate it and "see" (i.e., symbolize) what its pattern is and where it might fit in with other patterns of his experience to which he has never before related it.

Putting the matter in this way, it can be seen that what Freud struggled to preserve was a space in the therapy between the patient and himself (and within the patient himself) within which the patterns of the patient's feelings and relationships might be more clearly discerned. The enemy of this space was the patient's doing and striving after consummation. Everything was encouraged to enter this space, but only in a certain way, through saying; the rule for admission to this space was "no action." All this was for the sake of "that extra piece of mental freedom" that comes from symbolizing—from standing off and "seeing" the pattern of a structure rather than blindly realizing it or possessing it.

This holding off from action, which is one of the principle parameters of the analytic space, is closely similar to the progressive holding off from the object, which I have described as a precondition of symbol formation. As access to the object is curtailed during development, the space of doing becomes, in my language, a space of looking. This makes possible the development of symbols, by creating a space, first in reality, then in the mind, within which the object can be conceived of apart from the possibility of fulfillment with it.

From this point of view, the analytic space can be thought of as a space in which symbols are (to be) formed; the "no action" rule, which the analyst, where necessary, struggles to preserve, is protective of this function. It is not, however, a space for forming symbols in general, but a space for forming symbols of the self. *It is a space in which a self that was blindly lived will be transformed, through the analytic looking, into a self that is conceivable, a self that is known.*

HOLDING, HOLDING OFF, AND LOOKING

One of the difficulties of thinking about therapy in terms of this looking metaphor lies precisely in that distancing quality of looking which enables the object to be set at a distance and thus "seen" and symbolized. Looking can very easily become a flight from the immediacy of experience, and being looked at can be experienced as a demand never again to be this unnameable object that is revealed in the image at the end of the look. I have tried to unravel some of the complexities of this kind of looking in Chapters 2 and 3.

Therapy requires that the patient stay in touch with his experience. It is only when the seeing (knowing and symbolizing) can be brought into the closest possible relationship with the *prima materia* of experience that, in Freud's terms, the unconscious can truly be said to become conscious. Freud explored this issue (e.g., in his 1915 paper "The Unconscious") in terms of word and thing presentations. In Chapter 9 I tried to shift the language of this process into more object-relational terms, arguing that what was important was not just the relationship between word (symbol) and experience, but the relationship between the bringer of words and the subject who was to be objectified in these same words. I will now pursue that line of thought further.

A prerequisite for symbol formation is that something—a pattern or image of the object that is close to the experience of the object—can be held in the mind and contemplated in order that it can be matched with something else (in this case, the word) that is to be its symbol. What is this holding? And what determines whether the person can hold an experience in his mind or not?

Holding, to describe the complex functions of emotional and physical caring of the mother toward her baby, is a term that we owe to Winnicott (1971). We also owe to him that rich train of thought about the analytic setting, in which the analyst's background function, as opposed to his interpretative one, is seen as a symbolic or metaphorical extension of this maternal function. There may be Kleinian strands, too, in the concept, stemming from Bick's (1968) paper on the bounding function of the skin, and hence of tactile holding, in early ego development; and later from Bion's (1962b) writing about the "container" and the "contained."

The essence of Winnicott's idea of holding or containing can be summarized in the following way: it is the totality of the mother's caring and nurturing behavior with which she responds to her infant's needs. In that sense, it is another way of speaking about the way in which the mother "mothers." The "good enough mother" holds the infant in such a way that the infant never experiences a traumatic sense of "no mother." Separation occurs without the mother ever being "lost" or totally unavailable; as a result, the child comes to inhabit a space that always feels watched over or looked after by the mother. The other side of this is that the mother is not intrusive and does not force herself on the infant to satisfy her own needs. She is always able to put the infant's needs first. This results in the infant's ability to develop a space of separation from the mother that is always informed by her presence. It is safe, and the child has neither to look after himself nor constantly to watch out for dangerous gaps or impingements. This is the space of play, which, as we have seen in Chapter 14, is the space where the child becomes able to free the pattern of the object from the actual object and so form a first pattern-symbol of it.

All of this implies a situation where the infant's needs have been satisfied well enough. There is not so much frustration that the first sight of the object immediately engenders an instinctual craving for it—a desire to possess the object in either an attachment or an appetitive way. It is thus possible for the infant to pay attention to the pattern of the object without immediately wanting the object itself. The ground is thus prepared for the child to use the patterns of objects to explore and compare the larger world of objects that surrounds him.

We can think of this process as an early development of mind, created by the mother's satisfactory "holding." The child has been enabled to secure a space that is reasonably free from both internal threat (the infant's own ravening impulse) and external threat (the loss or impingement of the mother).

It is now possible to see what this "holding" in the mind, which is necessary for symbol formation, actually involves. It involves being able to contemplate a structure of action or feeling—to have it vividly present in the mind as an impression—without feeling impelled toward an actual realization of what is thus entertained. It involves being able to "hold off," to look at, and to maintain a sense of separateness from and of not having the object. All of this comes from the mother's satisfactory "holding" of the infant.

If we now return to Freud's patient and the therapist's struggle "to keep in the psychical sphere all the impulses which his patient would like to direct into the motor sphere," we can see a situation where not only the analytic space, but the psychic space also, is not "holding." There is a refusal of symbols and symbol making, because the need for some satisfaction with an actual object has become overwhelming. We could say that the mind, the space in which the object is not, has become an empty space, not a space of (recollected) maternal presence. Its need is therefore to be filled up with real (i.e., concrete) objects. As a result, there is an intolerance of symbolic objects, which are felt to be empty, hollow, and filled with nothingness, because they are not the thing to which they refer.

Freud's reaction to this situation is to reinforce the failing boundary with paternal prohibitions. The analytic space is then no longer a maternal space of playful exploration, but a stern paternal space in which a duty has to be fulfilled under pain of. . . . *The object must be given up.* It is the oedipal imperative, which guarantees a space for the word.

It can now be seen that the position of the father, the third position, has a double, or even a triple, aspect when we are considering the question of symbol formation, and indeed, the question of therapy. When the earlier maternal space of symbolic exploration—playing with the patterns of objects—is securely established, the third position of the father allows a great expansion of vision, which the exploring child may well seek out for himself. Its adoption will enhance the range and variety of patterns that can be seen and used, and the child will confidently explore the larger world the father thus opens up. Where the maternal space is still largely concerned with actual objects and satisfactions, or where the maternal symbols themselves are in danger of losing their differentiation from the object, the third position of the father becomes an imperative; and *not* having the object, a radical exclusion from the object, is compulsorily superimposed on an earlier situation. The paternal demand for the child to relate to the externally given symbol of the object is complied with but is always in danger of breaking down into an earlier, and still sought after, concrete mode.

A third possible scenario is that of the child embedded in a world of concrete relations with the mother that has been unsatisfactory or traumatic in some way. The patterns of object imagoes are still imbued with all their terrifying "objectness," and the child takes refuge from them in the paternally imposed separation and prohibition. There is a flight from overwhelming two-person, "hallucinatory" experience into the distanced world of looking and paternal symbols. This scenario might describe the patient who is always theorizing about himself, and who constantly inserts a ready-made structure of symbols and images between his own sentient self and the therapist. In this way, he avoids the terrors of reviving a two-person situation from which he has precariously escaped.

MATERNAL ACCEPTANCE—THE RETRIEVAL OF BANISHED SELVES

In Chapter 2, I described the scenario of the phobic patient, terrified lest a drama of abandonment, in the face of his own uncontrollable rage, should ever recur. I suggested that what such patients were struggling with was some aspect of themselves, which, at an earlier time, the mother had not been able to contain. She had not been able to "hold" the child through its impulsive expression, but had rejected or repudiated the child who behaved in this way. I put forward the idea that *what could not be contained was looked at*, not only now, by the patient himself, but originally, by the mother in relation to the child that was. This was a looking that banished the self in question behind a terrifying image of the self, which was then avoided in a phobic way.

If we consider what somehow has to be achieved with this kind of patient, we get a glimpse of the task therapy has set itself. We can say that the unconscious must be made conscious, or that the unconscious rage of the patient with his mother-analyst must be interpreted. But interpretation with such a patient will be experienced as a further terrifying looking. What has to be achieved is a resurrection of the banished self. A situation has to be created that is safe enough to allow this banished self to begin to emerge, in its subjectivity, into the light of day. This self has then to be allowed to be, and to be held, but at the same time limits have to be imposed as to what is tolerable: it is not a self that may be fully realized in action. This new sense of *holding* of the once banished self has to *precede* any renewed looking—premature interpretation would merely drive the self into hiding again. Only when the self has been drawn out by the safety of the therapy and the therapist's acceptance of what is "bad" can there be a re-viewing and a clearer understanding of this banished self and how it came to be the way it is.

The first looking by the mother had failed to create a true *symbol* of the self; it had generated only a terrifying *symbol-object* (the self through mother's eyes), which had to be banished, then avoided as though it were a real Other. The new looking by the therapist, which tries to understand the banished self in its context of earlier experience (the reason for the anger, the difficulties of the mother), may eventually enable the person to form a true symbol of this self—to give it a name and a place in the order of things. The rage may have to be given up as something that could still be consummated, but it can be accepted and will eventually find its reconciling place within a larger symbolic structure of personal history. The possibility of such a symbol being formed depends on the person becoming able to accept and tolerate what previously was unthinkable; this in turn depends on the therapist's being able to accept and tolerate and contain that which the mother, for her own reasons, had to reject. Looking after (rather than "looking at") the banished self allows a piece of personal subjectivity to be regained from behind its terrifying appearance. In this sense, therapy can be thought of as a process of retrieval—a gathering in of banished subjective elements from their diaspora, and a reuniting of them with a symbolic form. This is part of a maternal function that once more allows the self to *be* within a containing maternal place.

CONTAINMENT AND KNOWLEDGE— MATERNAL AND PATERNAL SYMBOLS

We need to look more closely at certain aspects of symbol formation in therapy in order to clarify the different kinds of symbols that might be formed and the various functions they might have in the person's overall psychic economy.

In the last three chapters, I have made much use of the distinction between a two-person and a three-person organization of experience. I have also tried to relate the different kinds of symbols the child is forming and using to this same distinction. Within the two-person organization, symbols are characteristically self-created, iconic, and nonverbal. They tend to be precariously separated from the object from which they are formed, and they are not yet fully representational. They do not serve the purposes of interpersonal communication; their primary functions are self-related, not Other-related. Their uses thus range from a primitive re-creation of the object, through an almost invocatory revival of the object's "presence," to a measuring and discovering function by means of which the world of objects can be explored. Within this sequence, I have suggested that we can also discern a maternal containing function. The transitional object, the bit of blanket, for example, can be thought of as "containing" the needed maternal presence; and the maternal presence, which is at the same time a part of the infant's subjectivity, can be thought of as dwelling in the bit of blanket.

Within the three-person organization, we can think of symbols that have their origin in a more radical separation from the primary object, a separation in which the third person, the father, has played a part. Characteristically, such symbols are made or acquired through an identification with the position of the third person, and may actually be the symbols and discriminations of the Other, as is the case with words. Their primary functions are rooted in the world of the Other: communication to the Other, bridging an established separateness; sharing an experience of common objects and their uses with the Other; learning about the world of the Other that exists independently of the child himself. Because it is the father who has been instrumental in establishing this separateness through the oedipal period, I have sometimes called these three-person symbols *paternal symbols*, contrasting them in this way with *maternal or two-person symbols*, which have their origin within the primary orbit of the mother. Having made this distinction, we have to remind ourselves that symbols are not indelibly determined by their origin, and their functioning can be changed by the organization of experience within which they find themselves. Thus words may often be used as maternal symbols, as in poetry, or in the expression of feelings; nonverbal symbols may at times aspire to a paternal mode that is more purely representational and communicative, as may sometimes be the case in artistic creation.

There are many ways in which this basic distinction might be relevant to therapy, but I want to focus here on only one aspect—the potential conflict in therapy between knowledge and representation, perhaps even communication (the paternal mode of symbols), and the containing, indwelling function of symbols (their maternal mode), which has more to do with "being" than with "knowing."

This potential conflict is illustrated within the opposing quotations at the beginning of this chapter. Freud is concerned with knowledge and representation—the primary aim of therapy is to know oneself, to make the unconscious conscious, to bring the word presentation into connection with the thing presentation. In the language that I have been using, the aim is to see, to gain insight, to stand back and use the patterns of distanced paternal vision to organize and structure and make sense of previously disparate and unintegrated elements. It is to bring the isolated two-person elements, which are closer to lived experience, into the organizing power of three-person vision. "Where id was, there ego shall be."

Winnicott, on the other hand, is concerned with something more intuitive and gestational. He holds, contains, stays with, remains nearby. He tolerates those deeper movements that do their silent forming in the darkness, or to use a phrase of Merleau-Ponty (1962), "in the silence of primary consciousness" (p. xv). He realizes that "light" and "seeing" and premature consciousness can be the enemy of this process; it is the *felt* joining together of things that has to precede their proclamation. This is the maternal and nurturing stance, which knows that "the heart has its reasons which reason knows nothing of," as Pascal noted in his *Pensees*. Insight, the seeing of forms from a distance, is here taking a second place to some more inchoate but tangible process of inner articulation, an articulation of forms that the subject still inhabits. The paternal capacity to separate out patterns from the maternal matrix has to be used sparingly lest it interfere with this more spontaneous process of creation.

There is no doubt that some therapists become overconcerned with imparting insight and giving interpretations to the patient. This may be particularly true in some forms of brief psychotherapy, where a barrage of interpretations may be made at the particular focus that has been selected. But it may also be true among some analysts who feel that every session has got to be tied up interpretatively if the patient is going to be "helped" to change. For such therapists, not interpreting means doing nothing; it is as though the maternal function is all but forgotten.

From the patient's point of view, the same conflict may be apparent. The analyst's interpretations are the most tangible things the patient can get hold of, and he may feel cheated if he does not get them in sufficient supply. On the other hand, it is clear that a patient can easily feel persecuted by interpretation; the interpretation is an impingement that intrudes upon some ongoing attempt to evoke or invoke some deeply felt experience.

We need to look more deeply at what is involved and to relate the maternal and paternal mode of therapy to symbol formation. When therapy is proceeding in one mode or the other, what is it creating?

It is much easier to say what is involved in the paternal mode. Here the patient and therapist are both occupying a position outside the structure that is being symbolized. What is being created, whether through a drawing out and putting into words, or through an imposition of some external pattern or form, is a separated pattern, a pattern of thought. An element of experience is being held at a distance and conceptualized. It becomes something that can be thought about and in this explicit way related to other things, to other elements of the patient's experience. The experience has at this moment been distanced; it is Other, over there; it is something that I am not. It has become easier to talk about but harder to feel. The sense of mastery of the experience can easily pass over into a further rejection of it, a leaving behind of something that is painful and hard to tolerate, an escape from being overwhelmed by an experience into the much "cleaner" and clearer "universe of things said." Leaving the chaos behind, assuming the freedom of the word, the separated symbol promises mastery and control as well as loss and deprivation of earlier riches.

What is it, then, that is being sought after, and sometimes achieved, in the maternal mode? I want to suggest that in this mode, the therapy is creating forms (maternal symbols) within which the presences of past objects can continue to dwell. By extension, what is also being created is a symbolic self, within which the subject can dwell—not as before, immediately, in the mode of the real, but mediately, symbolically, by a resonance of identificatory recognition, across the gap that separates the person from his own childhood and his own past. What is important here is not knowledge and understanding of reasons, but an encounter with and a recognition of a past self or past Other in a form that once again bestows being upon it.

When, in Chapter 14, I spoke of the "maternalizing of the world," I was trying to describe a mode of being in the world that was in continuity with the early transitional mode. The old pattern was found in a new object, so that the sense of loss and absence of the needed object was mitigated if not obliterated. This is basically the state of affairs in an uninterpreted transference—the past is re-created in the present. The old patterns are lived out (though not consciously recognized) in the new object or situation. What I am trying to describe now is the transformation of such transferences into something other than the separated patterns of insight and knowledge. Thinking in those terms seems to cause the past to disappear. It is no longer anywhere to be seen—it has been interpreted. Thinking in terms of the maternal mode of therapy, we can see that the past does not disappear, but is transformed. Having been resurrected in the transference, it is not then shooed away like the contents of the child's dream by the mother (see Chapter 13). Instead, it is given up as a real possibility—it has to accept the verdict of reality that it no longer exists. But it remains as a kind of shade or presence, maybe like the ancestors of ancient civilizations; not, however, as a shade walking the earth with no resting place and trying to be reincarnated in every new object or relationship, but as one with a peculiar kind of being that now has a place (a maternal "place") within the containing garment of the self. As the hymn puts it: "All is safely gathered in. . . ."

The maternal symbol, in this context, is forgiving and reconciling. All those parts of the self that had been banished and disowned, that were too "bad" to be allowed a place in the order of things or too much hated to be tolerated within the structure of the self—all these, through the maternal symbol, are regathered in, in a certain sense also "free from sorrow, free from sin" (as the hymn continues), not least because they can now be understood.

Once again, this returns us to the paternal mode of therapy and the clear understanding that this makes possible. I would not like it to be thought that I am rejecting the mode of insight, the separating power of the paternal symbol, which enables the pattern to be seen and thought about. Both maternal and paternal modes are necessary in the transformation of the self, just as, in my view, two parents are necessary for the development of the child and the separation of the child from the primary object.

I have stressed some of the dangers of unopposed interpretation, of a too ardent pursuit of insight and understanding. I should now redress the balance by saying something of the risks of an unopposed maternal therapy. Salient among these dangers is the risk of the patient becoming trapped in a maternal environment that is too comfortable and adaptive. Just as in ordinary development the child's separation from the mother is endangered by a father whose influence is absent or insufficient, so in therapy the patient may come to feel that the indulgences of therapy are preferable to the stringencies of ordinary life. Beyond this, the process of symbolizing may be seriously impaired. Not only will there be a relative absence of far-reaching understanding, but the transitional symbolic process may begin to slip back into a more concrete mode, where the actual therapist will be felt once more to *be* the mother who had been lost. When this happens, the separating edge between self and Other begins to disappear, and the creation of a symbolic home for the subjective self will cease. The therapist himself becomes the containing object, indispensable in perpetuity.

TRANSFERENCE INTERPRETATION: THE MOVE TO THE THIRD POSITION

I want to finish this chapter by considering more closely some aspects of transference in light of the ideas I have been developing. I will relate what

I am saying to the patient's experience of the transference within the therapy situation as the therapist shifts from a two-person to a three-person mode in the process of interpreting. What I say relates quite closely to what I have already discussed in relation to the concept of transference in Chapter 13.

At the beginning of the treatment, the therapist seems to be someone who is outside the patient's life. He is, in a sense, an observer of it and can be thought of as occupying the third position, originally held by the father in relation to the mother–infant pair. Before long, however, the patient begins to experience the therapist differently: the therapist begins to become a part of the patient's life, no longer just the observer of it. He is a new attachment figure, who increasingly may seem to promise a re-creation of the original dyadic (maternal) situation. Already the potential conflict between two-person and three-person organizations of the therapeutic field is apparent.

There now beings to be an inevitable tension between two different agendas. On the cognitive level, the patient is looking for structures of thought (paternal symbols) that make better sense of his world and his position within it than those he currently holds. In relation to this task, he seeks a guide—a temporary attachment figure—who will support him through the period of cognitive confusion and uncertainty that will develop, and will allow him to attenuate, at least temporarily, the bonds of attachment with current structures and objects. This aspect of the relationship with the therapist is often spoken of as the *therapeutic alliance*.

On a deeper level, however, the patient is searching for a more definitive love-object who will put right the legacy of wrongs and dissatisfactions he carries from his past into the present. At every turn, the fear of those same wrongs returning will determine the form of his feelings and communications. This is, of course, the arena of the transference—what is often called the transference relationship—where, in two-person terms, the therapist *is* that sought-after object. In the two-person mode (the transference relationship), the patient seeks real gratifications and fears real hurts from the therapist. In three-person terms (the therapeutic alliance), the therapist is the one who will convey knowledge (i.e., symbols), or at least he stands for the possibility of knowledge, of being able to know who that person is whom the patient wants and fears, and why he feels the way he does about him.

It is apparent, then, that just through being there the therapist is providing a great deal. As the one who is outside and Other, he is providing a place where the patient can stand, a place from which a view can be obtained. But by offering himself as a caring person who will listen and try to understand, even though he must never be what the patient wants, he becomes the focal point of all the unfulfilled longings and anticipated disappointments that have shaped that particular person but have never been spoken.

This revival of unspoken fears and longings is indeed the core of the therapy, its *prima materia*. Yet in a certain sense, the therapist's chair is always empty. At the moment when the patient would most wish his longing to be satisfied, the therapist is not there; he will not provide the satisfaction.

That was one way of trying to describe the situation, through not altogether satisfactory, as we will see. It suggests that the therapist is a nobody, the "blank screen" perhaps, which Freud once put forward as an image of the analyst's role.

Here is a further attempt to describe the situation. Let us suppose the therapist has two chairs. There is always one in which he is sitting and one invisible chair, alongside, which is empty. The patient talks, the therapist listens. The feeling of intimacy heightens. It is a two-person situation that ultimately will revive the deepest longings for the mother which lie buried at the core of everyone. And what happens?

At a certain moment, the therapist interprets. He offers some construction about the patient's feelings and longings. Suddenly he is not there; he is outside this intimate mother–infant situation, and he is inviting the patient to join him there: "Can you see what I can see from here? Don't you think that . . . ?" Perhaps the patient will be able to make that move and see something new. Or perhaps he will not. Perhaps he will be angry at the frustration, the disturbance of intimacy, of two-person closeness. The drama continues. The therapist hears the anger and frustration, the pain, the hurt, and the longing. And still he does not satisfy. Once again he moves to the other chair: "Don't you think that this anger that you feel . . . ?" Another interpretation, another view from outside the dyad, another construction from the third position.

Whose chair is that empty chair? I am suggesting that it is the father's chair situated outside the mother–infant dyad, in a place from which that dyad can be looked at.

I would not be the first to have noted this deep contradiction within the therapeutic enterprise, though it strikes me as a new insight to see the contradiction in this particular way. Therapy seems to offer the intimacy of a two-person relationship, a closeness that harks back to the first relationship with the mother, with the possibility of refinding or even improving on that earlier situation. At the same time, it offers the constant perspective of the third person, the father, who disallows that which is longed for and thereby creates a space for thought and for symbolizing and knowing what is lacked.

Trying to conceptualize this double aspect of the therapist's role seems to throw us into an either-or type of situation: either the therapist is being maternal, or he is being paternal, never both at once. Now it may be that therapists do tend to take a stance in one position more than the other— Freud and Winnicott may illustrate this. But equally, it is clear that, in practice, both functions coexist. If a patient really felt that the therapist's caring was just a tease, he would never risk bringing into the consulting room his deepest fears and hopes. Merely to know what one lacks is not a recompense for privation. If the caring mother was really abandoning the patient to the stern father every time an interpretation was made, the patient would not tolerate such an erratic maternal holding.

The answer to this apparent paradox is that the therapist does not stop caring every time he makes an interpretation. The temptation to describe the therapist as vacating the maternal chair when he makes the (paternal) interpretation arises from the fact that the therapist is indeed frustrating the patient *with respect to that which the patient is asking for* at the moment when he makes the interpretation. It is central to the whole conception of therapy that we owe to Freud that the therapist does not give the patient what he wants, but helps him to know what it is that he wants. As I have tried to make clear, however, the therapist's activity is not exhaustively described by his interpretations. He is *really* there, as Winnicott has helped us to realize, as a caring, holding, listening, feeling person who is attempting to sense what his patient is feeling and wanting. This activity is just as real, though more silent than, his actual interpreting.

The patient, of course, may not experience this, and this is one of the things that the therapist has to be aware of. The patient may feel that he is being abandoned when the therapist makes an interpretation, and this is more likely, the more sudden and erratic were the changes in the early mothering situation. Where, in Winnicott's terms, there was a gradual withdrawal of maternal adaptation, the person will not experience the temporary absence of the mother as an actual space or gap; but where the mother precipitated a sudden separation, then the child/patient will experience the "loss" of the therapist through interpretation as an actual, not a potential, space.

There is no doubt that we have to think of every interpretation as a separating experience, recapitulating in minuscule the birth of the self. Not only is it intended to separate a pattern from a lived experience in order to symbolize and know it; it temporarily separates the patient from his own self and his own involved two-person experience (with the therapist or with his own maternal pattern-symbols) by drawing him out from the dyadic matrix of therapy into the third looking position.

For a sensitive patient, this experience will be tantamount to being suddenly torn out of the "merged in" state, a painful repetition of earlier trauma. The distance between being merged into an experience and looking at it from the outside would be too great to handle. It could be compared to being jolted suddenly from a dreamlike state and forced to pay attention to "reality." To pursue the metaphor, the therapist's job, like the mother's, is gradually to wake the patient up, gradually to introduce a less adaptive "reality" into the "dream" of earlier experience.

When we try to conceptualize therapy, we seem to be faced by stark choices between maternal or paternal modes and a need to alternate between them. In practice, the moves may be much less clear-cut, and the therapist's sensitivity will try to ensure that transitions are gradual rather than sudden. When the patient is occupying a maternal space, conjuring up "presences" that move him, the holding mother-analyst will protect this space and the insubstantial fabric of experience from the forming and distanced pattern seeing of the father. When the patient is emerging from his "dream," the father-analyst will draw the patient further out of the dyadic matrix of *experiencing* into the paternal space of separateness and *seeing*, to share in the symbolic pattern making of thought.

THERAPY AS SYMBOLIC TRANSFORMATION OF THE SELF

I have presented an account of both therapy and symbol formation as unfolding between the twin poles of the mother and father. In this, they reflect development, where the father acts as a differentiating and separating influence on the child, who, psychologically speaking, starts life in a state of undifferentiation, a state of oneness or union with the mother. Therapy, in a very important sense, recapitulates the person's earlier development but at the same time offers the hope of a more favorable outcome.

The particular aspect of things with which therapy is concerned is the person's self, and it is within the person's self that we would expect to find the major changes wrought by therapy. I have argued that the self is a symbolic structure, and that the changes that occur in therapy are symbolic. More specifically, the changes we would hope to find in therapy would consist in an enlargement of the symbolic self, in such a way that its new structure more adequately contained and reflected the totality of the person's subjectivity.

In both this chapter and the last, I have presented a view of the self as formed in the space between the child and his objects, in the space that is opened up through their original separation and differentiation. I have emphasized the influences in this process that result in every self being a deformed and partial creation.

That which has distorted the self is, in the final analysis, the symbolic reflection of the Other. That which can undo this distortion is likewise a symbolic reflection. But in order for a new formation of the self to take place, there has to be a new subjective holding—an allowing of that in the subject which previously was not allowed—to be, and in a sense, to be born again.

It is this double aspect of self-realization that I have tried to relate to in this chapter, and this in turn has led to a view of therapy as involving not only a *transformative looking*, which creates new symbols, but a *containing holding*, which is a prior condition of this being possible. This has led me to emphasize the maternal and paternal aspects of both therapy and symbol formation.

It is in this light that the self can be seen to have both a containing and a denotative function. The self is not only something we can know (and which can be known), it is a structure in which the person dwells. It is more than a structure of paternal pointers; it is also a maternal home. In that "home," the person feels able to be himself—but only within the limits that the very structure imposes. And here lies the rub—that those limits may not be tolerable to the adult person and may lead to a chronic state of dis-ease.

I think one aim of therapy is to create a more fitting "home" for the subject to be in, though this home is also an object that the person has. It is a marriage of inner substance and outer form, a marriage in which the outer fits very closely with the inner to form a more integrated object than that which the person brought with him from childhood into adult life. The process of forming such an integrated object (self) depends on the therapist's empathic relating to the patient's subjectivity, and the holding and seeing functions that I have outlined. We can regard this process as reflecting the very early process of maternal adaptation to infant need that Winnicott has so beautifully talked about; and we can regard it as the heir in the mind of the actual process of maternal care in infancy, which in certain respects has never been "good enough." The finding of a "fitting" form for the self is the answer to a subjective need.

It must be part of that which we all long for to refind a state in which there is an answering call for every need. One way in which this need might express itself is in the search for a perfect form that would totally contain the self. This object would be a perfect union of inner and outer, and it would seem as though it had been made just for us. This thought leads in a number of directions. One, of course, is the impossibility of finding such an object. Nevertheless, I wonder if it is not the motive that keeps some people coming back for more and yet more analysis—in other words, analysis interminable. In a similar vein, I think of all those therapists trying to formulate and reformulate their theories, in order somehow to get them right, not to mention the actual work of therapy itself—that "impossible profession." This relation of the therapist to his theory and his theory to his own self brings me to the subject matter of the next chapter, where I discuss just what it is that is formed by the therapist's theory. Is it just the *patient's* "material," and indirectly the patient's self? Or is it, in a much deeper sense, the form of the therapist's own self that he finds in the mirror of the patient?

17   Theory and the Self

Ah, what a dusty answer gets the soul
When hot for certainties in this our life!
—George Meredith, "Modern Love"

IN THE LAST chapter I discussed the changing relations of the patient to his own self that were brought about by therapy. In these final chapters I explore the therapist's relation to his theories because there are parallels between this relation and that of the patient to his structure of self-images. In contrast to theories of the physical world, which only look outward, a therapist's theory also looks inward and mirrors the pattern of his own subjectivity.

This may, at first sight, seem an odd idea. A psychodynamic theory purports to describe, in schematic and generalized ways, the structures of the *other* person. But to put the matter in this way already highlights the fact that such a theory must look in two ways at once. It is Janus-faced and must give an account of the observer as well as the observed.

Psychodynamic theory occupies an interesting position in relation to the therapist. On the one hand, it mediates his relation to a group—a group of practitioners who all believe a similar theory. In this sense it exists "out there" as something that is independent of the therapist's self. On the other hand, it can be thought of as lying between the therapist and his patient, mediating that relationship, and forming and being formed (or re-formed) at that interface. Between these two, it occupies an essentially intimate relationship to the therapist's own self—it is "in there," part of him, inside him. This inner relationship to theory can be glimpsed in the fact that the therapist himself was once a patient and was inducted into the theory (at least in a subtle way) through his own therapy. It is this personal face of theory that is often ignored, and I shall tease out some implications of the view that a therapist's theory in many ways mirrors the structure of his own self.

My focus in this and the final chapter is on this subjective face of theory, although this does not mean I consider it to be the only face it has. I shall not be discussing the contentious and hotly disputed question of the scientific status of psychodynamic theories, nor shall I discuss how they may be evaluated by other than scientific means—by weighing of evidence, scrutiny of internal argument, and assessment of compatibility with available facts. What I hope to achieve is to open up debate in a neglected area and to raise awareness of the more subjective determinants of theory. In keeping with my theme of symbol formation, I shall devote some attention to the fact that theories may exist in different symbolic modes. I shall also discuss how such different modes or levels of theory profoundly affect the way in which both groups and individuals relate to them.

THEORY AS MIRROR OF THE SELF

We could begin to look at this personal, subjective face of theory in any of several ways. We could ask how psychodynamic theories are formed, how they are passed on within institutions and through therapy itself, how therapists come to select their theories from a range of possible ones, and how potential trainee therapists choose their theories by choosing a school or training institution. We shall examine each of these issues, and in so doing we shall have to confront the fact that psychodynamic theories are largely unverifiable. Although useful and often convincing, they are only ways of looking at human nature, not objective reflections of it. In the course of our exploration, we shall have to relate to the similarities between psychotherapy and religion, and the difference between dogma and fact. Finally, we shall have to note the contradiction between a *method*, which in its spirit is heuristic, and a *system of thought*, which tends toward institutionalized rigidity.

I shall start by considering the way in which a trainee psychotherapist becomes acquainted with psychodynamic theory, and how he comes to make an initial selection from the rich variety of possibilities.

The future therapist starts life as an outsider in relation to theory, but something catches his interest and he may explore further. He may read some Freud or Jung, or he may branch out into modern exponents of psychodynamic thinking. While some may give up at this point, others will persist in their reading and study because they have a sense that one or more of these theories are talking about real things and processes. A certain theory or writer portrays something that they can recognize. It has a feel of truth about it that makes them want to know more. Not without chance, but more often by self-selection, different individuals may thus gravitate toward different groups of theories. In this way, one person may train to be a Freudian, another a Jungian, and yet another opt for an existentialist framework. What determines this choice? It is not scientific evidence or verifiability. More likely, a person chooses that theory which "speaks to his condition." He feels a correspondence, or resonance, with one theory but not with another. In the final analysis, it is the feeling of personal affinity that is critical in his decision-making.

The same considerations apply in the next stage, after the student has made a general choice of direction. Within each school there are different theories and different writers, and once again the student takes to some of these but not to others. This is surely not a question of judging the truth of such theories but, as before, a matter of how they speak to us. One theory makes sense and helps us to understand ourselves; another does not. One theory touches us; another leaves us cold. Again it is a question of felt resonance or lack of it; as with people, we warm to one but not to another.

How are we to understand this feeling of resonance or affinity? In a very general sense, we have to return to the idea of fit. Theories are attempts to formulate what a person is and how he functions. They are more or less schematic images of the person, symbolic portrayals of a generalized human being. What determines our acceptance or nonacceptance of such images is, I believe, whether or not we can recognize in them something of ourselves. In this sense, a theory is like a mirror: if we cannot see in it a semblance of our own self, we will have difficulty integrating the theory into our own preexisting, although informal, theories (i.e., unconscious patterns) of human relationships.

Although psychodynamic theories all purport to give general accounts of human nature, they in fact show a range of different faces, and these faces, which highlight different features of the human being, different patterns of relationship and feeling, lend each theory a *specificity* that strongly influences our response to it. In spite of what their protagonists might say, it is not only, or even mainly, the clinical usefulness of these theories that determines what we think of them, but something much more personal that depends on whether or not they reflect, in some general sense, the way we feel ourselves to be. A theory thus offers an external form, which fits or fails to fit some important aspect of our own self.[1]

We see here a relation between theories and the self that is not often stated. The official relationship between a therapist and his theory is, I suspect, a relatively neutral one. The theory should be judged on how well it fits a whole spectrum of patients, not on how well it matches the therapist's own self. Yet it may be the case that the theory with which the therapist equips himself is itself influenced by the second of these considerations more than it is by the first.

MUTUAL MIRRORING BETWEEN PATIENT AND THERAPIST

This personal choice of theory based on the capacity of the theory to mirror the subject's own self has guided the young trainee to the point at which he must choose a therapist. How does he do this? Again, there may be the same mixture of chance and circumstance, but we have to wonder if the decisive factor may not in the end be something quite similar to the process of choosing a theory, a school, or a group. An initial interview is not a one-way process—it is a process of mutual assessment. The therapist may think he is assessing the patient (the trainee), but the patient will be assessing the therapist as well. Among other things, the therapist will try on his particular psychodynamic ideas for fit. He will certainly be doing this in his own thoughts, whether or not he attempts such matching in the form of a trial interpretation. If his ideas (based on his theories) begin to fit, this will be one of the things that reassures him that he can understand and work with this patient. If he feels in the dark at the end of

---

[1]It may be we feel that a theory reflects who we are; or it may propose an image of who we would like to be. It may offer a theory of therapy or of cure which answers to a felt need. But in each case the image is self-related. I am reminded again of Lacan (1949)—the infant's reflection in the looking-glass yields an image of not-yet-attained integration.

the interview, he will feel less certain and may consider that the patient is too deeply "defended" to use psychotherapy.[2]

The patient, for his part, will work more intuitively in relation to the therapist, but whether or not he feels understood by the therapist will have an important influence on his decision to go ahead. How much such a feeling will depend on any actual revelation of the therapist's ideas in what he says is doubtful. It is more likely that the patient senses something about the therapist, just as people do in any first encounter. In such situations we read elements of character and style in an immediate and prereflective way.

In the first meeting between therapist and patient (trainee), we can see once again the familiar process of pattern sensing and pattern matching. The therapist consciously (and probably unconsciously) matches his dynamic patterns with those of the patient; the patient unconsciously matches his inner patterns with something in the therapist. Each tries to find an echo in the other—the therapist, an echo of his theory; the patient, an echo of his deepest self.

If this mutual sounding is successful, if there is sufficient sense of fit, and thus of possible closeness, then a therapy will get underway. If there is not sufficient fit in either direction, there will be a sense of distance and a question about whether this particular combination of patient and therapist can evolve.

This may not be the only consideration that determines the setting up of a therapy. I am suggesting, however, that therapy is likely to founder where no such match or fit can be found, or felt to develop. It could be postulated that meaningful therapy can only occur in areas of overlapping pattern and sensibility between patient and therapist.

---

[2]The therapist's difficulty in making contact with the patient may indeed be because he is defended and is not revealing himself sufficiently freely. What I am drawing attention to is a different kind of possibility—namely that the therapist's structure is too unlike that of the patient for much understanding to be possible. An extreme instance of this might be if one tried to analyze a Martian. It may be that cross-cultural analyses could run into this kind of difficulty as well. The point I am making is really part of a larger one to do with the essential uncertainty that exists in the process of attributing agency or causation for what goes on in a dyad to one or other member of it—particularly when the attributer is himself a member of that dyad. Defense mechanisms in general readily lend themselves to this kind of unwitting abuse. The therapist attributes a defensive process when the difficulty lies in some other aspect of the interaction.

THEORY AS SUBJECTIVE STATEMENT

I will now discuss the way in which psychodynamic theories are made. This may enable us to see more clearly the subjective relation between a therapist and his own theory. I shall deemphasize the sense in which theory can be regarded as an objective statement delineating the structure of other persons. I will highlight instead the more subjective aspect of theory formation and suggest that theory can be seen as a subjective statement by the therapist, a symbolic formulation of his own psychic structure. From this point of view, the making of a psychodynamic theory is one way in which a therapist may realize his own self as an object of knowledge. Where theory arises in the clinical situation, the process of theory formation can then be seen as the other side of a process through which the patient's self, as object of knowledge, is realized.

If we look at the origins of psychoanalysis, we see that Freud's workshop, the place in which he forged his theories, was probably more his study than his consulting room. It has frequently been noted that the major features of psychoanalysis were already given in the *Project*. This is not to say that Freud's experience with patients was irrelevant, but to emphasize the important part his *self*-analysis played in the generation of his theories. That, and the correspondence with Fliess, the Other who enabled him to speak to himself, were critical in the development of his ideas. For example, the Oedipus complex, which for Freud became a kingpin of his theory, was something he first arrived at through an analysis of his own dreams. From this, he went on to find the same constellation of experience in his patients, and eventually to regard it as a universal of human development. Those who did not agree with him as to what constituted true psychoanalytic theory fell by the wayside: they either broke with him or were pushed out of the psychoanalytic circle.

Freud's definition of what constituted true theory was thus determined by himself; there were no external means by which his assertions could be challenged or refuted. It depended in the end on whether it was possible for others to see what he saw, or at least whether they could agree that they saw it. Power politics and the dynamics of father–son relationships came into the development of psychoanalytic theory from the start. This can be seen in the relationship between Freud and Jung. Jung was first of all drawn into the position of the favored son. Later, he stood up to the

I am suggesting, therefore, that the theory a creative therapist generates is not only, or not so much, a function of the patients whom he sees, but rather a function of his own psychic structure—in other words, a formulation of his own self. The therapist's theory is a particular mode of symbolizing that which he, the therapist, is. We might think of one person writing a novel, another a poem, another painting a picture. Each creation can be seen as a symbolic portrayal of the self. The making of a psychodynamic theory can be seen in a similar way. This does not necessarily invalidate such a theory; nor does it mean such a theory should be judged as a work of art. What it may do is heighten our skepticism of all theories by increasing our awareness of the privileged, yet limited, status of each of them.

It can now be seen why therapists often defend their theories so vigorously. They may think they are defending the truth, as did Freud. More likely they are defending themselves—their own personal truth— and that truth may or may not turn out to have more general validity. The position I am adopting, which underlines the situated and subjective basis of any theory, will not help us to determine which theories we should espouse. It may help us to be guarded about *believing in* any, and more tolerant of the diversity of theories and the practices to which they give rise. It may be that methods will be devised to determine whether one theory is more comprehensive than another; it is as unlikely that one theory will tell the whole truth, as it is that one witness could describe the definitive version of an event.

MIRRORING AND MERGING—
THEORY AS AUTOBIOGRAPHY

I have discussed the way in which a creative theorist may generate theory through his own self-analysis. The theory in this case forms an externalized symbolic structure that mirrors the structure of his own self. I now want to consider what goes on in the consulting room at the interface of patient and therapist. I would hardly get a hearing if I tried to argue that theory was entirely self-contained and had no phase in which it passed through the other person.

I have already argued that it is at the interface of therapist and patient that the patient realizes his self in a symbolic way. I shall now ask what

father and held out for his own point of view. There had t[...]
the ways because Jung could not bring himself to agree [...]
thereby sacrifice the integrity of his own vision. By the s[...]
course, Freud was unable to sacrifice the integrity of *his* vis[...]
no doubt he believed his vision to be the true one and was s[...]
the rupture with Jung that followed.

As is well known, Jung went on to develop his own theori[...]
own school, and for Jung, too, self-analysis and his work in[...]
private space was at least as important, if not more so, than the w[...]
he did with patients. It is clear from his autobiography (Jung 19[...]
he kept copious journals and diaries where he recorded his exper[...]
and it emerges that his personal conflicts were quite different[...]
Freud's, involving a life-and-death struggle with psychotic anxieties[...]
near-psychotic experiences that Freud could only dream of. To catego[...]
Jung's work in a few lines may be presumptuous, but I think it can[...]
said that if Freud's inner structures and conflicts were organized arour[...]
the axis of the father, Jung's revolved more crucially around the earlie[...]
more primitive axis of the mother.

It is possible to see now, in a way that could not have been understood
at the time, that Freud and Jung were talking about different areas of
experience and thus were groping toward theoretical formulation of
different aspects of (their own) psychic structures. Both were talking
about what they knew to be important from their own personal experience, and neither could see that their discourses might actually complement each other. Jung, as is well known, not only wrote about the
archetypes of the "great mother," which can now be seen as a way of
talking about the mother of infancy; he was equally concerned with "the
Self"—that image of wholeness toward which a person might strive. It
could thus be argued that Jung was speaking about areas of experience
that Freud and his associates failed to appreciate. Psychoanalysis had to
wait many years before it could remedy this hiatus. It needed its own
maternally biased therapists before it could listen to what had to be said
about such early experience and development. Klein's theories, for example, did not emerge until the 1930s and 1940s, and preoccupation with the
self and identity as key concepts (e.g., Erikson 1959, Kohut 1971) did not
surface until much later. Even then, as the rift over Klein's ideas in the
British Society showed, it was evidently still difficult to accept more than
one statement of what constituted the truth of the person.

the relationship is between this clinical formulation of theory and the parallel forming of the patient's self.

One possible answer is that the two processes are opposite sides of the same coin. The patient symbolically realizes his own self, and by the other side of a paired act of consciousness, the therapist realizes his theory.

There are many ways of talking about the therapist's activity in the therapy session, but we could think of the therapist as "hovering"[3] over the whole array of feelings and thoughts of both parties in the session, in a state of not knowing, but being ready to know when there is a sufficient coming together of all the disparate elements that go to make up the session. This activity of the therapist, in certain respects not unlike the process of understanding a complex metaphor, may lead to a "knowing" in the therapist, and this may lead to an interpretation, which may be "right" or "wrong." This "knowing" or "seeing" in the therapist, given through his interpretation, may in turn lead to knowing or seeing in the patient, by which he becomes able to realize some previously unrealized part of himself.

This is the paired act of consciousness—as the therapist realizes (and gives) an interpretation, so the patient realizes a part of himself. This process can be repeated an indefinite number of times, resulting in a cumulative realization of the self in the patient and a cumulative realization, a cumulative opus, of interpretations in the therapist.

Now, the relation of the therapist to his theory in this activity is a complex one, and although he may try "not to know," not to impose his theories too glibly on "the material" and thus on the patient, he will inevitably be guided by his theories. Yet the creative theorist may still be able to allow the material to generate new theory. There is a sense in which such a therapist rediscovers afresh the old theories in each new situation; yet there is still room for discovering them differently, or even

---

[3]The idea of hovering over the field is one that has been discussed by Padel (1985). He attributes the use of this metaphor in a psychological context to Rycroft in his book *The Innocence of Dreams* (1979). He in turn made use of Gerard Manley Hopkins's poetic image of the hawk in his poem "The Windhover." Padel sees the image of hovering as capturing the sense of an important ego function of scanning the field as a preliminary to making sense of it—hovering, scanning, and then swooping.

making new ones if he remains sufficiently open to what is going on. The enemy of creativity is premature closure.

It is out of this cumulative opus of interpretations that the therapist generates, if he is going to, his new or modified theory. Something dawns on him as he reflects on his growing understanding of the patient, a new insight, something that may be of more general significance. He finds himself linking it to aspects of his work with other patients, to bits of theory he already has, and maybe also to aspects of his own experience. The therapist's insight into *this* patient generalizes and becomes a new piece of theory.

This account of theory formation stresses that aspect of the process where the material that has to be formed lies "out there," in the patient's utterances or in the session. It seems to be something "other" that is the object of scrutiny. What I now want to introduce is the fact that one of the therapist's principal tools of understanding in the session is his capacity to *empathically identify* with what the patient is or might be feeling or experiencing.

This fact is extremely important. The therapeutic relationship is not, as I see it, first and foremost an *object* relationship. The therapist is neither doing to the patient, nor, in the ordinary sense of the word, being done to. He is not there to satisfy the patient's appetitive needs, or his own; indeed, this is expressly forbidden. He is there to put himself at the disposal of the patient—a parental function perhaps, but it is a knowing and understanding function, not an interrelating one. To make the contrast with an ordinary object relationship, we could say that the therapeutic relation is a self-to-self relationship. *The therapist uses his own self to reflect or to resonate with the patient's self, not to interact with him as an object.* In this sense, it is a narcissistic, mutually reflecting relationship; it satisfies narcissistic needs, not appetitive or object relational ones.

When Winnicott talks of psychotherapy as "a complex derivative of the face that reflects what is there to be seen" (see Chapter 16), he is talking of the therapist as a mirror to the patient, helping to create resonating symbolic reflections of the patient's largely unknown self. He is also talking about identification and empathy, because it is through these that the therapist functions when he achieves such a state of "primary maternal [or therapeutic] preoccupation."

It is thus through *identification* that the therapist gets close to his patient, not through touching or other means by which we normally establish contact and connection with each other. The therapist enters into the patient, but never becomes him and never loses sight of his difference and separation from him. This identification can be thought of as a juxtaposing of two selves, a part of the therapist with a part of the patient. Maybe, momentarily, there can be an illusion of oneness, when the therapist finds that part of himself that seems to fit the patient, but the part of the process that I want to highlight is the recurring *matching* that goes on between something in the patient and something in the therapist. It is not just a question of matching a pattern of behavior or feeling with a conceptual form, a bit of theory, although that can be part of it. It is rather a question of *matching an inner form of his own experience with something in the patient that resonates with that form.*

This mirroring process is officially one-way; the patient leads, the therapist follows. But might not the balance easily shift? Might not the therapist *want* to find something in the patient that mirrors and confirms some sentient form in his own self—whether it be some as-yet-unformed and inchoate part of himself, or some symbolized and highly formed part of himself that is already represented in his theories? Even if this does not happen, does not the process of matching that these affective identifications involve imply a kind of mirroring that is not just one-way? If the therapist offers the patient a (symbolized) bit of himself that seems to give form to something nascent in the patient, then by the same act, is not that which is emerging in the patient also a mirror, one that confirms something in the therapist, or even perhaps enables him to give form to something not yet spoken in himself? This could be particularly true where the therapist is groping for a new understanding not yet given in a satisfactory way within a piece of available theory.

This at last enables me to state the idea clearly that *every psychodynamic theory is a piece of autobiography: theory is the external, conceptualized, symbolic form of the therapist's own self.* Every new piece of clinical theory comes from an overlapping, perhaps even merging, of the therapist's self and that of the patient. Every piece of therapy that seems to confirm in a vivid way the "rightness" of a piece of theory is at the same time a confirmation of something in the therapist that is represented by that piece of theory. Just as the therapist is for the patient that Other who mediates to him (the patient) who he is by an ongoing process of symbolic reflection, so we might think of the patient, in only a slightly different sense, as Other to the therapist, mediating to him (the therapist), through what he produces in the session, that which may be forged into an image, at one and the same time a form of the patient and a form of the therapist himself.

The patient's utterances and behavior constellate, according to this view, something in the therapist that is part of the therapist's own subjective self. The therapist finds an interpretation that fits this activated structure in himself and offers it to the patient as the form that fits the patient's self. There is at that moment a concordance, or overlap, of two selves. Through this overlap the patient discovers who he is; the therapist confirms or refines, or even discovers, his theory. But on a deeper level, not stated in any theory, the therapist too realizes or extends his own symbolic transformation. That which leads up to the interpretation fosters a merging with the patient through identification; the interpretation, once found, again fosters differentiation and distance (separation) by symbolizing the way in which the insight applies to the patient in all his specificity, with his own particular biography and history. This work of linking the interpretation to the patient's detailed biography helps to obscure the degree to which it is also autobiographical.

This notion of theory as autobiography has intrigued me for many years. It seemed to be particularly clearly exemplified in the history of the psychoanalytic movement with its various schisms, and later convergences or rapprochement of ideas from different subgroups. Yet, as far as I know, it is not an idea that has been fully explored in the analytic literature. For this reason I was intrigued to find a recent paper by Simon (1988) that seemed to be moving in a similar direction. Simon called his paper "The imaginary twins: the case of Beckett and Bion." In it he explores in detail some major themes in Beckett's literary work and in Bion's theoretical work, and he demonstrates the extraordinary overlap of their concerns, expressed nevertheless in very different ways. The point of interest here is that, early in both of their careers, Beckett was in therapy with Bion. Subsequent to this there was no contact between the two men, although Bion apparently followed Beckett's work. Simon's thesis is that the therapeutic contact had a profound and prolonged impact on both men, which informed the work of both of them for years to come.

Simon writes:

> I will argue that in the years of their work together, something happened, or something "clicked," in their interaction and in the intersection of their life histories and temperaments. The work with Beckett, in an important sense, helped to set up a certain *programme* for Bion's psychoanalytic concerns over the next forty years of his life. Moreover, I will argue that in regard to certain themes and to certain forms of presenting these themes, the works of Beckett and Bion can be shown to run in parallel course, with Beckett struggling with certain problems about meaning, communication, affect, the origins and fate of human connectedness in his literary work and Bion pursuing these themes in his psychoanalytic writings and in his autobiographical-psychoanalytic writings. [p. 331]

Simon sees this as an instance of something he believes is not uncommon in the history of psychoanalysis—namely, a patient making a profound impact on an analyst, and in this way providing the material for long-term seminal work in formulating theoretical issues. He writes:

> Something unfinished, unsatisfying, unresolved, but intriguing and attractive, gets into the "system" of the analyst and does not let him alone. [p. 331]

This "something" is the stimulus for the analyst's extended working-out of new theoretical ideas. In trying to explain it, Simon refers to Bion's idea of an imaginary twinship, *introducing the idea that each saw in the other a reflection of himself.* Toward the end of the paper, he more explicitly states his view that what is involved in phenomena of this kind is a common core, an overlapping of inner structure:

> My claim is that there is an important gestalt, a gestalt of form and content common to Beckett and Bion. I also suggest, that in the encounter between the two . . . each intuitively apprehended the presence of that gestalt in the other, though neither could conceptualise it or formalise it. I would assume that the decision to go to the Jung lecture [Bion had apparently suggested that he and Beckett go together to a lecture that Jung was delivering at the Tavistock Clinic] represented a subliminal awareness that they needed someone to catalyse or crystallise their inchoate understanding, and that over the remaining

years each in his own way would work out and work in the implications of and exposition of that gestalt. [p. 349]

Simon's thesis thus has similarities to my own. But whereas he suggests that the process he describes is an occasional element in the development of psychoanalysis and psychoanalytic theory, I am suggesting that, in a more subtle way, it is a feature of every therapy that is more than just a fitting of someone else's theory to a patient's material. The occurrence of a gestalt that bridges two selves and helps to form or formulate both of them is, I would maintain, present in every therapy and perhaps in every interpretation.

THEORY AS OBJECTIVE STATEMENT

This chapter has led to a more complex view of psychodynamic theory than would usually be accepted. I am not suggesting that theory be viewed only from the subjective point of view. I am merely asking that we pay more attention to it. The aim of creating an objective theory might still be pursued as an ideal, yet paradoxically, that aim may only be furthered if we come to doubt more seriously that which we think we know.

The view that psychodynamic theory is a cumulative picture of psychological structure that transcends any particular individual rests its case on the idea that the theory has been built up through experience with many individuals over a long period of time. It transcends any particular theoretician for a similar reason—that it is a synthesis of the ideas of many different individuals. Theory in this sense might be thought of as an objective statement—if not scientific, at least honed and refined in the myriad consulting rooms of the world.

This "cumulative wisdom" view of theory may well deserve some recognition. There are, however, a number of points that might dampen our enthusiasm for too complete an acceptance of it. First, the larger areas of psychoanalytic theory have been mapped by relatively few creative individuals, whereas the mass of ordinary therapists have tended to confirm them. Second, the major thrusts of theory have tended to be formulated in relation to relatively few paradigmatic cases. Third, the process of confirmation of psychodynamic theory is highly problematic.

It is subject to all manner of doubts, not least because of the nature of psychoanalytic coteries and the dynamics of psychoanalytic training and institutions. Finally, to this we must add the whole subjective dimension of theory I have explored in this chapter.

In the next and final chapter I shall explore both the institutional and subjective dimensions of theory in further ways. In particular I shall discuss the part that theory plays in the economy of the therapist's self and in the life of institutions. This will involve looking in more detail at the symbolic mode or level of theory in the mind of the therapist and the way in which this will influence or impede his quest for an objective view of reality.

18 Theory and Reality

Human kind cannot bear very much reality . . .
—T. S. Eliot, "Burnt Norton"

All is safely gathered in . . .
—Hymn

THE DECONSTRUCTION OF REALITY

IT WAS IMMANUEL KANT who made the important philosophical
distinction between *phenomenal* and *noumenal* reality. The phenomenal world was the world we could know and experience; the
noumenal world was that which lay behind the phenomenal world.
We could neither experience it nor know it, but we could make inferences
about it. It was unknowable in any direct way.

This notion of two orders—a realm of knowledge and a realm of
reality—is crucially important in any consideration of symbols. Symbols
occupy a different realm from objects: the map is not the territory; the
symbol is not the object. The symbol can indeed only have its existence in
the space where the object is not.

This is the thesis that has underpinned my whole exploration of self
and symbol in this book, and it has been a major part of my concern to
spell out the conditions and achievements that make the development of
a symbolic world possible at all.

There is no doubt that the symbolic is a painful and hard-won achievement that introduces not only freedom but also uncertainty into the
world. To live in the "real" is to be certain of what is the case. The real is
the primary stuff of our experience. To live in the symbolic is to live in
doubt. It is to be in a state of uncertainty, of never knowing for sure, of
always considering that something could be other than how we see it. But
the symbolic is also a world of possibility, because the patterns with

which we operate within it now exist in ourselves, not out there in the world. They are no longer a part of the object but have become part of our subjectivity—something we can use as we think fit. It is now a question of how we *see* or *construe* the object (reality), not just a simple matter of the way it is.

This is an issue constantly confronted in therapy, at least indirectly. The patient says, "This is the way it is; this is the way it will turn out." He has certainty, even though it may be a certainty of misfortune. The therapist says, "Perhaps things are not quite so certain as you think; perhaps you only see them this way because . . ." It is then into this gap of uncertainty the therapist has opened up that the whole story (pattern, symbol) of the patient's life and experience can come to be conceived of. The patient may now realize that his former certainty was based on past experience, not on present probability. Where reality was, there transference (symbol) shall be.

From this point of view, the experience of transference unhinges the world—it deconstructs the world by separating the pattern of our life from its lived reality. It thereby creates a gap between the two orders. This gap or separation between symbol and reality is the condition of new possibility. But because it creates uncertainty, it arouses fear, and so the impulse to close the gap is strong.

This deconstruction of reality, brought about through separation of the pattern (symbol) from reality, is central to the whole therapeutic enterprise. It was addressed in a very interesting way by George Kelly, the originator of personal construct theory. Kelly once said that his philosophical position was one of "constructive alternativism." He would have agreed that we can never know what reality actually is. The best we can do is to say what the world is like—it is always *like* something else. Although he was not a psychoanalyst, he perceived that people spend much of their time construing the world in terms of patterns they are unaware of. They act into a world of nonverbal constructs that they take to be reality itself.

Kelly saw the therapist's job as one of helping the patient to construe things differently, of making different comparisons, or of making conscious comparisons instead of unconscious ones. He did not in fact see a great difference between helping a student with his research project and helping a patient with the project of his life. In each case it was a question of trying to make sense of (construe) something and then testing out the implications of one's view or hypothesis about the world. Constructs are always predictions, and man is essentially experimental in the way he sets about things. Kelly often used the metaphor of the scientist to capture this sense of man's searching and exploring nature.

In one of his papers, "The Language of Hypothesis: Man's Psychological Instrument" (in Maher 1969), Kelly addressed this notion in a novel way. He gave the example of taking something quite obvious—say, that the floor was hard—and he would say to the person: "Just imagine for a moment that the floor is hard! Just suppose that the floor is hard. What then? What would follow from this?" In a certain sense Kelly's question is nonsense. How can one imagine that something is the case, when we know it to be the case already? That precisely is the point. How can we begin to imagine—in other words, to entertain an idea of something in the symbolic realm—that presently exists only as part of our reality? This is the task of therapy and it is also the task of creativity—to envisage new possibilities by unhinging the pattern or symbol of an object from its embeddedness in the real.

These ideas led Kelly to speak of the *invitational mood* in psychotherapy. Therapy, according to Kelly, was not about suggesting to patients a different reality that they might believe instead of the reality they currently adhered to. It was about enabling or inviting them to enter the symbolic world of their imaginations so that they could envisage more possibilities for their lives than their current fixed views of reality allowed them.

Kelly's methods were not those of psychoanalysis, but I have found his ideas helpful and illuminating in thinking about what psychoanalysts do when they make interpretations and what they do when they make theories. The making of a theory, like the symbolic realization of the self in therapy, is a process of lifting patterns out from the real into a symbolic realm where there are no objects. The word *theory* comes from the Greek root *therio*, meaning "to behold or contemplate"; the Greek word *theoros* means "spectator." This derivation of the word *theory* is in keeping with my thesis that it is through looking and contemplating (and not being able to touch or do) that psychological separation from the object and separation of pattern (symbol) from object is achieved. If we are looking here for a psychoanalytic interpretation of reality, we might well wonder if reality—that which is forever beyond our grasp—is not related in some way to that which is enclosed within the oedipal circle.

Developmentally speaking, what goes on between the parents can only be imagined (symbolized), never experienced.

If what I have said throughout my presentation has helped to convey the arduous route that has to be taken toward a symbolic life, perhaps it will also help us to understand the precariousness of this achievement, and the ease with which such a developed and demanding capacity will revert to earlier modes of the process when under pressure. This regression of the symbolic toward the real is nowhere more apparent than in relation to theory. This can be seen both in the individual's relation to his own theory and in his relation to the theory of a group.

I shall consider these various modes and functions of theory under four headings: theory as doctrine, theory as refuge, theory and religion, and theory as dwelling for the self.

THEORY AS DOCTRINE

The idea of the *invitational* mood in psychotherapy is not one that would appeal to the doctrinal therapist. Such a therapist *knows*—he does not have uncertainty, he does not wonder. In spite of all his protestations to the contrary, such a therapist lives with the certainty of facts. Theory—the fleeting symbol or pattern that emerges from the object in contemplation of it—has been replaced by a new kind of reality. In doctrine, the symbolic form has reunited with the object and become the new reality. Doctrine—for which we might also substitute the word *dogma*—does not say what might be, what could be. It states what is.

The symbolic has here usurped the unknown. There is a tyranny of concepts over the more reticent substance of the real. A way of seeing has become the way it really is. Hypothesis has become fact. And all this has been achieved, not by a process of questioning reality, but rather by defiant assertion in the face of reality. The impossible goal of possessing the object symbolically has been achieved. And let anyone who doubts it shut up!

In this reification of theory, the line of difference separating symbol from symbolized has disappeared. The achievement by which the symbol of the object came to be formed by separation from the object has been lost. The object (reality) is now felt to be under the control of the concept (symbol), not any longer capriciously independent of it.

This substitution of certainty for uncertainty is probably the major gain from the maneuver; omnipotent control of reality by the symbol has been achieved by resurrecting the earlier transitional mode of subjective objects (Winnicott's term). Reality for the doctrinal therapist is what he says it is, what he wants it to be. The uncertainty of a vast and unknowable objective *reality* has been replaced by the certainty of symbolic *theoretical* relationships that have regressed to the concrete level of transitional functioning. Through this loss of difference, theories can now reassure us by their ever-present sameness, and patients can comfort us by conforming to our view and confirming our view of reality. Like the transitional object, theories will now comfort us when discrepancy and absence of the familiar object threaten our security. Within the familiar theory there are no nasty gaps; it presents us with a seamless fabric of reality in which we feel at home.

It is worth noting here that this regression of theory toward the "real" recapitulates, but in an opposite direction, the process of therapy, in which there had to be a painful unhinging of the subjective part of ourselves from its primary embeddedness in the "real" (for example, in the interpretation of the transference). That process gave us an "extra piece of freedom" by showing us that the world and the self were not fixed, as we had thought, but more various and therefore full of a greater number of possibilities. The regression of theory works in an opposite sense. It closes off possibilities, reducing the freedom of the world (in this case, the Other, the patient), and in our feeling gives us omnipotent control over it. Freedom and certainty are in inverse relationship to each other.

The institutional dimensions of this mode of theory are of great importance, although beyond the scope of this volume to explore in detail. I can, however, sketch an outline of the possible relationship between a doctrinal therapist and the body of institutionalized theory to which he adheres.

In drawing this outline we would have to remember that the therapist's theory is a part of himself as well as part of some external body of "knowledge" (I put "knowledge" in quotation marks because the issue here is not the truth of a theory but its acceptance by a group of people). We would have to suppose that the therapist's theory provided a symbolic form that fitted the therapist's self, and that this symbolic form was felt also to fit the self by each other member of the group. We could then argue that just as in the therapy situation, theory provides an intersubjective bridge between therapist and patient, so in the group of like-minded theoreticians the body of theory would exist as a kind of shared subjective object. This idea is not dissimilar to Freud's idea of the group—each member sharing or internalizing a common ideal.

The institutional theory now becomes a bond between the members, a shared confirmation of the self, one that must not be challenged or allowed to change. The theory becomes dogma—a statement about reality, not a theory about human beings. What gets lost in the awareness of each member is the subjective factor—the intimate relation the theory has to each one of the group and the coincidence or overlapping of symbolic reflections of the self of each member that exists within the shared group object.

The next stage of institutionalization of theory would have to take account of different factors. These would include the initiation of other members into the group and the means by which this was done. While a process of self-selection to the group might to some extent ensure that the novices to that group felt some resonance with the symbolic forms of the theory, the method of entry through training and personal therapy would also have to be taken into account. This is where the tyranny of defended theories would begin to take its toll and the trainee or novitiate would be increasingly exposed to assertions about his own reality that would leave no room for disagreement. When this happened, therapy would no longer be an *invitation* to the trainee/patient to contemplate the many-faceted reality of his personal experience but an exercise in *forcing* reality (the novitiate) to conform to the preordained pattern of the theory. Disagreement in this circumstance is bound to be resistance or defense (see Chapter 17, footnote 3), and challenging of basic assumptions would amount to heresy.

This is not to say that the novitiate will necessarily protest. What is at stake is not only his personal integrity, which might encourage protest; there is the contrary lure of omnipotent certainty and the comfort that this promises against the essential uncertainty of a person's being in the world. The person who allows himself to be indoctrinated is a more or less willing convert.

I have presented an extreme image of institutionalized theory and practice to try to illustrate its means and mechanisms. It does not necessarily mean that such a picture exists in the real world—the map is not the territory. What I shall argue is that psychodynamic theory exists permanently in a state of tension, slung between its hypothetical/objective moment and its personal/subjective one. The security needs of the subject will push it toward concrete certainty and the subjective pole (reification of theory); the need of the subject to discover the truth, to keep open a search for the real object, will pull it toward the symbolic and the hypothetical.

It might be said with Eliot that "human kind cannot bear very much reality," in the sense of an Other who is over and against us, not subject to our wishes, and always more various than our predictions and formulations of it. Under these circumstances, the pressure to "return to the mother" who made the world to be what we needed, to merge again with her as a reassurance against discrepant reality, must surely be very great. Although our capacity to tolerate separation from the object and the uncertainty arising out of its independence from us is a goal toward which psychoanalysis and most dynamic psychotherapies would aspire, it is an achievement that is variable between individuals, and within each of us at different times. We all are involved in a never-ending struggle to face reality.

THEORY AS REFUGE

The idea of theory as a refuge from reality—of theory as an alternative reality—has already emerged in what I have been saying. I have likened theory in this sense to the baby's transitional object—the bit of blanket that restores the feeling of continuity and familiarity in the face of change. The mother is gone; she is still here. Theory too can be a kind of solace—an illusion of predictability and order in a threatening world. That world can be the external world, but it can also be our own subjectivity that threatens us with chaos. This is the point at which theory links up with therapy—in a sense becomes therapy—where theory becomes a home for the self, a "place" in which the self can dwell.

Theory can exist for us in different ways, spanning the whole range of symbolic modes. I emphasize here the distinction I have made between maternal and paternal symbols (Chapter 14) and the different uses these symbols have in the economy of the self. The maternal symbol is a containing symbol. It perpetuates the maternal function of looking after the self. It is still in warm and close connection with the object it represents and serves to remind the subject so vividly of that absent experience that the boundary of separation is easily blurred. In relation to theory, this may be the form in which reality is first "captured"—the burgeoning poetic metaphor that ushers in the new insight. As such, the maternal symbol provides a space still warm with the imprint of the object and provides a place for the memory of the object to dwell. Theory in this mode *contains* the living substance of the self—not, of course, in reality, but in an illusory way.

The paternal symbol is a further development that has incorporated a more radical separation from the object into its constitution. It has bowed to the oedipal imperative—the "must nots," the "on pain ofs"— that bolster up the boundary against incestuous possession. Founded in separation, it forms bridges to the other person through communication. It allows us to talk about the objects we do not (and cannot) have. Theory in this mode is a set of ideas, of observations and reflections about the object, that we can share with others and use to enhance our understanding of it so that we can better predict its behavior. It may well be that paternal symbols have their major function in relation to separated objects. Their aim is to know, to direct, to point toward, and to establish orientation and adaptation in relation to the separated object. The separated object is one we cannot control, so in order to adapt to it we have to learn its ways and learn to communicate with it.

Theory exists in these ways in each of us, serving our different and changing needs in relation to the object. The greatest problems are created when we do not keep the distinctions clear. The problem with institutional and institutionalized theory is that the personal and maternal modes of theory are not acknowledged but are everywhere rampant. The theoretician in this case is looking after himself with his theory when he claims to be using it in the service of the object (of reality).

THEORY AND RELIGION

Wittgenstein (1922) said, "Whereof one cannot speak, thereon one must be silent." The skeptic might agree and would suggest that since there is no way of *proving* that psychotherapy, and especially psychodynamic theories, are dealing with real things, it would be better to pay no attention to them at all. This is just the kind of criticism that is also directed at religion. Yet for the practitioner of either discipline, such attacks do not have much effect. Just as the truly religious person says that he *knows* (Jung, the religious psychotherapist, often said this)—that it is part of his *experience* that God supports and gives guidance, for example—so the psychotherapist will say that he, too, knows from experience that certain phenomena he is talking about have a reality.

The link here is that both psychotherapy and religion deal with the ineffable. Both need to talk about that which, in Wittgenstein's terms, cannot be talked about. Both deal with things experienced but unseen. Religion locates these things in a supernatural realm; psychotherapy locates them in a natural one. Both deal with issues of truth, healing, and wholeness—matters of intense concern to the self. Finally, both deal with mental suffering and propose methods of "cure." With religion on the decline and psychotherapy on the increase, I would not be the first to suggest that psychotherapy might lay some claim to be the secular religion of the twentieth century. It is also probable that among its practitioners are many who in a less secular age might have numbered among the priesthood.

There is, however, an important difference between psychotherapy and religion. Usually, and certainly in its psychoanalytic forms, psychotherapy is informed by a scientific spirit. Even though it fails to be scientific in the experimental sense, it can be rigorous in its methods, and it strives to make its formulations within the framework of the possible, that is, of the natural. Although its canons for the marshaling and weighing of evidence may not be as rigorous as skeptics would like, it can strive to display evidence, and it can, at least in principle, reach a point of being able to say that one set of evidence is more persuasive than another. In the last resort, however, it remains a matter of persuasion, not proof, both in its practice and in relation to theory.

There is one further important link in terms of content. From an analytic perspective, both religion and psychotherapy deal with structures and experiences that relate to infancy and childhood, to issues of trust, love, and caring, and to issues of right and wrong in relation to figures that are larger than ourselves and on whom we are dependent for everything. Religion posits these as continuing and still available experiences of positive value that underpin our sense of our own worth and our social relations with others, provided we locate them where they belong—within the structures of religion rather than in the structures of the real world. "Render under to Caesar the things that are Caesar's, and unto God the things that are God's."

Psychotherapy, or at least psychoanalytic psychotherapy, views the matter rather differently. It sees such experiences as still alive but understands them as residues of childhood experience with parental figures. Finding them still located within the structures of ordinary social relations, it has regarded them as something to be plucked out, outgrown, and superseded to make way for the adult man. This has created a problem for contemporary man because these structures, clarified and identified by the symbolic transformations of the therapy process, now find themselves without any place in which to be. Their positive value as a cohesive force in society, which religion seems intuitively to have grasped, becomes undermined, because within our ordinary institutions of marriage, family, and the workplace they can appear as interferences in the smooth running of our current ideal of adult relationships. Nietzsche was concerned as to what would happen to man when he woke up and realized that God was dead. Jung repeatedly emphasized the problem that arose when the "archetype" (in my language, the unconscious structure of experience) came to dominate behavior. Perhaps in the end it has to be acknowledged that religion has found a solution to this problem, which, although it may not work for us, has yet to be bettered. By placing these still-present structures of experience in a special realm, it has ensured a continuing recognition of their value, while at the same time removing some of the more troublesome features of their continuing existence.

It is in relation to this need to contain archaic structures that psychodynamic theory, and particularly institutionally shared and revered theory, may unwittingly have assumed a quasi-religious function. I have sketched in some detail how the forms of theory may be well suited to reflect and contain the inner structures that they formulate, and also how the members of a group who share such theoretical beliefs may feel themselves to be united and bound together by this common symbolic structure that reflects (and at times contains) the self of each. If this be so, it can be more easily understood how the life of such a group, based on a kind of transpersonal unity of many selves (could one say a God-self?), begins to assume the customs and trappings of a religious order. For the truth of this group is no longer an objective truth; its mainstream life no longer consists in the sharing of common hypotheses about the real world; its truth has become an inner truth, a truth of the self that cannot be challenged. Its adherents *know* this truth beyond any shadow of doubt, and challengers of the new belief system have either to be excommunicated or converted. Theory has become theology, and the practitioners of the new order have become its high priests rather than its therapists. The system has become closed to external influence because the basic truths (concepts) have already been established and are beyond question. Any pretense to a heuristic or scientific attitude has given way to the hegemony of belief.

The irony of this for the psychotherapist is that it is just such unquestioned belief systems—those unconscious assumptions of the patient about himself and the real world—that psychotherapy attempts to loosen from the tenacious grip of the "real." Such, however, is the need of people for relief from uncertainty, that in the end the therapist himself succumbs to a new tyranny of the real in the form of his theoretical beliefs.

THEORY AS A DWELLING FOR THE SELF

My major concern in these final chapters has been to highlight the inner relation that exists between a therapist and his own theory and to show that this subjective, maternal face of theory may have far more powerful influence on individual therapists and institutions than is usually acknowledged. The relation I have described is one of correspondence: *the theory of the theoretician describes his own self.* Whether that theory also describes the self of others—be they patients or other therapists—is far more problematic. While the notion of overlapping selves, whether in therapy or in theory-orientated groups, allows for some possibility of generalization of theory across individuals, the hope of ever achieving one generally accepted dynamic theory seems extremely remote.

I started by describing theory as a schematic map of the self, in other words, as a cognitive, other-directed structure, set in discursive language. As I explored the theme, my metaphor spontaneously changed, and I started to talk of theory as a "home" or "container" for the self, a "place" for the self to be, and closer to sensory experience and memories of the flesh. This illustrates the way that theory exists on different levels, and although we can speak of theory as a structure of *ideas* that is independent of and separate from ourselves, we can still *feel* that the theory is a part of ourself, filled, as it were, with our own experience, our own flesh and blood. The first, discursive mode of theory is the mode of paternal symbols; the second mode I have termed "theory as transitional object." In this second mode, theory is a structure of inward-looking, maternal symbols concerned with the well-being of the self rather than with knowledge of the Other. In this mode, the symbol is heir of the mother who supports and comforts us and gives us the illusion that every part of us is accounted for and "gathered in." If not "free from sorrow, free from sin," as the hymn goes on, then at least in a safe "place" where mother is, and by extension, our own analytic mother and father, too. "Every hair is hair of the head numbered . . ." says Gerard Manley Hopkins. Or listen to T. S. Eliot as he affirms a similar deep gathering-in as he nears the end of his *Four Quartets*:

> And all shall be well and
> All manner of thing shall be well
> When the tongues of flame are in-folded
> Into the crowned knot of fire
> And the fire and the rose are one.

My metaphor shifts to a religious symbolism, following the direction so often taken by psychoanalytic theory in our minds. The containing circle, the space of the mother's arms, the need to be held, the state of being completely known and loved. Theory in this mode becomes a *mandala* of the self, to use Jung's term, a symbol of the wholeness of the self, a sacred object not to be tampered with. All its parts are in-folded, represented in the image, within the containing circle of the mother's arms. "And all shall be well and All manner of thing shall be well."

I spoke earlier in this chapter about the difficulty facing secular man as to where he could put the partially superseded but still loved presences of his archaic objects—parental and early self imagos—that in religious times would have found a home in that "special area" of religion. If the religious icons of those former times contained these precious and sometimes terrifying objects, and if theology was the discursive and coherent account of the place of these objects in the scheme of things, it would be difficult not to make one further link and to describe psychodynamic theory as the theology of secular man. It is not a theology that means much to the man in the street, but neither did the views of an Aquinas mean much to the peasant or the artisan. The people for whom it is really important are the psychotherapists—the priests of this new secular system.

This large new metaphor is one that has formed and asserted itself right at the end of this book, drawing together the religious references that have haunted my attempt to pursue a compelling idea through its multiple presentations. There is no room to explore it, and it stands as a risible or explosive image at the end of the text. It is an image that some will hate and many will refuse, but it seems to me to capture something of the devotion of the psychoanalytic enterprise and to explain the heavy seriousness of many of its practitioners. To be able to laugh at oneself is to be able to step out of one's role into the position of another, but to be unconsciously identified with that role is to be a prisoner of one's own forms.

Epilogue

> . . . *And the end of all our exploring*
> *Will be to arrive where we started*
> *And know the place for the first time.*
> —T. S. Eliot, "Little Gidding"

I STARTED THIS BOOK by considering the face and the part that the face plays in experience, especially early experience. I noted the almost complete absence of the face in psychoanalytic theory and speculated about some possible reasons for this omission. I suggested that a reinstatement of the face in the theory might bring about a rebalancing of the theory, a change in the way we think about human beings and what goes on in the analytic and psychotherapeutic settings.

I would not go so far as to suggest that I have achieved that aim, but it may be that I have made a start. The face, with its capacity to convey emotional expressions, is implicit in all the different looks that the mother makes in the direction of her infant or young child; much of what I have written is about the way in which such looks, and the views they convey, interact with and transform the primary substance of the child's impulsive action self. I have suggested, in effect, that the self as a symbolic object, which can be conceived of and related to as Other, is a product of such looking transactions at this interface.

In the beginning, that interface is between the infant and the mother; later it will be between the child and all his other significant objects. From here it is a short step to thinking about self-consciousness as the internalization of that interface, where we look through the eyes of the Other at ourselves. The space of our self-consciousness then becomes the internalization of an originally existing space between infant and mother, infant and father, infant and Other, bridged by an identification with this Other's view. In being self-conscious we are inevitably Other to ourselves.

If we accept this derivation of self-consciousness, we have to go a step further and accept that repression and other defenses also occur at this interface and can be thought of as forms of interpersonal action, not as faceless mechanisms.

Throughout the book have run the twin themes of separation and reunion. I have had in mind the longing for reunion, which is probably never superseded, and how we remain separate and avoid falling back into a state of oneness. More practically, I have been concerned with the question of how we keep in contact with the loved and needed object once we have separated both emotionally, and physically through locomotion.

It has seemed to me that the face stands in a pivotal position at every point along this developmental pathway. At the very beginning—before separation, before there is an object there at all—the mother's face is already there, as that which mediates attachment behavior and perhaps also as the first visual form of an early blissful experience. A little later, though still part of the attachment process, there develops that interactive smiling and looking between faces, the conversation of gestures between infant and mother, which I have suggested is important in laying the foundations of the self. As separation gets under way and the child begins to circle out from the mother, the mother's face is the beacon to which the child references back for orientation and reaction, and the conversation of smiles and other visually perceived facial expressions becomes the means of keeping in touch and making the distance tolerable. The very notion of keeping in touch seems to imply an annihilation of distance by such visual signaling.

The face has now become the focus of the infant's awareness of the mother, so long as separation is maintained. If the breast held the focus of attention in the beginning in relation to appetitive needs, or perhaps even then shared it with the face, it is certainly no longer so once distance is a fact. Object seeking, in contrast to satisfaction seeking, revolves around the face. It is the face that is searched for and then recognized; the face has already become the center of the person.

It is from this point that I have made a bridge to communication and the understanding of symbols. It may well be that the capacity to recognize patterns is an innate human characteristic. Nevertheless, the face is apparently one of the first patterns or gestalts to be recognized by the infant, and the refining of that pattern into a unique gestalt of the mother gradually follows. But the infant's relation to the mother's face does not end there. The infant or young child comes to search the mother's face for expressions, for emotional reactions to what he is doing. Although the child cannot yet perceive in such reactions a separated meaning, I have suggested that the relation between the face, as a conveyer of such messages, and the expression (the message) that fleets across the face may be a prototype that facilitates the child's later grasping of the relation between a symbol and the idea the symbol conveys. While the relation between a symbol and that which it symbolizes seems to imply a whole path of development in which separation from doing with the object may be the critical factor, the face is from the beginning an object that only yields itself to looking, not touching and doing. It thus has a unique position in the infant's experience and is well suited to mediate a line of development that starts with attachment, then goes on to nonverbal communication, which in its turn paves the way for speech. In speech itself, the face is still the center of visual attention, and a new conversation begins that serves to further strengthen and maintain the attachment bond.

It is not my purpose in these last comments to summarize a whole complex argument, but only to draw together the sometimes scattered bits of the whole that seem to offer a special importance to the face. In this regard, there is one aspect I have not really touched upon that might nevertheless prove a fitting thought with which to end. The unique configuration of the mother's face is a complex configuration that comes to represent the mother. Where there is any sense of threat, it becomes the one pattern that must be found, and nothing else will do. It is an absolute in the child's experience.

That is one part of what I want to say. The next relates to the issue of giving something up. Progression in development, as I have indicated in various places, nearly always involves a giving up of something *for the sake of* something else. What is it that induces the child to give this something up? It may be a threat, but that, after all, is not so far from the threat of losing the most precious object, namely, the mother. It is not always a threat, however; it may be love. The mother's face (dare I say it and thereby challenge the breast its pride of place) is the most loved object in the child's universe. The mother wants the child to do something, to try something (and, of course, later so does the father). Before that moment when the doing of the thing brings its own reward of some new achievement, it is, I would maintain, the mother's face that facilitates those leaps into the unknown that have to be made.

This brings us back again to the idea of maternal presence. Whenever we attempt any difficult or new undertaking, whenever we have to leap into some new organization of the world or experience, there is always a "giving up" and there is always a "for the sake of." Of course, we do the thing for ourselves, because we want to. But what determines our willingness to try, and what supports us in our leap, is, I would suggest, the mother's face, her continuing presence in our minds, and a knowledge in the depths of our being that she wants us to do it.

If some would find in these remarks a religious significance, I would not dispute it; for it is here, where words do not really count, in the preverbal core of the self, that religious faith and our basic trust in ourselves or life, or as much of it as we can muster, have their origins.

Postscript

Since writing this book, my attention has been drawn to a paper by Beebe and Lachmann (1988) entitled "The Contribution of Mother–Infant Mutual Influence to the Origins of Self- and Object Representations." It is too late to incorporate any reference to the work and ideas of these authors, but they strike me as sufficiently important and relevant to merit separate discussion even at this late stage.

Their paper is important in providing a window to the field of empirical infant research. Although I had some idea that this was a growing and important field, I had no conception of the relevance of its findings for anyone trying to understand the early structuring of experience in a dynamic way. It may be that other papers could have served the same function for me, but because it was this one, I owe it a special debt.

It is not my purpose to summarize this paper or the field it opens up, but to indicate some of the areas where I seemed to find a more substantial base for the ideas I have been putting forward.

Among these ideas is the central importance of the face in human experience and development, particularly the importance of early facial interaction with the mother. Curiously lacking in analytic literature, face-to-face interaction with the mother is here the focus of sustained research—it could even be said it provides a paradigm or model of the earliest phase of the social process. Together with vocal and various kinetic or "movement" interactions of mother and baby, it is regarded as forming the core of those representations that will structure all future interactions and provide a basic sense of attunement or nonattunement to other people. Beebe and Lachmann call these first representational structures *interaction structures*. They are "characteristic patterns of mutual regulations in which both infant and caretaker influence each other. The infant comes to recognise, remember and expect these recurring interaction structures" (p. 306).

A feature of these structures is that they do not depend on the prior development of symbols but are formed through an earlier and more basic process of pattern recognition in the different sensory modalities. Beebe and Lachmann refer to this early capacity to recognize and store patterns from experience as a "presymbolic representational capacity." Clearly this depends on a primary organizing of sensory data, and they suggest that this is the substratum out of which "abstracted prototypes," and eventually symbols, will be formed.

These early organizations of sensory data and the prototypes that emerge from them are closely similar to what I have called the stages of iconic or maternal symbol formation—in other words, to the growth of sensory (especially visual) patterns that represent the object rather than announce it (Chapter 14). Incidentally, Beebe and Lachmann reserve the term *symbol* for those arbitrary symbols of objects, especially words, that come from outside the subject and are part of the cultural heritage.

There is another area of overlap between the ideas I have presented and those arising from empirical infant research. This is most marked in the concept of *matching* or *fit*. The basic method of this infant research involves recording on film or tape, then analyzing in great detail sequences of mother–infant interactions—vocal interactions, face-to-face interplay, and various body-movement sequences in mother and baby. One of the major findings, not only of Beebe and Lachmann but of other researchers, too, is the extraordinary degree of matching or interlocking of mother and infant behaviors in the ordinary mother–infant relationship. Mother and infant react to each other's gestures and movements in exquisitely sensitive ways. The matching and adaptation of response is not just one way: the infant adjusts to the mother as much as the mother adjusts to the infant.

In my own ideas I have made reference to Winnicott, relating the ideas of match and fit to the preseparation phase, where the infant's well-being depended on a sense of maternal fit or adjustment to infant need. In the field of infant research we find similar ideas being generated directly from empirical observation and research.

There are differences, of course. Beebe and Lachmann are referring to a split-second adjustment of mother to baby and baby to mother on the behavioral level. So rapid is it that it often cannot be detected with the naked eye. Winnicott's ideas belong to a more intuitive and feeling level of interaction, in which the mother empathically adjusts to her infant's needs. Despite this difference, the convergence of concepts is striking. It seems, indeed, very likely that the adjustment observed by Beebe and Lachmann on the behavioral level will ultimately be found to correlate with the mother's adjustments to the baby's needs on a more feeling level.

In their discussion, these authors do in fact attempt a bridge from behavioral to feeling levels. While admitting that such bridging always involves a high degree of inference, they attempt to suggest some possible mechanisms.

Of particular interest is their attempt to link the findings of infant research to the communication of feeling states between adults. In this, they are not concerned with verbal communication about affects but with the more direct means by which one subject may come to share in the feeling state of another.

One of the possible mechanisms they mention in this regard has once again to do with matching. They cite evidence that when subjects identify with or empathize with each other, their behavior becomes more similar in various respects. This behavioral matching between adult subjects has much in common with the behavioral matching between mother and infant noted in infant research. Beebe and Lachmann believe that not only are these early matched interactions with the mother laying the foundations of shared subjective experience in that dyad; similar behavioral matching mediates the sharing of affective states in adult life as well.

Quoting evidence from Ekman (1983) and Zajonc (1985), they reach the following conclusion: if a subject matches, with his own *behavior*, the behavioral correlates of another subject's *emotion*, he actually reproduces in himself the autonomic activation of that emotion. For example, if one person is crying, another person who is relating to him will, through identification, reproduce in himself similar facial movements to those of the person who is crying. These movements may be subliminal, but will generate, in muted form, patterns of autonomic arousal and affective experience that echo those in the first person.

These ideas are of great interest in relation to such matters as projective identification and the communication of affect by primitive means, which I touched on in Chapters 10 and 14. I believe they provide a means though which a sensible critique of projective identification could be made, a subject about which analysts, according to Meissner (in Sandler 1988), talk so much "psychobabble."

There are two final areas I want to consider. The first concerns psychological separation from the mother; the second, the status given to the social in psychoanalytic theories.

Psychological separation from the mother implies an earlier state in which mother and child were still one or not yet separated in the infant's experience. This is a central concept in my work and underpins many of the arguments I make. There is a sense in which the observations of empirical infant research appear to undermine this concept. Stern (1985), for example, makes much of this and claims that the weight of infant research points to the infant's being aware of self and mother as separate objects virtually from the start. The notion of mutual adjustment—infant adjusting to mother as much as mother to infant—seems to him to imply this. Nevertheless, I think it can be argued the other way.

What this sensitive mutual adjustment of mother and infant highlights is the degree to which both together form a self-contained and self-regulating system. It is mother and infant *together* who function as a unit, a dyadic system; it is such things as level of activity, level of arousal, degree of engagement or disengagement between the partners, in the system as a whole, that act as the governing constraint on the behavior of each.

Where this differs from Winnicott's account is in the active part played by the baby in achieving the result. The question I would ask is whether this will really make much difference to the baby's experience. The baby still has to cope with periods of separateness from the mother. The sense of being part of an attuned system lasts only as long as the interaction with the mother continues. What Beebe and Lachmann do not discuss, at least in this paper, is how this passage from matched togetherness to solitary aloneness is negotiated. How does the baby cope with an absence of the mother that disrupts the mutually attuned system? Although the emphasis here is on a myriad of interdependent interactions, we can still wonder about the experience of the baby and ask if it may not still be meaningful to link this loss of the mother from the dyadic behavioral system with the more familiar concept of psychological separation.

My final point concerns the status of the social in psychoanalytic formulations—a theme to which I have returned throughout the book. I have indicated that I prefer those theorists who see attachment to the mother as a primary social element in our constitution, and I believe that the findings emerging from empirical infant research are strongly in favor of this view.

In the almost incredible degree of interlocking responsiveness described in this work, we see a sophistication of social equipment, at such an early stage of infant development, that it seems impossible to believe it could be other than a primary part of our constitution. It also strikes me forcefully that this apparently innate behavior is not only interaction but primitive communication; as Beebe and Lachmann suggest, it may also provide the basis of a continuously matched, and thus shared, affective experience.

References

Balint, M. (1952). New beginning and the paranoid and depressive syndromes. In *Primary Love and Psycho-Analytic Technique*, pp. 230–249. London: Tavistock, 1965.

—— (1965). *Primary Love and Psycho-Analytic Technique*. London: Tavistock.

Bateson, G. (1973). Style, grace and information in primitive art. In *Steps to an Ecology of Mind*, pp. 101–125. London: Paladin.

—— (1985). *Mind and Nature: A Necessary Unity*. Flamingo edition. London: Fontana.

Bateson, G., Jackson, D. D., Haley, J., and Weakland, J. (1956). Toward a theory of schizophrenia. *Behavioural Science* 1:251–264.

Beebe, B., and Lachmann, F. (1988). The contribution of mother–infant mutual influence to the origins of self- and object representations. *Psychoanalytic Psychology* 5:305–337.

Bertalanffy, L. von (1968). *General Systems Theory*. New York: Braziller.

Bick, E. (1968). The experience of the skin in early object relations. *International Journal of Psycho-Analysis* 49:484–486.

Bion, W. (1959a). Attacks on linking. *International Journal of Psycho-Analysis* 40:308–315.

—— (1959b). *Experiences in Groups*. London: Tavistock.

—— (1962a). A theory of thinking. *International Journal of Psycho-Analysis* 43:306–310.

—— (1962b). *Learning from Experience*. London: Heinemann.

Bleuler, E. (1950). *Dementia Praecox or The Group of Schizophrenias*. Trans. J. Zinkin. New York: International Universities Press.

Bollas, C. (1987). *The Shadow of the Object: Psychoanalysis of the Unthought Known*. London: Free Association Books.

Bowlby, J. (1969). *Attachment and Loss*. Vol. 1: *Attachment*. London: The Hogarth Press.

Breuer, J., and Freud, S. (1893–1895). Studies in hysteria. *Standard Edition* 2.

Buber, M. (1937). *I and Thou*. Trans. R. G. Smith. Edinburgh: T. & T. Clark.

Bullough, E. (1912). Psychical distance as a factor in art and an aesthetic principle. *British Journal of Psychology* 5:87–118.

Cassirer, E. (1946). *Language and Myth*. New York: Harper and Row.

—— (1953). *Philosophy of Symbolic Forms*. Vol. 1: *Language*. Trans. R. Manheim. New Haven: Yale University Press.

Cooley, C. H. (1902). *Human Nature and the Social Order*. New York: Scribner's.

Ekman, P. (1983). Autonomic nervous system activity distinguishes among emotions. *Science* 221:1208–1210.

Eliot, T. S. (1944). *Four Quartets*. London: Faber and Faber.

Erikson, E. H. (1959). *Identity and the Life Cycle*. New York: International Universities Press.

—— (1964). *Insight and Responsibility: Lectures on the Ethical Implications of Psychoanalytic Insight*. New York: Norton.

Fairbairn, W. R. D. (1941). A revised psychopathology of the psychoses and psychoneuroses. In *Psycho-Analytic Studies of the Personality*, pp. 28–58. London: Routledge and Kegan Paul, 1952.

—— (1952). *Psycho-Analytic Studies of the Personality*. London: Routledge and Kegan Paul.

Forrester, J. (1980). *Language and the Origins of Psychoanalysis*. London: Macmillan.

Fraiberg, S., and Freedman, D. A. (1964). Studies in the ego development of the congenitally blind. *Psychoanalytic Study of the Child* 19:113–169. New York: International Universities Press.

Freud, S. (1900). The interpretation of dreams. *Standard Edition* 4/5.

—— (1914). Remembering, repeating and working-through. *Standard Edition* 12:147–156.

—— (1915a). Observations on transference love. *Standard Edition* 12:159–171.

—— (1915b). Repression. *Standard Edition* 14:146–158.

—— (1915c). The unconscious. *Standard Edition* 14:161–215.

—— (1917). Mourning and melancholia. *Standard Edition* 14:239–258.

—— (1923). The ego and the id. *Standard Edition* 19:13–59.

—— (1924). The dissolution of the Oedipus conflict. *Standard Edition* 19:173–179.

—— (1925). A note upon the mystic writing-pad. *Standard Edition* 19:227–232.

—— (1930). Civilisation and its discontents. *Standard Edition* 21:64–145.

—— (1933). New introductory lectures on psycho-analysis. *Standard Edition* 22:3–182.

Fuller, P. (1980). *Art and Psychoanalysis*. London: Writers and Readers Cooperative.

Greenacre, P. (1949). A contribution to the study of screen memories. In *Psychoanalytic Study of the Child* 3/4:73–84. New York: International Universities Press.

—— (1957). The childhood of the artist: libidinal phase development and giftedness. *Psychoanalytic Study of the Child* 12:27–72. New York: International Universities Press.

Hobson, P. *On developing the capacity to symbolize*. Paper presented to the Independent group of psycho-analysts, London, October.

Hobson, R. (1985). *Forms of Feeling*. London: Tavistock.

Jung, C. G. (1953). *Psychology and Alchemy*. London: Routledge and Kegan Paul.

—— (1963). *Memories, Dreams, Reflections*. London: Collins and Routledge and Kegan Paul.

Keller, H. (1902). *The Story of My Life*. Garden City, NY: Doubleday.

Kelley, K., ed. (1988). *The Home Planet—Images and Reflections of Earth from Space Explorers*. London: Macdonald Queen Anne Press.

Kelly, G. A. (1955). *The Psychology of Personal Constructs*. Vols. 1 and 2. New York: Norton.

—— (1964). The language of hypothesis: man's psychological instrument. In *Clinical Psychology and Personality—the Selected Papers of George Kelly*, ed. B. Maher, pp. 147–162. New York: Wiley, 1969.

Kohut, H. (1971). *The Analysis of the Self*. New York: International Universities Press.

Korzybski, A. (1941). *Science and Sanity*. New York: Science Press.

Kuhn, T. (1962). *The Structure of Scientific Revolutions*. Chicago: University of Chicago Press.

Lacan, J. (1949). *Le stade du miroir comme formateur de la fonction du "Je"* (The mirror image as formative of the function of the "I"). In *Ecrits: A Selection*, trans. A. Sheridan, pp. 1–7. London: Tavistock, 1977.

Laing, R. D. (1960). *The Divided Self*. London: Tavistock.

—— (1961). *Self and Others*. London: Tavistock.

Langer, S. K. (1942). *Philosophy in a New Key*. Cambridge, MA: Harvard University Press.

—— (1953). *Feeling and Form*. London: Routledge and Kegan Paul.

Lemaire, A. (1977). *Jacques Lacan*. Trans. Macey. London: Routledge and Kegan Paul.

Lenneberg, E. (1967). *Biological Foundations of Language*. New York: Wiley.

Lidz, T., Cornelison, A. R., Fleck, S., and Terry, D. (1957). The intrafamilial environment of schizophrenic patients. II: Marital schism and marital skew. *American Journal of Psychiatry* 114:241–248.

Lynd, H. M. (1958). *On Shame and the Search for Identity*. London: Routledge and Kegan Paul.

MacLeish, A. (1960). *Poetry and Experience*. London: Penguin.

MacMurray, J. (1957). *The Self as Agent*. London: Faber & Faber.

Maher, B. (1969). *Clinical Psychology and Personality—The Selected Papers of George Kelly*. New York: Wiley.

Mahler, M. S., Pine, F., and Bergman, A. (1975). *The Psychological Birth of the Human Infant*. London: Hutchinson.

Mead, G. H. (1934). *Mind, Self and Society*. Ed. C. W. Morris. Chicago: University of Chicago Press.

—— (1956). *On Social Psychology—Selected Papers*. Ed. A. Strauss. Chicago: University of Chicago Press.

Menzies-Lyth, I. (1989). *The Dynamics of the Social*. London: Free Association Books.

Merleau-Ponty, M. (1962). *The Phenomenology of Perception*. Trans. C. Smith. London: Routledge and Kegan Paul.

—— (1964a). Indirect language and the voices of silence. In *Signs*, trans. R. McCleary. Evanston, IL: Northwestern University Press.

—— (1964b). On the phenomenon of language. In *Signs*, trans. R. McCleary. Evanston, IL: Northwestern University Press.

—— (1965). *The Structure of Behaviour*. London: Methuen.

Nagera, H., and Colonna, A. (1965). Aspects of the contribution of sight to ego and drive development—a comparison of the development of some blind and sighted children. *Psychoanalytic Study of the Child* 20:267–287. New York: International Universities Press.

Padel, J. (1985). Ego in current thinking. *International Review of Psycho-Analysis* 12:273–283.

Pines, M. (1984). Reflections on mirroring. *International Review of Psycho-Analysis* 11:27–42.

Rogers, C. R. (1961). *On Becoming a Person*. London: Constable.

Rycroft, C. F. (1979). *The Innocence of Dreams*. London: The Hogarth Press.

Sandler, J. (1988). *Projection, Identification, Projective Identification*. London: Karnac.

Sartre, J-P. (1957). *Being and Nothingness*. Trans. H. Barnes. London: Methuen.

—— (1976). *Critique of Dialectical Reason*. Trans. A. Sheridan-Smith. London: New Left Books.

Schafer, R. (1976). *A New Language for Psychoanalysis*. New Haven: Yale University Press.

Searles, H. (1963). The place of neutral therapist-responses in psychotherapy with the schizophrenic patient. In *Collected Papers on Schizophrenia and Related Subjects*, pp. 626–653. London: The Hogarth Press, 1965.

—— (1965). *Collected Papers on Schizophrenia and Related Subjects*. London: The Hogarth Press.

Segal, H. (1986). Notes on symbol formation. In *The Work of Hanna Segal—A Kleinian Approach to Clinical Practice*, pp. 49–65. London: Free Association Books and Maresfield Library.

Senden, M. von (1931). *Space and Sight*. Trans. P. Heath. Glencoe, IL: Free Press.

Simon, B. (1988). The imaginary twins: the case of Beckett and Bion. *International Review of Psycho-Analysis* 15:331–352.

Spence, D. (1982). *Narrative Truth and Historical Truth: Meaning and Interpretation in Psychoanalysis*. New York: Norton.

Spencer Brown, G. (1969). *The Laws of Form*. London: Allen and Unwin.

Spitz, R. A. (1955). The primal cavity. In *Psychoanalytic Study of the Child* 10:215–240. New York: International Universities Press.

——— (1946). The smiling response: a contribution to the ontogenesis of social relations (with the assistance of K. M. Wolf, Ph.D.). *Genetic Psychological Monographs* 34:57–125.

Stern, D. (1985). *The Interpersonal World of the Infant*. New York: Basic.

Sullivan, H. S. (1953). *The Interpersonal Theory of Psychiatry*. New York: Norton.

Suttie, I. D. (1935). *The Origins of Love and Hate*. London: Kegan Paul.

Szasz, T. (1963). The concept of transference. *International Journal of Psycho-Analysis* 44:432–443.

Trist, E., and Emery, F. E. (1970). *Towards a Social Ecology*. New York: Plenum.

Turbayne, C. M. (1962). *The Myth of Metaphor*. New Haven: Yale University Press.

Winnicott, D. W. (1951). Transitional objects and transitional phenomena: a study of the first not-me possession. In *Collected Papers—Through Paediatrics to Psycho-Analysis*, pp. 229–242. London: Tavistock, 1958. Also in *Playing and Reality*, pp. 1–25. London: Tavistock, 1971.

——— (1958). *Collected Papers—Through Paediatrics to Psycho-Analysis*. London: Tavistock.

——— (1965). *The Maturational Processes and the Facilitating Environment*. London: The Hogarth Press.

——— (1967). Mirror-role of mother and family in child development. In *Playing and Reality*, pp. 111–118. London: Tavistock, 1971.

——— (1971). *Playing and Reality*. London: Tavistock.

Wittgenstein, L. (1922). *Tractatus Logico-Philosophicus*. Trans. D. F. Pears and B. F. McGuiness. London: Routledge and Kegan Paul, 1961.

Wolff, P. H. (1963). Observations on the early development of smiling. In *Determinants of Infant Behaviour*, vol. 2, ed. B. M. Foss. London: Methuen.

Wright, K. J. T. (1969). An investigation of the meaning of change in a group of phobic patients using grid methods. Unpublished dissertation, University of London.

—— (1976). Metaphor and symptom: a study of integration and its failure. *International Review of Psycho-Analysis* 3:97–109.

Zajonc, R. B. (1985). Emotion and facial efference: a theory reclaimed. *Science* 228:15–22.

Index

This first edition of *Vision and Separation:
Between Mother and Baby* was finished in May 1991.

The book was commissioned by Robert M. Young,
designed by Wendy Millichap,
and produced by Bernard F. Horan
for Jason Aronson Inc. and Free Association Books.